D0216293

THE DEVELOPMENT OF
MATHEMATICAL SKILLS

THE DEVELOPMENT OF MATHEMATICAL SKILLS

edited by

Chris Donlan
University College London, UK

Psychology Press
a member of the Taylor & Francis group

Copyright © 1998 by Psychology Press Ltd.
a member of the Taylor & Francis group
   All rights reserved. No part of this book may be reproduced
in any form, by photostat, microfilm retrieval system, or
any other means without the prior written permission of
the publisher

Psychology Press Ltd., Publishers
27 Church Road
Hove
East Sussex, BN3 2FA
UK

British Library Cataloguing in Publication Data
A catalogue record for this book is available from the British Library.

ISBN 0-86377-816-X (Hbk)
ISSN 1368-2563

Typeset by Quorum Technical Services Ltd., Cheltenham, Glos.
Printed and bound in the United Kingdom by
Biddles Ltd., Guildford and King's Lynn

Contents

List of contributors

John W. Adams, Department of Psychology, University of York, Heslington, York YO1 5DD, UK

Mark H. Ashcraft, Department of Psychology, Cleveland State University, Cleveland, OH 44115, USA

Chris Donlan, Department of Human Communication Science, University College London, Chandler House, 2 Wakefield Street, London WC1N 1PG, UK

Ann Dowker, Department of Experimental Psychology, University of Oxford, South Parks Road, Oxford OX1 3UD, UK

Graham Hitch, Department of Psychology, University of Lancaster, Bailrigg, Lancaster LA1 4YF, UK

Derek Hopko, Department of Psychology, Cleveland State University, Cleveland, OH 44115, USA

Elizabeth Kirk, Department of Psychology, Cleveland State University, Cleveland, OH 44115, USA

Paul Macaruso, Massachusetts General Hospital, Psychology Assessment Centre, 5, Emerson, Suite 105, 55 Fruit Street, Boston, MA 02114, USA

Constanza Moreno, Child Development and Learning, Institute of Education, 20 Bedford Way, London WC1H 0AL, UK

Penny Munn, University of Central Lancashire, Department of Psychology, Preston, Lancs PR1 2HE, UK

Terezinha Nunes, Child Development and Learning, Institute of Education, 20 Bedford Way, London WC1H 0AL, UK

Bethany Rittle-Johnson, Department of Psychology, Carnegie Mellon University, Pittsburgh, PA 15213-3890, USA

Matthew Saxton, Department of Psychology, Royal Holloway University of London, Egham Hill, Egham, Surrey TW20 0EX, UK

Robert S. Siegler, Psychology Department, Carnegie Mellon University, Pittsburgh, PA 15213-3890, USA

Scott Sokol, Massachusetts General Hospital, Psychology Assessment Centre, 5, Emerson, Suite 105, 55 Fruit Street, Boston, MA 02114, USA

Catherine Sophian, Department of Psychology, 2430 Campus Road, University of Hawaii at Manoa, Honolulu, Hawaii 96822, USA

John Towse, Department of Psychology, Royal Holloway University of London, Egham Hill, Egham, Surrey TW20 0EX, UK

Naoki Ueno, National Institute for Educational Research, Shimomeguro 6-5-22, Meguro-ku, Tokyo 153, Japan

Karen Wynn, Department of Psychology, University of Arizona, Tucson, AZ 85721, USA

Preface

Far more psychological research has been generated in exploring the process of reading and its development than in exploring mathematical skills. Despite the notable contributions of individual researchers and their teams, the study of children's mathematics has traditionally seemed an item of low priority on the psychological research agenda.

In the last two decades a change has taken place. A new energy has been generated and there is a growing realisation that this relatively neglected area is both deserving of attention and likely to yield important new findings. The present volume aims to encapsulate some of the excitement that surrounds the current broadening of interest in children's mathematical learning, to offer a representative sample of the diverse theoretical orientations, research frameworks and methodologies currently employed, and to allow the reader to evaluate the strength of the evidence and the power of the insights that this collection of new and recent work brings together.

Some recurrent themes will be found in the chapters of this book. Arguments for an innate mathematical cognition are presented alongside competing but perhaps also complementary empiricist accounts. Wynn's nativist account of her influential body of work on infant numerical cognition (Chapter 1) is closely argued and firmly grounded in experimental evidence; she claims that an innate numerical competence serves as the foundation for mathematical development, but acknowledges that this basic foundation cannot explain the breadth of subsequent expansion. Sophian (Chapter 2) re-examines these issues and offers a sharply focused review of research (including her own) into the dramatic advances in counting skill that occur in early childhood. A developmental account of these changes must, Sophian claims, give prominence to socially-mediated activities.

The interaction between "pure" cognitive research and work within broader models of social cognition becomes apparent as the book develops. Munn (Chapter 3) provides an intriguing insight into the crucial but scantily re-searched area of pre-schoolers' use of numerical symbols. She gives the reader a careful introduction to the general importance of social context in symbolic function before presenting new and intriguing findings concerning young children's awareness of the function of numerical symbols, an important foundation for the subsequent development of arithmetical skills.

The cognitive framework supporting mathematical development is the subject of a penetrating review by Johnson and Siegler (Chapter 4). The authors focus on the fundamental distinction between conceptual and procedural aspects of mathematical knowledge. In some sense their chapter extends the "principles versus practice" debate (introduced by Sophian in Chapter 2) to cover not only counting skills but also a range of later acquired computational and reasoning skills. The complex pattern of findings, Johnson and Siegler argue, can best be explained by variation in the extent of environmental exposure that children receive to different sorts of mathematical experience.

The context of learning is repeatedly referred to as the source of individuals' accumulated knowledge. In Chapter 5 Ueno re-examines what may have seemed a commonplace notion. He rejects experimental methods, arguing that context only exists as defined (and redefined) by participants in interaction. Experimental design attempts to exclude interactive definition of participants' activities; therefore scientific findings are distortions of reality. Readers who are not familiar with this sort of view will find Ueno's explanation both accessible and powerful. All readers are likely to find his accounts of mathematical interaction in the workplace and at school refreshing and insightful.

The importance of cultural and linguistic factors in children's mathematical development is emphasised by a number of contributors. Towse and Saxton (Chapter 6) review the literature on international comparisons on mathematical attainment and examine in detail experimental evidence for and against the influence of number-specific language characteristics on numerical cognition. Towse and Saxton offer no simple conclusions; they provide for the reader a lucid account of the linguistic relativity viewpoint, as well as some evidence of its limitations, and demonstrate the considerable objections that stand against any unitary account cross-cultural variation in mathematical achievement.

Identification of cognitive systems supporting mathematical development is the goal of many contributors to this volume. By far the most clearly specified model reported here is the working memory model discussed by Adams and Hitch in Chapter 7. The authors present a lucid and authoritative account of the detailed literature that precedes their collaborative studies. The general claim is a strong one: that the role of working memory in the development of mental arithmetic skills is crucial. Intriguing evidence is put forward for the differential involvement of specific components of the working memory system. A further perspective on the influence of working memory in mathematical thinking is provided by Ashcraft, Kirk, and Hopko (Chapter 8). Following a review of the broad-ranging literature on anxiety and mathematics, they present evidence for a possible mechanism whereby anxiety specifically disrupts the efficient operation of working memory, with consequent effects on arithmetical performance. The research has been conducted with adult participants, but the developmental and educational implications of these findings are clearly spelt out.

Studies of children whose mathematical development is subject to special restriction through, for example, learning difficulties, sensory deficit or language impairments, may provide important indicators of processes underlying mathematical development in general. Macaruso and Sokol (Chapter 9) demonstrate the application of cognitive neuropsychological methods to this end. Basing their studies on a specific model of numerical cognition in adults, the authors present detailed reports of the patterns of intact versus impaired performance in individual secondary level students with specific learning difficulties. A strong case if made for the single-case approach, and a series of focussed research questions emerges, addressing both clinical and theoretical concerns.

Similar goals are pursued using a very different methodology in the next two chapters. Both Nunes and Moreno (Chapter 10) and Donlan (Chapter 11) use quantitative methods and group studies to examine the interdependence (or independence) of language and mathematical skill. The authors studied deaf children and language-impaired children, respectively. Although these groups differ substantially, and although the research frameworks of the studies are quite different, there is substantial agreement in the findings. Despite poor overall mathematical attainment, there is clear evidence for "normal" learning processes in some specific areas of numerical/mathematical knowledge, suggesting that language deficits may have differential effects on subcomponents of mathematical development.

The final chapter, by Dowker, provides a reminder that the componential nature of mathematical learning is amply demonstrated not only in patients and children with learning difficulties but in normally developing individuals. The fact that substantial discrepancies between, for example, calculation skills and arithmetical reasoning (note the elegance of Dowker's technique for eliciting this information) are rather easy to find may be surprising; it certainly offers discouragement to any unitary model of mathematical development.

Diversity is a characteristic of this book. Between "situated cognition" on the one hand, and cognitive neuropsychology on the other, there may be scant common ground! But acceptance of the complementarity of different perspectives may be essential for progress in towards a shared goal. Each chapter in this volume represents the refined product of a considerable investment of energy and expertise in pursuit of some important key to understanding children's mathematical skills. Where empiricist challenges nativist, or information-processing theory conflicts with structuralism, neither side is seen to win the battle. At best, contrasting perspectives may be clarified and strengthened through juxtaposition.

The present volume is, I hope, novel insofar as it brings together diverse current research approaches. The aims are: to provide for the reader a real sense of discovery, to invite re-examination of previous assumptions, and to encourage a willingness to tolerate uncertainty in the pursuit of a new and broader understanding of how children learn mathematics.

Pre-school mathematical understanding

INTRODUCTION

Chapters 1 and 2 offer the reader lucid and authoritative, but also contrastive accounts of early mathematical development. When Karen Wynn published a paper in *Nature* in 1992 under the provocative title "Addition and subtraction by human infants" she presented evidence that five-month old babies show suprise when their numerical expectations concerning the outcomes of events are violated. The innovative design of the 1992 study appeared to exclude explanations based on pattern recognition. Participants' reactions demonstrated their attention to cumulative sequences of events; Wynn claimed to have evidence that, before any sort of numerical language is acquired, infants are capable of encoding ordinal (numerical) information.

In our opening chapter Wynn presents the 1992 study and subsequent work within a thoughtful and broad-ranging literature review. The reader will welcome the clarity with which the methodologies as well as the findings of infant research are presented, as well as the detailed interpretation of findings.

Wynn takes a strong nativist position, arguing that human infants are innately endowed with arithmetical abilities. She makes it clear towards the end of Chapter 1 that she does not seek to explain all subsequent mathematical or even arithmetical development within the narrow confines of her model. However, it seems fair to conclude that Wynn's account entails a continuity whereby the enumeration system present in infancy supports the development of counting in early childhood, and therefore that innate structures are central to mathematical development in the pre-school years.

In Chapter 2 Catherine Sophian offers an equally thoughtful alternative account. Addressing the infant research, she proposes a perceptually based interpretation of findings, in opposition to Wynn, and suggests that definitive evidence for one or other position has yet to emerge. Sophian goes on to examine in detail the findings of her own and others' research into the development of counting. She shows that the refinements of counting skill that take place from 3 to 5 years of age are such as to test quite severely the constraints of an innate enumeration mechanism.

Sophian proposes that the developmental process is best characterised as a "virtuous circle" of interaction between the child's goal-directed numerical activities and the conceptual advances that these bring about. The goals or uses of counting clearly change as the child grow older, and a part at least of this change is, according to Sophian, the result of social interaction. Thus her account of pre-school mathematical development is a dynamic one within which the achievement of socially mediated goals is a driving force.

The final chapter in this opening section builds, to some extent, on the social orientation of Chapter 2. Penny Munn presents new research exploring children's acquisition of symbolic skills, in particular their use of written numerals, and the influence this new skill may have on the understanding of number in general. She presents intriguing evidence to support the claim that children's understanding of the function of numerical symbols is crucial in the development of a cognitive model of number. For Munn this cognitive model is essentially a social one, it is the product of negotiation and forms the basis of shared understanding of numerical communication. There is considerable force behind this argument, and it has powerful educational implications, especially within the United Kingdom where formal schooling starts at age five. Munn draws an important distinction between the socially mediated learning that takes place in the pre-school and the formal methods of teaching in school, noting that a quarter of children in her sample entered school before they had become aware of the function of conventional number symbols.

At a theoretical level Munn's proposal is far-reaching. She presents, in prototype at least, a theory of symbolic development within which emergent numeracy and literacy skills are grounded in social context. An important contribution of this chapter is its requirement that the reader consider at some length the complex meanings that attach to the simple written numeral, the function of which is taken for granted in much of the research that is to follow.

CHAPTER ONE

Numerical competence in infants

Karen Wynn
University of Arizona, Tucson, USA

INTRODUCTION

The abstract body of mathematical knowledge that has been developed over the last several thousand years is one of the most impressive of human achievements. What makes the human mind capable of grasping number? Philosophers and psychologists have long speculated about the origins of numerical knowledge and concepts. The empiricist account of how we possess such knowledge is that we acquire even the simplest understanding of numerical relationships from our observations of the world. The alternative is a nativist account in which some understanding of number is inherent in the structure of the mind.

Number is different from perceptual properties such as colour and size. As the 19th century philosopher and logician Gottlob Frege (1893) observed, number is not an inherent property of any portion of the physical world. That is, there is no one number that describes a particular portion of matter. To give an example, there may be three *dogs*—but that same group of dogs is also an example of some different number (probably twelve) of *paws*, of yet a different number of *hairs*, of an astronomical number of *molecules*, and so on. In short, there is no "right" number for describing that particular portion of the material world. Number is not a property of the physical world itself, but rather is determined as a result of how we choose to carve up the physical world into individual elements—as *dogs*, as *hairs*, as *paws*, and so on.

The basic empiricist story of the origins of numerical knowledge, found in both philosophy and psychology, is that we learn numerical facts by induction over observations of the world. The philosopher John Stuart Mill (1843) held that we can identify the number of a group of things by identifying the individual elements and arranging them, in our minds or in the actual world, into a recognizable pattern. We can recognise that there are *three* flowers, for example, by perceiving the individual flowers and realizing we can always arrange them in the same pattern, for example,

○
○ ○

We then go on to learn mathematical truths, such as that $1 + 2 = 3$, by observing it to be true over and over again, for many different objects. We observe that one flower (○) and two flowers (○ ○) make three flowers (○°○); that one cookie plus two more cookies make three cookies; that one kitten and two kittens make three kittens; and that in general, we can arrange our idea of one thing (○) and our idea of two things (○ ○) so as to make up our idea of three things (○°○). Finally, we induce, from observing many such examples, that it is *always* true that one and two make three.

Philip Kitcher (1984) is a contemporary philosopher who has proposed an alternative empiricist theory of the origins of mathematical knowledge. Kitcher's main thesis is that we learn the simplest of numerical knowledge by observing the results of our own actions, and we learn the rest from authorities in mathematics—parents and teachers, and ultimately mathematicians. The body of mathematical knowledge that has been developed through history was itself built (and is currently being expanded further) by experts in mathematics, who first learn from and then build on the knowledge of their predecessors, who in turn built on the knowledge of *their* predecessors, and so on. The whole chain of knowledge, both for individual people and over the course of history, is grounded in the activities of young children, who learn about the mathematical structure of reality through their actions and interactions with the physical world: "Mathematical knowledge arises from rudimentary knowledge acquired by perception. Several millennia ago, our ancestors set the enterprise in motion by learning through practical experience some elementary truths of arithmetic and geometry" (Kitcher, 1984, p. 5). Kitcher gives an example of the way in which we perceptually acquire a particular arithmetical truth through practical experience—namely, that $2 + 3 = 5$: "We recognize, for example, that if one performs the collective operation called 'making two', then performs on different objects the collective operation called 'making three', then performs the collective operation of combining, the total operation is an operation of 'making five'." (Kitcher, 1984, p. 108).

But for as long as there have been empiricist theories of how we attain numerical knowledge, there has also been a nativist alternative to the empiricist view: philosophers, psychologists and cognitive scientists have long argued that some understanding of number is inherent in the structure of the mind. For example, Kant (1781/1965) has argued that "Mathematical propositions are always judgements *a priori*, not empirical; because they carry with them necessity, which cannot be derived from experience." More recently, Chomsky (1980) has speculated that "It seems reasonable to suppose that this [number] faculty is an intrinsic component of the human mind ... the capacity to deal with the number system ... is surely unlearned in its essentials."

The debate over how mathematical understanding originates has been going on for many hundreds of years, but for most of this time has been limited to a priori and philosophical arguments. Within the past 20 years, however, experimental methodologies have been developed in psychology that allow us to investigate the minds of young infants, and so to obtain some understanding of the inherent structure of the mind prior to the influences of language and culture. In this chapter, I will review evidence showing that humans come into the world already equipped with the concept of number. They are able to distinguish different numbers of entities, and to recognize numerical equivalence across different instances. This ability to represent number applies to a wide range of different kinds of entities, and to entities perceived through different sensory modalities. Moreover, in addition to being able to represent number, infants are able to engage in processes of numerical reasoning—they can determine the numerical relationships that hold between different numbers. But this numerical competence is not unique to humans—I will next review evidence that many different animal species are also able to represent and reason about number. I will conclude by describing a mechanism that has been proposed to account for this numerical competence in human infants and nonhuman animals—a hardwired mental mechanism dedicated to enumerating and performing numerical operations—and discuss some limitations to this psychological foundation of numerical knowledge.

NUMERICAL COMPETENCE IN HUMAN INFANTS

Infants are sensitive to number

Findings over the past 20 years have shown that infants are sensitive to number. These studies use a *habituation* methodology. Infants tend to look longer at things that are new or unexpected to them. By accustoming, or *habituating*, infants to displays that have a given property, we can determine if infants are sensitive to this property by then presenting them with displays that do not have that property and seeing whether they look longer at these new displays.

In one study, 5-month-old infants were divided into two groups. The infants in one group were habituated to displays of 2 circular spots of light arranged in a line, whereas those in the other group were habituated to displays of 3 spots of light. Each baby was repeatedly presented with displays of 2 (or 3) spots, and the infant's looking time to each display was measured. (As an infant becomes accustomed to a display, he or she begins to lose interest in it and will look at it for shorter and shorter periods of time, indicating he or she is becoming habituated.) Once an infant was habituated, as determined by the decrease in looking time, the test phase began: the infant was presented with new displays, some containing 2 spots, some containing 3 spots, and his or her looking time to these displays was measured. The experimenters found that infants looked longer when they were shown a new number of spots than when shown the number they had been habituated to, indicating that they could discriminate 2 spots from 3 spots (Starkey & Cooper, 1980). In a second experiment conducted in a similar fashion, infants did *not* discriminate 4 spots from 6. Because the ratio of 2:3 is the same as that of 4:6, infants were apparently not distinguishing the ratio of dark-to-light in the displays or using a general "more-numerous/less-numerous" response, both of which would distinguish 4 from 6 just as strongly as 2 from 3. Rather, they were responding to the number of spots *per se*. In a separate study, similar results were obtained with infants of 1 to 3 days of age (Antell & Keating, 1983).

In another study, 7-month-old infants were habituated to visual displays of either 2 or 3 randomly arranged objects. The displays were constructed of photographs of various household objects that were different in each picture—for example, one picture might consist of an orange and a glove, the next might include a key chain and a banana, the next a bell pepper and a sponge, and so on (Starkey, Spelke, & Gelman, 1990). Moreover, the photographs of the different objects varied considerably in size, and the items were placed in a different spatial arrangement in each picture, guaranteeing that the overall configuration of the items changed from picture to picture. Following habituation, infants were shown test pictures of 2 items and of and 3 items, containing new objects not seen in the habituation pictures. Infants looked significantly longer at test pictures containing the number of items that differed from what they had been habituated to, indicating that they discriminated between the two numbers.

In an intriguing series of experiments (van Loosbroek & Smitsman, 1990), infants of 5, 8, and 13 months were habituated to displays of 2, 3, or 4 moving items displayed on a video screen, and then tested on the habituated number and its immediate neighbours. Each item was a random "checkerboard" pattern, constructed by randomly filling in a proportion of the rectangles defined by a 16 × 16 grid. Each pattern had its own path of motion on the computer screen. The different paths of motion occasionally intersected so that checkerboards would overlap each other on occasion. Thus, a static view of the display would not guarantee correct number information—the number of items could only be determined by watching the display in motion over time. Nonetheless, infants of all ages tested discriminated 2 from 3 and even 3 from 4, and the older two groups of infants also distinguished 4 from 5.

Infants are able to determine numbers of many different kinds of entities. Not only can they identify the number of items in perceptually very different displays of visual objects, from spots of light, to photographs of household objects, to computer-generated random "checkerboard" patterns, they can also determine numbers of *sounds*, as shown in a series of experiments by Starkey et al. (1990). In these experiments, 6- to 9-month-old infants were habituated to photographs of 2 items or of 3 items as described earlier. On habituation, they were presented with a black disk on a display stage. On some test trials, the disk would emit 2 drumbeats, on other trials 3 drumbeats, and infants' looking time to the disk was measured. It was found that infants looked longer at the disk when it emitted the same number of drumbeats as the number of objects they had been habituated to. That is, infants habituated to pictures of 2 objects looked longer at the disk when it emitted 2 drumbeats; infants habituated to pictures of 3 objects looked longer when the disk emitted 3 drumbeats.[1] In order for infants to show the observed pattern of preference they must have been sensitive to the number of sounds. Alternative explanations appealing to stimulus complexity or to preferred general levels of stimulation, rather than number of sounds, cannot account for this finding, as infants preferred both the *less* complex or stimulating 2-sound/2-object combination, and the *more* complex or stimulating 3-sound/3-object combination, to the intermediately complex and stimulating 2-sound/3-object and 3-sound/2-object combinations (see Wynn, 1992c).

Studies in my laboratory have examined infants' ability to enumerate physical actions in a sequence. A sequence of actions differs from a display of visual objects in several respects. In terms of everyday, moment-to-moment human perceptual experience, most objects exist continuously through time, but exist only at specific locations in space. At any given point in time, there is a specific spatial location in which that object exists. Sounds, on the other hand, tend to exist for a specific segment of time only, but need not be localized to a specific portion of space during the time that their existence is perceived. Though a sound must actually emanate from some location or object, it can be perceived independently of its location in a way in which an object cannot be. Thus, whereas spatial information is primary in the segmentation of objects, temporal information is primary in the segregation of distinct individual sounds.

Physical actions are different from both objects and sounds. Unlike objects, actions do not exist continuously through time and so cannot be segmented from each other without reference to temporal information. Unlike sounds, they cannot be perceived independently of a spatial location, because in order for an action to be perceived, the "agent" of the action—which is an object—must simultaneously be perceived. Therefore, whereas objects may be individuated primarily in terms of spatial information and sounds primarily in terms of temporal information, the individuation of actions requires an integration of spatial information over time.

In the first experiment (Wynn, 1996), two groups of 6-month-olds were habituated to a puppet jumping; for one group, the puppet jumped 2 times, for the other group, 3 times. On each trial, the puppet made the requisite number of jumps, pausing briefly between jumps, then stood still. Infants' looking time to the now motionless puppet was measured. Following habituation, both groups of infants received six test trials in which the puppet alternately jumped 2 times and 3 times. If infants are enumerating the jumps of the puppet, they should habituate to the number of jumps presented in the habituation sequence, and look longer on those test trials containing the new number of jumps. Figure 1.1 shows the testing apparatus.

To ensure that this predicted pattern of looking time could not result from infants' responding to the tempo (length of pause between jumps) or overall

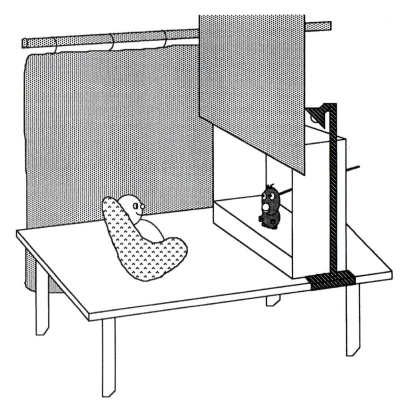

FIG. 1.1.   Diagram of Testing Situation and Apparatus in Wynn (1996). (Courtesy of *Psychological Science*).

duration of jump sequences rather than to the number of jumps, jump sequences were contructed as follows. Test jump sequences containing the old, habituated number of jumps had both a new tempo and new overall duration from the habituated jump sequence. Test jump sequences containing the new number of jumps had the same value on one of these dimensions as the habituation sequence, and the same value on the other dimension as the other test sequence. That is, for half the infants, both old-number and new-number test sequences were matched for overall duration (a new duration from the habituation jump sequence), with the new-number jump sequence having the same tempo as the habituation sequence and the old-number jump sequence having a new tempo. For the other half of infants, the two kinds of test sequences were matched for tempo (a new tempo from the habituation sequence), with the new-number test sequence having the same overall duration as the habituation sequence, and the old-number test sequence having a new overall duration. The speed and height of the actual jumps themselves never changed.

Results are shown in Fig. 1.2. Infants looked significantly longer at the puppet following a new number of jumps than following the old number of jumps, even though the old-number jump sequences were more novel on the bases of both tempo and overall duration than were the new-number jump

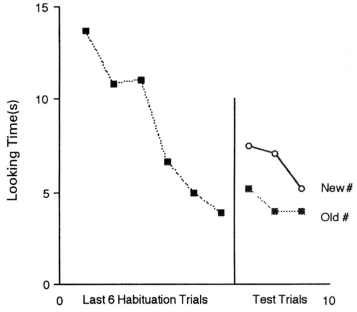

FIG. 1.2. Six-month-olds' looking times on last six habituation trials and on old- and novel-number test trial jump sequences in Wynn (1996), with sequences with motionless inter-jump intervals. (Courtesy of *Psychological Science*).

sequences. Thus, infants were able to identify the individual jumps in the sequence, and to enumerate them.

In a second experiment, we asked whether infants could enumerate even more complex action sequences. Again, one group of 6-month-olds was habituated to sequences of 2 jumps, another group was habituated to sequences of 3 jumps. Here, however, the puppet was in constant motion throughout the sequence—in between jumps, and briefly following the final jump of the sequence, the puppet wagged its head from side to side in an exaggerated fashion. Then it stood still, and the timing of infants' looking to the puppet began. In the test phase, as before, infants were presented with trials in which the puppet sometimes jumped 2 times, sometimes 3 times.

Again, infants looked longer at the test trials containing the new number of jumps, as shown in Fig. 1.3, showing that they discriminated the number of actions of the puppet.

Because the puppet was in constant motion throughout the action sequences, this meant that, in order to distinguish the different kinds of trials, infants were not simply enumerating the number of times the puppet moved—on every trial, the puppet had only a single period of motion, a complex one composed of several different aspects of motion and lasting several seconds. Instead, infants must have been enumerating entities considerably more complex than "period

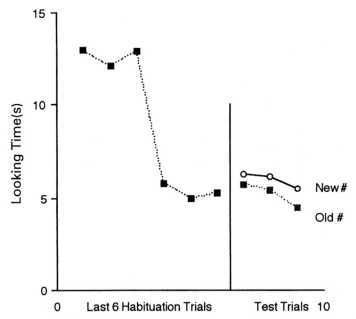

FIG. 1.3.   Six-month-olds' looking test times on last six habituation trials and on old- and novel-number test trial jump sequences in Wynn (1996), with sequences in which the puppet was in continuous motion. (Courtesy of *Psychological Science*).

of motion". There are several possibilities as to exactly what infants were enumerating. They may have been counting the jumps themselves—picking out the jumping actions of the puppet from the "backdrop" of head-wagging. Alternatively, they may have been counting the repetitive "jumping-followed-by-head-wagging" activity of the puppet. In either case, infants were enumerating individuals whose boundaries were determined by a complex analysis of patterns of motion over time.

The studies reviewed so far show that infants' numerical representations are abstract enough to apply to different situations and to different kinds of entities. Infants can represent numbers of physical objects and visual patterns, regardless of their colour, size, and configuration. They can also represent numbers of sounds, and numbers of actions. They can represent numbers of items presented simultaneously and numbers of items presented sequentially, numbers of items presented visually and numbers of items presented aurally. Finally, they can recognize numerical correspondences between different kinds of items; for example between a number of objects and that same number of sounds. These findings all indicate that infants have a capacity for representing numerical values independently of situation-specific or perceptual information. Human adults can enumerate virtually any kind of entity we can conceive of: animate and inanimate physical objects such as *dogs* and *cups*; collections of entities such as *flocks* and *armies*, actions and events such as *jumps* and *parties*; political and cultural entities such as *governments* and *religions*; abstract entities such as *opinions* and even entities defined by an absence of matter, such as *holes*. The empirical results reviewed here suggest that infants' enumeration mechanism may be equally general.

Infants can reason about number

However, there is more to numerical knowledge than the ability to distinguish different numbers. The ability to distinguish numbers does not entail an ability to reason about those numbers—to determine, for example, that 5 is larger than 3, or that 2 is composed of 1 and 1. To determine such relationships, infants must not only be able to construct mental representations of the relevant numbers, but also be able to manipulate these representations in numerically meaningful ways. There is empirical evidence that infants can determine the results of certain numerical operations on small numbers of physical objects.

Studies in my laboratory have been examining infants' numerical reasoning capacities. In one experiment, 5-month-old infants were divided into two groups. Those in the "1 + 1" group were shown a single item being placed into an empty display area. Then a small screen rotated up, hiding the item from view, and the experimenter brought a second identical item into the display area, in clear view of the infant. The experimenter then placed the second item out of the infant's sight behind the screen (this sequence of events is shown in the top portion of Fig. 1.4). Thus, infants could see the nature of the operation being performed, but could not see the result of the operation. The screen was then dropped to reveal an outcome of either 1 object (the Impossible Outcome) or 2 objects (the Possible Outcome). Infants in the "2 – 1" group were similarly presented with a sequence of events depicting a subtraction of one item from two items (shown in the bottom portion of Fig. 1.4). Again, after this sequence of events was concluded the screen rotated downward to reveal either 1 object (now the Possible Outcome) or 2 objects (Impossible Outcome) in the display case. Infants were presented with 3 test trial pairs; each pair of test trials contained one Possible and one Impossible Outcome, always in the same order (half the infants in each group received the Possible Outcome first, the other half, the Impossible Outcome first).

Sequence of events: 1+1 = 1 or 2

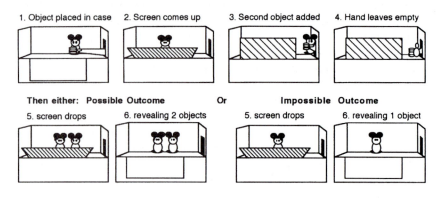

Sequence of events: 2-1 = 1 or 2

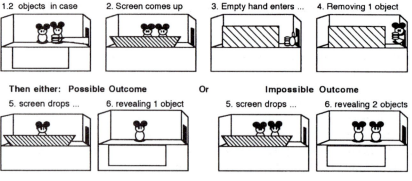

FIG. 1.4.   Sequence of events shown to infants in Experiments 1 and 2 of Wynn (1992a). (Courtesy of *Nature*).

Infants' looking time to the display was recorded when the screen dropped. Because infants tend to look longer at things that are unexpected or surprising to them, then if infants are able to compute the correct outcome of the addition or subtraction, they should look longer at the apparently impossible results than at the correct results. Thus, the two groups should show significantly different looking patterns. Infants in the "1 + 1" group should look longer when the result is 1 than when it is 2, whereas the "2-1" group should show the reverse pattern. (A pair of pre-test trials, in which infants were simply shown displays of 1 and 2 items, revealed that infants in the two groups did not differ in their baseline looking patterns to 1 and 2 items.)

This was in fact the pattern of results obtained. Infants in the two groups differed significantly in their patterns of looking in the test trials. Infants in the "1 + 1" group looked longer when the addition appeared to result in a single item than when it resulted in 2 items, whereas infants in the "2-1" group looked longer when the subtraction appeared to result in 2 items than when it resulted in a single item. Figure 1.5 shows infants' looking times to the outcomes.

One possibility is that infants were determining the exact result of the operation. That is, they were expecting 2 objects in the 1 + 1 situation, and 1 object in the 2 − 1 situation, and were surprised when that result did not obtain. However, another possibility is that infants were simply expecting the number to have been changed in some way as a result of the operation, without having expectations as to precisely what the result should be. In both groups, infants looked longer when exactly the same number of objects were revealed behind the screen as had been initially placed there prior to the operation. Infants in the 1 + 1 group, for example, may have looked longer at 1 than at 2 simply because they were surprised to see the initial number of objects unchanged. To put it differently, they may have been expecting "some number of objects other than one" rather than "two objects".

To distinguish between these two possibilities, another experiment was conducted in which infants were shown an addition of 1 + 1, but where the outcome was either 2 or 3 objects (see Fig. 1.6). In this case, both outcomes are different from the initial number of objects (one) placed in the display. Thus, if infants only expect *some change* to obtain as a result of the addition, they will not be surprised by either outcome. However, if they are computing the precise nature of the numerical change, they will be expecting 2 objects behind the screen and will look longer at the incorrect result of 3 objects. (A pretest condition showed that infants looked equally long at 2 and at 3 objects.)

This was the pattern of results obtained. Infants looked longer when the addition appeared to result in 3 items than in 2 items (see Fig. 1.7). That is, from two distinct experiences, each of 1 item, infants constructed an expectation of precisely 2 items. Thus, 5-month-old human infants are able to compute the precise results of simple numerical operations on small numbers of objects.

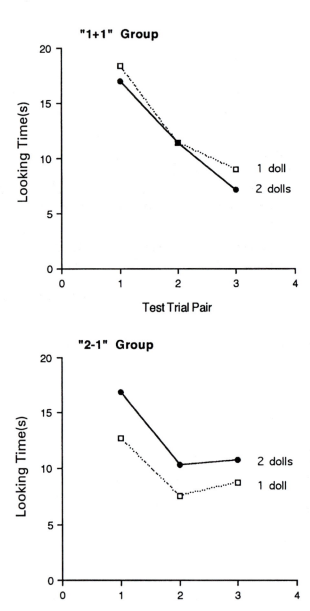

FIG. 1.5.   Five-month-olds' looking times to outcomes of 1 doll and 2 dolls following "1 + 1" versus "2 − 1" event sequences in Wynn (1992a).

Sequence of events: 1+1 = 2 or 3

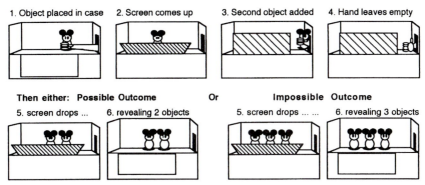

FIG. 1.6. Sequence of events shown to infants in Experiment 3 of Wynn (1992a).

These findings have been replicated in several different laboratories, using varying techniques and different stimuli. Uller, Carey, Huntley-Fenner, and Klatt (1996) presented 8-month-olds a situation in which one object was added to another and appeared to result in either one or two objects, and found that infants looked longer at the incorrect outcome. Baillargeon (1994) showed 10-month-olds situations in which one object added to another resulted in either two or three objects; again, infants looked longer at the incorrect outcome.

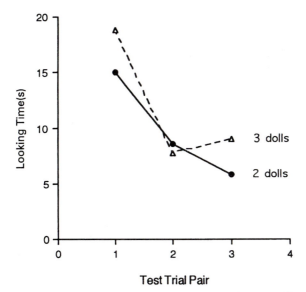

FIG. 1.7. Five-month-olds' looking to 2 versus 3 objects, following a "1 + 1" sequence of events in Wynn (1992a).

Moore (1996) presented 5-month-olds with "1 + 1" versus "2 – 1" situations as in Wynn (1992a) on a computer monitor. The "objects" were computer-generated random checkerboard patterns; the "occluding screen", a red square that descended from the upper portion of the monitor to "cover" the initial "objects", then rose up again following the addition or subtraction operation to reveal the outcome. Despite the change from actual objects in the real world to two-dimensional, abstract patterns, the same results obtained; infants looked longer at the numerically incorrect outcomes.

An experiment by Simon, Hespos, and Rochat (1995) shows that infants are not operating over visual aspects of the display rather than number. They presented 5-month-olds with "1 + 1" and "2 – 1" situations as in Wynn (1992a). In the outcomes, the identity of the objects was manipulated as well as their number. For example, infants might see an Ernie doll added to another Ernie doll resulting in: two Ernie dolls (number and identity correct); an Ernie doll and an Elmo doll (number correct but iₜ 'ity incorrect); one Ernie doll (identity correct but number incorrect); or one Elmo doll (number and identity incorrect). Infants looked longer at the numerically incorrect outcomes regardless of the identity of the objects, indicating that they were not attending to specific visual properties of the objects involved in developing their expectations.

In an elegant study, Koechlin, Dehaene, and Mehler (1996) tested whether infants might be responding on the basis of the presence or absense of objects in specific locations, rather than number. It is possible that infants might represent the precise spatial locations of objects in a display, and infer the spatial location to which an object is added or from which an object is removed. If so, infants might be surprised by the numerically incorrect outcomes, not because the wrong number of objects was revealed, but because a location was empty when it should have been filled, or filled when it should have been empty. To test this, 5-month-olds were presented with "1 + 1" versus "2 – 1" situations as in Wynn (1992a). However, all the objects were placed on a large revolving platform on the display, which was hidden when the screen was raised. This ensured that no object retained a unique, predictable spatial location. Regardless, infants showed the same pattern of results, looking longer at the numerically incorrect outcomes.

Similar abilities have also been shown in somewhat older toddlers, in a task requiring them to perform deliberate, consciously controlled motor actions based on their numerical expectations (Starkey, 1992). In this study, 18- to 35-month-old children saw from 1 to 5 identically coloured ping-pong balls placed into an opaque box which they could not see inside of. Next, they saw an experimenter add or remove a small number of balls. The children were then allowed to reach into the box to retrieve the objects. The box was constructed so that the children could not see into the box as they were reaching into it, and so that each reach into it allowed contact with, and removal of, only one object at a time. Thus, the number of reaches into the box that the children made indicated how many items they believed the box to contain. Even the 18-month-olds showed a knowledge of how many objects the box contained, when small numbers were involved.

The studies reviewed show that infants as young as 5 months of age are sensitive to the numerical relationships between small numbers, and able to compute the results of simple numerical operations. Infants can not only represent different numbers of entities, but they can reason about these numbers in numerically meaningful ways.

NUMERICAL COMPETENCE IN OTHER ANIMALS

The ability to represent and reason about number is not unique to humans. Numerical abilities have been shown in a wide variety of vertebrate warm-blooded species, both avian and mammalian. Studies show that, like human infants, animals can (i) distinguish between different numbers of entities; (ii) enumerate a wide range of different kinds of entities; (iii) recognize numerical correspondences between different kinds of entities; and (iv) engage in numerical reasoning, that is, determine the results of some numerical computations. There follows a brief review of some of these findings (for more detailed review and discussion, see Davis & Perusse, 1988, Gallistel, 1990).

Animals can discriminate numerosities of simultaneously presented objects. In one study, a raccoon was successfully taught, when presented with an array of 3 to 5 Plexiglas boxes each containing from 1 to 5 items, to choose the box containing 3 items; nonnumerical cues such as size, stimulus density, odour, and location of target box were controlled for (Davis, 1984). In another study, a chimpanzee was trained to pick out the correct Arabic number symbol when presented with arrays of 1 to 6 physical objects (Matsuzawa, 1985). In both of these studies, results generalized to novel items without additional training.

In a particularly compelling study, Pepperberg (1987) trained an African Gray Parrot to speak the appropriate number word when presented with up to 5 objects. Most interestingly, because the parrot had also been trained to "name" different kinds of objects, the parrot could be asked to identify the number of a subset of items of the display. For example, when presented with a tray with two corks and three keys randomly scattered over it, the parrot could successfully answer all three of the questions, "How many?" (correct answer: five), "How many cork?" (two), "How many key?" (three). Here, the parrot had to attend selectively to different aspects of the same display, based on the question asked of it. Again, results generalized to items not previously presented to the parrot for numerical evaluation. The flexibility of this controlled focus of selective attention indicates a general concept of number accessible to higher-level central processes.

In addition, many different species of animals are able to keep track of a number of sequentially occurring events. In one series of experiments (Platt & Johnson, 1971), rats were trained to press a certain number of times on a particular lever before pressing a single time on a second lever for a reward; penalties of varying degrees were imposed on the rats for pressing the second lever too early. Rats can learn this task with at least as many as 24 presses required (24 was the most tested). That their response was based on number of presses rather than on elapsed time is clear; when rats are trained to press for a certain amount of time, they continue to press for a certain extra *proportion* of the trained time on each trial in order to ensure that they have satisfied the criterion for reward; but when trained to press a certain number of times, they press a certain extra *constant number* of presses, independent of the required number (Mechner & Guevrekian, 1962). Similar abilities have been shown in pigeons, with a somewhat different task (Rilling, 1967; Rilling & McDiarmid, 1965).

Rats have also been trained (Davis & Bradford, 1986) to turn down the third, fourth, or fifth left-hand tunnel in a maze, and once trained, did so even when the distance between the tunnels was varied from trial to trial, and a corner had to be turned before the rewarded tunnel was reached. The rats could not simply have been running for a fixed length of time before turning left, or responding to some level of fatigue. They had to have encoded the numerosity of the tunnels on the left in order to succeed at the task.

Birds show similar abilities. In one experiment, canaries were successfully trained to select an object based on its ordinal position in an array (Pastore, 1961). Ten cubicles were spaced along a runway, and the canaries had to walk along the runway and choose the cubicle containing, say, the 5th aspirin in the series. Which cubicle contained the relevant aspirin was varied from trial to trial, ruling out any regularity of distance from the starting point. To control for the possibility that the birds might use rhythm as the basis of their judgements, the number of aspirins per cubicle ranged from 0 to 2, and the distance between cubicles varied from trial to trial. Given this, the birds must have been succeeding on the basis of the ordinal position of the aspirin.

Like human infants, animals are also sensitive to numerical correspondences across different situations. In several of the experiments reviewed in which animals were trained to discriminate different numbers of one kind of object, responses generalized to new kinds of objects without further training (Davis, 1984; Matsuzawa, 1985; Pepperberg, 1987). In an experiment by Church and Meck (1984), rats trained to respond to a certain number of auditory stimuli generalized when tested on a mixed presentation of auditory and cutaneous stimuli. And Meck and Church (1983) trained rats to respond on one lever when presented with two sounds or two light flashes, another lever when presented with four sounds or four light flashes. When tested with a mixed presentation composed of two simultaneous sound/light-flash pairings, they responded on the "four" lever, indicating that they recognized the numerical correspondence between four sequential sounds, or four sequential light flashes, and the mixed set of two sounds/two light flashes.

Furthermore, at least some species can compute results of numerical operations. The most conclusive evidence comes from studies with primates. In one study, Boysen and Berntson (1989) taught a chimpanzee to associate the Arabic numerals "0" through "4" with their respective numerosities. Without further training, she was able to choose the numeral representing the sum of oranges hidden in any two of the three possible hiding places in her pen. Most impressive of all, when the sets of oranges in the hiding places were replaced with Arabic numerals (one card with an Arabic numeral printed on it hidden in each of any two hiding places), she was immediately able to choose the Arabic numeral representing the sum of the two found numerals. That is, without training, she was able to operate over two symbols representing numerosities in such a way as to arrive at the symbol representing their sum.

In an extensive series of experiments, Hauser and his colleagues (e.g. Hauser, MacNeilage, & Ware, 1995) replicated and extended the addition and subtraction situations in Wynn (1992a) with rhesus monkeys and cotton-top tamarinds. In one experiment, rhesus monkeys were presented with a version of the "1 + 1" addition situation in Wynn (1992a). When shown 1 eggplant and then another eggplant placed out of sight inside a box, the monkeys looked significantly longer when only 1 eggplant was revealed than when 2 were, despite showing no preference in a control situation for looking at 1 eggplant over 2. In other experiments, monkeys were presented with a range of different addition and subtraction situations. In all cases, the subjects looked longer at the numerically incorrect results than at the correct results.

Suggestive findings have been obtained with other species. Rats appear to anticipate when they are approaching the required number of presses, when they must press a required minimum number of times on a lever to obtain a reward (Platt & Johnson, 1971). Rats will frequently check for the reward before they have given the required number of presses in situations when there is no penalty for checking for the reward too early, and on finding no reward, will return to the lever to increase their number of presses. Interestingly, the greater their number of presses before pausing to check for the reward, the smaller their number of additional presses is on returning to the lever. That is, they appear to know how close they are to the needed number, not only whether they have or have not reached that number yet.

The studies reviewed so far show that, like human infants, animals are able to determine numbers of many different kinds of entities with different perceptual properties, entities presented simultaneously and entities presented sequentially, entities presented visually and entities presented auditorily. Furthermore, like human infants, animals can engage in numerical reasoning; they can tell whether a given number is more, less, or the same as another, and in some instances can determine the precise results of numerical operations. These findings suggest the existence of an unlearned capacity for numerical representation and reasoning that is common to these different species. If the ability to represent and reason about number is of adaptive benefit, a mechanism designed specifically for determining and reasoning about number may have evolved through natural selection, perhaps at a distant point in evolutionary history shared by these different species (see Wynn, 1998). The next section presents a model for a mental mechanism that could perform such abilities.

A MODEL OF NUMERICAL KNOWLEDGE: THE ACCUMULATOR MECHANISM

Description of the model

This model was originally proposed to account for numerical competence in rats (Meck & Church, 1983), and has since been expanded to account for human infants' and adults' nonverbal numerical competence (Gallistel & Gelman, 1992; Wynn, 1990, 1992b).

There are a number of similarities in rats' ability to determine number and their ability to measure temporal duration. To account for these similarities, Meck and Church (1983) proposed that a single mechanism underlies both abilities, and expanded a model for measurement of temporal intervals (developed by Gibbon, 1981) to incorporate a counting component. Briefly, their proposed mechanism works as follows: a pacemaker emits pulses of energy at a constant rate, which can be passed into an accumulator by the closing of a mode switch. In its timing mode, the switch closes at the beginning of the temporal interval being timed and remains closed for its duration, passing energy into the accumulator continuously at a constant rate. Thus, the amount of energy in the accumulator varies in direct proportion to the length of the timed duration. The fullness of the accumulator after timing some duration can be compared with fullness values previously stored in memory, to determine whether the just-timed duration is longer, shorter, or the same as a duration associated with some event. In its counting mode, when an entity is experienced that is to be counted the switch closes for a brief, fixed interval and then opens again. Thus, when counting, the accumulator fills up in equal-sized increments, one increment for each entity counted; and its final fullness value varies in direct proportion to the number of entities so counted. This mechanism contains numerous accumulators and switches, so that the animal can count different sets of events and measure several durations simultaneously.

Evidence for functional similarity between rats' timing processes and their counting processes comes from several experiments (see Meck & Church, 1983). First of all, methamphetamine increases rats. perceptions of duration and of numerosity by exactly the same factor, suggesting that the same mechanism is affected in both cases. This effect could be explained on the model by the drug causing an increase in the rate of pulse generation by the pacemaker, leading to a proportionate increase in the final value of the accumulator regardless of the mode in which it was operating. Second, both numerical and duration discriminations transfer to novel stimuli equally strongly, when rats trained on auditory stimuli were then tested on mixed auditory and cutaneous stimuli. Finally, Meck and Church tested the following prediction: If the animal's decision is based on a comparison of the final value of the accumulator with a previously stored value of the accumulator, then one might expect there to be transfer from making an evaluation on the basis of the output of the timing process to making an evaluation on the basis of the output of the counting process, so long as the final output value of the accumulator in the two cases was identical. For example, a count that yielded the same final fullness value in the accumulator as a previously trained duration might be responded to as if it were that duration. This prediction was confirmed—when rats were trained to respond to a specific duration of continuous sound, they immediately generalized their response when presented with a certain number of one-second sound segments that had been calculated by the experimenters to fill up the accumulator to the same level as the level for the duration the rats had been initially trained on. Transfer was equally strong from number to duration. On the basis of these findings, Meck and Church concluded that the same mechanism underlies both counting and timing processes in rats.

On this theory, it is the entire fullness of the accumulator, comprised of all the increments together, that represents the numerosity of the items counted. This means that magnitude information is inherently embodied in the structure of the representations, which are themselves magnitude values—the fullness values of the accumulator. Thus the relationships between the representations exactly reproduce the relationships between the quantities they represent. For example, three is one more than two, and the accumulator mechanism's representation for three (the magnitude of fullness of the accumulator) is one more increment than the representation for two. Eight is four times as large as two; and the accumulator's representation for eight is four times as large as the representation for two (see also Wynn, 1992b,c).

Consider the information implicit in a system such as this, where the symbol for *one* is something like "–", that for *two*, "—", that for *three*, "——", and so on. A comparison of any two symbols will indicate whether the represented numerosities are the same or different. The symbols also carry, by virtue of their structure, information on whether one of the represented numbers is larger or smaller than the other, and by how much. If animals and infants possess such a representation of numerosity they may be able to determine more-than/less-than relations and to compute the results of additions and subtractions, *provided* they can operate over the representations in relatively straightforward ways.

For example, addition could be achieved by conjoining two (or more) representations together ($- + \underline{} = \underline{}$), or, more specifically, by either transferring the contents of two accumulators into an empty third accumulator, or "dumping" the contents of one of the accumulators into the other. A more-than/less-than/equal-to comparison of two accumulators A and B could be achieved by simultaneously "dumping" one increment from A and one from B; checking both A and B to see if either is empty; "dumping" another increment from each; checking each again; and so on. If A and B become empty at the same check, the 2 numbers are equal. If not, the accumulator that becomes empty first represented the smaller number. Exactly *how* much larger one is than the other (subtraction) would be indicated by the remaining fullness value of the nonempty accumulator. (To avoid loss of the initial values in the above operations, the mechanism could initially create "working copies", say A' and B', on which to carry out the operations.)

Implications of the accumulator model

The accumulator accounts for several aspects of animals' and infants' numerical abilities. First, the accumulator is a mechanism that determines discrete numbers of individual entities; it takes as input discrete *individuals*, not perceptual information. Therefore, it accounts for infants' and animals' ability to discriminate number *per se*, as opposed to nonnumerical properties of arrays such as light/dark contrast, configuration, contour complexity, physical magnitude (size, volume, height, etc.), and so on. Second, there is nothing inherent in the structure of the accumulator model to restrict the *kinds* of individuals it can count. Thus, it accounts for infants' and animals' ability to determine numbers of different kinds of entities. From an evolutionary standpoint, an enumeration mechanism with no structural limitations on the kinds of input it can take (beyond the requirement of *discrete inividual*) would be advantageous given the needs of animals to count different kinds of entities. Third, the accumulator also accounts for animals' and infants' ability to perform numerical operations and comparisons. The representations produced by the accumulator have a structure in which the numerical relations between different numbers are inherently embodied; thus, if animals and infants have suitable procedures for operating over these representations, such information will be available to them.

A prediction also emerges from the accumulator model. Because of variability inherent in the rate at which the pacemaker generates pulses and in the amount of time the switch closes for each increment, the exact fullness of the accumulator after counting a given number of items will vary from count to count. There will be a mean fullness value for each number, with the actual resulting fullness from counts of a given number being normally distributed about this mean. The variance of this distribution increases with increasing numerosity, due to the additive nature of the physical variability of the accumulator's functioning. Because of this, larger numbers will be more confusable with each other than smaller numbers having the same difference in magnitude, as higher counts have a greater variability than smaller ones.

Empirical findings confirm this prediction. In experiments in which rats are trained to press a lever a minimum required number of times in order to obtain a reward, the variance of their response increased with the required number (Platt & Johnson, 1971). In another experiment, in which rats were required to discriminate 2 from 3 and 3 from 4 sounds, all three subjects successfully discriminated 2 from 3, but only two learned to discriminate 3 from 4 (Davis & Albert, 1986). Similarly, in an experiment requiring squirrel monkeys to pick out the smaller of two simultaneously presented arrays of objects, subjects were able to distinguish 6 from 7 and 7 from 8, but only one subject was able to distinguish 8 from 9 (Thomas, Fowlkes, & Vickery, 1980).

Discrimination of number by human infants is also stronger with smaller numerosities. In a series of experiments by Strauss and Curtis (1981), infants discriminated 2 objects from 3 reliably, discriminated 3 from 4 only in certain situations, and did not discriminate 4 from 5; and in van Loosbroek and Smitsman (1990), infants discriminated 2 objects from 3 and 3 from 4, but only their oldest age groups (8- and 13-month-olds) discriminated 4 from 5.

Limitations to inborn numerical knowledge

Possessing an inborn mechanism for representing and reasoning about number does not imply unlimited numerical capacities. The existence of a framework of knowledge—numerical or otherwise—both enables the acquisition of knowledge consistent with the framework, and renders more difficult the acquisition of knowledge that does not fit the framework (see Gelman, 1991). That is, unlearned mental structures make some things easier to represent and learn, at the expense of making other things more difficult. The accumulator mechanism is no exception to this; there are limitations to the numerical knowledge that it supports.

First, there are limits to how the outputs of the accumulator can be manipulated, which in turn impose limits on the kinds of numerical information that can be obtained. In order to extract numerical information from the representations generated by the accumulator, they must be operated on in some way. For example, to determine the sum of two values, the contents of an accumulator representing the first value may have to be "poured into" an accumulator whose fullness represents the second value. Determining different kinds of numerical information requires different procedures, and we do not know just what procedures infants or animals have at their disposal. Many numerical computations—computing the product of two values, finding the greatest common factor of two values, determining whether a given value is prime, and so on—may require complex procedures that overstep practical limitations on the kinds of manipulations available to animals or infants.

Second, the accumulator mechanism only represents specific numbers themselves; it does not represent certain other mathematical concepts, such as *infinity*. Such concepts therefore would not be expected to be part of our initial numerical understanding, but probably result from the application of more general cognitive capacities. For example, Bloom (1994) has suggested that the concept of numerical infinity developed as a result of applying the iterative structure of language to the number naming system.

Third, the accumulator mechanism is designed to *enumerate* when in its counting mode. By virtue of its structure, it only represents numbers of whole, individual entities. This means it is built to represent positive integer values—the so-called "natural numbers". It is structurally incapable of representing other numerical values, such as negative numbers, fractions, irrational numbers, complex numbers, and so on. Interestingly, children seem to have great difficulty in initially learning to think about these other kinds of values. Fractions, for example, are notoriously challenging. Analyses of the kinds of errors children make in their reasoning about fractions show that across a wide variety of tasks, children persist in attempting to interpret fractions as discrete values for numbers of individual entities (that is, as positive whole numbers), and that this difficulty can last for several years (Gelman, Cohen, & Hartnett, 1989). From these findings, Gelman and her colleagues conclude that in order to become competent in manipulating and reasoning about fractions, children first have to expand their very notion of what it is to be a number—they have to go beyond the framework that "numbers are what you get when you count". The precise way in which children do this is not yet clear, but again, it is likely through the application of more general cognitive capacities (for example, processes of analogical reasoning as proposed by Gentner, 1983) that we achieve this conceptual expansion.

In this chapter, I have reviewed evidence that young human infants already possess a foundation of numerical understanding—they can represent and reason about discrete numbers of entities. Moreover, this ability is shared with other animal species, suggesting that some mechanism for numerical competence may have evolved far back in our evolutionary history. This initial numerical competence likely forms the basis for our further numerical knowledge—it would be very difficult to develop numerical understanding without an initial concept of number to build on to. But this initial basis is just that—a starting point. The abstract, complex, and richly elegant body of mathematical knowledge that has been developed by humans over the course of history goes far beyond these initial foundations. To understand how we have accomplished such an achievement, we will have to look to more general reasoning capacities of the human mind.

ACKNOWLEDGEMENTS

I am grateful to Paul Bloom for helpful comments on an earlier version of this chapter. This work was supported by an NICHD FIRST Award to the author.

NOTE

1. When, as in this experiment, test stimuli and habituation stimuli are presented in different perceptual modalities, infants typically look longer at the matching stimuli in the new modality rather than at the completely novel stimuli, possibly because the correspondence along a single dimension (e.g. number) between two very different kinds of stimuli (e.g. pictures and sounds) is inherently interesting to infants. Regardless of the direction of infants' preference in the test phase, the fact that this preference is systematically determined by their habituation experience shows that they are sensitive to the attribute under question, in this case number of sounds and number of objects.

CHAPTER TWO

A developmental perspective on children's counting

Catherine Sophian
University of Hawaii, USA

Is it necessary that a child recognize a group of four objects, let us say dots on a piece of paper, before he may be said to "know" four? Investigations have shown that the child may "know" four in some patterns of grouping and not in others ... should the standard be recognition of four in any and all possible groupings? ... Does a child really "know" four until he is able to assemble a group of four objects, to select four from a large number? Must he be able to distinguish four from three, from five, and all other numbers? Can he be said to have a "true" concept of four if he is not aware of all of its properties, e.g. that it is half of eight or a third of twelve, that it is twice two and the sum of three and one, and that it is the difference between ten and six and between five and nine? Must one not know that it is the square of two and the square root of sixteen, that it is the logarithm of 10,000? ... It is clear that there is no limit which may be set to the extension or perfection of concept. It is never complete, and the bounds of its development are limitless. (Douglass, 1925, pp. 444–445)

Douglass' query underscores the pervasiveness of change in numerical development. There is no single criterion by which we can judge whether a child has a concept of number, because number development is not a matter of acquiring any single concept. Even very young children may share some of the knowledge we as adults have about numbers, and yet their knowledge is also likely to differ from ours in important ways. Much of the study of numerical development, and particularly of the development of counting, has been directed toward asking whether, or when, young children acquire the aspects of numerical knowledge that are thought to play a central role in mature numerical abilities. This approach has been fruitful in uncovering the richness of early numerical knowledge, but it neglects an equally significant aspect of numerical development—change. Any satisfactory theory of development must tell us not only how children's knowledge originates but also how it grows. This chapter accordingly focuses on how children's knowledge about counting changes with age and what implications those changes have for a theory of early numerical development.

Most people think of counting as a verbal process, in which a string of number words is recited in a fixed order. Counting need not even refer to objects; for instance, an adult may ask a young child to "count to ten", just to practice the number sequence or to demonstrate that the child has learned it. Clearly, counting in this sense depends on verbal abilities and cannot be present in preverbal infants. However, in itself, recitation of the counting string is more a mnemonic feat than a numerical one; it is only when the elements of the counting string are used to enumerate some collection of items that a numerical operation is performed. If we focus on this kind of enumerative counting, it is possible to characterize it in an abstract way that does not rule out the possibility of preverbal counting. Gelman and Gallistel (1978) offered such an abstract characterization in formulating their "how to count" principles: These principles assert that counting requires taking a sequence of counting tokens in a fixed order (the stable order principle), mapping them onto the to-be-counted objects so that each object gets one and only one token (the one-to-one principle), and finally interpreting the last token used as a representation of the cardinal value of the whole set of objects (the cardinality principle). Given an abstract characterization of this kind, it is possible to ask whether children count even before they learn the counting string—using a sequence of internal numerical representations in place of the number words we use in verbal counting.

This question, and particularly the assumption that infants do indeed engage in a form of counting, has played a central role in contemporary theories of numerical development. The claim is not just that infants count, but that they do so on the basis of an innate mechanism that, because it embodies the critical principles of counting, provides a conceptual framework that helps older children learn to count verbally (Gallistel & Gelman, 1992; Wynn, 1992b). Because of the theoretical significance of this idea, this chapter begins with a careful analysis of the available evidence concerning infant numerical abilities. A central question in this analysis will be whether the evidence supports the conclusion that infants count, albeit in a nonverbal way, or whether number-related aspects of infant behaviour might be based on a more limited mechanism called subitizing.

Next I consider the evidence of developmental changes in children's counting over the pre-school years and even beyond, considering first developments related to the principles of counting identified in Gelman and Gallistel's (1978) seminal work, and then developments related to children's understanding of the functions of counting or the purposes it can serve. These findings underscore the developmental side of children's counting, and the need for a theory of numerical development that can account not only for what children know at an early age but also for how their knowledge changes with age.

The concluding section of the chapter, therefore, takes up the question of what kind of developmental theory can account for both the richness of children's early numerical knowledge and the continuing development of their knowledge over the pre-school years and beyond. I begin with an idea that underlies much of contemporary nativist theorizing, that the richness of children's early knowledge may reflect the operation of conceptual constraints that facilitate early knowledge acquisition. In light of the evidence of developmental change, however, it is important to consider the possibility that conceptual constraints on children's numerical learning may not be innate and unchanging but instead may themselves be subject to development. Specifically, I hypothesize that socially mediated goals may function as a source of changing constraints on children's numerical development, and I outline some ways in which an analysis of changing goals can help to elucidate early numerical development.

ORIGINS OF NUMERICAL KNOWLEDGE: WHAT DO INFANTS KNOW?

There is considerable evidence that infants are sensitive to numerical properties of the things they see and hear (see Chapter 1, for a detailed review). An influential hypothesis is that these numerical discriminations are based on a mechanism for nonverbal counting called the accumulator (see Chapter 1 for a full description). This mechanism satisfies the how-to-count principles, using the states of the storage device as an ordered sequence of tokens.

An alternative interpretation of infant numerical discriminations attributes them to a perceptual process known as subitizing. Subitizing is not yet fully understood, but it is thought to provide information about very small numerosities much faster than counting, probably by processing the items simultaneously rather than in succession. The existence of a subitizing process that is distinct from counting was inferred from marked differences in the speed and accuracy with which adults (Mandler & Shebo, 1982; Trick & Pylyshyn, 1993, 1994) and children (Chi & Klahr, 1975; Svenson & Sjoberg, 1978) enumerate arrays of one to three objects, as compared to larger numerosities. In general, reaction times increase with the number of items in a set to be quantified; it takes adults about 380msec longer, for example, to correctly quantify a set of seven than a set of six, or a set of six than a set of five (Mandler & Shebo, 1982). The increase is very slight, however, when the numbers are very small: A typical finding is that it takes adults about 40msec longer to respond correctly to three items than to two, or to two items than to one. Indeed, the current view is that even this small increment reflects the response choice part of reaction time rather than the time needed to process the stimuli. A method that involves limiting exposure time and asking at what exposure durations observers are able to quantify the sets accurately (cf. Trick & Pylyshyn, 1994) separates these two components of reaction time because it limits processing time without constraining the time taken to choose a response. Results from this method indicate that adults can quantify sets of three items within the same exposure time as sets of two or one.

One reason for thinking that subitizing rather than counting might be the basis for infants' sensitivity to number is that, until very recently (Xu & Spelke, 1997), all the available evidence indicated that infant numerical discriminations were limited to the same small numerical values as is subitizing in older children and adults. The largest numerical contrast for which successful infant discrimination has been obtained was three versus four items (Strauss & Curtis, 1981); and contrasts of four versus five (Strauss & Curtis, 1981) and four versus six (Starkey & Cooper, 1980); had failed to elicit significant discrimination. However, Xu and Spelke (1997) have now reported evidence that infants can make large-number discriminations when the numerical values are quite widely separated (16 versus 8). This finding, and its relationship to the earlier findings concerning infant number discrimination, clearly warrants further investigation.

Importantly, there is nothing inherent in the accumulator mechanism that would limit it to very small numerical values. Whereas subitizing is thought to be limited by characteristics of the perceptual system (e.g. the limited number of FINSTs, or mental reference tokens, in visual processing; c.f. Trick & Pylyshyn, 1993, 1994), within the accumulator theory effects of set size are explained by invoking variability in impulse size and the like. This variability accumulates as numerosity increases, reducing the discriminability of numerical values from each other. Thus, for example, the outputs of the accumulator for numerosities of six versus seven will be less discriminable from each other than those for numerosities of two versus three (Gallistel & Gelman, 1992). But this interpretation implies that discriminability should drop off gradually; it cannot account for a sharp loss of discriminability when numerosity exceeds three or four items. Thus, more research on infants' ability to discriminate among large numerical values, particularly research examining the degree of numerical contrast needed to elicit successful discrimination as numerical magnitude increases, would be useful in evaluating the accumulator hypothesis. It should be noted, though, that even if discrimination proves to drop off quite abruptly after three or four, that finding in itself would not rule out an accumulator mechanism. There might be limits on the number of impulses that the accumulator can store, which would generate restrictions on numerosity discrimination just like those that characterize subitizing.

A finding that has been taken as strong support for the counting position is that infants can identify numerical matches among sets that are presented in different modalities (Starkey et al., 1990). The evidence for this conclusion comes from a preferential looking experiment, in which infants heard a number of drumbeats and then were given a choice of two slides to look at. The number of items in one slide matched the number of drumbeats whereas the number of items in the other did not. Infants looked significantly longer at the slide that matched the drumbeats in numerosity than at the one that did not. Clearly, this result implies that the representation of numerosity infants generate when they see or hear a small number of items is not specific to the modality in which the items were experienced. Just as when we count verbally, to the same token (e.g. "three") whether we are counting pictures or drumbeats, infants too apparently arrive at a common representation when processing items presented in different modalities. Unfortunately, it is difficult to determine whether or not subitizing also generates a common representation regardless of input modality. Indeed, very little is known about the subitizing of stimuli presented through modalities other than vision. Insofar as the subitizing process is thought to be a perceptual and pre-attentive one, it is reasonable to expect it to be closely related to modality-specific perceptual processes. However, the fact that specifically visual processes are used to subitize visually presented items need not mean that the representation generated is modality-specific. After all, adults can very well subitize a set of visual stimuli and then report the result verbally. Why should not infants, similarly, be able to use visual processes to carry out a quantification but arrive at a modality-general representation of the numerical value that can then be compared to representations obtained by processing other stimuli in other modalities?

An important difference between the subitizing and counting hypotheses is in the richness of the numerical knowledge they attribute to infants. Subitizing is generally conceptualized as a very limited process, not only in the range of numerosities it can enumerate but also in the kinds of numerical information it provides. On the basis of subitizing alone, an infant would be able to tell that a set of three objects was different, numerically, from a set of two but not (at least initially) that it was numerically greater. Indeed, one hypothesis is that infants learn about ordinal relations by seeing what happens (via subitizing) as they add objects to sets or remove them (Cooper, 1984). Thus, for example, they may discover that three is more than two by observing that adding an object transforms a set of two into a set of three. The accumulator mechanism differs from subitizing in that it inherently provides relational information (Wynn, 1992b). The fact that three is greater than two can be determined directly by comparing the representations the accumulator generates for the two numerosities. Indeed, according to the accumulator theory, infants not only know that two is less than three, they know the basic arithmetic relations among small numbers, such as that one plus one makes two.

Cooper (1984) examined infants' ability to distinguish less-than versus greater-than relations between visually presented stimuli using an habituation

procedure. He presented pairs of slides in rapid succession, keeping the numerical relation between the two slides the same over a series of trials but varying
the specific number and type of objects involved. None of the slides depicted
more than four things, so they were all within the range of numbers that previous
research had shown infants can discriminate. Thus, on one trial infants might
see a slide depicting two objects followed in quick succession by a slide of
three; on another, a slide of a single object followed by a slide of three; and on
the next, a slide of two followed by a slide of four. In the test phase, a pair of
slides that involved a different numerical relation (e.g. two equal slides, or a
sequence in which the second slide depicted fewer objects than the first) was
presented to see whether infants would detect the change in the numerical
relation. Cooper found that 10- to 12-month-old infants did not react when he
switched from less-than to greater-than sequences or vice versa, but they did
react when the switch was from an unequal relation to an equal relation or vice
versa. By 14 to 16 months, infants reacted to both kinds of relational changes.
Thus, Cooper's data suggest that relational information such as less-than versus
greater-than is not inherent in infants' representation of numerical values.
Although they can judge whether or not two numerosities are the same from
an early age, it is only later that they distinguish between different ways of being
"not the same".

Wynn (1992a), however, reported findings that appear to show much greater
numerical knowledge in young infants. Her focus was on knowledge of basic
arithmetic relations, such as that adding one and one yields two. She showed
5-month-old infants either one or two objects, then screened them from view,
and as the infant watched either placed another object behind the screen or
removed an object from behind the screen. Finally, she removed the screen,
revealing either the appropriate number of objects or a different number, and
observed infants' reactions. Infants looked more at the uncovered objects when
their number was not consistent with the arithmetic operation they had just seen
than when it was. Specifically, they looked more at one object than at two after
seeing an enactment of the addition problem 1 + 1; and they looked more at
two or three objects than at one after seeing an enactment of 2 − 1. Simon et al.
(1995) replicated these results.

Although these findings are intriguing, they do not conclusively demonstrate
that infants have knowledge of arithmetic relations. An important alternative
possibility is that infant responses were based on same/different judgements
much like those underlying simpler numerical discriminations. Two of the three
contrasts in Wynn's (and Simon et al.'s) research pitted the correct arithmetic
result against the numerical value of the initial set (e.g. 2 versus 1 for the 1 + 1
episode), so that to discriminate between the alternatives infants had to know
only that the numerosity should be different after an object is added or taken
away than it was before. The only result, therefore, that implicates more than
a same/different discrimination is the finding that infants look longer at three

objects than at one after seeing a 2 – 1 episode. This finding is certainly of interest, but more controls are needed to ensure that it is not based on other factors, such as the novelty of the sets of three, which did not appear anywhere else in the experiment.

Another fundamental question is whether infants were quantifying the collections at all in the experiment. Simon et al. (1995) raise the possibility that infants might instead have been individuating and tracking the separate objects, reacting with surprise and increased looking when a new object mysteriously appeared or one that had been there disappeared. This possibility is very difficult to disentangle from the numerical interpretation within Wynn's paradigm, because the arithmetic operations are instantiated by actions carried out on objects. However, a method like Cooper's, involving the detection of numerical relations among arrays that are presented independently but in close succession, would not be amenable to this kind of interpretation. Clearly, converging evidence from different paradigms would be valuable in substantiating the conclusion that infants have arithmetic knowledge.

In sum, although there is considerable evidence of numerical processing in infants, there does not yet appear to be sufficient evidence to decide between competing theories as to the nature of that processing or the extent of infants' numerical knowledge. Do infants count? Theoretical analyses of the counting process, and accounts of a plausible nonverbal mechanism that embodies those elements, make it clear that this is a viable possibility. Pending further research, however, it is not possible to decide whether infants in fact do use a nonverbal counting process or a more limited subitizing mechanism. What we do know is that infants are able to detect the kinds of properties of events to which older children and adults might attach numerical representations. In particular, it seems clear that infants are able to individuate objects and notice when there are several different ones; and these individuated objects are exactly the sorts of units to which verbal counting is first applied.

PRE-SCHOOL DEVELOPMENTS: HOW TO COUNT, WHAT TO COUNT, AND WHY TO COUNT

The development of the how-to-count principles

Gelman and Gallistel (1978) argued that even before children have learned the correct counting sequence, they understand the conceptual principles that underlie counting. This claim is critical to their thesis that learning to count is not a purely empirical enterprise but reflects the operation of innate constraints that guide children's learning in fruitful directions. However, although there is considerable evidence that children's early counting conforms to the principles hypothesized by Gelman and Gallistel, it is more difficult to establish that young children understand the logical significance of those principles. This issue has been the impetus behind a good part of the research on pre-school children's counting.

In support of their conclusion that the principles precede correct counting and guide its acquisition, Gelman and Gallistel (1978) cited examples of children who counted idiosyncratically, yet in accordance with the principles. For instance, some children used either an incorrect sequence of number terms (e.g. "one, two, six") or nonnumber terms (e.g. letters of the alphabet) in their counting, yet abided by the stable-order principle in that they used their terms in the same order from one trial to another. Because children are unlikely to have seen other people count with incorrect sequences of number terms or with sequences of letters, these idiosyncratic but principled counts provide important evidence that children do not acquire the counting principles simply by mimicking adults. Thus, they support Gelman and Gallistel's contention that knowledge of the counting principles is not acquired in the course of learning to count but precedes and guides that learning.

Unfortunately, the use of counting terms in a stable order, even an unconventional one, does not in itself tell us whether children have any idea why a stable order is important. Conservatively, one might conclude that the children had learned that one of the things one does in counting is to recite a list, and along the way to mastering the correct list they sometimes came up with an incorrect one (either the alphabet, or a number list that contains some omissions). There is certainly nothing in the idiosyncratic counts that Gelman and Gallistel cite to suggest that children were actively generating a list to fulfil the requirements of "principle", as opposed to doing their best to remember a list that had been presented to them (Fuson, Richards, & Briars, 1982). Moreover, because only a few children generated idiosyncratic counts, it is difficult to draw general conclusions from them about children's knowledge of counting principles. Consistent with the view that idiosyncratic counts reflect partial memorization, Fuson et al. report that many nonconventional counts consist of both a stable and a nonstable portion, and that the deviations from the conventional count sequence in the stable portion predominantly consist of omissions (88%).

In order to function as a conceptual foundation for counting, all three of Gelman and Gallistel's how-to-count principles need to work together. Using the counting tokens in a stable order, for instance, is important only because it ensures that, when they are assigned in one-to-one correspondence to the objects being counted, the last one used will in fact be a correct representation of the cardinality of the set. The conclusion that the principles serve as a conceptual framework that guides children in learning to count, therefore, requires them to have all three principles at once. It is of course possible that they will make occasional slips in implementing the principles (skipping an object or counting one twice, for instance), but they should show some concern for all three of the principles and for how they fit together if the hypothesis that principles guide the acquisition of counting is correct.

The most troubling evidence in relation to this conclusion is that children often seem not to understand that the outcome of a count is bound to be the same each time a set is counted if the principles are followed. Consider, for instance, the following anecdote describing the counting efforts of a 4½-year old child:

> ... she had no difficulty in saying the number words ... Yet in counting the candies, she made many errors ... Her procedure was to point to each candy in its original location; she did not bother to push any candies aside after counting them. Because of this, she forgot which were counted and which were not. She counted several candies twice and several not at all, and as a result got different results each time. This inconsistency did not disturb her in the slightest. (Ginsburg, 1977, p. 11)

This child's errors in maintaining a one-to-one correspondence between her counting terms and the candies might be of little concern in themselves, as the child's pointing suggests that she understands the goal of pairing number words with objects, even if she has trouble achieving it. But the child's lack of concern with the inconsistent results raises questions about whether she understood the idea that the count should yield a single definite result.

Even clearer evidence that children do not always appreciate this point about counting can be seen in the following anecdote, again featuring a child who was over 4 years old:

> C: [Counts both rows and gets six.] What!?
> E: How come the red row has the same number of chips as the white row?
> C: I don't understand. Maybe if we count slower. Count the white ones slower this
>   time.
>
> (Wagner & Walters, 1982, p. 154)

This example comes from an intensive longitudinal investigation, in which children were visited at least twice a month for a 5-year-period beginning when the child reached 12 months of age. Both children's free play and their responses to a number of structured tasks designed to probe children's symbolic abilities were observed. On the basis of their observations, the investigators concluded that early number development is better thought of as a collection of developing concepts whose interrelations only gradually become clear than as the development of a single "number concept". Often the children in the study had difficulty coordinating different aspects of their number knowledge. For instance, the investigators noted "recycling errors", in which very young children reused numbers they had already assigned to objects, in order to finish counting a set; in one episode a child counted a set of seven objects, "1, 2, 1,

2, 1, 2, 3" (p. 143). Other counting errors appeared to be motivated by the child's expectation as to how a count should come out; thus, one child (3;5) counted a set of five objects, "1, 2, 5, 6, 7, 5 ... it's 5 cuz, I counted 5!" (p. 150).

These examples are interesting because they suggest that children try to satisfy some of the counting principles even as they violate others. In making recycling errors, children violate the stable-order principle in order to honor the one-one principle. In generating counts that distort the counting sequence to arrive at a desired outcome, they seem to be recognizing the cardinality principle yet violating other principles in order to get the results they want. These partially principled counts make sense as an accommodation to the young child's still limited mastery of the mechanics of counting: The child implements as many aspects of correct counting as he or she can, and fakes the rest. But it is difficult to see what the conceptual significance of the counting principles could be for children who violate one principle to satisfy another. What, for instance, could children who make recycling errors understand about why it is important to tag each and every object? Certainly, in the absence of the other principles, it does not make for a valid count. Thus, it seems likely that children's partially principled counts reflect their best efforts to reproduce characteristics of the counting they have seen other people carry out rather than *a priori* knowledge of the logical requirements of meaningful counting.

Counting permissions and developmental changes in what children count

In addition to the three how-to-count principles, Gelman and Gallistel also posited two other counting principles that function as "permissions" rather than "constraints"—instead of indicating what is necessary to generate a valid count, they indicate the permissible variations in the way things can be counted. One of these is the order-irrelevance principle, which indicates that objects can be counted in any order. The other, the abstraction principle, indicates that all kinds of objects can be counted: A collection does not need to be homogeneous, or composed of any particular kinds of objects to be countable. Each of these principles, too, has been the subject of some research, and in each case there is evidence that the principles are not fully in place in early counting.

Piaget (1973) tells an anecdote about a friend of his who, as a child of 4 or 5, apparently discovered for the first time the order-irrelevance principle:

> A friend of mine ... when he was about 4 or 5 years old ... started to amuse himself by placing some pebbles in a straight line and counting them, for example one to ten from left to right. After this he counted them from right to left and to his great surprise he still found ten. He then put them in a circle and, with enthusiasm, counted them—again ten so he counted them in the opposite direction and he found there were ten in both directions. He went on arranging the pebbles in all sorts of ways and

finished by convincing himself that the sum, ten, was independent of the order of the pebbles. It is evident that neither the sum nor the order are physical properties of the pebbles until such time as the child has actually arranged them or put them all together. (Piaget, 1973, p. 81)

This anecdote strongly suggests that the child did not acquire the order-irrelevance principle until after he had been counting for some time; indeed, the child appears to have discovered the principle by counting in different ways and observing the results obtained. Baroody (1993) obtained more systematic evidence on this issue in a study with 4-year-old children. He asked children to count a collection of objects; then, when they had finished, he asked them whether Cookie Monster could count the set in the reverse order and what number he would get if he did. All but one of the 29 children in the sample agreed that it would be possible to count in the reverse order. However, a substantial proportion of the children failed to predict the outcome of the reverse count correctly. Seven children were unable to recall the results of their original count in response to a follow-up memory probe, so that memory limitations rather than a lack of understanding of order irrelevance could be the basis for their failure to make a correct prediction. Of the children who demonstrably did recall the initial outcome, however, 27% nevertheless were unsuccessful in predicting the outcome of the reverse count.

Shipley and Shepperson (1990) addressed children's knowledge of the abstraction principle by investigating what kinds of things children count. In one experiment, they showed children between 3 and 6 years of age a pictorial array composed of several intact forks and two detached pieces of a fork that, if joined, would form a whole fork like the others. Children were instructed either to count the "things" or to count the "forks." Regardless of instructions, the younger children were not willing to count the two detached pieces of a fork as a single item; mostly they counted each part separately, so that an array of four intact forks and two half-forks led to a count of "six". In further experiments, the experimenter explicitly pointed out that the two parts together made one fork, and even modeled a count in which the two half-forks were counted as a single item, but the children still would not produce this kind of count themselves. Instead, they often excluded both of the part-forks from their count entirely, as if all they got out of the explanation was that the part-forks did not qualify as items to be counted.

Shipley and Shepperson (1990) also conducted an experiment in which they asked children how many "kinds of toys" there were in displays consisting of several duplicates of each of several toys. Only 2 out of 44 3- and 4-year-olds made a single correct response! Instead, they typically counted each individual item in the set, resulting in a quantification of the discrete objects, not the classes. However, performance improved markedly with age so that a majority of 5- and 6-year-olds were able to quantify the classes successfully.

Shipley and Shepperson's research calls attention to an aspect of the counting process that is not directly addressed in Gelman and Gallistel's principles—the segmentation of an array into units to be counted. In each of Shipley and Shepperson's experiments, children faced a choice between two alternative units—the discrete items (which are what the 4-year-olds typically counted), and some sort of aggregate (such as forks composed of two separate pieces, or classes composed of several like items). These are not just different kinds of things to count, they are different ways of segmenting the same array.

The segmentation process, like other aspects of counting, is subject to some constraints that must be met in order for counting to function as intended. In particular, all the items we count must be construable as equivalent units, they must have a commonality at some level of abstraction that allows us to think of each of them as an instantiation of whatever it is we are quantifying. We cannot include fork-handles as units equivalent to whole forks if we want to know how many forks are in an array. Moreover, we cannot switch units in mid-count; in Shipley and Shepperson's count-classes task, for example, it would not be valid to count some of the items individually and to group others together to be counted as a single "kind". Such a count would not correspond to any coherent quantification goal; having done it, we would not be in a position to say how many of anything are in the array. The fact that counting is a process of quantification or measurement, then, constrains the segmentation process in that it dictates that a uniform basis of segmentation must be used throughout any single count. Further, insofar as any specific count is directed toward a specific quantification goal, the units to be counted are constrained by that goal: The segmentation must partition the array into items that qualify as valid instances of what is being quantified.

Sophian and Kalihawa (in press) examined children's appreciation of these principles of segmentation, using a task in which children were asked to count arrays composed of objects that came apart into two pieces. Children saw arrays composed of some intact objects and some objects that were presented with the two pieces detached, but near each other; and they were asked to count either all the whole objects or all the pieces in the entire array. Even the youngest children in the study, 4-year-olds, adhered to the principle of uniform segmentation. None of the children produced a single count in which they counted one pair of separated pieces as pieces and another as a single unit, nor did they ever count one intact object as a pair of pieces and another as a single unit. However, there were marked age differences in children's adaptation of the counting units they used to what they had been asked to count. At 4 years, children typically did not differentiate between the two kinds of counts they were asked to produce: They segmented the arrays into the same types of units—whole objects for some children, pieces for others, discrete items (treating the intact objects as a single unit and the separated ones as two units) for still others—regardless of whether they were asked about the number of wholes or the number of pieces. Many of the 5-year-olds also counted this way. Some showed some differentiation between the problems, but typically they altered which parts of the array they counted as well as what sort of unit they used. Thus, when asked about wholes, they counted only the intact objects and treated them as single units; when asked about pieces, they counted only the detached objects and treated each piece as a unit. At 7 years, a majority—but still by no means all the children—adapted their counting appropriately in that they counted both intact and detached objects as single units when they were asked about wholes, and they counted both intact and detached objects as two pieces when they were asked about pieces.

Understanding the goal structure of counting

The difficulties young children have in selecting appropriate counting units call attention to the importance of understanding counting as a goal-directed activity and to possible developmental changes in that understanding. Counting is fundamentally a means of quantification or measurement, and all of its components derive their significance from this goal. The stable-order and one-one principles are important because they ensure that the last number in the count represents the cardinal value of the set (the cardinality principle), and the cardinal value of the set is important because it tells us how many we have of something we wanted to quantify. But do young children understand this goal structure? The evidence that they do not adapt their choice of counting units to the goal specified in a problem suggests that they may not. Several other kinds of evidence likewise support the idea that important developmental changes take place in children's understanding of counting as a means of quantification.

In a longitudinal study of very early counting, Durkin, Shire, Riem, Crowther, and Rutter (1986) observed systematic age-related changes in the kinds of counting toddlers produce. Many of the early counts they observed appear to be more social than quantitative in nature. Thus, children below 2 years of age typically produce number words either singly, in conversation, or as part of standard expressions such as "one, two, three, go". Recitation of the counting sequence first becomes common in the context of turn-taking with the parent, and these turn-taking recitations account for a substantial proportion of children's number word production between 21 and 30 months of age.

One way to clarify what children understand about the goals of counting is to see what kinds of situations will lead them to use counting. In one study of this kind (Sophian, 1987), 3- and 4-year-old children were asked to solve three basic kinds of numerical problems: (1) "How many?" problems, in which the child was asked how many objects were in a set; (2) "Put n" problems, in which the child was asked to put a particular number of objects into a set; and (3) "Make equal" problems, in which the child was asked to make a set that had the same number of objects as another set. Although the children were not explicitly instructed to count, the problems were designed so that counting was a potentially useful way to solve them. The results showed a definite progression with age in the range of problems for which children counted. All of the children counted on the "How many?" problems, but about on quarter of them—mostly 3-year-olds—did not go beyond that to use counting on any other problems. Of the children who did count on other problems besides the "How many?" problems, almost all counted on the "Put *n*" problem; only one child counted on the "How many?" and the "Make equal" problems but not on the "Put *n*" problems. There were also quite a few children—almost all of them 4-year-olds—who counted on all three types of problems in the study.

Restrictions on the ways young children use their counting have also been observed in many other studies (e.g. Hunting & Davis, 1991; Michie, 1984; Saxe, 1977; Schaeffer, Eggleston, & Scott, 1974; Sophian, 1995; Wynn, 1992d). Information-processing limitations may well contribute to these restrictions, but they do not appear to be the whole story. Counting to compare two sets, for example, may be difficult in part because it entails not only counting each of two sets, but also keeping track of the results obtained and comparing them. These demands could exceed the processing capacity of young children, accounting for their tendency not to count when they are asked to compare sets. However, children show marked limitations in their understanding of counting as a means of comparing two sets even when they do not have to carry out the counting themselves, suggesting that information-processing limitations are not the only problem.

Sophian (1988) asked children to watch a puppet count and to judge whether or not the way he counted was a good way to solve a problem that had been posed. Sometimes the problem was about the relation between two sets of animals, for example "Can every big horse have its own baby horse?", and sometimes it was about the total number of animals, for example "How many horses are there altogether?". Regardless of which problem was presented, sometimes the puppet counted all the animals together and sometimes he counted the two subsets separately. Children typically indicated that counting all the animals together was a better thing to do on the "How many" problems than counting the two subsets separately. However, they did not make the complementary judgement on the comparison problems. Three-year-olds tended to accept both types of counts on those problems, and 4-year-olds again judged counting all the objects together as better than counting the subsets separately. Thus, in their judgements of a puppet's counting as well as in their own counting, pre-school children showed much less understanding of counting as a way of comparing two sets than as a way of quantifying a single set.

Another indication that information-processing limitations are not the whole explanation for early counting restrictions is evidence that, in some situations in which pre-schoolers do not count spontaneously, they can improve their performance by counting if they are specifically told to do so. Sophian, Wood, and Vong (1995) provided evidence of this kind in a study in which children were asked to quantify a set that was hidden from view. A second set, which had been presented in one-to-one correspondence with the target set, remained in view. In one condition, children were explicitly told to count the visible objects before they were asked how many objects were in the hidden set. In a second condition, children were only asked to move the objects in the visible set—an activity that drew attention to each of the objects but not to the numerosity of the set. Because the objects remained in view, children could still count them when asked about the hidden set, but they would have to do so on their own initiative. Even the youngest children tested, 3-year-olds, made appropriate inferences about the hidden set when they were explicitly told to count the visible set. However, for the most part they did not count the visible set when they were not explicitly told to do so and thus performed less well in the "move" condition.

Several studies of children's understanding of the cardinality principle—the idea that the last number in a count quantifies the whole set—provide further evidence of age differences in children's understanding of the functions of counting (e.g. Bermejo, 1996; Frye, Braisby, Love, Maroudas, & Nicholls, 1989; Fuson, 1988; Markman, 1979). In these studies, children are asked how many objects are in a set they have just counted. The idea is that, if children understand the cardinal significance of the count they have just completed, they should answer with the last number from that count rather than recounting the whole set. On this task it proves to be the younger pre-schoolers who count and the older ones who do not. Thus, this research provides a nice complement to research on children's use of counting to solve different kinds of problems. Although young children show opposite kinds of behaviour in the two kinds of studies—failing to count when it would be helpful, in the one case, and counting when it is not necessary in the other—both sets of results support the idea that young pre-schoolers do not fully understand the quantitative function of counting.

IMPLICATIONS OF CHANGE FOR A THEORY OF NUMBER DEVELOPMENT

The research reviewed in the preceeding sections underscores two important questions for a theory of number development. First, what is the relation between infant numerical abilities and the development of verbal counting? And second, what developmental processes are responsible for the changes in children's counting over the pre-school period and beyond? Although it is clear that infants have important numerical abilities, it is not at all clear how much their processing of the numerical properties of the things they see and hear has in common with the counting processes used by older children. The available data are consistent with the accumulator model, which attributes to infants essentially a nonverbal form of counting, but they are also consistent with a subitizing account which posits much less continuity between infant numerical abilities and those of preschool children. Clearly, further research is needed to resolve this issue. At the same time, the evidence of later developmental changes in children's counting clearly has implications for the interpretation of the infant data. Whatever knowledge infants may share with older children, it must leave room for the developments we see when we study age differences in children's counting over the pre-school and early elementary school years.

An influential hypothesis, and one that has motivated much of the research on infants' numerical abilities, is that there may be important innate foundations for numerical development, particularly for the development of counting and related whole-number knowledge (Gallistel & Gelman, 1992; Wynn, 1992b). To the extent that, from an early age, infants show knowledge of properties of numbers that play an important role in later numerical development, it is plausible to hypothesize that that knowledge is grounded in innate structures that provide a biological foundation for numerical development. The accumulator is a model of how this could occur. The idea is that because the operation of the accumulator embodies important principles of counting, in particular the how-to-count principles identified by Gelman and Gallistel (1978), it directs children's attention to those same principles as they are learning to count verbally. On this view, verbal counting is not innate but its acquisition is facilitated by the presence of an innate structure—the accumulator—that directs children's attention to crucial features of the counting process.

The postulation of innate biases or cognitive structures that orient children's learning processes in a particular direction is an influential response to what is known as the "learnability" problem, the problem of explaining how children manage to master complex bodies of knowledge where the number of logical hypotheses to be considered is too great for learning to proceed effectively on a purely trial-and-error basis (e.g. Cosmides & Tooby, 1994). A classic example of the learnability problem arises in learning word meanings, because any episode in which a person speaks a word, even in conjunction with a pointing gesture, is consistent with a wide variety of interpretations for that word (Quine, 1960). It may be a name for the object pointed to, or for the substance of which the object is made, or for some part of the object, or for the position of the object, to name just a few. To account for word learning in the face of this problem, Markman (1990) postulated a collection of biases or assumptions that lead children to consider some interpretations before others in trying to figure out the meaning of a new word. In the same way, the accumulator hypothesis explains early numerical development by suggesting that children do not have to sort out all the complexities of the ways people use numbers at once; the accumulator directs their attention to the critical how-to-count principles and thereby facilitates learning.

This kind of explanation for learning in complex domains offers only a partial solution to the learnability problem, however. It reduces the initial learning problem, by suggesting that built-in constraints get the child going in the right direction, but it leaves us with the question of how children manage eventually to learn things that do not fall within the postulated constraints (Bloom & Kelemen, 1995; Sophian, 1997). Vis-à-vis numerical development, the accumulator model offers an explanation for how children initially learn to count, particularly how they acquire the how-to-count principles that the accumulator shares with verbal counting. But the problem is how to account for further developments, for aspects of numerical development that cannot be explained in terms of the facilitative role of the accumulator. Gelman (1991) considers this issue in relation to fractions, suggesting that it is because fractions do not work the same way as the accumulator that they pose so much difficulty for children. But even the developmental changes within children's counting in the pre-school period are beyond the explanatory scope of the accumulator model.

Consider, for example, the developments in children's ability to segment arrays into different types of counting units—to count parts of objects and aggregates as well as discrete items. There is strong evidence that infants have considerable innate knowledge about how to identify object boundaries (Spelke, 1990), and this knowledge could well provide the initial units on which the accumulator operates, accounting for the bias young children show toward counting discrete physical objects (Shipley & Shepperson, 1990). But how then do children learn to adopt other kinds of counting units? In particular, how do they arrive at the insight that the unit to be counted depends on the quantitative goal one has in counting? Learning to count units such as parts or aggregates appears to require overriding an initial assumption that what we count are whole things. Perhaps even more fundamentally, it requires replacing the assumption that countable units are defined by the physical properties of the things we are counting, and thus that number is inherent in the array, with a view of counting as a measuring process that quantifies an array in relation to a chosen unit of measure. The accumulator model has little to offer toward an understanding of how these changes come about.

To a large extent, mathematical learning can be seen as progressing from special cases to more general ones. Just as discrete objects turn out to be just one of many possible types of counting units, the counting numbers turn out to be just one kind of rational number, and linear equations turn out to be just one kind of equation. Accordingly, much of numerical development can be seen as a relaxing of constraints. But the problem is not just one of overriding old constraints, because with each new level of generality, the complexities of mathematical learning increase, so that the problem of explaining how learning is possible is no less challenging at the more advanced levels than at the initial ones. The same learnability argument that led to the postulation of initial constraints on learning, therefore, implies that there must be constraints on later learning as well. What we need, then, is a theory that is not limited to initial, innate, constraints but that can account for the progressive emergence of new kinds of constraints that make possible new kinds of numerical learning as the child develops.

Cognitive constraints are usually understood to be a kind of belief or expectation. In Markman's account of word learning, for instance, they are characterized as assumptions about the meaning of a new word. Similarly, Gelman and Gallistel's counting principles express general beliefs a child might hold about what is necessary for a count to be valid. Cognitive activity, however, is a function of desires as well as beliefs; it is goal-directed. Goals function as a source of cognitive constraints because they determine what we pay attention to. Even in infancy, the presence of an attractive goal object can have a strong impact on what infants learn from a series of demonstrations (Kaye, 1979). Likewise, the goals children have when they view a set of materials affect what they are able to remember from those materials (e.g. Geis & Hall, 1978; Istomina, 1975).

Goals derive in large part, although not exclusively, from social interactions. Social interactions influence cognition by shaping the activities in which children participate and the goals toward which those activities are directed. Because people interact in different ways with children of different ages, social interaction is adapted to the cognitive abilities of the child. Yet at the same time that interaction contributes to cognitive change. Thus, there is a dynamic relation between the goals and activities established through social interaction and children's developing knowledge and cognitive abilities.

Several researchers have provided information about age-related changes in the kinds of social interactions within which children engage with numbers. Durkin et al. (1986) have documented the kinds of recitative interactions in which parents, at least in some cultures, begin to engage their children as soon as the child has begun to produce number words, and they have also noted the marked age-related changes that occur even in the first years of life in the ways parents and children talk about numbers. Saxe, Guberman, and Gearhart (1987) have provided evidence of changes over the pre-school years in the kinds of numerical problems parents set for their children. There are also important differences between school-based interactions and the ways children engage with numbers outside the classroom, not least because of the emphasis in the classroom on written representations of numbers (Nunes, Schliemann, & Carraher, 1993). In all these interactions, children's goals may not be the same as their adult partners', but they are surely influenced by the ways the adult defines the interaction, and they surely change with age. As these changing goals direct children's attention to different aspects of numbers and the ways we use them, they therefore provide a rich set of changing constraints on their numerical learning.

In addressing the acquisition of aspects of numerical knowledge that do not fit well with hypothesized innate constraints, theorists often invoke the contribution of social and cultural processes, as well as biological ones, to numerical development (e.g. Elbers, 1991; Gelman & Brenneman, 1994; Resnick, 1994). The notion that socially defined goals function as a source of dynamic constraints on learning is consistent with this general idea. At the same time, because goals can derive from biological needs and functions (Cosmides & Tooby, 1994) as well as from social interactions, a goal-based account of numerical development need not draw a sharp demarcation between innate constraints and developmentally changing ones, or between biologically primary versus secondary kinds of numerical abilities (Geary, 1995). Throughout development, children's learning can be understood in relation to what they are trying to do and how that activity directs their attention.

Thus, in infancy, an important goal of early visual processing appears to be to identify distinct objects within the visual field (Spelke, 1990). This goal, and an attendent interest in individuating objects and tracking their movements, could account for the responsiveness of infants as young as 5 months of age to changes in numerosity (Simon, et al., 1995; Wynn, 1992a). On this view, very early numerical discriminations may not be based so much on attention to aggregate numerosity as on attention to individual objects. That goal, however, in conjunction with some limited enumeration processes, is sufficient to allow the child to notice some numerical regularities, such as that adding an individual to a group of two produces a group of three. These regularities may engender new interest in quantification as a goal in its own right.

The goal of quantification, in turn, engenders interest in number words, which are used to describe these quantities. In the second and third year of life, children primarily use number terms incidentally or in conversation rather than in a counting string (Durkin et al., 1986), perhaps reflecting this early goal. But enumeration without counting is limited to very small sets, so encounters with the words for larger numerical quantities, in conjunction with the goal of applying them to the appropriate quantities, could lead to the formation of enumeration as a goal. Counting then flourishes—but at first only in the form of counting one set at a time. The early limitations on children's numerical functioning—for instance, their inability to use counting relationally (Sophian, 1987)—can thus be understood as a reflection of the constraints of thinking about numerical activity solely in terms of enumeration. But the goal of enumeration is itself a developmental construction, and as it gives way to new goals the constraints it imposes will likewise give way to new constraints.

Soviet researchers have attached particular importance to developmental changes in children's ability to subordinate activities to new goals in a strategic manner (e.g. Istomina, 1975). This development is illustrated by the emergence of mnemonic strategies, which entail doing something (such as repeating a word) not for its own sake but for its impact on the goal of remembering. The emergence of strategic behaviour, therefore, is taken to reflect an important developmental change in the kinds of goals children are able to construct.

Sophian et al.'s (1995) evidence of developmental changes in children's use of counting points to changes in counting that parallel these changes in mnemonic behaviour. Just as the children in Istomina's research had difficulty subordinating verbal activity to the goal of remembering, Sophian et al. found that young pre-schoolers had difficulty counting one set as a means of drawing an inference about another, corresponding, set. The children counted when they were told to do so, and it helped them solve the inference problems, yet they did not engage in counting on their own initiative as a means of solving the problems. These findings directly parallel the evidence for "production deficiencies' in research on children's use of mnemonic strategies (Flavell, 1970).

These findings are relevant to children's numerical learning because counting is a potentially powerful way of learning about numerical relations. Gelman (1982), for instance, showed that children's conservation performance improved when they were asked to count the sets before and after the transformation. Other researchers have also found counting-based training procedures to be effective in improving performance on numerical comparison tasks (Clements, 1984; Cowan, Foster, & Al-Zubaidi, 1993; Saxe, 1979). But outside of an experimental context, if children cannot themselves generate the goal of counting sets as a basis for comparing them, they will not have the opportunity to learn in this way. Thus, there appears to be a dynamic relation between children's conceptual knowledge about numbers and their goal-based numerical activities: Conceptual advances facilitate new goals and corresponding activities, which in turn provide the input for further conceptual advances.

Clearly, much further work is needed to develop a complete account of the role of changing goals in numerical development, and to evaluate its validity. The value of the proposal, for now, lies primarily in pointing a way out of the fundamental impasse to which accounts based on innate competences lead us. Instead of positing static constraints, and then worrying about how children transcend them, we can locate the constraints that make learning possible in the intrinsically dynamic goal-oriented activities of the child. To account for children's eventual mastery of what is initially difficult, we do not need so much to posit that they override initial constraints as that they construct new goals that no longer entail those constraints. Those new goals grow in part out of the very activities engendered by the old goals and in part out of the child's engagement in new kinds of socially mediated activity.

CHAPTER THREE

Symbolic function in pre-schoolers

Penny Munn
University of Central Lancashire, UK

INTRODUCTION

The focus of this chapter is young children's progression in symbolic function from resemblance-based number symbols (iconic tallies or pictograms) to conventional symbolisation (numerals). Figure 3.1 shows the varying forms of young children's written number representation. Longitudinal data summarized here suggest that the acquisition of conventional number symbols in early childhood is indicative of a general shift into symbolic function. However, the important progression is not in the *form* of the symbols that children use—whether they are based on resemblance or on convention. The real progression lies in the *function* that the symbol has for the child's action—whether it's used as a mere accessory to action or as an integral part of the child's cognitive model. It is argued that the development of symbolic function can have a marked impact on number understanding in childhood through its role in providing a common cognitive model that underpins novice/expert communication about number.

Very young children undoubtedly have distinctive ways of thinking. Since Piaget first began to document the nature of this early thought (Piaget 1926, 1929; Piaget and Szeminska, 1941, 1952), many authors have extended the description of small children's singular thought processes. Thus Carey (1985) has described how young children's thinking about bodily processes (including illness) focuses on social rather than physiological function. Damon (1990) has described how young children's thinking about themselves and their relation-

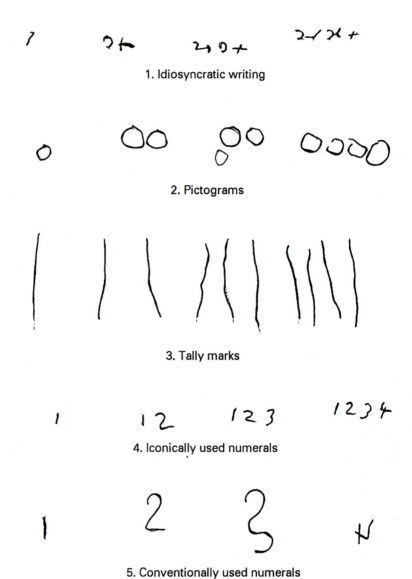

1. Idiosyncratic writing

2. Pictograms

3. Tally marks

4. Iconically used numerals

5. Conventionally used numerals

FIG. 3.1. Ways of representing one, two, three, and four blocks.

ships focuses on physical rather than psychological aspects of their experience. Baron-Cohen (1995) and Harris (1995) have described in some detail how young children lack the complex thinking about other people's minds and goal-states that are an integral part of mature social interaction. Despite controversy over Piaget's initial claims (for instance, that young children's inability to "decentre" was the central cause of childish thinking) it remains true that small children's thinking is quite different from that of adults and older children. Yet some similarities are to be found in the principles that govern the thinking and reasoning of both children and adults and these have given rise to doubt about some aspects of the programme of cognitive developmental psychology. Although we may document differences between adult and child thought processes, it is possible that these differences may not be absolute but may originate in the different social contexts and activities of adults and children. One major difference between older and younger children's behaviour relates to literacy. The acquisition of the ability to read and create symbols marks a qualitative difference in experience that is developmentally very important. One of the factors governing pre-school children's psychological function consists of their relative inability to participate in the literacy that pervades the culture and thinking around them. In this chapter I shall relate pre-school children's use of symbols to current ideas about the way symbol systems contribute to adult thinking and consider the way early number understanding may be affected by symbolic function.

My description of developments in numeric symbol use draws heavily on two empirical studies. The first set of studies was conducted by Hughes and his colleagues in the 1980s (Hughes, 1983, 1991, 1986). The second was my own longitudinal study of pre-school literacy and numeracy conducted in the early 1990s (Munn, 1994, 1995). This study followed 56 pre-schoolers through their final year of nursery school and first term of primary school. During four visits (one per term) I interviewed each child individually about reading and number. The children (31 boys, 25 girls, 46 months old on average at the start of the study) were selected from 8 pre-school centres that varied in size and organization. Nearly three-quarters of the children came from families living on low wages or benefit. One of the children had a first language that was not English. No other children in the sample were from ethnic minority groups.

As it was the pre-school context that was the focus of the study the age of the children mattered far less than their experience of formal schooling. The children were all receiving their pre-school education in centres that were independent of primary schools. Sample attrition due to children moving away or parents refusing consent after the move to primary school was 14%. Children were interviewed once each term in the final year of pre-school and again at the end of their first term in primary school about number, reading, and writing.

Storybook reading.   The children were invited to read from a beginning reader, were read a story, and then asked to read it again. They were asked to point to where the story had been read from and then to the words.

Counting and number words.   The children were asked to count as high as they were able (i.e. to recite the number words) and to count a row of blocks. They were asked to give the interviewer a successively larger number of blocks.

Recording quantity.   The children were given small pieces of card and a stubby pencil and asked to label the quantity of blocks (1, 2, 3, and 4) in a set of four tins. A secret addition was introduced to the labelled tins and the children were asked to search for the tin to which the extra block had been added.

Teacher questionnaires.   The children's primary teachers returned questionnaires on progress at the end of primary 1 in the June following the fourth visit.

The focus of this chapter is the progression in symbolic function I found in these children's responses. Two major questions are addressed:

1. Do nonconventional symbols really function as "precursors" in form to conventional symbol use, as Hughes' work suggested? The finding that quite young children can record number in the form of tallies or pictograms has led to speculation that this "natural" symbolizing activity should be integrated into classroom number activities (Atkinson, 1992).

2. What role does a child's developing symbolic function play in the development of number understanding? Current notions of the development of number understanding emphasize the role of concrete activity in a child's number ability. Number symbols are usually regarded as devices for recording concrete activity. To what extent do number symbols become an integral part of children's numerical thought?

These questions are addressed in the general theoretical context of social cognition in which cognitive models are viewed as having a primarily communicative function.

WHAT IS A SYMBOL?

A symbol is something—a mark, drawing, sound, object, etc. that stands for something else. This relation of "standing for something else" can be achieved in more than one way.

Iconic symbols

A symbol can resemble the thing that it stands for, as a drawing, painting or schematic design does. Such iconic symbols usually have one or more points of correspondence with the thing or idea that they represent, such that they represent only part of the whole. A drawing of a face, or an animal, for instance, might give only an outline and a few key features—just enough to convey "catness" or the individuality of the person depicted. Similarly, iconic symbols for number (such as tallymarks or pictograms) would show the quantity of objects represented—just enough to convey "threeness", for instance.

Conventional symbols

A symbol can also stand for a thing or idea without resembling it in any way. In this case the link that provides the meaning is established arbitrarily—purely by convention. The process of establishing the link between a conventional symbol and its referent is inherently social. Some community of shared meaning has to be established in order to assign meaning to a symbol, and the person wanting to understand the symbol must become part of that community in order to access the meaning. Some religious symbols such as a cross or a pentagram are examples of symbols specific to certain social groups: To understand the meaning of the symbol one must be inducted into the practices of the group. Letter symbols such as ü or ø are specific to certain linguistic groups and make no sense without some experience of the language they represent. Number symbols are largely universal, and can be interpreted by anyone practised in the conventions of number. Mathematical symbols, however, like + require a socially based initiation into the practices of mathematicians. At the earliest stages of number learning small children become inducted into the symbolic practices of their community in much the same way as they learn about the linguistic practices that relate to letter symbols. However, the two symbol systems (numerals and letters) are very different in the type of meaning that they represent, and in the syntactic rules that establish how they must be read and written.

Symbolic function and verbal meaning

We have a very clear picture of the earliest development of symbolic function in relation to verbal meaning. Initially, children's experiences with storybooks and environmental print exposes them to the link between symbol and meaning. Repeated exposure aids the development of the idea that printed letters communicate meaning. This understanding is crucial: It entails a shift in perception from people to symbols as the origin of communications. Once children have grasped the role that print plays, they have the contextual understanding to begin learning just how the letter system works (Clay, 1979). Initially, they use the gross visual appearance of printed artefacts to identify meanings. This route to understanding can result in extensive sight-reading of individual words. Sooner or later, skilled reading development demands that children understand the letter-sound correspondence rules that dictate the form of individual words. The development of skilled reading therefore involves a wide range of linguistic functions—communicative competence, understanding the communicative purpose of symbol systems, auditory and visual working memory, and a grasp of the complicated letter-sound correspondences that govern the formation of written words (Bryant, 1993).

Symbolic function and numeric meaning

The "syntax" of numerals—the precise rules that govern the relation between form and meaning—is quite different from that governing the way the alphabetic writing system is used to form words. It is a schoolchild's first task in learning about symbols to understand that there are two quite distinct rule systems to be learned. After the transition to school children begin to grapple with many aspects of these symbol systems whose meaning is governed by convention. They bring to this task all their previous experience of symbols with meanings governed by resemblance.

HOW DO CHILDREN BEGIN TO GRASP THE IDEA OF SYMBOLS?

Both mental and social abilities are needed to understand symbol systems. Understanding that a mark can represent an idea or a thing—can contain meaning—is a cognitive achievement in itself, and remembering the rules for creating (i.e. writing) or decoding (i.e. reading) symbols entails considerable cognitive effort. However, a child needs to do more than understand the process of symbolization and remember the decoding rules. The child also needs a cognitive model of the world that is shared with those who write or read these same symbols. This is true both for iconic and conventional symbol systems. A line-drawing of a cat will only evoke "catness" in someone who has had considerable experience of the real thing: It is this experience that is drawn on when a few simple lines evoke the memory of a cat curled up asleep, or walking away with its tail in the air. It is the same with the meaning created by arbitrary symbols such as letters; decoding ability can be severely limited by a vocabulary that is too small. It is one thing to decode printed words, but only experience (and therefore inclusion in the cognitive model) of the word and of the thing or idea that it represents will allow the reader to share the meaning that the writer intended.

Cognitive models of number

An expert's cognitive model of number incorporates the number words, the abstract number referents (including number bonds), and the number symbols. It functions to coordinate, direct, and activate numerical goals. In adults, numerical goals will typically involve actions such as counting, comparing, calculating, reading, writing, and communicating. The basic model of number, containing representations of number, number words, and written number symbols, governs all these activities. It also functions to interpret others' numerical meaning in conversation, reading, and writing. An expert's model of number will contain ready-made metaphoric links among the different levels of representation and between the different meanings that number words and symbols can take. It is the possession of this shared cognitive model of number that establishes intersubjectivity between people and allows them to communicate about number.

Young children have a novice's version of this cognitive model of number. They quickly grasp the varying meanings of the number words and develop a cognitive model that is based on their social function in everyday interaction (*"I am four, you are three. I'll decide what we play"; "We need three things for this game. I'll get them"*). Children take a number of years to develop a language-based model of the number system. During this time they also experience the numeral system, which is part of the adult cognitive model of number.

The pre-schooler's understanding of number symbols

We know a great deal about children's early understanding of the letter system and how their intuitions about letters gradually develop into understanding of letter-sound correspondences. There is also a growing literature on infants' numerical cognition (see Chapter 1) as well as substantial research into children's counting (see Chapter 2). In contrast to our knowledge of these areas, we know very little about how children begin to grasp the function and structure of the numeral system. Their early experience of numerals has not been extensively studied, but is presumably as important as are early experiences of books and environmental print to reading development. Children in Western cultures are inevitably exposed to numerals in many different contexts, and these numerals have as many different meanings as do spoken numbers. Whereas children are accustomed to working out varying meanings of the same number word by attending to the context of the utterance, it is not so simple to deduce the many meanings of a written numeral. First, there is the difference between numerals that have a *cardinal* meaning—as in, for instance a card instructing you to "draw three apples"—and the *non-cardinal* meanings, ranging from numbers on buses and house doors to the numbers that label the television channels. Secondly, there is the difference between *"count"* and *"measure"* numbers (examples of "measure" numbers would be points on a weighing scale, thermometer, clock or oven). "Count" and "measure" numbers have little direct correspondence—"measure" numbers are actually a metaphoric use of counting in which numbers are applied to continuous rather than discrete quantities. "Count" numbers correspond to things that really exist (as discrete quantities), but the meaning of "measure" numbers relies on a mutual understanding of the metaphoric projection of the count numbers onto infinitely divisible matter. It also relies on a joint understanding of the implicit use of a scale that orders the number correspondences, given that there are no discrete objects to perform this function (see Lakoff & Nunez, 1997 for a discussion of the role of metaphor in mathematical communication). It follows then that children will not understand the referent of a "measure" number until they have acquired the measure metaphor that underlies this use of number, along with concepts of scale to interpret the measure unit—something that usually happens around age 7. Adults and older children can skip happily from one kind of numeral meaning to another, using the context to decide the referent of the numeral currently being presented. Very young children have no such ability, and it is not clear how they learn that one function of numerals is to represent cardinality, as it is a function that is not very common in everyday life outside the context of written arithmetic. Virtually the only situations in which young children experience numerals with a cardinal referent are those traditional teaching contexts in which numerals are illustrated with quantities, and situations in which the children themselves are writing numerals that they have decided beforehand will have cardinal meanings. All other contexts in which children encounter numerals have a mixture of cardinal, noncardinal, and measure meanings for numerals, with cardinal meanings being comparatively rare. It is difficult to see, then, how children can learn the arithmetical (or cardinal) meanings of single-digit numerals from environmental exposure alone. Learning number symbols is more problematic than learning number and with such a large gap between number learning and number symbol learning, it is small wonder that some children end up treating quantities and their symbols as completely different entities (Ginsburg, 1977).

THE COGNITIVE AND THE SOCIAL

How, then, does knowledge of number symbols begin to be incorporated into children's cognitive model of number? It is a common claim of cognitive anthropologists that cultural artefacts shape thought processes. This notion has wide currency: Maths historians, for instance, invariably point to the introduction of the arabic numeral system as an essential factor in the development of modern mathematics. They claim that the thought processes central to the required calculations would be impossible without the elegant Indian system of base-10 numerals using spatial position to code value (Menninger, 1958; McLeish, 1993; Wilder, 1968). Similar thinking has prompted the many studies of reading development in cultures using logographic script, where a single symbol stands for an entire idea (e.g. Kimura & Bryant, 1983). There is little scope for cross-cultural comparisons of number development; Saxe's studies of Papua New Guinean populations provide an insight into the limitations of prehistoric counting systems based on body parts, but these are insights into an ancient number system rather than into the shaping of thought processes by written symbol systems. There is little in the field of numeracy development akin to the studies of children learning alphabetic and logographic scripts that illuminate the mental processes involved in reading. There is some evidence that variation in number practices results in variations in the mental representation of number. Stigler, Chalip, and Miller (1986) show that abacus training in Taiwan produces a markedly different representation of numerical calculations to that seen in the West. Some historical evidence for script-dependent variation also comes from Pullan (1969) who investigated number practice in the centuries before arabic numerals were universally accepted in Europe. He cites evidence to show that "reckoning" was carried out swiftly and accurately with physical aids, the rather clumsy Roman notation being used merely to record the end-result of the sum. Arabic numerals, of course, permit the use of the numerals themselves as objects in the mental calculation and the argument is that it is this design characteristic that opened up the possibility of modern mathematics. This point about the inherent nature of the numeral system is not controversial and most maths historians make it, thus giving the notation system a central role in the historical development of number concepts.

Taiwanese children and medieval merchants alike might have based their cognitive models of number on physical manipulation of objects, but it is not the *logic* of the physical manipulation that fosters this development. Both the Eastern abacus and the medieval counting board become integrated into a cognitive model through the social practices of counting and calculating that are focused on them. It matters that the counting objects are part of the adult world. Classroom aids to counting have a quite different social status and produce quite different cognitive models. Such aids are often seen as "babyish" or the domain of the incompetent, and so they do not attract the kind of social interaction that will foster the development of a cognitive model. The physical aids Cobb and Bauersfeld (1995) described in their account of an experimental "inquiry maths" classroom (hundreds boards and "strips and squares" activities) are quite different from the usual classroom aids in that they are the focus of shared social practices that are deliberately fostered by the teacher. This quality of social interaction is enough to give these aids sufficient status to be integrated into a cognitive model, and to enable children to manipulate models based on both physical and symbolic representations of number.

Inquiry maths classrooms are quite rare and it is more usual to find that the cognitive model constructed around the numeral system predominates in classrooms. This numeral-based cognitive model may explain why it can be difficult for children to switch back and forth between concrete and symbolic numerical models (see Hughes, 1986, for examples). It is likely that children form two cognitive models: one based on interaction around concrete objects and another based on interaction around numeric symbols. Adults usually expect children to see the logical similarities between the concrete objects and the numeric meaning expressed by symbols as though the logical structure were physically present. However, what is not widely understood is that inferences are often derived from the cognitive model that people use to create meaning, not from the logical structure in itself. Although there are logical similarities between the classroom aids and the numeral system, it is not the logical structure that people use when they make inferences. Adults use the logical structure for only the most primitive reasoning; anything more complex brings their socially constructed cognitive model into play. For instance, most people have difficulty with if-then connectives and the logical structure these create when the context is arbitrary (i.e. where there is no culturally derived cognitive model to supply ready-made connectives).

D'Andrade (1990) gives the following examples to illustrate the difference a well-established connection can make to this type of inference:

Given: If Roger is a musician then Roger is a Bavarian.
  Suppose: Roger is not a Bavarian.
  Then: (a) It must be the case that Roger is a musician
             or
             (b) Maybe Roger is a musician, maybe he isn't
             or
             (c) It must be the case that Roger is not a musician.

The logical form of this is noted for its difficulty. Only 15% of undergraduates correctly solve the completely decontextualised problem and only 53% correctly solve the contextualised problem above. However, 96% of undergraduates correctly solve the following problem, which is identical in form:

Given: If this rock is a garnet then it is a semiprecious stone
  Suppose: This rock is not a semiprecious stone
  Then: (a) It must be the case that this rock is a garnet
             or
             (b) Maybe this rock is a garnet and maybe it isn't
             or
             (c) It must be the case that this rock is not a garnet.

D'Andrade's explanation of this difference is that the cultural schema that links the categories "garnet" and "semiprecious stone" provides a shortcut; the inference is derived from this cultural link rather than from the logical structure of the problem.

There is little reason to suppose that children's cognitive systems operate on different principles to those of adults. It would follow that where children find logical inferences about number difficult, they will fall back on their socially constructed cognitive model, relying on the links formed within this model. Take, for instance, the difficulties that Hughes (1986) describes in children translating from written sums to Dienes blocks. Michael (top maths group) is well able to do multidigit addition, but when he translates his sums into blocks he uses the same "magical logic" that Nunes' Brazilian street traders used on their school sums (Nunes et al., 1993). Stephen (middle maths group) tries to lay out a concrete analogue of his multidigit subtraction by mimicking the layout (surface form) of his sum. Angela (middle maths group) tries to use the rules governing multidigit subtraction on her block representations of quantities. All these children had cognitive models of number that had been constructed in the context of talking and writing about numerals, and it was these models (rather than "logic") that they drew on when they were faced with the novel problem of creating a concrete analogue of a written sum. The fact that their cognitive models turned out to be unreliable in these instances could mean *either* that they did not have an appropriate cognitive model *or* that their metacognitive faculty was not yet functioning well enough to select the appropriate model. My point here is that children will build their cognitive models around the social context of their teaching/learning, not around abstract logical structures. This will mean that models with similar logical structures (e.g. numeral systems and Dienes blocks) will not necessarily be linked in children's minds. For most children, one cognitive model of number will be created around the verbal number system, another around objects used in counting and calculating, and yet another around number symbols. Unless adults (as in Cobb's experimental classroom) deliberately foster a cognitive model that links objects with symbol systems, children will find it hard to see how the logical structure of concrete objects maps onto that of numeric symbol systems.

NUMBER SYMBOLS AND NUMBER UNDERSTANDING

If number symbols are integrated into a common cognitive model that aids numerical reasoning, does it follow that an understanding of numerals aids the development of number understanding?

There are two theoretical viewpoints on this. The first, articulated by Nunes and Bryant (1996), holds that an understanding of number symbols is not necessary for the initial development of number skills. Their evidence consists of the finding that number skills are present in the absence of skill in generating multidigit numerals, but not vice versa. In this view, number understanding is based on a mental representation of quantity and the mental representation is not affected by knowledge of numeric symbolism. The second viewpoint derives from Vygotsky and his colleagues, who regarded the number symbols as a cultural memory-aid that did help with the early development of cognitive function. The evidence on both sides is inconclusive. Nunes and Bryant point out that understanding the base-10 structure of the number system is crucial both for generating multidigit numeric notation and for the ability to add and subtract multidigit numbers. Nunes' studies tested Luria's suggestion that this structure is understood through learning to write multidigit numbers. She found that children and adults who had not been taught how to write numbers were quite able to understand the additive composition of number—a basic understanding of the way numbers decompose into and are made up of other numbers. Moreover, she found that it was essential for children to understand the additive composition of number in order to generate multidigit numerals accurately before being taught these. In this view, physically based number representations form the basis of children's understanding of number symbols.

Vygotsky and Luria (1930/1993) investigated a quite different aspect of number symbolisation. Their concern was not with number skills, but with the cultural development of memory. They looked at what they called children's transition from an "immediate recall" system to a "notation" system. Their method was to ask children to recall a list of numbers read out to them, then, when the child realized that this was a difficult task, to provide various objects to help. The children were given a variety of things—a piece of rope, some wood shavings, a pile of grains, some feathers, a piece of wood, a piece of paper. Vygotsky and Luria found that initially the children would use the objects to tally the number words. They would make rips in the paper, knots in the rope, or pile the objects up to represent the numbers they were to remember. Older children, who had started school and knew the notation system, would tear out the shape of a numeral, arrange the rope in the shape of a symbol, or arrange the objects in the shape of a numeral. Vygotsy and Luria give very few details of their experiments but note that this new technique resulted in a "tremendous increase in the number of items recalled" and concluded from this and other results that the effect of school (and symbolizing ability) was to transform natural memory into an infinitely more powerful "cultural memory".

These two positions are extremes of the theoretical continuum and neither study really addresses the issue of the relation between symbolic function and number understanding. If we look carefully at the ways that pre-schoolers have of developing symbolic numeric function, then it may be possible to untangle some of the complexity in the relation between numeral use and number understanding and to produce a better description of the ways in which symbolic function might aid numeric understanding. In the main body of this chapter I shall outline some evidence that understanding symbol systems might play a role in the pre-school development of number understanding.

RESEMBLANCE-BASED SYMBOLS IN PRE-SCHOOL

The study of number understanding in young children has been dominated by a Piagetian perspective. Current shifts towards sociocultural perspectives on knowledge acquisition have enabled Margaret Donaldson and her colleagues (Donaldson, 1978) to research the cultural knowledge that young children bring to well-defined school subjects such as mathematics. This research has resulted in a wider understanding of young children's propensity to use iconic (resemblance-based) symbols to encode numerical meaning before learning the conventional numeral system, and in the documentation of a general shift from resemblance-based to convention-based symbol use that coincides with formal school instruction (Hughes, 1986). Hughes found that young children often had their own particular way of representing quantity before they learned to write conventional numerals. Hughes and Jones interviewed 96 children aged from 3 to 7 years. They asked them to "put something on the paper" to show how many bricks were on the table using the quantities one, two, three, five, and six. They divided the children's responses into four main categories.

Idiosyncratic responses were not meaningful to the adult reader. These responses could include children's "pretend" writing, hieroglyphs, scribbles, random letters, or drawings that did not represent the quantity shown

Pictographic responses consisted of drawings of the blocks that included information about quantity as well as information about size, shape, etc.

Iconic responses consisted of tallies or more elaborate shapes that did not reflect the shape or configuration of the blocks; these recordings reflected only the quantity.

Symbolic responses consisted of responses in which either the numerals or the written number words were used to represent the quantity.

There was a marked shift with age in the children's use of these systems, shown in Table 3.1. Hughes and Jones made a theoretical distinction between "tallies" and "pictograms" (calling only the latter "iconic") because of the supposedly more abstract nature of tallies; these representations supposedly provide information *only* about quantity, not about the objects themselves. Pictograms, on the other hand, appear less abstract because they give information about shape, size or appearance. This categorization according to "abstractness" may be misleading and there may be more similarities than differences between Hughes' tallying and pictographic categories. Both, for instance, are physical records of the act of counting and this similarity in function may be more relevant than the differences in appearance. If Hughes' data on pictograms and tallies are combined into one category of "iconic" then the picture is simplified to one in which iconic responses (signifying "visual records of

Table 3.1
Percentage of children in each response category:
Hughes and Jones Task 1 (adapted from Hughes,
1986, p. 60)

	Age			
	3/4	*5*	*6*	*7*
Symbols	10	30	50	50
Iconic	30	12	0	7
Pictographic	25	45	50	43
I & P combined	*55*	*57*	*50*	*50*
Idiosyncratic	30	3	0	0

counting") are equally common at all ages. There is an increase in symbol use and a decrease in idiosyncratic responses, but Hughes' data are cross-sectional, so we do not know whether the children progress directly to conventional symbols or whether the "iconic" responses are a necessary step towards understanding conventional symbolic notation.

There is, then, a shift to the use of numerals around school entry, but we have very little information on children's early grasp of number symbolism beyond the description of this shift by Sinclair, Siegrist, and Sinclair (1983) and Hughes (1986). This situation contrasts starkly with the detailed knowledge we have about children's earliest understanding of letter symbols, which includes studies of the hypotheses young children make about the relation between letters and spoken words (Ferreiro & Teberosky, 1982). We do need to know just how children develop an understanding of numerals—this is apparent from studies of older children that show that their number knowledge can be dissociated from their numeral use, often with bizarre results for mathematical performance (Carraher, Carraher, & Schlieman, 1985; Ginsburg, 1977). The frequent reports that some children have specific difficulty in dealing with symbolic representations of number suggest that literacy is linked to numeracy in some fundamental way. The nature of this link, however, remains open to question. Although Hughes' data showed that children have personally meaningful ways of writing quantity before they use the conventional notation, it leaves a number of questions about early symbolism unanswered—most notably, whether the resemblance-based symbols naturally lead on to the conventional symbolic forms and whether the shift in form is developmentally meaningful.

Hughes' data were derived from a situation in which the children were conforming to an adult's request to "put down how many there are on paper". This was not a task that provided the children with a clear-cut reason to record quantity, and may have affected the results. With no clear communicative purpose incorporated in the writing task, the children may well have been responding to the request "how many?" with a record of the physical act of counting rather than with a representation of the quantity (before children have an understanding of cardinality the typical response to "how many?" is to produce a count sequence). Hughes remedied this himself later with the "tins" task, in which he involved the children in a game of guessing how many bricks were inside a set of closed tins. The task of putting the quantity down on paper is easily presented in this context as an aid to remembering something that is hidden. With this task, Hughes did find differences in the pattern of responses. There were far fewer "iconic" representations from pre-schoolers, and none at all from 5 year-olds. In the context of this game, those children who had drawn iconic representations or numerals were able to identify the quantities hidden within the tins, whereas children who used "idiosyncratic" writing could not. Hughes found that this recognition persisted a week later, suggesting that the children's writing (both iconic and numeric) was truly communicative. He also found that children who used "idiosyncratic" representations could be shown how to use the iconic recording, and could learn to read it in the same way as the children who had produced it spontaneously.

Mental activity in reading and writing symbols

Even this improved task, however, contained some ambiguity about the nature of the symbolic activity involved in the children's spontaneous recording of quantity. Were the children really "reading" the iconic symbols they had written, or were they merely repeating the counting procedure in response to the question "how many?" as they would do if the bricks had been visible? This difference between "reading symbols" and "counting marks that stand for objects" seemed to me to be crucial in describing the development of symbolic function. The second possibility is quite different in quality. It requires only a transfer of some counting principles to paper. It does not entail an understanding that the tally marks can be used to communicate a specific quantitative meaning. I designed a version of Hughes' "tins" task that would show a little more of the mental activity that went with the children's writing and reading of quantitative symbols. I reasoned that a task like Hughes' recognition of symbol meaning only required that the children *associate* the result of their counting with a written symbol. A task that required a child to *discriminate* between a symbol that correctly represented a quantity and one that did not would be a far better test of the child's thinking—of the cognitive model being used to interpret the symbol. In other words, the important question was not whether the children could say that a particular configuration "meant" a particular quantity, but whether the child's symbol became part of his or her numerical thinking.

The task I designed was similar to Hughes' "tins" game. First the child counted one, two, three, and four blocks into four tins, then I shuffled the tins and the child played a guessing game about how many blocks were in each tin.

When the child clearly understood the difficulty of knowing how many were in each tin, I introduced labels and pencil and invited the child to "write down how many there are in here". With the tins closed once more and the labels attached, the children were again asked how many blocks there were in each tin.

It was the next stage of the game that introduced a numerical goal, and the crucial question of whether the children's written record would enter into their goal-directed numerical activity. A "secret addition" to the child's carefully ordered sequence of one, two, three, and four blocks would produce the numerical goal of finding the quantity to which something had been added. I did this by persuading the children to cover their eyes and pretending that my teddy bear accomplice had hidden a block in one of the tins. (The accomplice teddy bear is useful where one needs to distract attention from the agency and intention of the adult experimenter. All the children I interviewed happily went along with Teddy's pretended actions). In each case, the extra block was hidden in the tin containing two blocks. The question "In which tin did Teddy hide the block?" elicited the numerical structure shown in Fig. 3.2.

The goal was quite clearly unrealizable without recourse to an independent record of the original contents. The problem did not tax the children's number concepts overly, because it only required "two" to be distinguished from "not-two". The secret addition game was only played with children who had number concepts of two or more and who had "read back" their written record on request.

Two categories of response

As I had anticipated, the question "Where did Teddy hide that block?" gave clear indications of the mental activity that accompanied the children's symbolic and numeric actions. There were two categories of response. In the first, which I labelled "nonfunctional" writing, the written symbol was not incorporated into the numerical problem. In the second, which I labelled "functional writing", the child's written symbol became incorporated into the numerical problem and was used to solve the question.

Children in the first group, whose responses categorized their writing as "non-functional", were clearly puzzled by the problem. They searched each tin, counted the blocks inside, but they did not examine the labels they had written

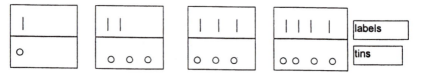

FIG. 3.2. Problem structure of secret addition task.

to check the present state of each tin against its previous state. Some of these children pointed to a tin and said "it's in that one" (sometimes they did this to each tin in turn) but their responses to the probes ("How did you know that?", or "How could you find out?" if they admitted they did not know) showed that they depended for knowledge on another agent rather than on a written symbol. Most children in this category were quite incoherent in response to the probe, but some were quite adamant that the answer could be found only by interrogating the teddy bear or guessing. It did not occur to them to check the labels on the tins; their writing was simply not incorporated into the problem space they had created.

Children in the second group, whose responses categorized their writing as "functional", involved their written recording in the search for the hidden block. After examining the tins, children in this group pointed to the tin they had labelled "two" and announced "That's the one". The probe "How did you know?" elicited clear references to their written record in such statements as "Cos that says two" or "Cos look, there's two and there's three".

Patterns over time

The pattern over time was for more of the children to acquire this tendency to involve their written record in the numerical goal. Once they had acquired this feature they rarely lost it, showing that it was a true progression in mental function and not a situational feature sometimes present, sometimes not. Those children who used their written records in this way were also quite clear when probed that their knowledge was derived from the symbols they had created, not from communicating with another agent. The pattern of change confirmed that pre-school children gradually become able to integrate their written symbols into their "cognitive model" and to use this to direct and activate numerical goals. The speed and certainty with which some of the children in this category announced "There it is" the moment they opened the tin labelled "two" confirmed that their writing was beginning to function as part of a cognitive model—as a mental short-cut that relieved them of the necessity of exploring every logical possibility before drawing their conclusion.

What about the change in form that seemed to take place in Hughes' cross-sectional study? Recall that there seemed to be a shift with age from idiosyncratic to resemblance-based to convention-based recording. There was a similar pattern in the younger sample I followed, with idiosyncratic, iconic figures (both tallies and pictographs), iconically used numerals, and numerals appearing in succession (see Fig. 3.1).

Such a progression would accord with some theoretical intuitions about the nature of symbols and confirm that resemblance-based symbols are a sort of "half-way house" to the more difficult arbitrary symbols. The longitudinal data offers the opportunity of looking at whether the children did move from idiosyncratic to iconic to conventional ways of writing quantity. Table 3.2 shows the percentages of my sample progressing from different symbol forms.

Although these figures give some support to the idea of the resemblance-based (iconic) symbols being a "half-way house" this was clearly not the case for the children who proceeded directly from their idiosyncratic writing to using numerals, with no "iconic" stage in between. The longitudinal design also gave the opportunity to check whether all the children moved from nonfunctional to functional symbols. Table 3.3 shows the percentages of children progressing in symbolic function.

The progressions in function were relatively straightforward, with only two children wavering: One child started out using nonfunctional iconic symbols, became a functional numeral user, then switched back to nonfunctional iconic symbols again. The second child started out using functional idiosyncratic symbols, switched to nonfunctional iconic symbols, and then became a functional numeral user.

Progression in form seemed to be loosely connected with progression in function, in that changes in the use of the symbols were accompanied by changes in the category of symbol used. (Chisquare for function by writing style = 23.8, $P < .001$; Munn, 1994).

Association between mental function and form of symbol

As Table 3.4 shows, very few of those children who used iconic strategies involved their writing in the task. Iconic notation was in fact no better in this respect than pretend writing or hieroglyphs; these "idiosyncratic" methods of recording were functional in roughly the same proportion as "iconic" recording. In contrast, all but one of the 20 who used numerals to write quantities incorporated their writing into their mental activity in this numerical task.

The pattern of association between the style of the children's writing and their response category showed an intuitively surprising result, but one in keeping with the notion that numeric notation becomes integrated into a socially constructed cognitive model. If it was only the logic of number that was

Table 3.2
Progression in form (%)

No progression	22
(Iconic/ idiosyncratic writing throughout)	(14)
(Numerals used throughout)	(8)
Idiosyncratic writing → numerals	22
Iconic writing → numerals	35
Iconic numerals → numerals	9
Other	12

Table 3.3
Progression in function (%)

No progression	55
(Nonfunctional throughout)	(31)
(Functional throughout)	(24)
Nonfunctional → functional	41
Functional → nonfunctional	4

involved in the numerical task outlined in Fig. 3.2 then clearly a system of tally marks or pictograms would be just as effective as the conventional numeric notation. However, it was not just the logical structure that was important; it was the extent to which the written symbols became part of the child's cognitive model of number. Although it is possible for nonconventional notation to become part of a cognitive model, and for conventional notation to be ignored and not used, there was a very powerful effect whereby conventional numerals were usually incorporated into the cognitive model, whereas iconic and idiosyncratic notation were not.

Other associations

There were also associations between children's functional use of notation, their print concepts, and their use of counting in response to a "give a number" request (see Munn, 1994). This suggests that children's early learning about symbols is continuous across the domains of reading and number. Learning that symbols are involved in storybook reading can transfer to a numeric context. Equally, learning that the number words can be used to solve a problem can transfer to the context of using a written symbol to solve a problem. Information from the teachers about the children at the end of their first year of formal schooling showed that there was a strong connection between not developing functional number symbols and doing poorly in basic school subjects (Munn, 1995).

Table 3.4
Number of children in each response
category: "Tins" task with secret addition
at time 3

	Nonfunctional	Functional
Idiosyncratic	5	1
Iconic	14	4
Numerals	1	19

COGNITIVE MODELS AND NUMERICAL INFERENCE

The association between the functionality and conventional form of the children's symbols suggests that the principles governing their thinking are similar to those that govern adults' thinking. In the same way that most adults rely on a socially constructed cognitive model to make logical inferences, so access to the social convention of numeric notation is capable of supporting children's numerical thought and making problem solving easier. It is not the notation itself that is responsible for this effect; if it were, then the iconic notation that contained the number logic in visual form would have been read as frequently as the numerals. It is the cognitive model that is constructed while the number symbols are learned that is responsible. If iconic representations were an important part of our culture, then children would also construct cognitive models around the learning of them. I have no doubt that the children could have been taught, or even prompted, to read the information in these iconic labels. However, the point is that they did not do this spontaneously, whereas they did read their numerals quite spontaneously. This difference suggests that it is not the physical or logical characteristics of the number symbols that are important to the children's thinking, but the social fact that these are the symbols owned by the powerful, numerate people who teach them.

Children can be taught to use tally systems. Hughes achieved this with all the pre-schoolers in his sample, and no doubt if I had explicitly shown the children how to compare their iconic notation with the quantities in each tin they would have constructed a cognitive model that included such notation. However, the children's thinking would then not depend on the logical characteristics of the notation system—the 1:1 correspondence between tallymark and object—but on the social processes whereby the notation system's meaning had become established. Social interaction, imitation, and social marking are all important ways whereby symbols become established as part of children's cognitive models. Remember that these children were all pre-schoolers and had not been exposed to formal teaching about number or writing. The results—the association between numeral use and mental activity that incorporated written symbols—suggest that powerful processes are at work whereby children form cognitive models of number around the notation systems that they learn from expert number users.

Once the children had started school, and had some contact with formal teaching, the association became weaker. After the children started school there was a marked increase in the proportion using conventional numerals and in the number who ignored these numerals in their problem solving. This suggests that the slow, informal, affect-laden processes of pre-school learning were more powerful than the formal methods of teaching used in school. These "school" methods can lead children to rote-learn numeric forms without relating them to quantities

MODEL OF SYMBOLIC DEVELOPMENT

There are two separate associations evident in the data. The first—between understanding the communicative function of print in story books and using numerals communicatively—points to the learning about symbol systems and their use that takes place in the context of reading and transfers to a numeric context. In the "prefunctional symbol" phase the children's responses showed that they thought of people as the only source of knowledge. Whether this was knowledge of stories or knowledge of hidden actions, it seemed inconceivable to them that information might be sought from printed symbols. Once the children had grasped that information might be stored in printed symbols—information that was quite independent of human action and knowledge—there was a qualitative change in their responses both to the story interview and to the number problem. Those children who used numerals functionally were using them as numeric objects—a use that contrasted strongly with the more common non-functional use of iconic symbols.

The second association—that between using numerals communicatively and quantitative counting—points to a link between symbolic function and children's use of the counting system. How was it that counting out blocks to "give a number" was so strongly associated with functional use of number symbols? It seems that in our culture fluency with the linguistic aspect of number is invariably accompanied by well-developed symbolic function. There is no evidence that one causes the other, and it may well be that both are caused independently by a third factor, such as high-quality educational experience. However, the possibility remains that functional symbols in themselves might help children to integrate counting conventions with number logic more quickly than would happen otherwise.

The evidence presented here—the difference between early iconic/ idiosyncratic writing and the use of numerals—suggests that pre-school children's understanding of numeric notation does indeed have a bearing on their number understanding. It suggests that there is something about the known communicative value of conventional numerals that aids children in their understanding of the abstract qualities of number. Functional number symbols may help, particularly, in developing children's understanding that number systems are used to solve problems, that recording something in written form is also a convenient way of remembering it, and that arbitrary symbols can be used as numeric objects.

The model of symbolic development in Fig. 3.3 was derived from the data on the pre-school children.

At Level 1, children act within the objective world, responding to external behaviour and objective features of phenomena. Of course, the child experiences culturally organized symbols, and may understand and respond to some. However, the child's actions (including problem-solving actions) do not yet

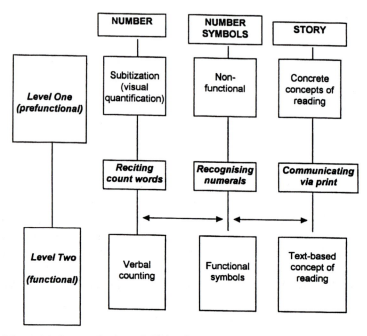

FIG. 3.3. Model of progression in symbolic function.

incorporate written symbols. Thus, if children at this level are asked to read a story they look to a person to find out what the story is. If they are asked to give a number or to find a quantity they look to the objects themselves for the solution.

At Level 2, children act within the symbolic world incorporated within their cognitive model and begin to respond to hidden cultural meanings. Their actions begin to incorporate symbol systems. A request to read a story results in pretended engagement with the print. A request to give a number or find a quantity results in objects being matched to symbols and compared.

CONCLUSIONS

Overall, the evidence is that important developmental shifts take place before school in relation to children's symbolic function—an aspect of their mental activity that is distinct from, but related to, the form of the symbols that they use. In this section I shall address the bearing this has on the two questions that were posed in the introduction, and the importance of symbolic function in the pre-school and early school years.

Do nonconventional symbols act as "precursors" of early symbolic activity?

A variety of symbolic forms precede children's use of conventional numeric symbols: idiosyncratic (pretend writing, scribble, hieroglyphs), iconic (pictograms, tallymarks), and iconic-numeric (numerals used iconically; number 4 in Fig. 3.1). A substantial number of children know about numerals from an early age. Most children shift into using conventional number symbols before they are formally taught them in school. Once children start using them, these conventional symbols rapidly become functional. The important development lies in the *function* of the symbol—its role in the child's mental activity—and not in its form. As the children matured they began to use their symbols as an integral part of the cognitive model of number that guided their actions. For most of the children this happened around the time they began to use conventional symbols. For a minority of children the new function was added to their "primitive" idiosyncratic or iconic forms. The nonconventional symbols were not developmental "precursors" because there were no causal relations between the children's use of these forms and the later development of symbolic function. In the early stages of developing symbolism (Level 1) the children used whatever forms were meaningful to themselves. At Level 2 the child's perception of the communicative value of the number symbols became important, but this still allowed for variation in the actual form of the symbols that functioned as an integral part of their planning and thought.

What role does symbolic function play in developing number understanding?

The evidence that there is a developmental shift in symbolic function around school age suggests that it plays a role in number understanding that neither Vygotsky nor Nunes and Bryant took account of. Vygotsky emphasized the power that the form of the number symbols had, and the role that this played in children's memory strategies. He emphasized the differences between "primitive" and "sophisticated" cultures and projected these onto children's use of symbols. He emphasized the "primitive" nature of the iconic system and assumed that the step from iconic to symbolic was indicative of mature symbolization. Although this may be incidentally true for many children, it is the integration of the symbol system into the child's cognitive model that aids development, not the relative sophistication of the symbol system used. This integration provides the child with the earliest experience of memorization and problem solving in symbols.

Similarly, Nunes and Bryant's demonstration that number knowledge precedes the ability to generate multidigit numerals has little to say about the nature of children's number use. Neither of these arguments touches on the role that symbols play in children's cognitive models of number, as what has been assessed is symbol knowledge (or lack of it), not the way the symbol functions for the child.

Possibilities

Vygotsky and Luria saw conventional numerals as a "cultural memory aid" but they did not investigate the possibilities that functional symbols, of whatever form, create for a child learning about number. Number symbols are memory aids, and they are also aids to problem solving. The functional use of number symbols takes a child one step closer to the adult's cognitive model of number—one in which number symbols are so closely linked with quantities that the two are sometimes not distinguished in everyday language. The possession of an adult-like cognitive model gives a child many more chances of accurately interpreting an adult's communication about number and thus extending his or her knowledge. Shared cognitive models permit the intersubjective understanding that is essential to interpret ambiguities in meaning, and to communicate effectively one's own knowledge of number. This, then, is the importance of symbolic function in children's early number development: that it allows children greater communication about number with expert users.

THE IMPORTANCE OF SYMBOLIC FUNCTION

The symbolic function that I have described in this chapter is a very simple aspect of number thinking, and one that is usually taken for granted. I have pointed out that it is essential for communication with expert number users; without it, a child will have difficulty interpreting meanings that encompass both symbols and quantities. (See Cobb & Bauersfeld, 1995, for examples of typical classroom interactions that show instances of ambiguous, context-dependent numerical meaning.) It is evident that this function is highly related to the development of literacy in pre-school and to the metalinguistic understanding that children bring to the classroom when they first enter school. It is, therefore, a particularly important consideration in teaching number to children who have difficulties with language or with symbols. The UK number curriculum expects that 5 year-olds have already developed this adult-like cognitive model. For many children who have not (around a quarter of my sample did not develop this function by school age) the expectation is that the process of schooling will help them to develop it quite rapidly. However, it is not the lack of symbolic function in itself that will affect children adversely; it is the lack of teacher-child intersubjectivity that follows which will lead to loss of confidence. The resulting poverty of communication will have a knock-on effect as children will develop an awareness of their own lack of understanding and may eventually resort to coping strategies that alienate them from an understanding of number. The importance of symbolic function as a prerequisite to schooling lies in the quality of adult-child social interaction that it can foster in the classroom.

ACKNOWLEDGEMENTS

The study of pre-school literacy and numeracy was supported by ESRC grant no. L208252005 and was part of the ESRC programme Innovation and Change in Education. Thanks are due to the pre-school centres who took part in the study and to Strathclyde Region Education Department for help and cooperation.

Mathematical understanding and mathematical performance

INTRODUCTION

Drawing together the findings of research carried out by different researchers at different times and with different participants is often difficult for a new reader who may be struggling to understand methodologies and analyses with which he or she is unfamiliar. Many readers will welcome Bethany Johnson and Robert Siegler's contribution (Chapter 4) for this reason. But their review is much more than just a synthesis of findings. They have framed the review to address a specific research question that is now seen to underlie much of the work that has been carried out in the field during last two decades: What is the relationship between conceptual and procedural knowledge?

Since the much-cited work of Gelman and Gallistel was published in 1978, and counter-proposals were made by Fuson and colleagues (e.g. Fuson, 1988), there has been wide-ranging debate about the precedence of principles versus practice, or vice versa. Does children's knowledge of a certain numerical principle precede or succeed their practical experience of the operation of the principle? Although the question has been asked in a variety of contexts, Johnson and Siegler are the first to produce a systematic review that applies the question to a range of issues covering a wide age span in mathematical development. The incisive summary which they have produced gives deep consideration to the subtle and changing relation that may hold between conceptual knowledge and procedural skills, concluding that the structure of the environment within which learning takes place is of great importance.

We make repeated reference to the importance of context in mathematical learning, but how is the context to be defined? Is it best described physically, in terms of the materials that are available, for example, in the home, nursery school, or classroom? Is the social context more important, that is, the family,

the playgroup, the teacher and classmates? Is the linguistic context also important, the words and symbols, the special language of mathematics? In Chapter
5 Naoki Ueno presents a radical redefinition of context, rejecting all sorts of
experimental approaches and relying instead on observational techniques applied to mathematical operations *in situ*. Ueno is working within a tradition
drawing strongly on principles of Conversation Analysis. Here the turns of each
participant are defined by the responses they elicit: My comment to you is
intepreted in terms of your reaction (a raising of the eyebrows, for example!).
The context of our conversation is defined according to the rules we jointly
define.

Ueno succeeds in drawing the reader towards a new appreciation of context,
and in particular towards an appreciation of the function of culturally defined
tools (units of measurement, numerical statements) in mathematical communication. His examples of mathematical actions in the workplace and in the
classroom are both revealing and contrastive: In the former we see the effectiveness of shared understanding of a tool (a wooden pallet for lifting tins); in
the latter, we observe uncertainty in the definition of context, a lack of shared
understanding between teacher and student(s). Ueno's viewpoint is challenging. It draws attention to the pitfalls that surround research into children's
mathematics, where the agenda of the experimenter and the participant may
barely intersect!

In Chapter 6 John Towse and Matthew Saxton address the issue of cultural
context very broadly. They take as a starting point the much-publicised international comparisons of mathematical attainment. How can we account for the
observed differences, notably the consistent deficits shown by school children
in the United States compared to Asian counterparts? The authors offer a
principled review of studies of comparative attainment and explore in some
detail research, including their own, which addresses the intriguing issue of
"linguistic relativity" as it applies to numerical vocabulary. How far does
cross-linguistic variation in the structure of number words influence the development of numerical concepts? The question is an enticing one, as Towse and
Saxton amply demonstrate. Their findings lead to a cautious conclusion that
emphasizes the complexity of cross-cultural comparison and questions the
validity of any unitary explanation.

Although Towse and Saxton reject the linguistic relativity hypothesis as an
account of cross-cultural difference, they do not discount the possible influence
of linguistic characteristics on numerical processing. At a psychological level
the case is not proven one way or another. In terms of development, the issue
is extremely important, and emerges clearly in Section 4 of this volume.

CHAPTER FOUR

The relation between conceptual and procedural knowledge in learning mathematics: A review

Bethany Rittle-Johnson and Robert S. Siegler
Carnegie Mellon University, Pittsburgh, USA

INTRODUCTION

This chapter examines the relations between children's understanding of mathematical concepts and their ability to execute procedures that embody those concepts. Delineating how these two types of knowledge interact is fundamental to understanding how development occurs. After all, concepts and procedures are much of what children learn in the course of development, and without question, they develop in tandem rather than independently.

The literature on this topic presents a paradox, though. Pre-schoolers often are described as having sophisticated conceptual understanding that guides their generation of procedures in such domains as counting (e.g. Gelman & Gallistel, 1978) and simple addition (Geary, 1995). In contrast, school-age children are described as having impoverished conceptual understanding that leads to their generating flawed and illogical procedures for solving multidigit subtraction problems, decimal fraction problems, and other mathematical tasks (e.g. Hiebert & Lefevre, 1986; Kouba, Carpenter, & Swafford, 1989; Resnick & Omanson, 1987). Why should older children's conceptual understanding and procedural skill seem so much less adequate than that of younger ones?

One prominent effort to resolve this paradox is the *privileged domains hypothesis* (Geary, 1995; Gelman, 1993; Gelman & Meck, 1992). Within this view, a few early-developing mathematical competencies are evolutionarily privileged, in the sense of being especially easy to learn. These competencies are ones that have potential evolutionary importance, that are learned by children in diverse cultures at about the same age, and that are consistently learned at young ages. Counting and simple arithmetic are the most commonly cited examples of privileged domains of mathematics (along with a basic sense of cardinality and ordinality). Pre-schoolers are said to understand the goals and constraints of accurate counting and to understand the qualitative effects of addition and subtraction of one item before they utilize correct procedures in the domains (Geary, 1995; Gelman & Gallistel, 1978; Gelman & Meck, 1983; 1986; 1992; Greeno, Riley, & Gelman, 1984; Wynn, 1992a).

The privileged domains approach has been best developed in the context of counting. Children have been hypothesized to possess a set of five, innate, principles (Gelman & Gallistel, 1978). These principles are: (1) the one-one principle: every object should be tagged with a unique counting word; (2) the stable order principle: a single set of count words must be used consistently; (3) the cardinality principle[1] the last count word used represents the number of items in the set; (4) the abstraction principle: any collection of objects can be counted; (5) the order irrelevance principle: objects can be counted in any sequence. This early conceptual understanding is said to guide the acquisition of procedures in the domains. Areas of math taught beyond first grade, on the other hand, are considered to be nonprivileged, leading both concepts and procedures to develop more slowly in them. Thus, the privileged domains approach explains the paradox in terms of children having special conceptual understanding of the early-developing domains, and this special conceptual understanding allowing more rapid acquisition of procedures in these than in other domains. The approach also predicts that in evolutionarily-privileged domains, conceptual understanding should precede skilled execution of the relevant procedures.

This privileged-domains approach has not been accepted by all investigators. A number of researchers have suggested an alternative perspective that we have labeled the *frequency of exposure hypothesis* (e.g. Baroody & Gannon, 1984; Briars & Siegler, 1984; Frye et al., 1989; Fuson, 1988). Within this perspective, what differentiates the early-developing competencies is the many opportunities that the environment offers for observation and imitation. For example, young children see numerous examples of counting in everyday life. General imitative capacities may allow children to learn to count in the way they have seen other people do. Experience in using, and seeing other people use, counting procedures in varied situations may allow children to abstract its conceptual underpinnings. Thus, in contrast to the privileged-domains approach, the frequency-of-exposure approach predicts that procedural skill in counting should develop before conceptual understanding of the underlying principles. The perspective also predicts that procedures should be acquired before the underlying concepts in domains other than counting that also present extensive opportunities for observation and imitation.

The issue of the developmental relation between understanding concepts and implementing procedures is of practical as well as theoretical importance. The widespread observation that many children perform poorly in school mathematics highlights the need for improved instruction. Historically, instructional reform has wavered back and forth between emphasizing procedures and emphasizing concepts (Hiebert & Lefevre, 1986). It has become clear that neither type of mathematical knowledge should be taught to the exclusion of the other. How to design instruction that will inculcate both types of knowledge is less clear, however. A better understanding of the interaction between knowledge of concepts and procedures may aid development of more effective teaching techniques.

Potential relations between conceptual and procedural knowledge

Before proceeding further, it seems advisable to indicate what we mean by conceptual and procedural knowledge. We define conceptual knowledge as understanding of the principles that govern the domain and of the interrelations between pieces of knowledge in a domain (although this knowledge does not need to be explicit). In the literature, this type of knowledge is also referred to as understanding or principled knowledge. We define procedural knowledge as action sequences for solving problems. In the literature, this type of knowledge is sometimes referred to as skills, algorithms, or strategies.

How might conceptual and procedural knowledge be related? Four types of relations seem possible:

1. Procedural knowledge develops before conceptual knowledge.
2. Procedural knowledge develops after conceptual knowledge.
3. Procedural and conceptual knowledge develop concurrently.
4. Procedural and conceptual knowledge develop iteratively, with small increases in one leading to small increases in the other, which trigger new increases in the first.

Unfortunately, current theory and empirical studies have only addressed the first two of these potential relations. The reason lies in the logistic difficulty of adequately testing the third and fourth possibilities. Each of them requires repeated assessments of both conceptual and procedural knowledge from before the time that either is present to the time when both reach high levels of mastery. Further, measures of procedural and conceptual competence must be sensitive enough to detect gradual increases in knowledge. It is unfortunate that such studies have not been undertaken, because the fourth possibility, an iterative relation between procedural and conceptual mastery, seems an especially plausible path of development. However, because such assessments have not been conducted, this review will focus on the first two possible relations: procedures being acquired before relevant concepts or after them.

The review focuses on research in the five mathematics domains that have been studied most often in this context—counting, single-digit addition, multidigit addition and subtraction, fractional arithmetic, and proportional reasoning. Examining these five domains allows us to draw conclusions regarding the circumstances under which concepts precede procedures and those under which procedures precede concepts, and may also help in resolving the paradox described earlier.

Structure of the chapter

Studies in the five domains are discussed in the order in which the computational skills are acquired (from counting to proportional reasoning). Within each domain, we group studies by the type of evidence they provide. Table 4.1 lists, in order of increasing strength, seven types of evidence that could be obtained about the relation between conceptual and procedural knowledge of mathematics. The table also provides, in parentheses, the brief headings by which the types of evidence will be referred to subsequently. We will briefly describe each type of evidence.

TABLE 4.1
Types of evidence that could be obtained regarding the relation between conceptual and procedural knowledge

1. Use of routine procedures that do not violate concepts of the domain (*Procedures do not violate concepts*)
2. Possession of both conceptual and procedural knowledge as indicated by performance on independent tasks (*Knowledge of both concepts and procedures*)
3. Positive correlation between individual children's conceptual and procedural knowledge (*Positive correlations between knowledge of concepts and procedures*)
4. Consistent order of acquisition of conceptual and procedural knowledge (*Order of acquisition*)
5. Possession of one type of knowledge predicts acquisition of the other (*Predictive relation*)
6. Effective interventions increase both conceptual and procedural knowledge (*Interventions increase knowledge of concepts and procedures*)
7. Possession of one type of knowledge is causally related to acquisition of the other (*Causal relation*)

Procedures do not violate concepts

This type of evidence indicates that children can successfully implement the typical procedure on a routine task. The procedure is consistent with the concepts of the domain, suggesting that children may understand the concepts underlying the procedure as well. This type of evidence provides only weak support for conceptual understanding, however, because children could have learned the procedure without understanding it. Further, conceptual and procedural knowledge are assessed on a single task, so the developmental relations between the two cannot be discerned.

Knowledge of both concepts and procedures

Some of the problems with the first type of evidence are avoided by assessing children's conceptual and procedural knowledge on independent tasks. On one task, children solve problems designed to elicit the procedure; on the other, they perform tasks designed to tap conceptual knowledge. Four types of measures have been used most often to independently assess conceptual knowledge: (1) evaluation of novel procedures used by others, (2) adaptation of a routine procedure to a novel task, (3) verbal explanation of why a procedure works, and (4) representation of a concept with concrete materials or alternative notations (e.g. creating a concrete representation of a multidigit number). By requiring children to demonstrate their conceptual knowledge on a novel task, overestimates of conceptual knowledge are reduced. However, when both types of knowledge are present, or both are absent, we do not learn about their order of acquisition.

Positive correlations between knowledge of concepts and procedures

Support for linkages between the two types of knowledge comes from evidence that individual children's success on measures of conceptual and procedural knowledge are positively correlated. However, such evidence does not reveal the order of acquisition of conceptual and procedural knowledge.

Order of acquisition

A consistent order of acquisition of conceptual and procedural knowledge within a domain indicates which type of knowledge develops first in that domain. Most studies in this category are cross-sectional and demonstrate that children of a certain age tend to have one type of knowledge but not the other.

Predictive relation

Evidence that acquiring one type of knowledge predicts future acquisition of the other type of knowledge suggests that a causal relation may be present. For example, children's performance on measures of procedural knowledge may predict their success on measures of conceptual knowledge several months later. However, a third variable, such as IQ or motivation, may account for the apparent relation. Thus, this evidence does not provide strong support for a causal relation.

Interventions increase knowledge of concepts and procedures

Intervention studies typically address what types of instruction increase children's conceptual and procedural knowledge. Evaluating what elements of instruction facilitate children's acquisition of conceptual understanding or procedural skill in a domain can suggest causal relations between the two types of knowledge. However, if such studies lack control groups, as often is the case, drawing causal conclusions is perilous.

Causal relation

In these studies, children are randomly assigned to intervention and control groups, children in the intervention group receive instruction in one type of knowledge, and children in both groups are immediately or subsequently tested for knowledge of the other type. For example, randomly chosen children might receive instruction in concepts within a domain. If this instruction resulted in increased procedural ability relative to the control group, this would indicate a causal role of understanding concepts for gaining procedural knowledge.

In reviewing studies from the five domains of mathematics, it became apparent that different goals had motivated research in different areas. As shown in Table 4.2, while there is evidence in each domain for the positive correlations between conceptual and procedural knowledge and for the order of acquisiton of the two types of knowledge, the distribution of studies that provide evidence of the other types vary with the domain. Most research on pre-schoolers' knowledge of counting and single-digit addition has been conducted by developmental psychologists who were primarily interested in describing the typical course of development. Thus, evidence in these domains falls primarily within the first four categories. In contrast, most research on elementary school children's knowledge of multidigit arithmetic, fractional arithmetic, and proportional reasoning has been conducted by educational researchers, whose primary interest was describing and improving learning from instruction. Evidence in these domains is more likely to fall within the

TABLE 4.2

Distribution of studies in each domain across the seven types of evidence

	Procedures do not violate concepts	Know concepts and procedures	Positive correlation	Order of acquisition	Predictive relation	Effective intervention	Causal relation
Counting	Gelman & Gallistel, 1978	Gelman & Gallistel, 1978; Gelman & Meck, 1983; Gelman et al., 1986	Cowan et al., 1996	Wynn, 1990; Fuson, 1988; Frye et al., 1989; Briars & Siegler, 1984; Baroody, 1984, 1992; Cowan et al., 1996			
Single-digit addition			Baroody & Gannon, 1984; Cowan & Renton, 1996	Baroody & Gannon, 1984; Cowan & Renton, 1996; Siegler & Crowley, 1994			
Multidigit arithmetic		Fuson & Kwon, 1992; Fuson, 1990; Davis & McKnight, 1980	Resnick, 1982; Cauley, 1988; Hiebert & Wearne, 1996	Hiebert & Wearne, 1996	Hiebert & Wearne, 1996	Hiebert & Wearne, 1996 Fuson & Briars, 1990; Resnick & Omanson, 1987	
Fractional arithmetic			Byrnes & Wasik, 1991	Byrnes & Wasik, 1991		Byrnes & Wasik, 1991	
Proportional reasoning			Dixon & Moore, 1996; Ahl, Moore & Dixon, 1992	Dixon & Moore, 1996			

later categories. Therefore, the types of evidence discussed vary with the domain. We begin with the earliest developing of the five competencies—counting.

COUNTING

By the age of 3, many middle-class children are skilled counters of set sizes up to 10. In trying to explain this early competence, Gelman and Gallistel (1978, p. 204) concluded: "... one could argue that skill in reciting counting word sequences precedes and forms a basis for the induction of counting principles. We, however, advance the opposite thesis: A knowledge of counting principles forms the basis for the acquisition of counting skill." They posited that children's rapid acquisition of counting could not occur if they did not have conceptual knowledge to guide this acquisition.

As noted earlier, Gelman and Gallistel (1978) hypothesized five counting principles that they believed guide children's acquisition and execution of counting: the one-one principle, the stable order principle, the cardinality principle, the abstraction principle, and the order irrelevance principle. Subsequent research has focused on whether understanding of these principles emerges before or after children become skilled in executing the counting procedure. Below, we consider the types of evidence available in this domain.

Procedures do not violate concepts

The initial evidence that young children understand principles underlying counting came from 2½ to 5-year-olds' adherence to the principles in their routine counting (Gelman & Gallistel, 1978; Gelman, 1978). The children tended to assign one number word to each object, suggesting that they understand the one-one principle. Children also used a systematic set of number words across counts, even when the count order was not the conventional sequence. For example, a child might count "1, 2, 5, 6" and use this same count sequence across many counts. This behaviour adheres to the stable order principle. Children were said to understand the cardinality principle because they often repeated or emphasized the final count word when asked "How many are there?" Children also did not hesitate to count sets that included different kinds of objects, suggesting that they understand the abstraction principle. Understanding of the order irrelevance principle could not be assessed within routine counting; Gelman and Gallistel's (1978) argument that young children understand this principle was based on the type of evidence discussed in the next section.

Knowledge of both concepts and procedures

Although adherence to the principles in routine counting suggests that pre-schoolers understand the counting principles, the children could just be following social convention and imitating the typical counting procedure. Successful performance on independent measures of conceptual understanding, such as adaptation of procedures to novel tasks or evaluation of novel procedures, provides stronger evidence.

To assess understanding of the order irrelevance principle, Gelman and Gallistel (1978) asked 3- to 5-year-olds to begin counting in the middle of a row of five objects (the *constrained counting* task). Over three-quarters of the 4- and 5-year-olds successfully adjusted their counting procedure on at least 60% of the trials, but only 31% of 3-year-olds were successful on the task. When asked to count smaller sets (three objects), 75% of 3-year-olds used a successful procedure on all three trials if they were allowed to repeat a trial (55% were successful on their first attempts) (Gelman, Meck, & Merkin, 1986). These results suggest that many 3- to 5-year-olds understand the order irrelevance principle.

Most 3- and 4-year-olds' also recognize that counting an array in the reverse direction should not affect its cardinality (Gelman et al., 1986). A puppet first counted an array of seven objects and answered a "how many" question correctly by repeating the last count word. Then the puppet counted the array in the opposite direction and surreptitiously double counted an object so that when asked "how many?" the puppet answered "eight". Most 3- and 4-year-olds (70% and 80%, respectively) judged this second response to be incorrect, although few of them indicated that they noticed that the counting from right to left was wrong. Rather, the authors suggested, the children expected the second count to yield the same result as the first because they appreciated the irrelevance of counting order.

Some studies of 3- to 5-year-olds' evaluations of novel counting procedures suggest understanding of other counting principles as well (Gelman & Meck, 1983; Gelman et al., 1986). In these studies, the children's task was to judge the acceptability of a puppet's counting. On some trials, the puppet counted in a standard, correct fashion. On others, the counting was non-standard but correct. Such counting involved the puppet assigning a number word to each object but starting its count in the middle of the row or counting every other chip and doubling back to count the remaining chips. There were also several types of incorrect counts, in which the puppet's counting violated basic counting principles. Violations of the one-one principle involved the puppet skipping or double counting an object. Violations of the stable order principle involved the puppet using an unconventional sequence of number words. Violations of the cardinality principle involved the puppet saying a number other than the last count word when asked "How many are there?" In Gelman and Meck

(1983) and Gelman et al. (1986), most children at each age successfully identified correct and incorrect counts, suggesting that they understood the underlying counting principles.

Positive correlations between knowledge of concepts and procedures

Four-year-olds' procedural skill in counting is positively correlated with their conceptual understanding of order irrelevance and cardinality (Cowan, Dowker, Christakis, & Bailey, 1996). To assess procedural skill, the 4-year-olds were asked to count a row of 10 objects. To assess understanding of order irrelevance and cardinality, the children were presented with a *counting prediction* task. On it, children were asked how many objects there were and then were asked "We got N counting this way (left to right)—what do you think we would get if we counted the other way?" Children who understood order irrelevance and cardinality should recognize that cardinality does not depend on the order in which objects are counted, so they should repeat the last count word from the forward count. To guard against a bias to just repeat the last count word, children also had to succeed on a subtraction task where an item was taken away from the array after the forward count. Cowan et al. found that procedural skill in counting was positively correlated with success on this measure of understanding of order irrelevance and cardinality.

Order of acquisition

Gelman and her colleagues reported that even 2½-year-olds adhered to the counting principles in their routine counting and that children as young as 3 years demonstrated understanding of the principles on novel tasks. However, studies by other researchers, using both similar and dissimilar methods, indicate that many 3-year-olds, and some 4-year-olds, do not understand many of the counting principles, and that counting skill precedes understanding of counting principles.

First consider the cardinality principle. Several studies demonstrate that 2½- to 3½-year-olds often count accurately but do not understand cardinality. For example, Wynn (1990) found that older 2-year-olds and younger 3-year-olds often counted accurately but failed both of two tasks designed to assess understanding of the cardinality principle. On one of these two tasks, the *"how many" task*, children were asked how many there were after they had counted objects, actions, or sounds. If they repeated the last count word, they were credited with a cardinality response. On the other measure of understanding of cardinality, the *"give-a-number" task*, children were asked to give a puppet a certain number of toys. Counting out the correct number of objects was taken as evidence of understanding that counting establishes cardinality.

Most of the children counted small set sizes accurately. However, on the "how many" task, children younger than 3½ gave a cardinality response on only 19% of trials. Similarly, on the "give-a-number" task, all children under 3½ simply grabbed a handful of objects. They did not use counting to generate a set with a specific cardinality. On follow-up questioning, half of these children clearly violated the cardinality principle by adjusting their counting to tag the last item with the requested number. For example, a child grabbed three items when the experimenter asked the child for five objects. When the experimenter then asked the child to check that she had given five objects, the child re-counted the objects "1, 2, 5". Finally, performance on the two measures of cardinality was positively correlated, supporting the assumption that both tasks assessed understanding of the cardinality principle. Thus, older 2-year-olds and younger 3-year-olds counted accurately but did not show understanding of cardinality.

Further evidence that 2½- and 3-year-olds do not understand the cardinality principle comes from Fuson (1988). Children were asked the standard cardinality question "How many are there?" Sixty-five per cent of the children repeated the last count word they had used. However, half of these children could not demonstrate that their answer to the "how many" question referred to the whole set, even when asked to choose whether their answer referred to the whole set or just to the last item in the set. In addition, children sometimes gave responses on the "how many" question that completely violated the cardinality concept (e.g. counting "1 2 3 6 7 8 9 1 2" and reporting that there were two objects). Fuson concluded that children under 4 years do not understand that the last count word used represents the number of items in the entire set.

Similarly, Frye et al. (1989, Experiment 1) found that even 4-year-olds, who count very accurately, often have limited understanding of the cardinal goal of counting. They presented the children with three questions intended to assess their understanding of cardinality: "How many are there?", "Are there x counters?", and "Please give me x counters." The 4-year-olds answered the "how many" question quite accurately, did moderately well on the "are-there-x" task, and performed poorly on the "give-me-x" task. Thus, they only consistently answered the question that parents and teachers typically use to elicit counting, "How many are there?" This suggested that for 4-year-olds (and presumably younger children), counting is a relatively inflexible procedure, to be utilized in response to a specific question, rather than a flexible tool for establishing the cardinality of sets.

Counting skill also precedes understanding of counting principles other than cardinality. Frye et al. (1989; Experiment 2) examined 3½- and 4-year-olds' understanding of the one-one, stable order, and order irrelevance principles (as well as the cardinality principle). First, the experimenter assessed the children's ability to execute the counting procedure by asking them to count sets of 5 and 15 stickers. Then the tests of conceptual understanding were given. The experimenter demonstrated four types of counting procedures used by Gelman and Meck (1983): the standard-correct, nonstandard-correct (order irrelevant), one-one-violation, and stable-order-violation procedures. After demonstrating a count, the experimenter made a correct or incorrect assertion about the counting procedure ("I think I have counted right [or wrong]. Have I?") or the cardinality ("I think there are [x]. Are there?"). The child was asked to decide if the experimenter was right or wrong, so on half of the trials, the child had to contradict the experimenter to be correct. This allowed Frye et al. to test for a potential bias toward agreeing with the experimenter.

The children did not discriminate strongly between correct and incorrect procedures. When evaluating the novel counting procedures, they accepted valid, nonstandard counting orders on only 53% of trials and accepted incorrect counts that violated the stable order and one-one principles on 39% of trials (chance performance was 50%). Children also frequently accepted the experimenter's claim regarding the cardinality, even when they correctly judged the procedure that yielded the response to be incorrect. In addition, a Guttman scale analysis revealed that children counted accurately before they correctly evaluated novel counting procedures. Finally, children's performance was not lower when they had to contradict the experimenter, thus ruling out children's unwillingness to contradict the experimenter as an explanation for the results. These results indicate that even though 3½- to 4½-year-olds count accurately, they have a limited understanding of the underlying principles.

Using a similar task, Briars and Siegler (1984) also found that children accurately execute the counting procedure before they understand the one-one and order irrelevance principles. Children of ages 3 to 5 years first counted a row of 10 chips. They then watched a puppet count using the standard correct procedure, one of several nonstandard correct procedures, or one of several incorrect procedures that violated the one-one principle. As a group, 3-year-olds did not discriminate between nonstandard correct counts and incorrect counts. Only a third of them rejected at least 75% of violations of the one-one principle. Especially important in the present context, children executed the counting procedure correctly before they understood the one-one and order irrelevance principles. Half of 3-year-olds who counted accurately did not correctly evaluate the novel procedures, and none of those who counted inaccurately evaluated the procedures correctly.

Gelman et al. (1986) suggested that subtle differences in questioning style and scoring criteria between her studies and that of Briars and Siegler (1984) may have led to the discrepant findings regarding 3-year-olds' knowledge of the counting principles. However, replication and extension of Briars and Siegler's results in both of the experiments by Frye et al. (1989), and Wynn's (1990) similar results using other assessment measures, support Briars and Siegler's conclusion that children count accurately before they understand the counting principles.

Further evidence that children can count accurately before they understand order irrelevance and cardinality comes from 4- and 5-year-olds' difficulty with the counting predictions task. As noted earlier, this task requires children to predict the result of counting a row of objects from right to left immediately after counting from left to right. Instead of just saying the last number in the original count, many 4- and 5-year-olds count again in the reverse direction or offer a number other than the last count word (Baroody, 1984; 1992; Cowan et al., 1996). This suggests that they have limited understanding of order irrelevance and cardinality. The same children often succeed on the constrained counting task used by Gelman and Gallistel (1978) to assess children's understanding of order irrelevance, a finding that suggests that this task is not a sufficient test of children's understanding of the principle.

Gelman et al. (1986) suggested that children may interpret the counting prediction question as a challenge that implies their first answer was wrong. Within this view, failure to know the result of the right to left count in advance reflects a misinterpretation of the task rather than a lack of conceptual understanding. They reported that children did much better when the question format was reworded to avoid any reference to the initial count, and thus avoid challenging children's initial count. However, both Baroody (1992) and Cowan et al. (1996) failed to replicate this finding. At best, 4- and 5-year-olds' understanding of order irrelevance and cardinality is not strong enough to allow them to cope with even small deviations from the way in which counting is usually requested.

Summary

Some early evidence suggested that 2½- to 3-year-old children might understand the counting principles when they first learned to count. However, more recent research, utilizing a diverse set of methods, indicates that children count skillfully before they understand the underlying concepts. A number of studies have found that some children use the correct procedure but do not understand the underlying principles. No studies have found that children understand the counting principles but do not count accurately. Thus, knowledge of the procedure for counting precedes understanding of the underlying concepts.

SINGLE-DIGIT ADDITION

Middle-class children learn to add before entering school, usually by using the *sum procedure* (counting from one). This procedure typically involves representing each addend on their fingers and then counting the raised fingers. By kindergarten or first grade, many children invent the *min procedure*. This typically involves counting on from the larger addend, for example adding 2 + 5 by counting "5, 6, 7" or "6, 7".

Primary concepts in addition include the necessity of representing each addend once and only once and the irrelevance of the order of the addends. A more abstract form of this second concept is the *commutativity principle*, the idea that changing the order of the addends does not change the sum. Research has examined the relation between conceptual understanding of addition and use of the min procedure, though not between conceptual understanding and use of the sum procedure. We will review the several types of evidence available regarding understanding of addition concepts and ability to execute the min procedure.

Positive correlations between knowledge of concepts and procedures

Baroody and Gannon (1984) assessed kindergartners' understanding of the commutativity principle and their use of the min procedure. On one task used to assess understanding of commutativity, children were quickly shown pairs of addition problems such as 2 + 4 and 4 + 2 or 4 + 5 and 1 + 5, and then were asked to judge whether the two problems would yield the same or different answers. On a second assessment of understanding of commutativity, the kindergartners were asked to solve the problem 6 + 4, and then were asked whether 4 + 6 would yield the same answer (without computing a second time). Children were considered successful on this task if they responded quickly and accurately to the judgement question and did not overtly compute the answer. To measure procedural knowledge of the min procedure, children were asked to solve problems with the smaller addend first (e.g. 2 + 6). Children who succeeded on the commutativity tasks were more likely to predominantly use the min procedure in their own solution efforts than were children who did not (43% vs. 24%).

Similar positive relations between understanding of commutativity and use of the min procedure were obtained by Cowan and Renton (1996). To assess kindergartners' understanding of commutativity, the experimenter gave the child and herself counters of two colours, and stated how many of each she and the child had. On some trials, the sets had both addends in common (e.g. 2 yellow and 13 blue counters versus 13 yellow and 2 blue counters); on other trials the sets had only one addend in common (e.g. 2 yellow and 15 blue counters versus 15 yellow and 15 blue counters). The counters were placed in boxes, so the children could not count them, and the children were asked if they had the same number of counters as the experimenter. On the task used to assess knowledge of the min procedure, children were asked to solve problems with the smaller addend first and to describe on each trial which procedure they had used. Once again, children who succeeded on the commutativity tasks were more likely to use the min procedure to solve these problems than were children who did not (61% vs. 27%).

Order of acquisition

Both Baroody and Gannon (1984) and Cowan and Renton (1996) found that children usually understood commutativity before they generated the min procedure. In each study, almost half of the kindergartners who did not yet use the min procedure succeeded on an assessment of understanding of commutativity, and in Baroody and Gannon (1984), about a third of the children succeeded on both of the conceptual understanding measures. However, these results must be interpreted with caution. The conceptual tasks could overestimate understanding of commutativity because children could be responding based on the addends matching rather than the similarity of the sums (e.g. they could recognize that 2 and 13 are in both problems, and therefore respond that the answer would be the same, without understanding that their sum must be the same).

Most 5-year-olds also appear to understand other concepts underlying addition before they generate the min procedure. Siegler and Jenkins (1989) observed that 4- and 5-year-olds did not generate incorrect procedures in the period leading up to their discovery of the min procedure. Rather, their procedure generation seemed to be constrained by an understanding of the goals that an acceptable addition strategy must meet. To test this hypothesis, Siegler and Crowley (1994) asked 5-year-olds to evaluate novel procedures that did or did not adhere to constraints on legitimate addition procedures. The min procedure, sum procedure, and an illegitimate procedure in which one addend was represented twice were demonstrated, and children were asked to rate each procedure as "very smart", "kind of smart", or "not so smart". Several days later, the children solved addition problems and reported on each trial which procedure they used. As a group, kindergartners who did not yet use the min procedure evaluated it to be as good a procedure as the sum procedure, which they did use. They also rated the min procedure as a smarter procedure than the illegitimate procedure, indicating that they were sensitive to constraints on legitimate procedures. Children who used the min procedure produced almost identical judgements; they also rated the min and sum procedures as equally smart and the illegitimate procedure as less smart. Thus, most kindergarten children seemed to understand the importance of representing each addend once and only once and the irrelevance of addend order before they generated the min procedure.

Summary

Research on the relation between conceptual and procedural knowledge of single-digit addition indicates that conceptual and procedural knowledge are positively correlated. It also indicates that most 5-year-olds understand the concepts underlying addition before they generate the min procedure.

MULTIDIGIT ADDITION AND SUBTRACTION

Children spend several years learning multidigit addition and subtraction. They must learn the carrying procedure for addition and the borrowing procedure for subtraction. Understanding these procedures requires understanding of the concept of place value. A digit's place in a number determines its value—each position in a multidigit number represents a successively higher power of ten. Thus, the numeral "2" in 23 represents the value "20", not "2". A multidigit number can also be represented in different ways. For example, 23 can also be represented as 1 "10" and 13 "1's".

Many children have difficulty understanding place value, and they frequently use multidigit addition and subtraction procedures that reflect their lack of understanding of it. For example, second-graders often do not correctly carry when adding multidigit numbers (Fuson & Briars, 1990). Instead, they either write the two-digit sums beneath each column of single-digit addends (e.g. 568 + 778 = 121316) or ignore the carried values (e.g. 568 + 778 = 1236). In subtraction, children often use "buggy" procedures, and the bugs often persist for several years (Brown & Burton, 1978). For example, in the smaller-from-larger bug, children subtract the smaller number from the larger number, regardless of whether the larger number is in the minuend or subtrahend (e.g. 250–197 = 147).

To assess and teach concepts underlying multidigit addition and subtraction, educators and researchers often use concrete referents to represent the multidigit numbers. Base-10 Dienes blocks are the most commonly used representation. A set of Dienes blocks includes 1×1 "units", 1×10 "longs" (rectangles composed of 10 units), 10×10 "flats" (squares composed of 10 longs), and $10 \times 10 \times 10$ "blocks" (cubes composed of 10 flats). Units, longs, flats, and blocks represent the values one, ten, one hundred, and one thousand, respectively.

A number of types of evidence regarding the relation between conceptual and procedural knowledge of multidigit arithmetic have been reported. We will discuss each in turn.

Knowledge of both concepts and procedures

Cross-cultural comparisons of Korean and American elementary school children have revealed considerable national differences in both conceptual and procedural knowledge of multidigit addition and subtraction (see Chapter 6). Fuson and Kwon (1992) asked Korean second and third graders to solve two- and three-digit addition and subtraction problems that require carrying or borrowing. Then the children were presented several measures of conceptual understanding: ability to identify correctly and incorrectly worked out addition and subtraction problems, to explain the basis of the correct procedure, and to indicate the place value of digits within a number. Almost all of the Korean children solved the problems correctly and also succeeded on all of the measures of conceptual understanding. Stevenson and Stigler (1992) reported similar competence in first- through fifth-graders in Japan and China.

On the other hand, a number of studies reviewed in Fuson (1990) indicated that American children, ranging from second to fifth grade, frequently lack both conceptual and procedural knowledge of multidigit addition and subtraction. Lack of conceptual understanding was evident in findings that almost half of third graders incorrectly identified the place value of digits within multidigit numbers (Kouba et al., 1989; Labinowicz, 1985), and in findings that most second- through fifth-graders could not demonstrate or explain ten-for-one trading with concrete representations (Ross, 1986). Lack of procedural knowledge was evident in findings that children of these ages frequently erred while using paper and pencil to solve multidigit addition and subtraction problems (Brown & Burton, 1978; Fuson & Briars, 1990; Kouba et al., 1989; Labinowicz, 1985; Stevenson & Stigler, 1992). Taken together, these results suggest that conceptual and procedural knowledge are related, in that Asian children have both and American children lack both.

The limitations of American elementary school children's conceptual and procedural knowledge of multidigit subtraction was further illustrated by the findings of Davis and McKnight (1980). These investigators selected third- and fourth-graders who subtracted correctly when there were no zeros in the minuend but who had difficulty with borrowing across zeros. The experimenter asked the children to solve a subtraction problem that required borrowing across zeros (e.g. 7002–25). Then, the children were presented tests of conceptual understanding, among them creating concrete representations for multidigit numbers using Dienes blocks, solving an analogous borrowing task of making change (e.g. "How many ten-dollar bills could you get in exchange for a thousand-dollar bill?"), estimating the size of an answer, and using mental arithmetic to figure out an answer. When children succeeded at any of the conceptual tasks, they were encouraged to use this knowledge to work further on the subtraction problem.

All of the children initially failed to solve the subtraction problem involving borrowing across zeros. Many children succeeded on the first two, but not the latter two measures of conceptual knowledge. However, even when they understood a relevant concept, none of the children used the knowledge to correct their buggy procedures for subtracting across zeros. These results suggest that their concepts of place value and subtraction were insufficient to support broad procedural skill.

Positive correlations between knowledge of concepts and procedures

Preliminary evidence suggested that children's knowledge of multidigit arithmetic concepts and procedures was not related. In detailed, year-long assessments with four second- and third-graders, Resnick (1982) measured conceptual understanding by having the children represent numbers in concrete forms, teach a puppet to add and subtract using Dienes blocks, and identify the tens and ones in a written number. The children also solved two-digit addition and subtraction problems with paper and pencil and with Dienes blocks. The child with the weakest conceptual understanding adopted the carrying and borrowing procedures on written problems sooner and more accurately than the three children who demonstrated considerable conceptual understanding. This suggested that procedural and conceptual understanding were unrelated (or even negatively related).

Contrary to these results, two larger studies of multidigit arithmetic indicate that although individual children may occasionally deviate from the norm, conceptual and procedural knowledge are positively correlated. Cauley (1988) grouped second- and third-graders as complete users, partial users, or nonusers of the borrowing procedure, depending on their performance on 10 subtraction problems of varying difficulty. Then the children watched a puppet incorrectly solve three subtraction problems, after which they were asked to evaluate the procedure and show the puppet the correct procedure. After correcting the puppet, the children were systematically probed for their concepts of the borrowing procedure with questions such as "How much did you borrow?" and "What did you do with it?". Procedural skill level was positively correlated with how well children answered these questions. Partial and complete borrowers did better on the measures of conceptual understanding than children who did not use borrowing.

Results from a longitudinal study that followed children from first grade to the beginning of fourth grade also provide evidence for a positive correlation between conceptual understanding of multidigit addition and subtraction and the ability to invent and adopt computational procedures (Hiebert & Wearne, 1996). The assessments of conceptual understanding included asking children to identify the number of tens in a number (e.g. how many 10s in 54), to represent the value of each digit of a multidigit number with concrete materials, and to represent a multidigit number with concrete material in multiple ways. Children participated several times each year, and older children were asked to represent larger numbers. Procedural knowledge was assessed through performance on two-digit addition and subtraction story problems. The problems were presented orally, and the children were given paper and pencil to use if they wished. The procedures children used were classified as the standard algorithm or as an invented procedure that took advantage of the base-10 system, such as counting on by tens or decomposing the addends into tens and ones and combining each separately.

At each assessment, the authors selected children who demonstrated high or low levels of conceptual understanding (*understanders* versus *nonunderstanders*) based on criteria that shifted with grade. Across the assessment periods, understanders were much more likely to invent successful multidigit addition procedures before instruction and to adopt and explain the algorithm for multidigit subtraction soon after instruction.

Order of acquisition

In this same study, individual profiles revealed that some children understood concepts first whereas other children used a correct procedure first (Hiebert & Wearne, 1996). The authors identified when each child was first classified as an understander and when each child first used a correct addition and correct subtraction procedure. For both addition and subtraction, more than one-third of the children demonstrated procedural skill before conceptual understanding. In contrast, about two-thirds of children were classified as understanders by the time they first used a correct multidigit addition or subtraction procedure. Unfortunately, these results combine children who demonstrated understanding before they used a correct procedure with children who demonstrated understanding and used a correct procedure for the first time during the same session. For this latter group, the order of acquisition of concepts and procedures is unknown. Nevertheless, children clearly varied in whether they learned concepts or procedures first in multidigit arithmetic.

Predictive relation

In Hiebert and Wearne (1996), early conceptual understanding predicted future, as well as concurrent, procedural skill. Children who were classified as understanders in December of first grade steadily increased their procedural skill over time. Those who were classified as nonunderstanders in December of first grade had much flatter learning curves. Further, 86% of the most procedurally skilled subjects at the beginning of fourth grade had been classified as understanders in first grade.

Interventions increase knowledge of concepts and procedures

Studies aimed at improving teaching of multidigit addition and subtraction typically emphasize linking steps in the procedures to the concepts that support them. In general, these teaching techniques successfully increase both conceptual and procedural knowledge. Although these findings demonstrate a positive correlation between the two types of knowledge, they do not provide causal evidence, because they do not randomly assign children or teachers to treatment and control groups, and they do not separate the impact of increasing conceptual understanding from that of increasing procedural skill.

Hiebert and Wearne (1996) presented children either alternative or conventional classroom instruction on place value and multidigit addition and subtraction. The instruction was part of the classroom curriculum, so children were not randomly assigned to instructional group. Alternative instruction focused on contextualizing problem situations, representing quantities with Base-10 Dienes blocks, and having children create and discuss their solution procedures. The teachers introduced the standard algorithms as viable alternatives, but not as prescribed ways to solve the problems. Specially trained teachers, rather than the normal classroom teachers, presented the alternative instruction. In contrast, the normal classroom teachers presented the conventional instruction, and followed standard methods prescribed in the textbook. Although children in this group received some instruction on place value and the justification for the procedures, most lessons emphasized learning the correct procedure. In particular, the teacher often demonstrated a procedure and then had the children practice it on workbook pages.

Compared to children who received conventional instruction, children who received alternative instruction from first through third grade differed on four measures. Their procedural skill for solving subtraction problems was higher. They demonstrated the subtraction procedure more effectively using concrete materials. They scored higher on the conceptual knowledge tasks at the end of the third grade, although not before then. Finally, instruction influenced the order of acquisition of concepts and procedures. Seventy-two per cent of children who received alternative, conceptually oriented, instruction were classified as understanders by the time they used correct addition and subtraction procedures, compared to 46% of children who received conventional, procedurally oriented, instruction.

These results must be interpreted with some caution. The teachers who provided the alternative instruction were not classroom teachers, and may have differed in knowledge of math, enthusiasm for teaching this unit, or other variables. Further, children in the alternative instruction group had more experience with tasks closely related to the conceptual assessment tasks. In particular, they had much more experience manipulating concrete representations (although the particular concrete referent was different on the assessment tasks).

On the other hand, other investigators also have reported success with conceptually-based instruction. In Fuson and Briars (1990), everyday classroom teachers presented first- and second-graders with alternative instruction on addition for 3–6 weeks, with the exact length depending on ability level of the class. Second-graders received an additional 2–4 weeks of instruction on subtraction. Children used blocks to explore the meaning of multidigit numbers and to represent carrying and borrowing. Children were then taught the addition (and subtraction) algorithm by having them alternate between carrying out a step with the blocks and immediately noting the effects of this action in the written problem. Before and after instruction, all children completed written assessments of conceptual and procedural knowledge; some children were individually interviewed at the time of the post-test as well. The test of conceptual knowledge included five aspects of understanding of place value and of multidigit addition: translating from words to numbers (e.g. translating 6 hundreds, 4 tens, 5 thousands, and 7 ones to 5647), doing a similar task where the number form required trading (e.g. translating 2 thousands, 16 hundreds, 1 ten and 4 ones to 3614), choosing the larger of two numbers, vertically aligning addends with different numbers of digits, and solving addition problems with three addends that required carrying twenty instead of ten (e.g. $24 + 13 + 8$). The tests of procedural competence included addition problems that required carrying and an addition problem with two ten-digit addends. Second-graders performed parallel tests for subtraction including subtraction problems with zeros in the minuend (e.g. 205–24). Some children were also individually interviewed. They were asked to judge the correctness of written solutions to multidigit problems and to justify their answers.

From pre-test to post-test, both conceptual and procedural knowledge improved considerably. Many more children correctly solved the addition problems on the post-test; accuracy on the test of conceptual understanding rose from near 0% to over 90% from pre-test to post-test for the second graders. The first-graders' performance on the test of conceptual understanding was not reported, but both first- and second-graders who were interviewed correctly evaluated and justified the worked-out procedures orally. Although there was no control group, recall that US second- through fifth-graders who receive traditional instruction generally have limited conceptual and procedural knowledge of multidigit arithmetic (Fuson, 1990). The second-graders and high-ability first-graders in this study demonstrated procedural and conceptual understanding that well exceeded that of other US children their age. Thus, instruction that explicitly mapped concepts to procedures appeared to help children to understand and adopt the correct procedure. Earlier studies by Fuson (1986) and by Swart (1985) reported similar success for this instructional approach with children of the same age.

Resnick (1982) found similar instruction to be effective in pilot work with second- and third-graders, but Resnick and Omanson (1987) did not have comparable success with older children who already used buggy procedures. Fourth- through sixth-graders who used faulty subtraction procedures participated individually in two 40-minute sessions. In the first session, they learned to subtract using Dienes blocks; in the second session, they alternated between carrying out a step with the blocks and immediately noting this action on the written problem. On the conceptual understanding tasks on the pre-test and post-test, children were shown worked-out examples of subtraction problems. Then they were asked to represent the borrowed quantity with blocks, and to explain how much was borrowed and how the value was distributed. On the procedural knowledge task, they solved written subtraction problems that required borrowing.

Post-test performance was more accurate than pre-test performance on the tests of conceptual understanding. However, 8 of the 9 children continued to use buggy procedures. For example, children created accurate concrete representations of subtraction problems, but they did not solve the same problems correctly. These results differ from those of Fuson and Briars (1990), and are particularly surprising because the children were older and received individual, rather than classroom, instruction. However, the length of instruction was much shorter, and a long history of use of buggy procedures may have hindered learning.

Summary

Second- through fourth-graders' understanding of multidigit addition and subtraction tended to be correlated with their procedural skill in the domain. Most children showed understanding of multidigit numbers concepts prior to, or concurrent with, beginning to use a correct procedure. However, a significant minority of children used a correct procedure first. This was especially true of children who received conventional instruction that emphasized practicing procedures. Instruction that emphasized concepts of place value and how they relate to steps in a procedure usually led to increases in both conceptual and procedural knowledge.

FRACTIONAL ARITHMETIC

Before children receive extensive instruction regarding fractions, they often think of them in terms of parts of a whole, and arbitrarily define the unit as the number of elements identified in the problem. For example, one child insisted that if you begin with 4/4 and take away 1/4, then you have 3/3 because "that's the number of how many pieces you have in the whole thing each time" (Mack, 1993). Children can sometimes use informal understanding to solve problems presented in meaningful form such as "How many cookies would you have left if you had four cookies and ate 7/8 of one cookie?" However, the same children often cannot solve similar problems presented symbolically (Mack, 1990). Moreover, many children incorrectly generalize whole number procedures and simply add or subtract numerators and denominators (e.g. 5/7 + 1/3 = 6/10). To understand fractional arithmetic, children must enrich their understanding of what fractions represent and link this understanding to symbolic representations. For example, they must learn that the two numbers within a fraction represent a single quantity, that units equal in size are necessary for adding and subtracting fractions, and that the same amount can be represented with fractions that include different numbers (e.g. 1/2 = 3/6). Three types of evidence have been obtained regarding the relation between conceptual and procedural knowledge of fractional arithmetic.

Positive correlations between knowledge of concepts and procedures

Byrnes and Wasik (1991; Experiment 1) found that fourth- and sixth-graders who had a better conceptual understanding of fractions were also more success-ful at adding and multiplying them. Understanding of basic fraction concepts was assessed with questions that asked children to identify the written fraction that represented the shaded portion of an object, to choose an alternative pictorial representation of a depicted fraction (e.g. three shaded circles out of four is the same as three shaded squares out of four), and to compare the magnitudes of two fractions presented in word problems. Procedural skill was assessed with questions that asked children to add or multiply fractions that had unlike denominators.

Scores on the conceptual and procedural assessments were positivey corre-lated. When the age groups were considered separately, the correlation was significant for sixth-graders but not for fourth-graders. The nonsignificant relation for fourth-graders may simply reflect a loss of power because of the smaller sample size. Alternatively, it may be due to fourth-graders having received instruction on fraction concepts but not fraction computations whereas the sixth-graders had received instruction on both.

Order of acquisition

In the Byrnes and Wasik study, 81% of the children performed above chance on assessments of conceptual understanding, but only 6% performed above chance in solving the fraction addition problems. All of the few children who used a correct addition procedure also succeeded on the conceptual measures. Thus, conceptual understanding of simple fraction concepts seemed to precede procedural skill in adding fractions. Unfortunately, the measures of conceptual knowledge used in this study did not assess understanding of many concepts that are integral to fraction addition, such as the importance of having equal-sized units. Thus, whereas simple fraction concepts develop prior to use of a correct procedure for adding fractions, understanding of more difficult concepts that underlie fraction addition may or may not precede procedural skill.

In contrast, over two-thirds of the children performed above chance on both the fraction multiplication problems and the assessments of conceptual knowl-edge. An additional 16% of children were successful in solving the problems but did poorly on one or more of the conceptual knowledge measures. None of the children appeared to be successful on the conceptual assessments but unsuccessful in solving the problems correctly.

This much greater success in solving multiplication problems probably arises because some children treat the numerators and denominators within fractions as separate whole numbers, multiply them, and thus reach the right answer for the wrong reason. Consistent with this interpretation, children often use a parallel procedure of adding numerators and adding denominators in fraction addition, although in this case, the procedure results in a wrong answer. Also supporting the interpretation, even fourth-graders who had not received instruction on fraction computations, and who did not understand basic fraction concepts, solved fraction multiplication problems correctly.

Interventions increase knowledge of concepts and procedures

Byrnes and Wasik (1991; Experiments 2) assessed fifth-graders' conceptual and procedural knowledge before and after a 20-minute lesson on adding fractions. The lesson distinguished fraction addition from whole number addition and taught the lowest-common-denominator method for adding fractions. Children completed the conceptual and procedural assessments at pre-test and at a post-test that was given five days after instruction. The conceptual knowledge assessment included the three tasks described in the previous section (Experiment 1 of the study) as well as two new tasks: a *symbolic representation task*, which involved writing a fraction to represent a fractional amount described in a story, and a *nonidentical, equivalent fractions task*, which involved choosing a numerically different, but equivalent, pictorial representation of a fraction (e.g. when presented an exemplar circle with one of four equal parts shaded, choosing the alternative with two of eight triangles shaded).

Accurate execution of the fraction addition procedure increased from pre-test to post-test. However, performance on measures of conceptual knowledge did not improve. The lack of progress in conceptual understanding may have in part been due to performance on four of the five measures of conceptual understanding already being high on the pre-test. However, conceptual understanding also did not increase on the one task on which initial performance was relatively low: the nonidentical, equivalent fractions task. Thus, instruction on a procedure and on the distinction between fractions and whole numbers increased procedural, but not conceptual, knowledge.

A Guttman scale revealed a hierarchical ordering of the conceptual and procedural skills. At post-test, children who added fractions correctly were above chance on all items, or all but the nonidentical, equivalent fraction items, on the conceptual knowledge measure. This finding is consistent with Byrnes and Wasik's findings in Experiment 1 that understanding of basic fraction concepts precedes use of the correct procedure for adding fractions. Further, fifth-graders' success on the assessments of conceptual and procedural knowledge were strongly correlated after the instructional session, replicating the earlier finding that the two types of knowledge are positively correlated.

Summary

Fourth- through sixth-graders' understanding of fraction concepts was related to their use of correct fraction computation procedures. However, many children understood basic fraction concepts but did not add fractions correctly. Instruction on the fraction addition procedure was effective in increasing procedural skill, but had no impact on the already high understanding of simple fraction concepts. Understanding of more advanced concepts that are integral to addition of fractions was not assessed. In multiplication of fractions, children use a correct procedure before they understand what fractions are, probably because a simple extension of the procedure for multiplying whole numbers works for fractions. Thus, in addition of fractions, conceptual knowledge emerged first, but in multiplication of fractions, correct procedures were seen first.

PROPORTIONAL REASONING

Children often reason informally about outcomes that are dependent on two dimensions. For example, when children bathe or wash the dishes, they must adjust the water temperature by altering the temperature and quantity of water. Children also use proportions when they think about concepts such as speed, fairness, and probability. However, these evaluations rarely involve precise numerical scales, but instead usually rest on intuitive estimations (as when children compare the probability that each of two excuses for not doing their homework will have the desired effect, rather than making the teacher even more annoyed). In middle school, children also learn formal mathematical procedures for calculating and comparing proportions. For example, the weighted averaging procedure is used to calculate the outcome of combining two proportions.

Positive correlations between knowledge of concepts and procedures

In Dixon and Moore (1996), students in 2nd, 5th, 8th, and 11th grades, as well as in college, predicted the temperature that would be produced by combining two containers of water that varied in amount and temperature. Each participant performed under two conditions. In one, two containers of water were presented pictorially and described without numerical specification of their amounts or temperature. The temperature of the water in each container was depicted on a thermometer that did not include numbers; instead it included a picture of a snowman at one end and a picture of a fire at the other. The initial quantity of water was always the same in both amount and temperature; the added quantity varied in both qualities. Participants estimated the outcome of adding the contents of the containers by adjusting the thermometer that depicted the temperature of the water in the initial container (that now was said to contain both the initial water and the added quantity). In the other condition, the task was analogous, but the quantities and temperatures in both containers were described numerically (e.g. 1 cup at 60 degrees) and presented pictorially with thermometers and containers marked with numerical scales. Students in this condition were also verbally encouraged to find the answer mathematically. Thus, the first condition assessed qualitative or conceptual understanding, and the second condition assessed quantitative or procedural understanding.

Based on previous research, Dixon and Moore proposed that four principles guide proportional reasoning on this temperature mixture task. The Above-Below principle states that the final temperature should always change in the direction of the temperature of the water that was added. The Range principle constrains the final temperature to be between the temperatures of the water in the two containers. The Crossover principle indicates that the amount and temperature of the added water exert an interactive influence on the final temperature (i.e. the greater the quantity of the added water, the greater the effect of its temperature). Finally, the Equal-Temperatures-Equal principle indicates that when the initial and added water temperature are the same, the final temperature equals the initial one.

Children's judgements in the intuitive condition were scored for consistency with each principle. Thus, performance in this condition gauged children's conceptual knowledge of the mixture task. Children were also grouped based on whether the procedures they used in the numerical condition incorporated quantity appropriately (according to the Crossover principle) and produced answers that were between the temperatures of the water in the two containers (according to the Range principle as well as the Above-Below principle on some trials). Thus, performance in this condition indicated children's procedural knowledge of the mixture task.

Dixon and Moore (1996) found that children whose math procedures violated a principle in the numerical condition had lower scores for that principle in the intuitive condition than did children whose math procedures did not violate the principle. Thus, procedural skill was positively correlated with conceptual understanding.

Ahl, Moore, and Dixon (1992) reported similar results using the same proportional reasoning tasks with fifth-graders, eighth-graders, and college students. For both the intuitive and numerical conditions, students' judgements were scored for consistency with principles similar to the ones described earlier. Then, children were classified as following one of six hierarchically-ordered sets of principles in each condition. Children usually adhered to similar principles in both conditions.

Order of acquisition

Dixon and Moore (1996) also found that conceptual understanding of the mixture problems was considerably more advanced than ability to use correct procedures to solve the problems. Children's answers were much closer to the correct answer in the intuitive condition than in the numerical condition. In addition, many children seemed to understand a principle, as reflected in performance in the intuitive condition, but used a procedure that violated the principle in the numerical condition. Almost no subjects who did not understand a principle used a procedure consistent with it. For example, the Crossover principle is a key concept underlying the correct procedure, weighted averaging. Even second graders frequently estimated answers in the intuitive task that were consistent with this principle, but none of the second- or fifth-graders, and very few of the eighth-graders, used the correct procedure.

Summary

By second grade, most children demonstrated intuitive understanding of proportional reasoning. However, most did not use correct computational procedures until eleventh grade. Conceptual knowledge was positively correlated with procedural skill, but understanding of concepts developed much earlier.

DISCUSSION

In this concluding section, we first summarize the pattern of results across the five domains. We then propose four principles that can be used to predict whether conceptual or procedural knowledge will develop first on a task. Next, we return to an issue raised at the outset of the chapter: Why younger children tend to understand the concepts that underlie the mathematical procedures they learn, whereas older children tend to lack understanding of the concepts relevant to the mathematical procedures they learn. Finally, we offer suggestions for future research.

Overview of results

Correlations between conceptual and procedural knowledge

Across a wide range of ages, mathematical domains, and assessment tasks, conceptual and procedural knowledge are positively correlated. In all of the domains examined, children who better understood concepts also tended to solve problems better.

Resnick's findings on multidigit addition and subtraction (Resnick, 1982; Resnick & Omanson, 1987) are one exception to this conclusion. They are widely cited in the mathematics education literature as evidence that children's understanding of math concepts are not linked to their problem-solving procedures. However, more recent research on the same task with larger samples (Cauley, 1988; Hiebert & Wearne, 1996) indicates that the two types of knowledge are related in this domain as in others. Children sometimes have conceptual knowledge that they do not use to solve problems (Davis & McKnight, 1980). Sometimes they know the correct procedure without understanding the concepts behind it (Cauley, 1988). Nonetheless, as a general rule, children who have greater conceptual knowledge also have greater procedural knowledge.

Temporal relations

Ironically, counting, the domain in which children have been most often hypothesized to understand concepts before using correct procedures, is one of two domains reviewed in which there is strong evidence that procedural skill develops first (see Table 4.3). Although some research suggested that 3-year-olds both used a correct counting procedure and understood counting principles, multiple studies from a variety of sites indicate that many 3-year-olds, and some 4-year-olds, counted accurately but did not understand concepts underlying counting. At no age did any of the children possess conceptual but not procedural knowledge of counting (see Chapter 11, for contrasting findings in children with specific language impairments).

The other domain in which procedural skill precedes conceptual understanding is multiplication of fractions. Although most children demonstrated both conceptual understanding and procedural skill in the domain, a small proportion of fourth- and sixth-graders multiplied fractions correctly but did

TABLE 4.3
Overview of the order of acquisition of conceptual
and procedural knowledge in the different tasks

Task	Order of acquisition
Counting	Procedures 1st
Fraction multiplication	Procedures 1st
Proportional reasoning	Concepts 1st
Fraction addition	Concepts 1st
Single-digit addition- min procedure	Concepts 1st
Multidigit addition & subtraction	Variable

not understand the entities they were multiplying. None of the children showed the opposite pattern. Most likely, children who multiplied fractions correctly but did not understand basic fractions concepts adapted the procedure from whole number multiplication without understanding why the procedure was appropriate.

In four other tasks, conceptual understanding tended to precede procedural skill. First, most second-, fifth-, and eighth-graders understood the principles of mixture problems that required proportional reasoning, but they did not use correct calculation procedures. Understanding of principles of proportional mixtures preceded use of correct averaging procedures by many years. Second, most fourth-, fifth-, and sixth-graders understood basic fraction concepts but were unable to add fractions with unlike denominators correctly. The few children who added fractions correctly also understood basic fraction concepts. Third, most kindergartners understood the concepts underlying addition before they invented the min procedure. Fourth, many first- through third-graders understood concepts of multidigit addition and subtraction by the time they used a correct procedure. This was particularly true of children who received alternative instruction that focused on multidigit number concepts and how they could be used to invent procedures.

These patterns did not always hold for all children. At least one-third of children correctly added and subtracted multidigit numbers before they understood multidigit number concepts. Variability in the emphasis of classroom instruction partially accounted for this variability in the learning of multidigit arithmetic. Most children who received conventional classroom instruction that emphasized practicing procedures used correct procedures before understanding multidigit numbers. Children who received alternative instruction in multidigit arithmetic were much less likely to learn the procedures first. Nevertheless, approximately one-quarter of the children who received conceptually oriented instruction adopted a correct procedure before understanding multidigit number concepts. Thus, there also seem to be individual differences in the order of acquisition of conceptual and procedural knowledge within a domain.

A potential confound threatens the validity of drawing conclusions about the order of acquisition of any two variables. The temporal relation that appears may simply reflect differences in difficulty of the tasks rather than developmental differences in the order of acquisition of conceptual and procedural knowledge (Flavell, 1971). Children would succeed on the easier assessment before they succeeded on the harder assessment, but this would not reflect the true relation between conceptual and procedural knowledge. Well-designed assessment measures, especially ones that assess multiple aspects of understanding of a concept, can reduce, but not eliminate, the threat of this potential confound.

Causal relations

A major gap in the literature is the lack of direct causal evidence regarding how acquisition of concepts and procedures influence each other. To draw causal inferences, we need experiments in which children are randomly assigned to groups, in which one type of knowledge is inculcated, and in which changes in the other type of knowledge are then examined. Nevertheless, suggestive evidence regarding causal relations can be taken from predictive relations in longitudinal studies and from less controlled intervention studies.

Predictive relations were examined in the context of multidigit arithmetic. Conceptual understanding of multidigit numbers predicted future procedural skill in multidigit addition and subtraction, suggesting that conceptual understanding caused children to gain procedural skill. However, correlated factors such as IQ or general math ability, rather than conceptual understanding of multidigit arithmetic *per se*, may have caused the predicted relation to appear.

Evidence from the intervention studies that have been done is also less than ideal. In multidigit addition and subtraction, integrative instruction on place value and the links between concepts and procedures increased knowledge of both concepts and procedures among first-, second-, and third-graders. This conceptually oriented instruction seemed to be more effective than conventional instruction that focused primarily on procedures. Similar instruction increased conceptual, but not procedural, knowledge in a group of fourth-through sixth-graders who already used faulty multidigit subtraction procedures. Thus, integrative instruction may be most effective when presented before children have extended experience using faulty procedures. However, because these studies lack systematic and controlled comparisons, causal conclusions cannot be drawn.[2]

Predicting the developmental relation between conceptual and procedural knowledge

Findings from the five domains examined in this chapter are not consistent with the view that in privileged domains, conceptual understanding precedes and guides acquisition of procedural skill (privileged-domains theory). In the domain most often described as privileged, counting, procedural skill developed before, rather than after, the corresponding concepts.

In contrast, the general pattern of results found in the review can be predicted quite well from children's frequency of exposure to relevant skills. The complexity of the data, however, indicates that the simple frequency of exposure hypothesis presented in the introduction needs to be elaborated to better account for the findings. In Table 4.4, we outline four general principles for predicting when children will understand key concepts first and when they will learn related procedures first. The predictions are specific to understanding the

TABLE 4.4

Four principles for predicting the order of acquisition of conceptual and procedural knowledge.

Children will understand key concepts before they use the target procedure if:

1. The target procedure is not demonstrated in the everyday environment or taught in school (e.g. min procedure for single-digit addition)

OR

2. Children have frequent experience with relevant concepts, either in their everyday environment or in the classroom, before the target procedure is taught (e.g. proportional reasoning, conceptually oriented instruction in multidigit addition and subtraction)

Children will use the target procedure before they understand the relevant concepts if:

3. The target procedure is demonstrated frequently, either in the everyday environment or in formal instruction, before children understand key concepts in the domains (e.g. counting, procedurally oriented instruction in multidigit addition and subtraction)

OR

4. The target procedure is closely analogous to a procedure in a related domain and can be induced from that procedure before children understand key concepts in the domain (e.g. fraction multiplication)

---

concepts directly relevant to the target procedure, not more tangentially related ones. This specificity is necessary to make precise predictions.

Under two conditions, children should understand key concepts in an area before they learn the target procedure. The first instance is when children do not witness examples of the target procedure in the everyday environment or in school. Procedures such as the min strategy for single-digit addition are not modelled by most caregivers, teachers, or textbooks. Thus, the prediction is that children will understand key concepts in these domains before they invent the min procedure. Consistent with this prediction, most kindergartners understood concepts underlying addition before they invented the min procedure. Similar predictions would apply to other tasks that fit the criteria of this principle. One example is the mathematical equivalence task $(a + b + c = a + \_)$. Instruction is typically not given on this task, so children should understand relevant concepts, such as the meaning of the equal sign, before they solve the problems correctly. Recent research supports this prediction (Rittle-Johnson & Alibali, 1998).

A second condition under which conceptual understanding should emerge first is when children have frequent experience with domain concepts before the target procedure is taught. This exposure can either come from the non-school environment or from conceptually oriented instruction. One example from everyday experience is proportional reasoning. Children have considerable everyday experience with proportional reasoning, and by second grade, they are able to make reasonable estimates on a mixture task. These estimates reflect an intuitive understanding of the interaction between two variables. However, the weighted averaging procedure that formalizes this interaction is not taught until middle school, and children almost never use it before this point. Thus, children understand key concepts of proportional reasoning long before they learn correct mathematical procedures for solving problems in the domain.

Relevant experience with underlying concepts also can come from formal instruction. Children who received conceptually oriented instruction on multidigit addition and subtraction in school usually understood multidigit number concepts by the time they used correct procedures. This instruction emphasized the conceptual underpinnings of multidigit numbers and avoided prescribing algorithms for solving the problems. In general, instruction that spends a substantial amount of time inculcating concepts in a domain before introducing formal procedures should lead children to understand these concepts before the corresponding procedures. This prediction is consistent with current ideas for reform in mathematics education (e.g. Hiebert & Carpenter, 1992).

In contrast to these conditions, two other conditions lead to children acquiring procedures before they understand relevant concepts. The first situation is when children see frequent examples of the target procedure before they understand key concepts in the domain. In the everyday environment, caregivers frequently demonstrate counting and the sum procedure for adding. In the classroom, teachers often demonstrate more advanced math procedures and ask children to practice using them. These readily available models allow children to adopt the correct procedure even if they do not understand the supporting concepts. Consistent with this prediction, children learn to count before they understand counting concepts. Further, a majority of children who receive procedurally oriented instruction on multidigit addition and subtraction learn the procedures before they understand the relevant concepts.

The other condition under which procedural knowledge generally emerges first is when children already know closely analogous procedures and can use them to induce the procedure of interest. In these cases, some children will be able to induce a mathematically correct procedure even though they do not understand why it is appropriate. Examples of such analogies are inferring how to multiply fractions from the standard whole number multiplication procedure, inferring how to subtract multidigit numbers that do not require borrowing from the single-digit subtraction procedure, and inferring how to add decimals with an equivalent number of decimal places from the algorithm for adding multidigit whole numbers. In support of this prediction, some children multiplied fractions correctly before they understood even basic fraction concepts. This same result did not occur in fraction addition, where the correct procedure cannot be readily extrapolated from the standard algorithm for whole number addition.

Similar explanations may account for individual differences in the order of acquisition of conceptual and procedural knowledge. The typical learning sequence within a domain did not hold for all children. Children's different experiences with concepts and procedures, both inside and outside of the classroom, may help to explain this variability. Individual differences in how children utilize their experiences may also have an impact. Some students monitor their understanding and explain things spontaneously to themselves as they read or solve problems, while others do not (Chi, Bassok, Lewis, Reimann, & Glaser, 1989; Pirolli & Recker, 1994; Renkl, 1997). Thus, variability in amount of exposure to concepts and procedures, along with variability in how students use this information, may account for individual differences in whether children learn concepts or procedures first within a given domain.

Resolving the paradox

Environmental, rather than biological, differences related to the particular domains of mathematics may explain the paradox of young children so often being depicted as competent in mathematics whereas older ones are depicted as incompetent. Contrary to the privileged-domains hypothesis, early understanding of counting concepts did not appear to guide acquisition of the counting procedure. Thus, special conceptual understanding of early-developing competencies does not appear to underlie the more rapid acquisition of procedures in these domains.

Rather, the frequency of exposure to concepts and procedures in each domain may be the key determinant of younger children's greater conceptual understanding of the procedures they acquire. As described in the introduction, young children have many opportunities to observe and imitate counting and simple arithmetic procedures. For example, frequent experience in using, and seeing other people use, counting procedures may allow children to abstract the underlying concepts, leading to early conceptual understanding as well as procedural mastery. In contrast, school mathematics attempts to convey a great number of procedures and concepts in a relatively brief time, so children have far fewer opportunities to observe or practice the relevant concepts and procedures. Thus, young children may appear competent in early mathematics because they have frequent experience with the relatively few concepts and procedures they are learning, whereas older children may appear incompetent in later mathematics because they do not have much experience with each of the much greater number of concepts and procedures they are learning.

A second factor that appears to contribute to the paradox is that the criteria used to classify children as procedurally skilled are often more stringent for older children. If 3-year-olds count by assigning approximately one number word to each object, or if they use a fairly systematic, albeit nonconventional, number string, they are often credited with being able to count. In contrast, elementary school children who use buggy subtraction procedures, which deviate from the standard algorithm only on the most demanding problems, are not considered to know the multidigit subtraction procedure.

A third factor that has contributed to the paradox involves what counts as news in the field of developmental psychology. Demonstrating that young children have little mathematical understanding, or that older children have considerably more, fails the "Grandmother Test"; everyone's grandmother already knows this. Demonstrations of conceptual competence in young children are more surprising, as are demonstrations of conceptual incompetence in older children. The more surprising findings seem likely to be more widely discussed and better remembered. Thus, newsworthiness, rather than the actual competence of younger and older children, probably have contributed to the pervasive impression that younger children have surprisingly much understanding and older ones surprisingly little.

Thus, at least three factors—greater exposure of young children to the procedures and concepts they are learning, less stringent criteria for young children to be classified as competent, and greater newsworthiness of demonstrations of young children's competence—seem to have contributed to the paradox of young children being depicted as mathematically competent and older ones as mathematically incompetent.

Suggestions for future research

Although conceptual and procedural knowledge can be related in at least four ways (p. 77), current research only directly addresses the two global relations of concepts preceding procedures or procedures preceding concepts. The current research also suggests that conceptual and procedural knowledge do not develop concurrently because one type of knowledge often develops before the other. However, the possibility of an iterative relation between conceptual and procedural knowledge remains untested. In particular, learning may typically involve a hand-over-hand interaction between conceptual and procedural knowledge, such that small increases in one lead to small increases in the other, which trigger new increases in the first, and so forth. To evaluate whether incremental, rather than global, changes underlie the development of conceptual and procedural knowledge, three changes are needed: (1) more detailed task analyses to identify the concepts that are essential for understanding a given procedure; (2) repeated assessment of children's knowledge; and (3) use of true experimental designs.

To assess conceptual knowledge comprehensively, careful task analyses should be conducted to identify the essential concepts that underlie a procedure. Delineating such component concepts is a crucial first step toward assessing them. Because multiple concepts typically underlie a procedure, these analyses will highlight the need for multifaceted measures of conceptual knowledge. To capture gradations of understanding, measures should also be continuous, rather than dichotomous. Multifaceted and continuous measures, based on detailed task analyses, will allow detection of gradual changes in children's understanding.

A second key to ascertaining whether conceptual and procedural knowledge develop iteratively is to examine performance repeatedly during the learning process. Microgenetic methods provide a means to this end. In them, children are followed for a protracted period of time, and knowledge is assessed frequently relative to the learning rate (Siegler & Crowley, 1991). Although this method has historically been used to study procedural development, there is no obvious reason that it could not be used to study conceptual development as well.

Finally, causal evidence is needed. Research that uses true experimental designs is crucial to understanding the causal relations between concepts and procedures. Presently, we only have suggestive evidence for the impact of gaining one type of knowledge on the acquisition of the other.

CONCLUSION

Children's understanding of mathematical concepts is positively correlated with their ability to execute procedures. In some tasks, conceptual understanding precedes procedural competence; in other tasks, the order is reversed. Four general principles can be used to predict when children will understand key concepts first and when they will use the relevant procedure first. These predictions are primarily based on the relative timing and frequency of children's exposure to procedures and concepts. Our review also suggests a resolution for the paradox of young children so often being depicted as competent in mathematics whereas older ones are depicted as incompetent: Young children appear competent in early mathematics because they have extensive experience with the procedures and concepts they are learning, whereas older children appear incompetent in later mathematics because they do not have much experience with the procedures and concepts they are learning. The general lesson seems to be that the structure of the environment has a large impact on the developmental relation between conceptual and procedural knowledge.

ACKNOWLEDGMENTS

Preparation of this chapter was support by a graduate fellowship from the National Science Foundation to the first author and by National Institutes of Health Grant HD-19011. We thank Martha Alibali, David Klahr, Vladimir Sloutsky and Herbert Ginsburg for their helpful comments on earlier versions of the manuscript.

NOTE

1. This was originally termed the "cardinal" principle, but the more current term "cardinality" will be used in this chapter).

2. Outside of the five domains reviewed in this chapter, one study has provided suggestive evidence that increasing conceptual knowledge leads to procedure generation. Perry (1991) found that instruction on the concept of mathematical equivalence led a substantial minority of fourth- and fifth-grade students to generate a correct procedure for solving equivalence problems.

CHAPTER FIVE

Doing mathematics as situated practice

Naoki Ueno
National Institute for Educational Research, Tokyo

INTRODUCTION

In this chapter, I report some observations on activities utilizing mathematics. The observations demonstrate the ad hoc, improvisational and indexical or contextual properties not only of "doing mathematics" in the workplace, but of "doing mathematics" in classrooms and experimental settings of cognitive psychology.

Before going on to make observations of doing mathematics, I will try to formulate the notion of context by contrasting the traditional view of cognitive science with the view of situated cognition and actions. The reason I start by formulating the notion of context is that the issue of "context specificity" in cognition is always confused unless the different meanings attributed to "context" from different theoretical viewpoints are clarified.

According to the situated view mainly based on ethnomethodology and Conversation Analysis (Garfinkel & Sacks, 1970; Heritage 1984; Suchman 1987), the term "context" can be formulated as shown in the following.

First of all, the situated view claims that context is not something given. Context is neither in the mind nor in the environment. Context is not merely something like a static framework for interpreting information. Rather, context is situatedly organized by participants of an activity with various artifacts or resources in an ongoing activity. In short, context can be regarded as a kind of acting or interacting rather than a kind of entity residing in the environment or in the mind. In this way, an expression of "doing context" or "acting context" is appropriate rather than an expression of merely "context". This point makes a great contrast with that of the traditional view such as Script theory (Schank & Abelson, 1977). In the traditional view of cognitive psychology, context is, after all, regarded as a kind of knowledge in the mind or as a framework for interpreting inputted information. Otherwise, in the traditional view, context is regarded as part of a given environment. For example, as Lave (1988) pointed out, according to the traditional view, task instructions and problem content described in the report of an experiment are the "context" of a problem-solving activity. In short, in the traditional view, context is a static framework or something given inside or outside of the mind rather than something interactively organized by participants in an ongoing activity.

Second, in the situated view, the meaning of a speech, action, and use of tools are always "indexical", that is, dependent on context while that speech, action, and use of artifacts will "reflexively" constitute the context of other speech, actions, and tool use in a sequence of interaction. For example, in the case of production of speech, which Heritage (1984) formulated as "doubly contextual", a subsequent utterance not only relies on existing context for its production and interpretation, but that utterance is in its own right an event that shapes a new context for the action that will follow it. The reflexive or doubly contextual relation of context and utterance in organizing a context is observed not only in the case of production of speech but also in the cases of other kinds of action or use of tools. Rephrasing Bateson's (1979) formulating context, a message or an action can become a marker that defines or makes context intelligible. Formulating the reflexive relation of action and context in the situated view also results in great contrast with the view of "contextualism" that refers only to context dependence of an utterance or action.

Third, according to the situated view, while talk, action, and use of tools of participants become some of the resources for organizing a context, they simultaneously socially display participants' way of understanding the context. Let us look at an example of conversation. In an experiment on problem solving, after a short chat, an experimenter marks the opening up of a new context by saying "So, now I will explain the task. The task is ...". If the subject says "yes" with a nod and adopts a position that is attentive to the experimenter, then, at this moment, the responses of the subject can be interpreted not only as displaying his or her understanding of what the experimenter said but also as displaying his or her agreement with and understanding of the opening up of the new context. Given these displays, the experimenter may continue his explanation, although subsequent responses of the subject such as irrelevant talk or response may display his or her disagreement or misunderstanding of the context. On the other hand, if the subject tries to keep chatting or does not adopt an attentive position, the experimenter has to restart his or her talk again to organize the new context. We do similar things in everyday conversation in order to organize a context and to display our understanding of a context to each other (Goodwin, 1981). In this way, participants in an activity socially display to each other not only their understanding of an utterance but also their understanding of an ongoing context.

Fourth, as shown in the earlier example, context is interactively organized, understood, and formulated by participants in an activity. They utilize various resources rather than having these objectively defined by researchers. This is true in the case of an unit of context or in the case of a boundary of contexts. In everyday activity, boundaries of contexts are marked in various ways with various resources by participants. Furthermore, understanding a boundary of contexts is interactively displayed by participants in an ongoing activity again and again by repairing the organization of context.

In the following sections, I apply these perspectives on an analysis of action and context to cases of "doing mathematics" in various practices.

CALCULATION AS SITUATED ACTIONS

The solution of the dieter in context

I start this section by considering some math activities of dieters observed by De la Rocha (1986), cited by Lave (1988).

According to Lave, in the Weight Watchers dieting programme, new members were asked to prepare their lunch to meet specifications laid down by the observer. In this case, dieters were to fix a serving of cottage cheese; the amount allotted for the meal was three-quarters of the two-thirds of a cup the programme allowed. After muttering something, suddenly one of the members announced "I got it". Then he filled a measuring cup two-thirds full of cottage cheese, dumped it out on a cutting board, patted it into a circle, marked a cross on it, scooped away one quadrant, and served the rest.

Lave (1988) formulates this case such that "take three-quarters of two-thirds of a cup of cottage cheese" was not just the problem statement but also the solution to the problem and the procedures for solving it. The setting was part of the calculating process and the solution was simply the problem statement, enacted within the setting.

The issue in this case is how the context of diet training would be organized. In addition to instructions asking to fix a serving of cottage cheese in a specific way, "the structuring resources", such as plenty of real cottage cheese, measuring cups, a cutting board in the kitchen, and the time the task was given, would mark the context of diet training. It seems that, exactly in this context, the statement "take three-quarters of two-thirds of a cup of cottage cheese" could be read as a solution and the solution was enacted with various tools and an object in the setting. The meaning of that solution is socially observable certainly in the context of diet training. In this context, this solution appears to be not only unique but natural. (If the same calculation was executed in front of a teacher, in a classroom lesson on fractions, it would appear to be a funny, inappropriate, or primitive solution.) Simultaneously the solution itself would organize, display and maintain the context of weight watch training by reading the problem statement as the solution, and by enacting this statement with tools and an object in the setting. Further, this solution organized various tools and the object in the setting as resources for the calculation.

In short, in this case, the organized context with instructions along with what Lave calls the prepared "structuring resources", provide the solution. The example shows that the solution, in a specific way with specific artifacts, is strongly connected to organizing a specific social context. Utilizing a specific procedure and tools in calculation socially displays that a specific context is organized and maintained. This is also true in the case of the school-like situation. For example, in an experiment, adults who had attended school for a couple of years in Tanzania were given a set of school-like word problems. They tried to use school-like written maths to solve the problems, even though the procedures were inaccurate (Kawatoko, in press). Outside the test session, they may use different forms of calculation. However, by utilizing written maths, they display their understanding of the context and attempt to organize a context relevant to a school-like test session. Here the issue is not a solution to the problem itself but a "relevant" solution in a test session. In short, a test session marked by the experimenter's instructions, the form of a given problem, available artifacts, and other markers give directions leading to a relevant interpretation of the problem and a relevant solution in that context. In that context, utilizing written maths socially displays a person's understanding the context and, at the same time, it becomes an action that organizes and maintains the context of a test session.

Calculation in the context of distribution and exchange

Kawatoko (1996) reports the use of various artifacts such as documents, computers, a blackboard, and artifacts for computation in a refrigerated warehouse in Japan. This research project was jointly conducted with Ueno (1996) who was mainly focusing on the interaction in the field office as the "coordination center" of distribution and exchange of frozen seafood.

The refrigerated warehouse we observed is located in a large city in western Japan. The business of the warehouse is the storage, distribution, and exchange of frozen seafood. The process of selling frozen seafood at a central wholesale market involves complex exchanges between different kinds of workers.

Different kinds of orders are sent from wholesalers to the warehouse. One is called an "input order" or "load order", and the other is an "output order" or "remove order". An input order is sent to the field office of the refrigerated warehouse by fax or telephone about 7 to 10 days before the load is actually carried into the warehouse. A blackboard placed in the field office is used to record these input orders; this procedure will be described in some detail later. For input orders that are imminent, workers have to rearrange the space in the storerooms. The blackboard is also used for supporting communication among workers on three shifts: a daytime shift, a nighttime computer operating shift in the office, and a nighttime load-handling shift. The work of rearranging the space in the storerooms for input orders is the responsibility of the workers on the daytime shift, whose workload related to output orders is relatively light.

In this workplace, as described by Kawakoto (1996), the same person is in charge of the nighttime shift and the daytime shift every other week. Thus, even the worker in the nighttime shift often sees the space in the storeroom in the context of in-loading such as rearrangement of loads and also sees the blackboard in various courses of actions.

In this context, workers utilize a "pallet-unit" as the artifact for making the quantity of loads, the space, and the action visible. Following Kawatoko's description, let us look at a way of utilizing a "pallet-unit" in this workplace.

On 21 March, there was a description on the blackboard as follows:

3/22(Fri.) 823 princess codfish 10k 1416C/T (20 feet 2 container)
These goods are bonded. M-20, S-587, 2S-809

The inscription means "1416 10kg cartons of princess codfish will be carried in two 20-foot containers on 22 March, Friday. The 1416 cartons comprise 20 cartons of middle-size fish, 587 of small size and 809 cartons of double small size. These goods will be located in the bonded warehouse".

This input order shown on the blackboard had been sent from the owner of the loads one week earlier. Until the day before the scheduled date of in-loading, the inscription on the blackboard was as shown above. On 22 March, the actual date of in-loading, around eight o'clock in the morning, another inscription was added:

S-587 36 × 6 + 11 2S-809 36 × 22 + 17

"S-587 36 × 6 + 11" means that, first, the number of S size is 587 cartons, and second, if 1 pallet carries 36 cartons, then the 587 cartons are equal to 36 × 6 pallets plus 11 cartons. In this description, the quantity of goods is represented by the number of pallets. One pallet constitutes one unit. With this pallet-unit calculation, one can calculate the space that is required for the placement of loads. For example, in the case of "princess codfish S-587 C/T = 36 × 16 pallets + 11 cartons", if you place 4 pallets in one row, and pile up 2 more pallets on top of each pallet in the row, you will need the space for 1 row, 4 pallets and 11 cartons to place the whole load.

Here, the number of cartons inscribed on the blackboard is transformed and read as the number of pallets and the space needed for that number of pallets. Usually, the number of cartons and the way of piling up on one pallet are dependent on the way of packing, on the weight of one carton, and on whether the seafood is frozen or dried. Regarding "princess codfish", the workers talked about it in the morning meeting as follows:

> The goods are dried and sent to the factories for further processing. The weight of each carton is about 10 kilograms, that is heavier than an ordinary carton. So, only six cartons per layer and five or six layers per pallet, that is 30 or 36 cartons total, can be piled up on each pallet. This time, since a lot of cartons will be in-loaded, three pallets should be piled up in each array. Then, the load (weight) on the bottom pallet will be great. The supporter should be built up.

Here, the supporter means the metal frame attached to a pallet for reducing the load on the bottom pallet.

This above example shows that a pallet is not only the tool for carrying and piling up cartons, but also the measurement artifact that constitutes the unit of piled cartons. The unit can be easily transformed into the occupied space and the quantity of work. The quantity of loads carried by a truck is transformed into the number of pallets. The representation of the number of pallets constitutes the perceptual field for organizing the course of actions of calculation of space and of rearrangement of loads in a storeroom. Thus, pallets become the unit of space for placing the loads and the unit of actions such as the work of loading. For example, when the workers read the load-in order form and prepare for in-loading, they calculate the number of pallets from the number of cartons, and then they figure out, from the number of pallets, how many journeys they have to make with the fork-lift truck. Here, we see the seamless transactions between the pallets as artifacts and the planning activities that those pallets have organized.

As shown in the observation of Kawatoko, calculation with a pallet is one of the tools for jointly organizing a specific course of actions by making a space, a quantity of work, and a projective course of action visible or by constituting the perceptual field for such organization. At the same time, in that specific course of actions, calculation with a pallet has a meaning. In other words, in the context of distribution and exchange of frozen seafood, calculation with a pallet-unit has a meaning. At the same time, the calculation is part of the resources for organizing the context of distribution and exchange.

Hutchins (1988) described the computational technology of the piloting task within which navigational pilots make use of the time/distance/speed nomogram and the three-minute rule. Hutchins formulated the role of these artefacts as follows: "... these tools transform the task the person has to do by mapping it into a domain where the answer or the path to the solution is apparent."

According to Hutchins, the artefacts are needed because of the difficulty people have with the use of algebraic reasoning and arithmetic or the use of tables of distances, rates, and times (see Chapter 3, for discussion of the importance of familiar contexts in problem-solving).

However, it seems that whether or not "the path to the solution is apparent" is dependent not on the solution or the artifact for the solution itself but on an organized context where computation and artifacts for computation are embedded. Depending on context, the use of algebraic reasoning and arithmetic may make the path to the solution apparent. In the case of pallet calculation, the system of computation will be completely obscure without the context of organizing space, time, and actions of distribution and exchange. The same is true in the case of computation in piloting. Even the simple "three-minute rule" is difficult to understand without the context of the piloting task and the conventions of ship navigation. Furthermore, problem solving by computation is not a self-contained activity. As calculation with pallets shows, the forms of computation and of artifacts for computation are strongly connected to the organization of space, time, and actions. The computation is organized according to the unit of space, time, and action, and space, time and action are organized by the computation and its unit. Thus, in a warehouse, the computational artifacts and skills, and the activity of organizing space, time, and actions shape each other. For this reason the use of the pallet-unit in the warehouse makes the path to the solution apparent.

SITUATED MEASUREMENT

In this section, I will show how lathe technicians organize their actions of measurement for fine cutting. This observation is reported by Ueno (1996). Before going into the detail, let me briefly explain a lathe and the work of cutting metal.

What is cutting metal with a lathe?

In cutting metal with a lathe, a metal workpiece of column shape is attached to a chuck with a jaw, as shown in Fig. 5.1. There are two basic procedures. The workpiece is slightly shaved down with a cutting tool, and a hole is drilled into its base. Precision is essential. It is often required to process the product within – 2/100mm to + 2/100mm or within – 3/100mm to + 3/100mm tolerance. Considering the diameter of a hair is approximately 5/100mm, the processing has to be extremely fine.

There are various types of lathe including the manual lathe (illustrated in Fig. 5.1), the cam-following lathe, and the computer numerical control (CNC) lathe. In Japan, CNC machines were introduced in many factories 15–20 years ago, but manual machines are still utilized in all factories. In this section, I show

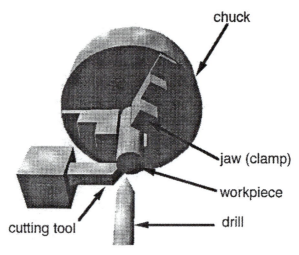

FIG. 5.1. Manual lathe.

how a technician cuts a metal workpiece with a manual lathe machine and demonstrate the situated nature of cutting metal.

Cutting and measurement

In the process of cutting, depending on the situation, technicians utilize various kinds of measuring tools, such as vernier calipers, micrometer, plug gauge, and dial gauge. There is also a scale on the handle of any lathe that moves a cutting tool. This scale, which shows the degree of movement of the cutting tool, can also be regarded as a kind of measuring tool. In addition, the "perceptual feeling", with or without tools such as a magnifying glass, is also a resource for measurement. For example, technicians often make a workpiece revolve and check the fluctuation of revolution in order to judge variation of around 5/100mm. Although novices may perceptually discriminate the degree of fluctuation, one cannot, without experience, calibrate one's perception of the fluctuation. This is also true in the case of utilizing a micrometer. According to the finger pressure pushing the spindle of a micrometer, one will obtain a different measured value. One needs the experience of coordination of perception-action-tool in order to know what degree of finger pressure pushing a micrometer spindle is close to the standard and appropriate for measuring.

Although the degree of uncertainty differs according the instrument of measurement, every tool shows some error. Moreover, the edge of a cutting tool is often chipped or worn away while cutting a workpiece. Thus, reading the scale on the handle of a lathe that moves a cutting tool has a different meaning according to the quality of the cutting tool. In addition, a workpiece is expanded or reduced by the heat of cutting. It is from this combination of errors that technicians have to measure an accurate degree of cutting of the workpiece. In other words, one cannot rely only on one resource for measurement. A technician uses various resources for measurement according to the situation.

The meaning of measured value is different depending on the type of the measuring instrument, and the previous course of actions and the context. For example, as pointed out, as the degree of uncertainty differs according to the measuring instrument used, the meaning of the same measured value differs for each instrument. The margin of error of vernier calipers is ± 0.1mm, that of a micrometer is ± 0.05mm, and that of a plug gauge for measuring the diameter of the hole is ± 0.02–0.03mm. In this way, if one obtains a precise dimension with vernier calipers or with a micrometer, the measurement may indicate overcutting rather than precise cutting. As shown later, a technician changes a measuring tool according to the phase of cutting. Thus the meaning of measured value depends not only on the measuring instrument, but also on the phase of cutting indicated through various resources.

The meaning of measured value also depends on the previous course of actions. Let me offer an observation. A technician was making repeated fine cuts and measuring with a micrometer. The degree of movement of the cutting tool was measured on the scale of the lathe handle. At one moment, immediately after measuring the workpiece with a micrometer, the technician observed the edge of the cutting tool with the magnifying glass and clicked his tongue. Then he substituted a new cutting tool for the clipped cutting tool. How did he know that the cutting tool was clipped? At the beginning of the job, a certain degree of movement of the cutting tool would result in an exact size of cut as measured by the micrometer. However, suddenly, the same degree of movement of the cutting tool did not give the same result. This previous course of action involving measurement and cutting made the technician reason that the cutting tool might be clipped. In this case, what was measured is not the workpiece but the condition of the cutting tool. Thus, according to the previous course of actions, even an object of measurement may be replaced.

The way of "reading" the scale on the lathe handle for movement of the cutting tool is also dependent on the phase of cutting. For example, when one sets up a new cutting tool for fine cutting, one can expect the precise degree of movement of the cutting tool to be registered on the scale. On the other hand, when one utilizes an old cutting tool for rough cutting, the scale on the handle does not indicate the precise degree of movement of the cutting tool.

These two examples show that the measurement of a workpiece measures not only the condition of the workpiece but also the condition of the cutting tool or of the machine, according to the previous course of action.

The meaning of measured value is embedded in the phase of cutting while the phase of cutting is also implied through the measured value and other resources. Regarding the phases of cutting, some typical phases such as rough cutting and fine cutting are socially observable. However, these "phases" or "contexts" in the cutting process are not given. Each phase of the process is organized by a technician and has to be marked with some resources. The boundary between phases also has to be organized and marked with some resources. Measuring instruments, measured value, and other presetting, such as the type of cutting tool and the condition of presetting, become resources that mark the phase and the boundary between phases of cutting process.

Let us consider one further observation. First, the technician made a hole with a drill, and measured the size of the hole with vernier calipers. Then, he switched to a finer cutting tool for the drill and measured it again with vernier calipers. After repeating this process, he exchanged the cutting tool, and again, he measured the size of the hole with vernier calipers. After that, he again moved to a finer cutting tool and measured it with a micrometer. And finally, he repeated the process of cutting and measured the hole with a plug gauge.

In this process, some phases of cutting such as the rough cutting, the semi-rough cutting, the fine cutting, and the final fine cutting are observable through the combination of the cutting tool, the measuring tool, and the measured value at that time. The measured value in the context of utilizing specific cutting tools and specific measuring instruments indicates which phase you are in and whether or not you should go to the next phase.

On the other hand, the meaning of measured value is embedded in the phase of cutting. For example, in the phase of semi-rough cutting where vernier calipers are utilized, over 0.2–0.3mm should be left. If not, the lathe may be overcutting. A remainder of 0.2–0.3mm in this context indicates that you should go to the next phase of the semi-fine cutting. In this way, the meaning of measured value and the phase at the present time are reciprocally organizing each other. The meaning of the measured value can be specified in the context of the phase at that time, and the phase at that time can be precisely specified through the measured value at that moment. Measurement has to be done with the appropriate measuring instrument at the appropriate time.

Finally, a technician organizes his perceptual field with various resources in order to make the state of cutting visible. In turn, the state of cutting made visible with various resources becomes the context for specifying the meaning of each resource. In this way, this organized perceptual field displays the projective course of the activity.

To summarize measurement actions, one must use the appropriate measuring instrument according to the phase of cutting such as rough cutting and fine cutting. At the same time, the type of measuring instrument one uses shows the phase of that cutting. Thus, the meaning of measured value on a specific measuring instrument at some moment is specified in the previously identified and organized "phase" while that measured value in the phase indicates whether or not one is in the same phase.

The popular view is to characterize everyday work practices as "situated actions" — and to distinguish these from scientific practices characterized as "abstract thinking". However, as shown by Garfinkel, Lynch, and Livingston (1981), and in Lynch, Livingston, and Garfinkel (1983), we can see the situated nature of actions for observing and experimenting in various scientific practices. As Jordan and Lynch (1993) show, the reproduction of standardized or mainstream experimental procedures in the domain of molecular biology is accomplished by situated practice in each laboratory. Even though there is a standardized manual for experimentation, it is merely utilized as one of the resources for producing the result. Thus, the situated nature of activity is the same in the case of measurement activities in experimental sciences as in everyday work practices of the type outlined earlier (Lynch, 1991).

SITUATED CONTEXT OF CONVERSATION IN CLASSROOM MATHS

How is a context organized in the classroom?

Let us take a look at a conversation in a third-grade maths classroom. The teacher asked how much change there was in two shopping tasks, using a drawing on a blackboard as shown in Fig. 5.2. The teacher then asked the students to identify similarity between the two problems. The meaning of similarity was the main topic in the teacher-student interaction that followed. Finally, what the teacher asked became apparent, that, is both of problems could be described as "money presented – price = change", although this meaning did not appear to be shared with the students at the outset.

The teacher asked the "similarity" question as follows: "So, well, these two people's shopping, (.) something similar?"

This question about the similarity of the two word problems, is embedded in the previously established context such as calculation of change in shopping as shown in the drawing on the blackboard. At the same time, this question appears to mark the opening up of a new context. In other words, the question appears not only to ask something but to tell something about context. Borrowing Bateson's (1979) terminology, this question can be regarded as a context marker or a metamessage that tells about something about the context.

After the teacher's question, some students offered answers as shown below. These students' answers appear to display their ways of understanding the context as well. In other words, the task here was for students to identify any noticeable similarity between problems or within a problem. The answers can be regarded as a kind of metacommunication that includes not only the students' answers to the question but also their understanding of the context. In this way, the students participate in organizing a context with the teacher.

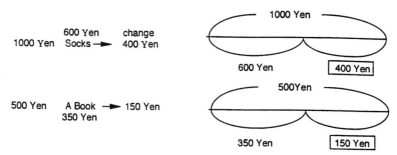

FIG. 5.2. The blackboard description.

C1: Something, the change is written in squares.
C1: Three-hundred-fifty and one-hundred-fifty, fifty and fifty.
...
C5: Both are more than half.
...
C6: The bottom is less, but five hundred and five hundred make one thousand ...
Three-hundred-fifty and three-hundred-fifty make six hundred.

After some students answered as shown above, the teacher started rephrasing the question. This is a kind of repair in conversation and the repair appears to display that the teacher's context is not shared with that of the students and that the intended task here is not enumerating similarities but pointing out a relevant specific similarity.

T: You're thinking about it in a complicated way. Wait a little bit. Yes, Yes, OK. I will try to write it down. You know. You do not need to think it in a complicated way. At the beginning, this, starting, starting was a line. Piiiiii (draws a line under 1000 yen and 500 yen), yes, what you start with, what you start with, both are drawn with lines. Yes, Yes (draws elliptical lines around prices and change), I do not know where the line goes exactly, the place is different. Anyway, we've done it this way. And both, the top and the bottom, have the same thing, the number is different, but is there a same thing? Are the numbers the same? Are they? What is the answer ?

Soon after the teacher's question, one student answered as follows:

C8: Maybe, it is different(.) well,(.) well, the money owned at the beginning is written on top, and, and.
T: The money owned at the beginning is written on top, Yes.
C8: And, well, buying, the money for buying, well, the money for buying, well.
T: What was it? A pair of socks and a book.
C8: A pair of socks and a book are written in the left side and the change(.) is on the right side.

This part of the transcript shows that when a student began to describe the similarity using words such as "the money owned at the beginning", "the money for buying" (the price), and "the change", the teacher joined in the answer. In this way, the teacher displays agreement.

By utilizing words from the students' answers, the teacher formulated the similarity of the problems, displaying that she agrees not only with the students' answers but also with their ways of understanding the context. Thus, a specific context now appears to be established.

This transcript shows, first of all, that a question posed by a teacher may have two meanings. One, it asks a specific question. Two, it marks a specific context or its starting. Students' answers may have two meanings as well. One meaning is a specific answer to the question, and the other displays ways of understanding that context. This is also true in the case of a teacher's evaluation of students' answers. A teacher's implicit or explicit evaluation shows not only whether or not the student's answer is correct, but also whether or not his or her answer is relevant in the context.

However, an independent utterance of a participant does not in itself show the double meanings of question and answer shown earlier. The meaning of utterances and a way of understanding the context only become apparent through interaction. For example, the students' answers themselves do not show whether or not the context marked by the teacher is shared with the students. The teacher's rephrasing of the question after the students' answers makes apparent that the context is not yet shared.

In this way, one utterance can be regarded as an action of organizing a context or a context marker, and as a marker of understanding a context. Interaction socially displays participants' understanding a context to each other and marks the kind of context. The transcript also shows that the business of organizing context is interactively accomplished by each participant's display of understanding of context. A teacher cannot organize a context alone. By displaying a way of understanding a context, students also participate in organizing that context in the classroom.

Situated organization of conversation in the classroom

Post hoc analysis suggests that classroom conversation, exactly as everyday conversation, is well structured. In other words, it appears to be composed of units of context between which the boundaries are obviously apparent. Furthermore, a hierarchical relation of contexts in classroom conversation can be observed. For example, the classroom conversation I observed can be regarded as being composed of some major units or contexts and the relation between these contexts can be formulated.

However, as Suchman (1987) and Schegloff (1982) pointed out in the following extracts, the "structure" of classroom discourse described earlier is an ad hoc, discursive accomplishment.

> While the organization of this and any interaction can be analysed post hoc into a hierarchical structure of topics and subtopics, or routines and subroutines, the coherence that the structure represents is actually achieved moment by moment, as a local, collaborative, sequential accomplishment. This observation stands in marked contrast to the assumptions of students of discourse to the effect that the actual enactment of interaction is the behavioural realization of a plan. Instead, every instance of coherent interaction is an essentially local production, accomplished collaboratively in real-time, rather than "born naturally whole out of the speaker's forehead, the delivery of a cognitive plan". (Suchman, 1987, p. 94)

> "If certain stable forms appear to emerge or recur in talk, they should be understood as an orderliness wrested by the participants from interactional contingency, rather than as automatic products of standardized plans. Form, one might say, is also the distillate of action and interaction, not only its blueprint. If that is so, then the description of forms of behaviour, forms of discourse ... included, has to include interaction among their constitutive domains, and not just as the stage on which scripts written in the mind are played out. (Schegloff, 1982, p. 89)

Certainly, as Mehan (1985) pointed out, variations of a three-part initiation-reply-evaluation sequence can be repeatedly observed in classroom conversation (as shown earlier) although the evaluation phase may not be so direct as in Mehan's case. According to Mehan, in this sequence called an "elicitation sequence", first, a teacher initiates one unit of sequence by asking a question. After that, students make some reply, and finally, the teacher evaluates students' replies. However, as Schegloff pointed out, this pattern should be understood as an orderliness wrested by the participants from interactional contingency, rather than the automatic products of standardized plans.

Constituting the meaning of problems in the classroom

In the previous section, I focused on how the context of a maths lesson is socially constituted. In this section, I analyse how the meaning of a math problem is organized within a lesson.

Let us consider as an example the following multiplication word problem: "There are 3 boxes of chocolate with 8 pieces in each box. How many pieces of chocolate are there altogether?"

If one presents the problem in this form to other people in another place, it will sound quite odd. If your friend sets you this problem in a bar, you may regard it as a riddle, part of a quiz, or a kind of joke. If the same problem were presented in an office, it would be extremely difficult to identify what kind of event was occurring. In this case, you might get angry with the person who gave you the problem. If a mother gives the problem to her 9-year-old child at home, it will be regarded as a marker to show that a multiplication lesson has started, although the child may not agree to organizing such a context at that time. Thus, all word problems in maths textbooks will appear strange without the context of a lesson in the classroom or at home. At the same time, presenting such problems will be a marker for organizing a specific lesson context, as long as it is given to an appropriate person in an appropriate place and at an appropriate time.

A context organized as a lesson is especially powerful for interpreting word problems. For example, in a lesson or a test session, even the following word problems are often interpreted as making sense.

Type 1. You buy nine packs of chewing gum each with five pieces. How much?
Type 2. There are four apples and seven oranges. Multiply them and get the answer.
Type 3. There are eight pupils of 6kg (about 13.2 pounds) each. How much will the total weight be?

According to Arimoto (1991), in the ordinary test situation, over 50% of fifth graders provided solutions for type 1 problems and over 90% of students provided solutions for type 2 and 3 problems. When asked to check the word problems from a teacher's point of view and to point out errors, if any, about 14% of fifth-graders succeeded with the type 1 questions, 35 percent succeeded with type 2, and 74 percent succeeded with type 3.

First of all, these results show how students were understanding the context of this test session of multiplication calculation. In a lesson or a test session, a question or problem given by a teacher does not ordinarily ask for new information but rather requires students to display their knowledge or competence, as shown by Mehan (1985). Many students in the test situation in Arimoto's research displayed that they understood this context as a test session by solving the "strange" problems. Fifth-graders differ in this respect from pre-schoolers who have rarely participated in such a situation. Pratt (1988) demonstrated that pre-schoolers often understand the questions or the problems in a Piagetian conservation experiment, not as the specific question in a test session but as ordinary questions in everyday conversation. According to this account, pre-schoolers who conserve understand the context of a test session requiring a display of knowledge or competence, whereas nonconservers deal with the test context as an ordinary conversation context in which a question is a request for information unknown to the questioner.

Second, these results also show how students were understanding the context of multiplication calculation in the word problems in this test sessions. In other words, students' actions of solving the strange word problems socially displayed their way of understanding the context of calculation. For example, for students who solved all the word problems except type 1, the issue here was whether or not it was possible to calculate the solutions. Students who solved only type 3 problems demonstrated an additional concern that the result of calculation should be an "arithmetically" meaningful quantity. For about 36% of students who did not solve any type of problem the task also entailed deciding whether or not the quantities referred to in the word problems were real.

These results show that fifth-graders neither lack a skill of "reality monitoring" nor lack understanding of meaningfulness of word problems. If they are asked directly, or if a different context for asking about the reality of quantities is organized, as shown in Arimoto's second study, it is not difficult for students to point out the unreality of an elementary school student weighing 6kg. In fact, one of the students pointed out that "a student weighing 6kg" is not strange because it is in a maths problem. Here he claims that a student weighing 6kg is possible in the context of math word problems although he knows it is unreal. Students' responses show their ways of understanding the context of the word problems rather than indicating any lack of reality monitoring or of meaningful understanding. In the context of ordinary word problems they display their understanding of the relevant meaning by an action of solving or of refusing to solve.

Summing up, the examples indicate that the meaning of maths word problems is indexical, for example, that is dependent on the context of a lesson. The same maths problem will constitute quite a different meaning without such a context. In a lesson in the classroom or a similar context, the meaning of a maths word problem may be constructed as shown in the response of the students to the "strange" problems. At the same time, a word problem, including its forms of talk or of description, will be one of the resources used for organizing the specific context of a lesson, accompanied by other resources. Furthermore, the action of solving a problem will contribute to organizing the context as well. Solving a problem is an action of organizing the context as it socially displays how one understands the context. The same is true for other kinds of maths problems in textbooks.

CONCLUSION

As shown in the previous sections, "doing mathematics" is always embedded in a context not only in the workplace but in classrooms. Even the use of skills and knowledge often regarded as "abstract" or "general" is embedded in context and situatedly accomplished even though organized contexts differ from workplace to school. At the same time, specific artifacts and procedures for doing mathematics are part of the resources used to organize specific social contexts such as distribution and exchange, production, and school lessons, rather than convenient tools available everywhere. Specific artifacts and procedures of calculation and measurement have been organized dependent on specific practices, and these artifacts and procedures have been utilized for organizing specific courses of actions in these practices. Thus, according to the situated view, decontextual skills and knowledge have no place. If there are such things, they should be regarded as phenomena researched under the pathology of communication as conducted by Bateson (1972).

Anderson, Reder, and Simon (1996) argue that a view of situated learning that does not recognize transfer of abstract knowledge is wrong because the empirical evidence demonstrates transfer of cognitive skills and concepts. In this claim, Anderson et al., tacitly presuppose that cognitive psychology and situated cognition share the dichotomy of context specific versus context free, or domain specific versus domain general. In fact, the issue is broader than this.

According to the situated view, transfer occurs by organizing a specific context. Transfer in an experimental situation means that a subject successfully shares a context with an experimenter. Whether or not transfer occurs is dependent on how context markers are concealed. For example, as Cole (1988) found, if you explain the concept of transfer to an audience and then present a series of problems, transfer between problems will easily occur in the audience. On the other hand, in an experimental study of transfer, the purpose of the experiment is ingeniously concealed from the subjects. In this situation, the task for subjects is to find out hidden context markers. Furthermore, in an experiment, the boundaries of opening up and closing the experimental context are clearly marked and organized. In this organized context, things the subject is permitted to ask the experimenter are quite different from things permitted outside the context. After the experiment, in many cases, subjects can ask about the purpose of the experiment. A subject and an experimenter can repair their ways of understanding a context to each other exactly as in everyday conversation. However, in an experiment, the resources a subject can use are carefully managed. Moreover, subjects in transfer experiments do not try to use the transferred skills and knowledge beyond the experimental situation. In other words, "abstract" or "transferred" knowledge is meaningful only within the context of transfer experiment.

As Lave pointed out, in research on the transfer of knowledge "responsibility to describe and analyse the context of activity is confined within the boundaries of task instructions and problem content, and the resulting silence about the experimental situation is then extended to the unanalysed situation outside the laboratory" (Lave, 1988 p. 40). Indeed, how the context in an experiment is interactively organized and managed by a subject and an experimenter has never been the target of analysis in traditional cognitive psychology.

Learning skills and knowledge cannot be separated from learning to organize a context. Learning maths in the classroom also includes learning about context just as in the case of doing maths in workplace and in the case of everyday conversation (Goodwin, 1995). School learning of concepts, calculation, and measurement cannot be separated from learning to organize a context with a teacher in the classroom. Understanding maths concepts is always accompanied by organizing a specific context or a specific language game. Wittgenstein (1958) and Goodwin (1995) argue that the meaning of a name is not its bearer, but rather mastery of the practice required to use that sign competently within a relevant language game. It is possible to make a paraphrase of this argument that the meanings of calculation, number, maths concept, and measurement are not their bearers, but rather the mastery of the practices required to use those signs, tools and procedures competently within a relevant language game.

CHAPTER SIX

Mathematics across national boundaries: Cultural and linguistic perspectives on numerical competence

John Towse & Matthew Saxton
Royal Holloway University of London, UK

INTRODUCTION

Methods used to teach maths to children in Taiwan and Switzerland—and in class-rooms throughout Britain for much of the century—are to be formally endorsed by Gillian Shephard, the Education and Employment Secretary, later this week ... In identical maths tests, English pupils lagged two years behind their peers in other European and Pacific Rim countries. Furthermore, their performance has declined since the late Sixties when the Plowden report on primary education led to the widespread adoption of so-called "child-centred" methods ... *Daily Telegraph*, 3 June, 1996

Traditionalists who hope to use an academic's research to force a return to the teaching methods of the 1950s are wrong. Professor David Reynolds, author of the research showing the benefits of whole-class maths teaching, said yesterday he did not want to see a return to the past. His comments came as the chief inspector of schools, Chris Woodhead, [said] that schools should turn their backs on modern lessons based on group work. *The Independent*, 6 June, 1996

... Colin Richards, a former senior advisor at Ofsted, criticises [Chris Woodhead's] "narrow, utilitarian view of what primary education is all about", and says that too much prescription about teaching methods will turn schools into dull, arid places. Mr Richards disputes the validity of international comparisons: "It is invalid to assume you can take any one particular factor from another culture and transplant it more or less intact.." *The Guardian*, 3 June, 1996

Inspectors have criticised maths teaching in inner cities—some schools are not even teaching times-tables. They say educating deprived children is no excuse for low standards and warn that big variations in teaching quality must be addressed if Britain is to catch up with competing countries. *The Independent*, 25 September, 1997

Cross-cultural comparisons of mathematical performance make "hot news". As the quotations reveal, newspaper reports in Europe and the United States often betray the widespread concern that national levels of mathematics attainment in children may appear inadequate when set against the achievements of their contemporaries in other parts of the world. In taking up quite diverse positions over the issue of cultural influences in mathematics learning, media coverage also reveals the complexities of interpreting what is known about cross-cultural comparisons. For example, the conflicting viewpoints expressed in the first three media extracts were based on the same research review (Reynolds & Farrell, 1996). Furthermore, politicians and educational practitioners have at their disposal findings from a wide range of research traditions concerned with the teaching and learning of mathematics—pedagogical, sociological, and psychological perspectives among them. With such an abundance of different approaches, it is perhaps not surprising that no consensus yet exists on what leads to proficiency in mathematical understanding. It is nevertheless possible to identify a number of interesting cross-cultural findings that have emerged, and assess their contribution to our understanding of children's mathematical cognition.

In this chapter, we will review key cross-cultural research from a psychological perspective, and provide an analysis of the extent to which valid inferences can be made about the causal chain of events that lead to cultural differences. Findings will also be used to highlight a number of possible explanations for the cultural differences in mathematical performance that have emerged. Particular attention will be paid to the differences that exist between children from East Asia and children from the United States and Europe. This special focus is warranted by the great preponderance of research in this area, and by the fact that performance differences tend to be especially marked across this particular cultural divide. Within this framework, several factors pertaining to the general cultural milieu of school education will be considered, including pre-school education, attitudes to learning of parents and children, and even the possible influence of language on maths performance. By contrast, important issues concerning the discrepancy between formal (taught) knowledge and informal ("street") knowledge will not be considered here (for detailed treatments of this topic, see, for example, Nunes et al., 1993).

In broad outline, we will argue that reference to cultural and linguistic differences in mathematics cannot easily be attributed to a single factor, at least not in any meaningful way. Even where the term "culture" is used as a term in order to invoke a consistent and coherent frame of reference for describing patterns of behaviour and learning, it clearly denotes a complex web of factors. As a consequence, any simple or global account of cultural influence on the development of numerical competence is unlikely to be satisfactory. And while attempts are still being made to identify the list of "ingredients" that potentially contribute to cultural and linguistic influences in the numerical domain, it is apparent that there is a still greater task: that of explaining the ways in which these ingredients interact and combine to produce particular levels of mathematical skill.

CROSS-CULTURAL DIFFERENCES IN MATHEMATICS PERFORMANCE

A central, undisputed finding from much cross-cultural work is that children from Japan, Korea, and China consistently outperform their American and European counterparts on tests of mathematical ability. So great is the discrepancy generally reported that some investigators have been moved to suggest that "poor performance by American students on tests of mathematics and science has reached the level of a national crisis" (Stevenson et al., 1990a). However, it is useful to be able to distinguish between general cross-cultural disparities—the notion that one group is more able than another across the spectrum of cognitive tasks; for example, contentious accounts of genetic differences in intellectual abilities (Lynn, 1982)—and more specific differences in numerical competence.

There are a number of reasons for favouring the view that national identity impacts on number skills more than in other areas of school curriculum. For example, Stevenson et al. (1990a) showed that reading attainment scores for US, Japanese, and Taiwanese children differed less dramatically than the corresponding differences in mathematics scores. For reading, they argued that although Taiwanese and Japanese children tended to score highest, they also had a disproportionate number of low achievers. In other cases, researchers have argued that there are domain-independent differences; for example, Takeuchi and Scott (1992), reported that Japanese pre-schoolers and first-year primary school children show higher scores on verbal, nonverbal, and quantitative tests than Canadian children. Nonetheless, during early school years, differences in number skills become the pervasive cross-cultural finding. Taken as a whole, therefore, it certainly appears reasonable to conclude that it is in the mathematical domain where the advantage enjoyed by Pacific Rim countries is consistent and very often dramatic in extent.

Harold Stevenson and his colleagues provide perhaps the most extensive research programme in this area. Several studies have documented cross-cultural differences in Taiwan, Japan, and the United States for a large number of children (often measured in thousands) across a 10-year period (e.g. Stevenson, Chen, & Lee, 1993; Stevenson, Lee, & Stigler, 1986; Stevenson et al., 1990b; Stigler, Lee, Lucker, & Stevenson, 1982; Stigler, Lee, & Stevenson, 1987). These researchers have adopted a number of approaches. In one report, they administered a battery of mathematical tests to children, reflecting a wide range of mathematical concepts and skills taught all three countries, namely: computation; estimation; graphs and tables; mathematical operations; measurement; number concepts (for example, understanding the principles and mechanisms of addition or fractions); spatial relations; visualization (involving the prediction of orientation of geometrical shapes); word problems and mathematical speed tests. The results were dramatic. Only on "graphs and tables" questions, and here only among 10- to 11-year-old children, were the American children able to achieve a superior mean score to Chinese children (a difference that was not significant). As can be seen in Fig. 6.1, in nearly all other cases the Chinese children showed a strong and reliable performance advantage.

A broad indication of cross-cultural differences can also be obtained by calculating the top and bottom 100 scores, across all subjects. In the absence of national differences one would expect 33 children from each country in each performance section. In fact, in a separate study to that discussed earlier, Stevenson et al. (1990a) administered a range of mathematical questions and reported that, of the 100 lowest scores at the first grade (age 6 to 7 years), 56 were American children. In the fifth grade (10–11 years) this preponderance was even more severe, with 67 US children in the bottom 100. By contrast, there were only 14 US first-grade children among the top 100 scores, and only 1 US child among the top 100 scores by the fifth grade. What is more, Taiwanese children tend not only to be more accurate in solving maths tasks, they also complete these questions more rapidly than American children. For example, Taiwanese first-graders (aged 6–7 years) completed nearly three times as many addition problems as the US children in the time allowed (Stevenson et al., 1990a).

The general mathematical superiority of Japanese and Taiwanese children is also underscored when one considers results from those children who were tested on three separate occasions over a 10-year period. For in these cases, it was found that the performance gap between the American and East Asian children widened between 1980 and 1990 (Stevenson et al., 1993). In other words, American children started out at a lower baseline, and they were outstripped by an increasingly large margin throughout their school careers. Only at the very bottom end of the distribution do the cross-cultural differences begin to fade away, according to some investigations. Thus, Brown (1996)

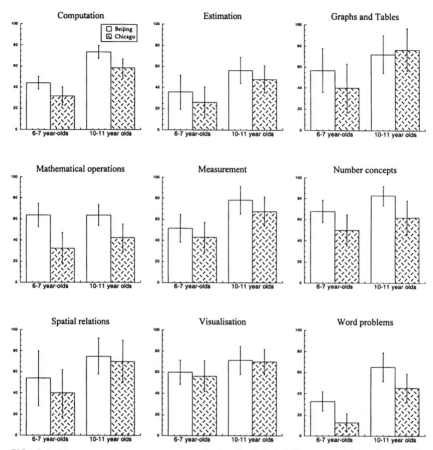

FIG. 6.1. Percentage correct responses on tests of mathematical ability among children from Beijing and Chicago (data obtained with permission from Table 1, Stevenson et al., 1990b). Unshaded areas indicates children from Beijing, cross hatched shading indicates children from Chicago. Error lines encompass 2 standard deviation from mean.

critically evaluated two international assessments of mathematics skills, and reported that, at least in the case of the Second International Mathematics Study, the lowest 10% of students perform at a comparable level in all countries. Overall, though, the abiding message from these and other, related, studies is that East Asian children enjoy a decided advantage over their American contemporaries in terms of mathematical knowledge and skills (e.g. Comber & Keeves, 1973; Garden, 1987; Glaser, 1976; Hatano, 1982; Husen, 1967).

Methodological issues in the comparison of national groups

The work of Stevenson and colleagues also provides an instructive example of how to go about making cross-cultural comparisons in the first place. The potential difficulties of such an enterprise become apparent when one considers that no two countries are likely to cover the same mathematical content in the classroom, and topics are often covered at different levels of difficulty. There is therefore the risk that a topic will be essentially unfamiliar to some children, but form a central and well-covered area for others. In such circumstances, it would be surprising if cultural differences did not emerge.

Reynolds and Farrell (1996) point out a number of additional issues that create problems for large-scale international comparisons of performance. For example, in some international surveys, such as those carried out by the International Association for the Evaluation of Educational Achievement, subject selection involves recruitment of a large number of children from a small number of schools, which makes the representativeness of the sample questionable. Often in surveys of this type, there is little account taken of educational policies that may affect how children progress through the school (e.g. instances where children repeat a year). Added to which it is more than possible that international differences will exist concerning the fundamental aims, learning objectives, and expected outcomes of mathematics curricula. Issues such as these have led to some sharp criticism of the value of some international surveys on mathematics (Brown, 1996) because they may not be comparing like with like.

Stigler et al. (1982) approached the problem of test content by devising questions based on analyses of relevant maths textbooks from all three countries involved in their study. Texts were analysed for the presence of specific mathematical concepts and skills, in addition to noting the grade and semester in which they featured in the curriculum. Of the 320 topics identified in this way, it emerged that 204 (64%) of them were shared by all three countries (Japan, Taiwan, and the United States). In fact, only 26 of these topics appeared at the same time in all three curricula, but this factor was taken into account by weighting item difficulty according to which semester a given topic was introduced in a particular country.

In compiling the final version of the test, attention was also paid to the accuracy of translations and the appropriateness of the cultural content of the problems. With regard to the selection of participants, the US children who participated in the Stevenson et al. (1990b) study were from Minneapolis, with the effect that they were drawn from largely American-born, English-speaking families. The area's relative economic strength, the social stability of communities, and not least the nationally high educational standards of children from this area served to produce a US sample comprising relatively high achievers.

Consequently, any cross-cultural deficits in the American children would be likely to represent a conservative estimate of national underperformance.

As a final point, we note that wider mathematics surveys have often compared not only US, British, Chinese, and Japanese children, but other national groups as well (see Reynolds & Farrell, 1996, for a useful review). These have invariably confirmed the high achievement level of East Asian children, and the under performance of US children in particular (with British children doing only slightly better). The relative performance in other countries (e.g. trends towards high achievement in Hungary and Switzerland and lower performance in Portugal and Israel) offers a further important perspective on levels of achievement. Their diverse mix of educational and cultural values gives a potentially fertile research base for developing accounts of effective learning. This wider potential has yet to be fully exploited, however.

EXPLAINING PERFORMANCE DIFFERENCES: (1) CULTURAL INFLUENCES

Although the occurrence of a cross-cultural gap in maths performance is by now beyond dispute, the attempt to account for why this gap exists has turned out to be a far more difficult endeavour. An immediate problem is presented by the large number of different explanations that have been advanced in the literature. The remainder of this chapter will be devoted to some of these possibilities, including: the influence of pre-school education; the quantity and quality of maths teaching; the strategies used in solving problems; the attitudes of teachers, parents, and children to learning maths; and the influence of language on the cognitive representation of number.

The investigation of all of these factors tends to rely on the strategy of first highlighting reliable differences between two (or more) cultures in, say, the amount of time spent learning maths. Typically, the next step is to argue for the relevance of this factor as an underlying cause of maths performance across cultures. This basic methodological orientation has yielded many valuable insights on the issues surrounding cross-cultural differences in the acquisition of mathematical skills and knowledge. At the same time, however, it is apparent that evidence consistent with one particular explanation rarely allows one simultaneously to rule out competing explanations. Of course, it is more than likely that many variables interact to produce the observed disparities in performance. In our present state of knowledge, however, it is not possible to establish which variables exert the greatest influence. Nor have many attempts been made to consider how particular variables interact with one another to produce their effects on children. It is therefore incumbent on future research programmes to make explicit the links between particular cultural practices and the development of psychological mechanisms in children relevant to the acquisition and deployment of mathematical knowledge and skills.

Pre-school experience

The research discussed in the previous section was conducted with school-age children, but it is possible, of course, that the cultural differences identified were already entrenched before children even started mainstream schooling. If that proved to be the case, then whatever responsibility they do carry, schools alone cannot be blamed for failing some children (Stevenson et al., 1990a). It is necessary, therefore, to consider the potential influence of children's pre-school experiences with mathematical concepts.

One possibility is that the amount and type of mathematical input supplied by parents varies across cultures. A study conducted by Durkin et al. (1986) is relevant in this respect because they found that number words are sometimes used in rather ambiguous ways by parents when talking to 1- and 2-year-old children. In English, for example, adults use "one" as both a (deictic) pronoun (e.g. "One must not throw food") and a number (e.g. "Put two in. That's one, that's one"). Confusing use of number words may represent an (albeit small) illustration of how pre-school experience can affect introductions to number concepts. Likewise, Blevins-Knabe and Musun-Miller (1996) found a significant relationship between the frequency of number use by parents and early mathematical performance in US children. In addition, experience in the home may also be supplemented by more formal pre-schooling classes. For example, anecdotal accounts often point to an especially well-organized and extensive system of early education in countries like Japan (where children may attend pre-school, or *yochien*). Empirical studies of the impact of home and pre-school environments are, however, very limited (but see Stevenson et al., 1990a, for evidence that length of pre-school experience among Chinese children was predictive of later school success).

An alternative research strategy that *has* been pursued, however, is to examine children's performance at the very beginning of their school careers. Typical in this vein is the study undertaken by Miura et al. (1994) (described in more detail later). The children in this study were chosen on the basis that the key concept being tested (the notion of place value) had not yet been introduced in the context of classroom teaching. It was also assumed that children had received no exposure to the concept of place value prior to schooling, but in the absence of specific information on individual participants' previous experience, this conclusion is perhaps unwarranted. For example, the Japanese school curriculum assumes that children will only be able to count up to 20 by the end of the first semester. However, the children in Miura et al.'s study had no special difficulties in identifying numbers in excess of 40. One cannot assume, therefore, that children's mathematical knowledge simply mirrors or corresponds to minimum targets within the school curriculum. In general, it is clear that cross-cultural differences not attributable to formal schooling should be investigated further, in order to establish the precise origins of children's performance in pre-school experience.

Pedagogical influences

In this section, the influence of classroom teaching on maths performance will be considered. In so doing, it will become apparent that cultural differences exist both in terms of the quantity and quality of teaching available. One method of assessing the quality of teaching available is to examine the kinds of teacher-pupil interactions that take place, in order to assess how they might affect children's performance. One can also scrutinize the quality of teaching materials available to children. The quantity of teaching will be considered in terms of the amount of time children are actually engaged in learning mathematics in the classroom. More subtly, it will be revealed that differences also exist in terms of the amount of practice children undertake for particular mathematical concepts, with direct implications for their success on related tasks.

In a revealing study, Perry, Van der Stoep and Yu (1993) investigated teaching styles in Taiwan, Japan, and the United States. In particular, they examined the methods used to teach the concepts of addition and subtraction in the classroom. It was found that differences existed in the kinds of questions directed at children. Asian teachers in particular produced relatively high levels of what Perry et al. termed "conceptual questions", which require children to integrate information and draw inferences. For example, children might be asked to compare solutions across different problems, or explain differences between mathematical operations. The US teachers, by contrast, often phrased computational questions in a framework where the arithmetic context was arbitrary and unfamiliar. These findings may surprise many people because the stereotypical view of the Japanese classroom conjures up an image of students, seated at rows of desks in rigid lockstep fashion, engaged in endless repetition of rote-learned facts. Of course, it remains for future research to quantify the extent to which styles of pupil-teacher interaction impact directly on subsequent maths performance. These findings are consistent, however, with the view that the acquisition of mathematical concepts is facilitated by methods encouraging children to go beyond simply finding the correct solution to individual problems and to think more deeply about the mathematical concepts involved. This is likely to be the case whether conceptual understanding is fostered in whole-class teaching or within small groups.

A further interesting point of contrast across cultures lies in the teaching materials used by children in learning mathematics. Specifically, it has been revealed that textbooks vary both in terms of content and the ways in which they present information. Thus, Mayer, Sims, and Tajika (1995) found that Japanese texts provide more in the way of instruction than American texts, and that there are more worked-out examples underpinning mathematical operations. Moreover, in Japanese texts, the accompanying illustrations were more likely to be directly relevant to the concepts being taught. In contrast, up to 20% of the space in American texts was taken up by "attention-grabbing graphics that, unlike those in the Japanese books, are interesting but irrelevant" (Mayer et al., 1995, p. 449). Furthermore, the use of concrete analogies to explain mathematical processes is more consistent in Japanese texts (thereby allowing the child to focus attention on the relevant concept). American texts, on the other hand, devoted more textbook space to series of exercises, which pupils were expected to solve unaided.

American textbooks have also been criticized for presenting material that underestimates children's abilities. For example, Stigler, Fuson, Ham, and Kim (1986) examined addition and subtraction word problems—that is, situations where the child is expected to translate a written problem or story into an appropriate mathematical expression (e.g. $6 + 2 = $) and then derive an answer. Textbook word problems of this kind tended to be of the simplest form, even for later grades, and Fuson (1992) argues that they should not take priority over "mathematical marks" problems, but should instead be introduced at a later stage in learning, in order to consolidate the meaning of mathematical formulae. From this standpoint, Fuson (1992) argues that American textbooks fail American children by not building on the knowledge they bring to formal classroom learning. As a further illustration of this tendency, she observes that young children tend to be quite advanced in their ability to count objects before the first grade, yet they are presented with only small object sets for counting in typical text illustrations. It may well be the case, therefore, that the abilities of American children are not being challenged or extended greatly by the teaching materials available to them.

Variation in the quality of teaching and teaching materials across cultures is compounded by variation in the amount of time spent learning mathematics. Significant differences have been found both in terms of the allocation of classroom time to maths, and the ways in which that time is used. For example, Stevenson et al. (1986, p. 231) observe that "in some of the American classrooms, no time was devoted to mathematics during the approximately 40 randomly selected hours when an observer was present." Furthermore, there were strong indications that teaching time was used less efficiently in US schools than in Taiwan or Japan. In some cases, American children known to be at school were not even present in the classroom, but were instead running an errand for the teacher, or otherwise occupied elsewhere in the school. For American fifth-graders, absenteeism of this kind occurred on 18.4% of occasions, compared with a figure of less than 0.2% for Taiwan and Japan. Compounding this difference in time spent studying mathematics at school, there are reports confirming the additional amount of homework given to East Asian pupils, particularly among older children (Fuligni & Stevenson, 1995).

Strategies in problem-solving

Fuson and Kwon (1992) provide a detailed consideration of addition and subtraction skills among Korean children (7- to 9-year-olds). They presented two forms of arithmetic tasks. First, children were presented with two- and three-digit addition and subtraction problems, which involved "trading" between columns. Second, they were provided with examples of sums that had previously been completed; in such cases, children were asked to determine whether the solution was correct or not. Some of these completed examples incorporated common errors made by US children on addition and subtraction tasks. The data showed that the Korean children were highly accurate, both at solving the problems themselves and also in verifying answers that were given by others. Furthermore, the justifications for their choice of arithmetic processes were conceptually sophisticated, and they revealed a good understanding of the multidigit number system. Korean children's facility with the concept of place value was attributed, in part, to the influence of stock phrases that make the notion of trading explicit in Korean (c.f. the notion of "carrying" in English).

A common error made by US children on subtraction problems was to subtract a smaller number from a larger number when the smaller number is on top, as in the following:

$$
\begin{array}{r}
43 \\
-17 \\
\hline 34
\end{array}
$$

One might characterize errors of this kind as rule-based, in this case, concerned with identifying the appropriate subtraction sequence. Notably, Korean children made no errors of this type, a fact that indicates their greater understanding of subtraction. Through whatever means, Korean children aged 7–9 years possess a thorough understanding of the arithmetical process, and can deploy solution strategies effectively and flexibly. One is thus testing more than children's knowledge of place value concepts in posing multidigit number problems.

Attitudes to learning

Beyond the purely pedagogical concerns outlined in the previous section, other, more socially based differences have been identified as contributing to the differential in maths performance. In particular, the attitudes of parents, teachers, and children towards mathematics and learning have been examined. For example, Hess, Chang, and McDevitt (1987) explored some of the factors that mothers in China and the United States consider important for the success of their children in mathematics. Success was attributed to five different factors, namely, inherent ability, personal effort, training at home, training at school, and luck. It was found that Chinese mothers considered lack of effort to be largely responsible for low performance, whereas American mothers empha-sized the child's innate ability and poor school training more strongly. This finding has been replicated by Stevenson et al. (1990a) with samples drawn from Taiwan, Japan, and the United States. This latter study also found that children's attitudes closely mirror those of their parents, with US children attributing success to natural ability, whereas the Taiwanese and Japanese children stressed the importance of hard work and effort for success.

In a follow-up to their original study, Stevenson et al. (1993) found that when the same children were questioned again five years later, these cultural differ-ences were maintained. It was also found that American families were more satisfied with children's progress in maths than their East Asian counterparts, a finding that supports a picture of misplaced complacency among US mothers and their children. Stevenson et al. (1990a) have also argued that US children grow up in an environment where there is relatively little family involvement in their education, and less interest in academic achievement. In contrast, Japanese and Taiwanese parents not only show a commitment to their chil-dren's success, but they also provide the social resources to facilitate this development, and children grow up in a cultural environment that stresses numerical proficiency (Hatano, 1990). In conclusion, the findings on parental attitudes provide a clear basis for constructing an explanation of cross-cultural differences in terms of motivation to succeed.

EXPLAINING PERFORMANCE DIFFERENCES: (2) LINGUISTIC INFLUENCES ON NUMERICAL CONCEPTS

While many researchers have focused on the teaching of maths, or more generally the environment in which that teaching takes place, there has also been interest in the possibility that the medium in which number concepts are grounded—the language for mathematics—may be relevant to the develop-ment of mathematics skills and the use of numbers. In particular, we will examine the intriguing suggestion that certain aspects of East Asian languages like Chinese, Korean, and Japanese may confer a special advantage on children in the acquisition and representation of mathematical concepts. In this regard, interest has centred largely on the concept of place value, that is, the idea that the position of a numeral in a multidigit number affects its value. Thus, in the base-10 system, the digits 4 and 5 in "45" have quite different meanings, because of their relative position. Many studies have demonstrated that the notion of place value poses particular problems for European and American children, with many 9-year-olds still experiencing difficulties (e.g. Baroody, 1990; Jones & Thornton, 1993; Kamii, 1986).

Cross-cultural research on the role of language in children's understanding of place value is based on the observation that the number-naming systems in Chinese-based languages are highly regular for numbers up to 100 (see Table 6.1). Moreover, the number of tens is made explicit in the names for two-digit numbers. For example, 57 in Japanese glosses as "five-ten seven" (*go-juu nana*), and 26 can be represented as "two-ten six" (*ni-juu roku*). The only minor exception to this straightforward pattern is that numbers between 10 and 20 are read as "ten-something" (e.g. 14 as "ten-four") rather than "*one*-ten something"—that is, there is an omission of the decade value in this particular case.

The strict regularity of Chinese-based languages stands in stark contrast to the numerous irregularities apparent in other number-naming systems such as English and French (see also Saxe, 1982, for a consideration of a quite different naming system among the Oksapmin of Papua New Guinea). For example, some English number names seem, to modern ears, quite arbitrary, with the number of tens and units they represent being obscure (e.g. "eleven", "twelve"). Similarly, morphophonological irregularities are present in several decade names. Thus, two, three and five are corrupted in "twenty," "thirty," and "fifty," respectively. In addition, although units of ten are explicitly marked, the morpheme changes from "-teen," for the numbers thirteen to nineteen, to "-ty" in the numbers from twenty to ninety-nine. Of course, both of these forms differ from the more basic "ten." A final source of irregularity is apparent in the order of units representing tens and ones. Thus, in teen numbers, a "ones-then-tens" order is apparent, whereas for higher numbers up to 99, the order is reversed.

One potential consequence of regularity in the Chinese-based number-naming system is that the "number vocabulary" might be relatively easy to acquire, because new numbers can be inferred rather than having to be learned individually. Miller and Stigler (1987) explored this possibility when they asked Taiwanese and American children between 4 and 6 years of age to recite numbers to as high a value as possible. They found that the Taiwanese children were more accurate in their counting, and also counted to larger numbers before

TABLE 6.1
Number names across languages

English	French	Japanese
one	un (or une)	ichi
two	deux	ni
three	trois	san
four	quatre	shi
ten	dix	juu
eleven	onze	juu-ichi
twelve	douze	juu-ni
twenty	vingt	ni-juu
twenty-one	vingt-et-un	ni-juu-ichi

stopping. They also noted that both American and Taiwanese children tended to stop counting as they approached a decade boundary (e.g. 39), suggesting that further responses may have been impeded because they did not know what decade name to use as a continuation. In addition, Miller and Stigler (1987) reported a different pattern in the counting sequence errors that children made. The most frequent type of error made by American children, in particular, was to skip a number in the sequence (see also Siegler & Robinson, 1982). These errors may be engendered by the need of American children to learn more number names, rather than acquire the rules for generating them, as would seem to be the case for Taiwanese children. On the basis of their findings, Miller and Stigler (1987) argue that English speakers have an additional linguistic hurdle to overcome before numbers can be used or transformed in mathematically appropriate ways (see also Miller, Smith, Zhu, & Zhang, 1995). The Chinese-based languages, by contrast, may facilitate the acquisition of multidigit number names at an earlier stage. The intuitive appeal of this interpretation is undeniable, although it has yet to receive direct empirical support.

The possible influence of language on not just the acquisition of numerical vocabulary, but also on mathematical cognition, has been explored in a series of experiments conducted by Irene Miura and colleagues (Miura, 1987; Miura, Kim, Chang, & Okamoto, 1988; Miura & Okamoto, 1989; Miura, Okamoto, Kim, Steere, & Fayol, 1993; Miura et al., 1994). Specifically, language has been implicated as a causal factor in explaining the superiority enjoyed by East Asian children on tasks requiring knowledge of place value concepts. The argument, then, is for a form of linguistic relativity, where language is considered to influence cognition (see for example Bloom, 1981; Brown & Lenneberg, 1954; Brown, 1976).

The claim for an effect of language on children's conception of place value and the base-10 system is based on responses made by children (between approximately 6 and 7 years of age) to a number-matching task. Children are presented with an Arabic numeral (for example, 42) and are then asked to "show" or represent the number with a set of cubes. In so doing, children have at their disposal a large set of individual cubes ("ones"), as well as blocks, each comprising 10 cubes. Children's responses were categorized in one of three ways. Taking our example of 42, a base-10 response would involve a collection of four 10-blocks with two single ones. A Unit response would comprise a collection of 42 individual ones cubes. A Non-Canonical response, meanwhile, involves the use of one or more blocks of ten but also more than 10 units (e.g. two ten-blocks and 22 individual ones cubes). Following their initial response, children were then asked if they could use the cubes to represent the number in an alternative way, thus providing an index of how flexible children are in their thinking.

The consistent pattern that emerges is that Chinese, Korean, and Japanese children produce significantly more base-10 responses than children from the

United States, France, and Sweden. That is, the Asian children display a strong preference for representing multidigit numbers with the appropriate number of tens and units. For the non-Asian children, on the other hand, Unit responses were predominant. Miura et al. (1994) reviewed a number of factors that might influence the child's responses on the number-matching task, but placed greatest emphasis on the possible influence of language. Their argument is that multidigit number names in the Chinese-based languages allow children to represent numbers directly in terms of their component tens and ones. Thus, it is argued that "variability in mathematics performance may be due to differences in cognitive representation of number that is affected by numerical language characteristics that differentiate Asian and nonAsian language groups" (Miura et al., 1994, p. 402).

Questioning the influence of linguistic relativity

Evidently, Miura et al.'s data are consistent with the linguistic relativity hypothesis. At the same time, however, their experimental paradigm does not allow one to rule out numerous alternative explanations. As already mentioned, much research in this field relies on the basic strategy of inferring an association between differences along one dimension (mathematics performance) together with differences along another (in this case, language). The fundamental problem here is that the association between language and cognition is not demonstrated directly.

One way of strengthening the conclusion that language influences numerical thought is to collect converging evidence. That is, one can seek other data that may confirm the influence of language on children's responses, thereby exploring whether the linguistic relativity hypothesis provides a satisfactory account of performance in the number-matching paradigm. To this end, we carried out an extension of the Miura et al. matching task in a study with English-speaking children from Britain (Towse & Saxton, 1997). The children (of approximately 7 years of age) were presented with a scenario in which they were asked to help a teddy bear, by showing him the meaning of written two-digit numbers with cubes. In one condition (termed here the baseline condition), there were single unit cubes and blocks of ten (as in previous studies). In an alternative situation, however, children had available unit cubes, blocks of ten cubes, and blocks of twenty cubes (we term this here the "twenty cube" condition).

The rationale was that incorporating blocks of twenty cubes changed the relationship between number names and the physical representations that were available. That is, for the twenty cube condition the identification or naming of numbers in the twenties such as "24" could now explicitly cue the use of a multi-unit block, in the same way that a multidigit numeral is held to cue a ten-block response for Asian children ("24" as *two-ten*-four"). It is important to note that in both conditions teen numbers were also included in the set of trials, as these values (e.g. "15") do not give a language-based cue to a block response. Thus, evidence for the importance of language structure on mathematical representations would be obtained if children used twenties blocks for numbers in the twenties, but units on the teen numbers.

Two aspects of children's responses were noteworthy. First, in the baseline condition, we found that children's responses involved a significant predominance of unit representations—essentially replicating previous studies. More specifically, response types were highly consistent across all experimental trials, that is, for both teen numbers and non-teen numbers. Rather than finding teen numbers conceptually harder to represent with base-10 blocks, children essentially responded to all types of numbers in the same way. Thus, children's concepts of numbers as measured by this task are general, rather than specific to particular number names and their structural characteristics.

The second major finding was that providing additional multi-unit cubes had a substantial effect on children's responses. As Fig. 6.2 illustrates, in the condition with blocks of 20 cubes available, there was a higher incidence of multidigit block use for representing numbers (both teens and non-teens). That is, in the twenty blocks condition, children were significantly more likely to construct responses using multidigit blocks, and less likely to use units alone. In addition to this finding, it is also possible to categorize performance on the basis of preferential responses on smaller (teen) and larger (twenties) numbers separately. This allows for a stricter criterion of possession of a multi-unit conception; one that requires a preference for using blocks specifically on trials

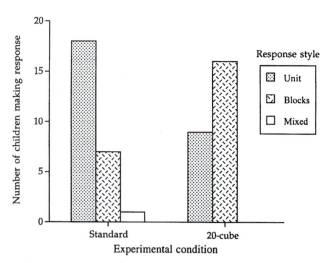

FIG. 6.2. Modal response style to requests to match numerals with tokens among British children. Children had available either unit and 10-block cubes ("standard" condition), or unit, 10-block, and 20-block cubes ("20-cube" condition). See text for more details.

involving teen numbers (where the lexical link between name and cube set is not apparent). In this way, one denotes as unit strategists children who made either unit responses throughout or unit responses on for the majority of teen numbers. Re-analysis of the data in this way showed, in the baseline condition, 18 unit and 8 block strategists, and in the twenty block condition, 10 unit and 15 block strategists. The association between response style and the provision of blocks remained significant, χ^2 ($df = 1, N = 51$) = 4.4, $P < .05$. This supports the conclusion reached in Towse and Saxton (1997) that the experimental situation affected how children interpreted task demands.

Thus, contrary to the idea that the English speakers faced a language-based hurdle through a poor linguistic correspondence between name and block concept, we found that an additional set of blocks produced a uniform shift in the response strategies. Another way of looking at these findings would be to say that a relatively simple alteration to the experimental materials had prompted children to respond in a significantly different way on the number-matching task. This latter perspective raises doubts about one aspect of the number-matching task: the assumption that it provides an appropriate and stable measure of how young children represent numbers cognitively.

Further experimental work has confirmed and extended the conclusion that children can be strongly influenced by subtle shifts in the instructions provided at the outset. In Miura et al.'s (1994) original study, the researcher first demonstrated how to represent numbers with the cubes by giving children two examples. The numbers chosen were 2 and 7, both of which require ones cubes only. These examples (however unwittingly) may have cued some children to follow the experimenter's example and use ones cubes in their own collections. Further, British and American children may have been particularly susceptible to this effect if they lacked practice and confidence in working with numbers and numerical tokens. Towse and Saxton (1997) tested this possibility with 6- and 7- year-old British children by creating an experimental condition in which one of the examples given to children ("13") involved the use of a block of ten. As in the conventional testing procedure, children then represented various written numbers using either units, or units and blocks of ten.

Following this single practice trial involving a two-digit numeral, children were significantly more likely to use blocks of ten in their own responses than was the case with standard instructions involving single-digit numbers. This held true even when children were confronted with larger test numbers (e.g. "65"). Such an effect underlines the possibility that children's responses are influenced, at least in part, by their perception of the experimental requirements (e.g. forming numbers with unit cubes) as well as by underlying "cognitive representations" of multidigit numbers.

In order to assess whether Japanese children are also affected by the experimental cues in the number matching paradigm, a group of 7-year-old mono-lingual Japanese, together with 6- and 7-year-old British children, were asked to represent a range of two-digit numbers in a separate study (Saxton & Towse, 1998). We once again varied the practice examples to children, showing either single-digit numbers or including a two-digit number. Unlike the previous study, however, this experiment used single cubes to stand for sets or blocks of ten. That is, children were told that cubes of a particular colour represented a value of ten units whereas other cubes had a unitary value. In this way, children's ability to represent numerical quantities was stretched by avoiding direct physical cues to numerosity.

Figure 6.3 illustrates the significant effect of instruction on the response styles adopted by children. For all groups, the appropriate use of base-10 representations (i.e. the ten-value cubes) increased following the inclusion of a multidigit number prompt prior to the experimental trials. Interestingly, in the prompt condition there were no significant differences between any of the groups in terms of preferred representational strategy. That is, cross-cultural performance differences diminished to nonsignificant levels when children were first shown an example of ten units being used. Furthermore, subsequent measures of these children's comprehension of multi-unit representations mirrored the production trials just described (Saxton & Towse, 1998).

The finding that Japanese children were affected by the instructions is revealing, because one would not expect such an improvement in performance for Japanese children if language played such a significant role in their responses. After all, according to Miura et al. the Japanese number language

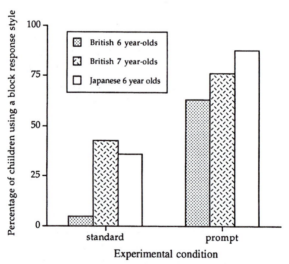

FIG. 6.3. Percentage of children preferentially using blocks of cubes to represent numerals (data from Saxton & Towse, 1998). Experimental trials either followed two single-digit examples ("standard" condition) or followed a single-digit and two-digit example ("prompt" condition). Data are reported for British 6-year-olds, British 7-year-olds, and Japanese 6-year-olds.

system is viewed as making the task particularly transparent, thus allowing children to exploit their sophisticated cognitive representations of multidigit numbers. Thus, one would predict relatively high levels of base-10 responding whatever the cue provided by the experimenter. Overall, these findings make it harder to accept that the Japanese and English children necessarily differ in terms of their underlying cognitions—there must be other factors at play. The Japanese superiority in the standard paradigm (with a low number prompt) is therefore not easily attributed to the direct influence of language.

In the context of the argument presented here, it is interesting to note that in the reports of Miura et al. (1993, 1994) the performance of French children was at least as good, if not superior to, that of the US sample. French speakers might be thought to have even greater difficulties than English speakers, as, for example, two ("deux") and twenty ("vingt") appear quite distinct, and larger numbers have irregular forms (e.g. "70" is "soixante-dix", or "sixty-ten"). Thus, the impact of language does not seem to explain fully all linguistic samples tested with the number-matching paradigm. By the same token, it does not appear to provide an account of the relative mathematical success in international surveys of children from, for example, Switzerland and Hungary (Foxman, 1992).

If language does influence mathematical cognition, in the way suggested by Miura et al., then it appears that more direct evidence is required. It is also apparent that their argument is restricted to particular linguistic samples, and to the relatively narrow domain of place value understanding. It will be recalled that the Asian superiority for computation and number concepts is matched by an equivalent advantage for many other aspects of mathematical knowledge, including measurement, spatial relations, visualization, and estimation (see Fig. 6.1; *pace* the view of Miller et al., 1995). The pervasive occurrence of performance differences across such a broad spectrum makes it increasingly difficult to maintain the view that language is a primary determinant of mathematical cognition.

Neither can the language argument explain the view that the advantage enjoyed by Asian-language children in arithmetic appears to be a recent historical phenomenon (Geary, Salthouse, Chen, & Fan, 1996). Geary et al. have reported that whereas US and Taiwanese children differ in their mathematical attainment, US and Taiwanese adults perform at very similar levels. Moreover, Geary et al. take pains to show that this effect is not simply due to a decline in performance with age among Taiwanese subjects.

Nonetheless, there are salient questions about base-10 thinking that remain in the light of the cross-cultural studies considered here. At the very least, it appears that Japanese children display a greater flexibility in overriding the influence of a low number prompt to produce base-10 responses; one possibility, as mentioned earlier, is that greater exposure to number work and use of cubes contributes to this phenomenon. However, thus far the arguments have generally focused on the legitimate *interpretations* that can be made from task performance. Given the cultural and developmental differences commonly obtained in studies of place value, a focus on the *mechanisms* of conceptual change might be particularly informative, both within and across cultures.

In addition, there is much potential merit in a fine-grained analysis of place value understanding, considering multiple ways that multidigit numbers may be understood by children (see Fuson, Smith, & LoCicero, 1997). In this chapter, we have merely considered responses in terms of unit and multi-unit conceptions of number, because this has been sufficient to evaluate experimental hypotheses. Although satisfactory for present purposes, it is worth acknowledging that this approach provides a rather blunt instrument. Other psychological tasks and situations may expose more subtle and varied mental representations between these coarsely defined extremes of unit and multi-unit conceptions; one could, for example, look to evidence on multi-unit thinking garnered from direct questioning or analysis of children's errors in transcribing spoken to written numbers (e.g. Baroody, 1987; Young-Loveridge, 1991). On a point of methodology about the number-matching paradigm, it is perhaps worth emphasizing the great sensitivity shown by children to minor shifts in instructional cues. Considerable care is therefore required in testing children from different nationalities, particularly if different investigators are involved. Minor changes in instructional or testing emphases may have a substantial impact on children's preferred responses.

Language and numerical processing

Although language may not have a direct bearing on the form in which numbers are represented, it remains possible that it exerts an influence on the processing of numerical information. Miller & Zhu (1991) presented adult American subjects with an unusual task in which two-digit numbers were to be read out in reversed form (thus "61" was to be read as "sixteen", "18" as "eighty one"). They found that there was a delay associated with the process of reversing a number into a teen form (61 to "sixteen"). Reversing a teen number itself (18 to "eighty one") was actually less of a problem than reversing other numbers (e.g. "36" read as "sixty three"). Further experimental work showed that this difficulty in reversing into teen numbers was removed when stimulus numerals were presented in mirror-imaged form (i.e. visually transformed). Significantly, the reverse-into-teen effect was found with Taiwanese subjects when they were asked to respond in English, but it disappeared when responses were given in Chinese. On the basis of these findings, Miller & Zhu (1991) suggest that the morphological structure of some English number names (i.e. teens) can influence the processing of numerical information. That is, English teen number names were considered to be difficult items to retrieve and produce as spoken output.

Although it is evident that Miller and Zhu (1991) have established that not all two-digit numbers are equally easy to reverse, the broader implication of their data is unclear. For example, their task involves reading a numeral and responding with a name that is a transformed version of that numeral. Teen number names in English are rather unusual in morphological terms, however, as they comprise a single word form (cf. the single word "sixteen" and the two words "sixty one"), and there may be something about the nature of the reversal operation in such a case that is particularly time-consuming. In a related vein, the reversal task has a substantial attentional component or "stroop-like" quality (see MacLeod, 1991), insofar as one must overcome a tendency to name the item, and instead name a transformed version of the stimulus. Indeed, the idea that individuals need to prevent an overlearned cognitive action (naming a number) is reinforced by the finding that reversal delays were different for mirror-image stimuli. That is, being less familiar, mirror-image numerals would be less strongly associated with particular responses.

Accordingly, one (rather intricate) explanation for the difficulty with accessing teen names found by Miller and Zhu (1991) reflects the attentional processes in their task. In retrieving a name, the target item must be selected while related nontargets must be inhibited. Furthermore, the inhibition of nontargets may be a process that varies according to the number of nontargets being suppressed. With an increase in the number of items or nodes that must be suppressed, inhibitory action on these nodes becomes diluted. In the conventional naming situation, because there are far fewer teen numbers than non-teen numbers, teen number names would be inhibited quite strongly when a non-teen number is presented. This would then make the reversal task difficult because the (now appropriate) teen name to be retrieved has been inhibited quite strongly by the number stimulus. By contrast, when a teen number is presented, non-teen numbers are more weakly inhibited (this inhibition being diffused over many items), allowing the more rapid activation for the appropriate non-teen number name in the reversal task.

It should also be borne in mind that these number reversal data are really germane to the question of whether the structure of number names influences the course of (a series of) cognitive processes. This is rather different from the claim that the structure of number names can influence the internal representations of numbers, or concepts held about numbers (cf. Miura et al., 1994). To use an analogy, communicating in a particular language may affect how a thought is phrased, via the use of idiom and particular vocabulary items. Nonetheless, communication through different languages can produce the same semantic content. Thus, one needs to be able to distinguish the *how* of a thought or cognitive representation, from the *what* (or *content*) of such a representation. Miller and Zhu report data directed at the first issue, whereas Miura and colleagues consider the second.

CONCLUDING REMARKS

In respect to the specific role of language in cultural differences on mathematics, it would be fair to characterize our own position as agnostic. It should be emphasized, perhaps, that the empirical work we have reported does not demand that one dismiss the possibility that language shapes the way children understand multidigit numbers. However, the data do strengthen the argument that the evidence for the impact of language is not entirely convincing and can be given alternative interpretations. To add to these qualms, there appears to be no metric, at present, by which the influence of language can be properly gauged independently of other factors. This does make the hypothesis a rather circular one—language differences are used in order to account for mathematical performance differences, and levels of mathematical performance are used to confirm the effect of language. Taken as a whole, and in the context of research from other areas, we suggest that studying the many non linguistic influences on mathematical attainment may provide a more productive avenue for understanding cultural differences.

One positive message from this chapter is to note that psychologists are far from being blind to cross-cultural variety in numerical skills. Indeed, there is an awareness of the great value of cross-cultural data for understanding the development of mathematical skills (just as there is interest in using cross-cultural mathematical differences to investigate the mechanisms underlying arithmetic computations; Geary, 1996; LeFevre & Liu, 1997). National differences in approaches to mathematics provide an intriguing "natural experiment" on children's acquisition of this important skill, and clearly some educational programmes are much more successful than others. Careful study of children's performance, their antecedents and consequences, afford an important opportunity to develop and refine accounts of the conditions under which learning takes place, and the efficiency of that learning. However, it should also be apparent that this "experiment" has many (uncontrolled) variables, quite likely to interact in complex ways. Thus, the identification of issues relevant to cross-cultural performance, hitherto an important research focus, may represent only a starting point from which the relationships between factors can be appreciated and modelled. Thus, it appears increasingly to be the case that multidimensional approaches will be required in order to deliver a coherent and comprehensive account of the impact of culture on mathematics.

ACKNOWLEDGEMENTS

We are grateful to Una Hutton and Peter Towse for helpful comments made during the preparation of this chapter.

Working memory and mental calculation: Effects of age and anxiety

INTRODUCTION

Specification of cognitive systems underlying development is often problematic. Change is an integral part of development, and highly specified models may lack the flexibility needed for developmental research. The working memory model introduced by Baddeley and Hitch in 1974 may be the exception that proves the rule. There is a developmental progression in the specifications of the model, and a body of research addressing issues in memory development and language acquisition from this standpoint (e.g. de Ribaupierre & Hitch, 1994; Gathercole & Baddeley, 1993). It is surprising that relatively little work has yet explored working memory and mathematical development.

John Adams and Graham Hitch (Chapter 7) give us an accessible but still detailed account of the general and specific models of working memory within which their work is located. The first experimental findings which they report establish a strong correlational link between their measure of "addition span" and calculation speed. The details of the findings and their interpretation are extremely well considered and repay careful reading. The fit to the general working memory model is very close. Further investigations explore the specific role of the "phonological loop" in the development of arithmetical skill. Detailed interpretation of findings here is equivocal. But still there is strong support for the model.

Later in this volume (Dowker, Chapter 12), and elsewhere, studies of children's arithmetical skill have attempted to test the involvement of working memory using a digit span task. It should be noted, however that digit-span is a unitary task with no concurrent load, and as such may be an inappropriate measure. The findings reported by Adams and Hitch seem likely to lead to further detailed investigations.

Adams and Hitch found age-related differences in the link between addition speed and span, and offered an explanation in terms of variation in working memory capacity. New research reported by Mark Ashcraft, Elizabeth Kirk, and Derek Hopko in Chapter 8 examines the ways in which working memory capacity might also be affected by anxiety. The problem of anxiety in mathematics is so great as to have generated not only a research literature of its own, but also specific assessment procedures designed to identify sufferers. Ashcraft and colleagues provide the reader with a useful review of the area before going on to introduce their novel hypothesis that maths anxiety reduces performance by imposing "artificial" limits on working memory capacity. The hypothesis is closely argued and the early findings are consistent with a mechanism whereby anxiety disrupts capacity by introducing distracting extraneous thoughts. In line with predictions, the restrictive effects of anxiety are found to be significant when concurrent processing (e.g. "carrying" in mental arithmetic) is required.

This research into the cognitive mechanisms through which maths anxiety restricts performance is quite new. So far, findings are based solely on studies conducted with adult participants. The developmental implications are important, however, and it may be that research into the onset of maths anxiety during the school years will benefit from a focused approach based on Ashcraft and colleagues' current work.

CHAPTER SEVEN

Children's mental arithmetic and working memory

John W. Adams & *Graham J. Hitch***
**University of York, UK*
***University of Lancaster, UK*

INTRODUCTION

Mental arithmetic is a common but important everyday skill. In formal education the child's acquisition of this skill is given considerable weight, second only to learning to read and write. A major factor contributing to efficient arithmetic performance is the memorization of number facts (e.g. Ashcraft, 1992; Siegler & Jenkins, 1989). Ashcraft, Donley, Halas, and Vakali (1992) argue that there is a clear distinction between integer-pair problems such as 2 + 3 and multidigit calculations like 14 + 27. The first are the basic addition facts that typically become overlearned during schooling, the integer pairs and their sums being stored in long-term memory. Retrieving the answer is normally quick, accurate, and relatively effortless. However, multidigit calculations are not usually performed by recalling the answer from long-term memory. Even if it were possible to memorize the answers to all possible problems, the time it would take to do this would be far too great. For this reason we tend to rely on algorithms that enable answers to be generated. Thus, multidigit additions usually require retrieval of the basic facts as part of a solution procedure that may involve carry operations and the storage of partial results (e.g. retaining the sum of the units while adding the tens). In general, procedures for multidigit calculation seem likely to demand a flexible operating space in which to combine ongoing processes with the handling of partial results. As Ashcraft (1995, p. 12) observes, "... the field has now begun to examine [arithmetic] performance in terms of the involvement of working memory".

It should be noted that the foregoing account of the difference between single-digit and multidigit calculations is a considerable oversimplification. For example, Baroody (1983, 1994) has pointed out that fact retrieval can be slow and inaccurate whereas procedural strategies can be fast and efficient. Also, LeFevre, Sadesky, and Bisanz (1996) have reported that in certain situations, adults may revert to using nonretrieval strategies such as counting. These qualifications are important, and suggest that the role of working memory may not be restricted to multidigit mental calculations, even in well-schooled adults.

The present discussion uses the model of working memory proposed by Baddeley and Hitch (1974). This model is supported by a large body of empirical evidence gathered from normal adults, neuropsychological patients with selective lesions and normally and abnormally developing children (see e.g. Baddeley, 1986, for a review). A full description of the model is given by Baddeley (1986). In outline, it consists of three components, termed the central executive, the phonological loop, and the visuospatial sketchpad. The central executive acts as a limited capacity attentional system, which initiates and controls mental operations. As such it fulfils a number of executive control functions (see Baddeley, 1996). Its primary role is to resource the competing demands of information processing and temporary information storage necessary for performing complex cognitive tasks such as reasoning or language comprehension. This involves coordinating the activities of the other components of the model, which act as limited capacity, modality-specific "slave systems". The visuospatial sketch pad is dedicated to storing and manipulating spatial or visual information, and the phonological loop is concerned with the maintainance and processing of verbal material using a speech-based code. A consequence of the limited capacity of working memory is that when a complex cognitive task overloads one or more subsystems, performance becomes impaired.

It is important to note that the term working memory has also been used to refer to the system for combining temporary storage and mental operations, without commitment to the assumption that it consists of specialised subsystems (see e.g. Daneman & Carpenter, 1980; Just & Carpenter, 1992). Where the distinction between this less specific interpretation of working memory and the Baddeley and Hitch (1974) model is important for following the present discussion it will be made clear.

WORKING MEMORY AND CALCULATION PERFORMANCE

Some of the earliest work on the role of working memory in arithmetic was carried out by Hitch (1978a, b, c). In one study, adult subjects solved orally presented multidigit additions of the form 425 + 63 (Hitch, 1978a). The most frequently used calculation procedure here is to follow the standard right-to-left algorithm, by adding first the units, then the tens, and finally the hundreds. In some conditions subjects were required to write their answers in right-to-left order (i.e. units, tens, hundreds), and in others the order was from left-to-right (hundreds, tens, units). Given the same order for output as for calculation, partial results can be reported as soon as they are calculated. However, when writing the answer in the opposite order to that of calculation, a mental transformation is required that imposes extra delays between the generation and output of partial results. Thus, the two conditions differ in the demands they place on working memory (in its general sense). Other experimental conditions varied the amount of visual support given on paper to augment the oral presentation (one, both, or neither operand), and the number of carry operations. Providing external information was assumed to reduce the load on temporary storage in working memory, whereas carrying was assumed to increase it, through the need to keep track of the carry.

Results showed that the number of errors increased when subjects were required to write their answers in the opposite order from that of calculation. There were also more errors when the amount of visual back-up was reduced, and when the number of carry operations was increased. Thus it appears that working memory can be overloaded by three aspects of mental calculation; the retention of temporary information, the length of time of that retention, and the number of operations involved in the calculation (Ashcraft, 1995). Interestingly, errors associated with the effects of output order, amount of visual back-up and carrying could be accounted for by assuming that temporary information is lost from working memory according to a simple decay function (Hitch, 1978a).

Ashcraft et al. (1992) highlighted two limitations in Hitch's studies. First, there was no reported analysis of the specific arithmetic facts that constituted the multidigit additions, (for example the problem 324 + 253 contains the basic addition facts 3 + 2, 2 + 5, and 4 + 3). Evidence from chronometric studies, (e.g. Ashcraft, 1982; Groen & Parkman, 1972) demonstrates that basic addition facts vary systematically in both their latencies and error rates. Larger sums are associated with longer latencies (i.e. the "problem-size" effect). If loss of information from working memory is sensitive to the duration for which information must be maintained, mental calculation errors should be sensitive to the size of the integers (even when there is no carrying). Relatedly, Hitch offered no insight into whether the retrieval of basic addition facts involves working memory resources. If this were shown to be so, then the problem-size effect suggests that some facts would be more difficult to retrieve and demand more resources than others.

Since this early work by Hitch (1978a, b), only a few studies have directly examined the role of working memory in multidigit arithmetic (Ashcraft et al.,

1992; Brainerd, 1983, 1987; Ellis, 1992; Fayol, Abdi, & Gombert, 1987; Hitch, Cundick, Haughey, Pugh, & Wright, 1987; Lemaire, Abdi, & Fayol, 1996; Logie, Gilhooly, & Wynn, 1994; see also Butterworth, Cipolotti, & Warrington, 1996). Some of these have focused on adult performance and are not directly applicable to children because of age differences in calculation processes and in working memory. For example, there are important changes in the way basic number facts are processed during initial learning (see e.g. Siegler & Shrager, 1984), and the degree to which working memory resources constrain mental arithmetic may be greater for children, as such constraints are more severe (see e.g. Hitch & Halliday, 1983). The need to identify the role of working memory in children's arithmetic is underscored by studies of children with learning deficits in mathematics, some of which have observed correlations with measures of working memory (e.g. Geary, 1990; Geary, Brown, & Samaranayake, 1991; Hitch & McAuley, 1991; Siegel & Ryan, 1989). However, interpreting such relationships is difficult in the absence of clear ideas about the precise role of working memory in children's arithmetic.

In order to discuss recent studies of the role of working memory in children's arithmetic, it will be helpful to describe some previous research on the role of working memory in cognitive development.

WORKING MEMORY AND COGNITIVE DEVELOPMENT

Case (1985, 1995) has put forward the view that working memory, in its general sense, plays a critical role in cognitive development. Many cognitive tasks that children learn to perform require the combination of temporary information storage with mental operations, and Case proposed that these two functions compete for a common pool of limited capacity resources. A consequence of this position is the prediction of a strong interdependence between processing and remembering, such that the more resources are required for operations, the less are available for short-term storage. Information processing will break down and errors will occur when the total resource demands of a cognitive task exceed the capacity of the workspace. Case (1985, 1995) proposed that cognitive development is made possible by a gradual increase in the efficiency of using the central workspace.

A study conducted by Case, Kurland, and Goldberg (1982) highlighted the importance of the speed of information-processing operations as a possible determinant of efficiency. Two of their experiments involved a novel "counting span" task in which children were asked to count the number of dots on each of a series of cards, while at the same time remembering the totals of previous counts. This task was designed so as to combine mental operations (counting) with temporary information storage (count totals). Counting span was defined as the maximum number of cards for which previous count totals could be recalled without error. Each child's speed of counting was measured by recording the time taken to count the dots without any requirement to remember previous totals.

In their first experiment, Case et al. (1982) discovered an approximate linear relation between counting span and counting time between the ages of 6 and 12, such that older children's higher spans could be predicted from their faster counting. In order to investigate whether the relationship had a causal basis, and was not simply a correlation, Case et al. (1982) carried out a second study where they manipulated an individual's processing speed. This was achieved by teaching adults to count using nonsense syllables instead of numbers, a much slower and less efficient process than normal counting. The experimental procedure was otherwise the same as for the children. The results showed that requiring adults to count in this unfamiliar way slowed their mean counting speed close to that of 6-year-olds. Significantly, their mean counting span was also reduced to a value similar to that of 6-year-olds.

Case et al. (1982) interpreted their results as indicating that the speed of mental operations reflects how much of the central workspace is required for operations. Thus, faster operations require less workspace, leaving more available for information storage. The systematic relationship between counting speed and counting span was taken as consistent with the hypothesis that the size of the workspace does not change during development, but that the efficiency with which it can be utilized increases, as in Case's general theory of cognitive development (Case, 1985; 1995).

It is important to emphasize that Case et al.'s (1982) notion of the central workspace is a general-purpose view of the nature of working memory resources. According to Case (1995) it can be regarded as a possible account of the central executive component in the Baddeley and Hitch (1974) model of working memory. However, the role of the various subsystems of working memory in counting span has not yet been fully analysed.

Although Case et al.'s (1982) seminal study provides significant evidence to support the role of working memory resources in a counting-based cognitive task, their approach raises a number of questions. One of these concerns the interpretation placed on the relationship between speed and span. Recently, Towse and Hitch (1995) argued for an alternative interpretation by pointing out that counting speed might affect the extent to which traces of count totals undergo decay in working memory, with slower counting allowing more time for decay. This is similar to the idea proposed earlier by Hitch (1978a, b) to account for errors in mental calculation in adults. It contrasts with Case et al.'s (1982) assumption that counting speed reflects the amount of working memory capacity required for the execution of counting operations.

To pit these two explanations against one another, Towse and Hitch (1995) measured counting span for different materials for which the time taken in counting and the cognitive difficulty of the counting operations were independently manipulated. Both explanations predict that increased cognitive difficulty should slow the speed of counting and thereby reduce span. The results supported this expectation. However, the decay model predicts that increasing the duration of counting operations while holding difficulty constant will also reduce span, whereas according to Case's capacity trade-off model, there is no reason to expect span to change unless counting difficulty changes. The results were consistent with trace decay and inconsistent with capacity trade-off. Thus, although it is clear that counting span reflects a constraint arising from working memory, Case's theoretical interpretation of the basis for this constraint is not well supported.

A second problem with Case et al.'s (1982) study is that even though children are likely to be familiar with keeping track of count totals, the counting span task is nevertheless somewhat artificial. Given that a working memory constraint should generalize to all cognitive tasks involving the combination of mental operations and temporary information storage, it should be possible to replicate Case et al.'s (1982) findings in a more naturalistic task such as mental arithmetic, the focus of the present discussion.

EXPERIMENT 1: WORKING MEMORY AND CHILDREN'S MENTAL ADDITION

Adams and Hitch (1997) reported a study exploring whether working memory constrains children's ability to perform multidigit mental additions. The investigation adopted the methodology used by Case et al. (1982) to study counting span. One of its aims was to explore whether there is a relationship between span for mental addition and the speed of addition operations, analogous to that between counting span and counting speed. It was assumed that if mental addition is constrained by working memory, then "addition span" should be related to addition speed by a similar function.

In order to establish a suitable measure of span for mental addition, problem complexity was incremented progressively in order to establish the level at which the child's performance broke down. In the absence of a detailed model of children's addition, complexity was defined empirically rather than theoretically, as illustrated by the rows in Table 7.1. As might be expected, however, the ordering of the levels was related to the number of operations required to implement "standard" calculation algorithms and the total number of digits.

In order to examine the variation of addition span with changes in addition speed, two factors were studied. The first, following Case et al. (1982), was children's age. It is widely accepted that during the formal schooling process children's strategies for adding pairs of integers undergo qualitative change from dependence on slow, algorithmic counting procedures to faster and more accurate retrieval of stored "number facts" from long-term memory (e.g.

TABLE 7.1
Incrementation of levels of addition complexity for three
degrees of operational difficulty

Addition Complexity (Level)	Operational difficulty		
	Easy	Hard	Carry
1	8 + 1	3 + 5	5 + 9
2	21 + 7	22 + 6	23 + 9
3	122 + 3	123 + 4	127 + 4
4	31 + 26	76 + 23	51 + 66
5	231 + 16	233 + 45	296 + 21
6	611 + 136	574 + 422	628 + 931
7	2412 + 123	2242 + 527	2834 + 624
8	4813 + 1152	3623 + 5356	1512 + 5842

Ashcraft, 1990; Ashcraft & Fierman, 1982; Hamann & Ashcraft, 1985; but see Baroody, 1994, for an alternative interpretation). Thus, the speed at which the children can efficiently solve an addition operation is expected to increase as they get older. The second factor was the difficulty of the arithmetical operations of combining integer pairs. These could involve generating a carry or, if not, could be relatively easy or relatively hard in accordance with the "problem-size effect" (Ashcraft, 1992, 1995), whereby larger digits take a longer time to add. The columns in Table 7.1 illustrate these three conditions; they are described in more detail later. To summarize, therefore, the effects of changes in addition speed were investigated by examining mental addition span for children of different ages and for additions varying in operational difficulty.

Each child was tested under two conditions of problem presentation. Oral presentation was assumed to maximize the demands on working memory as this method of presentation requires temporary storage of the addends. A visual presentation procedure was also used in which the addition problem remained continuously available for inspection during the calculation. In this condition, the addends themselves did not need to be remembered. Thus, if children's mental addition performance is constrained by working memory, their visual spans should be higher than their oral spans. An alternative possibility is that mental addition span is limited by children's knowledge of how to perform multidigit additions, that is, their arithmetical competence. In this case there would be no reason to expect addition spans to be any higher for visual than for oral presentation. Some form of competence limitation seems inevitable early on in schooling, when algorithms for multidigit addition are still being learned.

To summarize, the main aim of the investigation was to address the role of working memory (in its general sense) as a constraint on children's mental addition performance. Two converging strategies were adopted to explore this issue. One investigated whether there is an empirical relationship between mental addition span and integer addition speed of the type shown previously for the counting span task (Case et al., 1982). The other tested the prediction that visual mental addition spans would be higher than oral spans, reflecting reduced demands on temporary information storage in the visual presentation procedure.

Method

The study was carried out at a large primary school in the Lancaster area (further details are given in Adams & Hitch, 1997). In a within-subjects design, 80 children, 20 from each of the four primary years (Year 3, approximately 8 years old, to Year 6, approximately 11 years old inclusive) were presented with both oral and visual speed and span tasks in a single session. Each task was performed in each of three conditions of difficulty of the elementary operations used to construct the additions (see later). Half the subjects received the visually presented tasks first, half the oral. Addition problems for visual presentation were written onto pastel coloured cards in standard horizontal format (e.g. 723 + 813 =) using a black marker pen. The numerals were approximately 45mm high.

The speed task consisted of three lists of ten integer-pair additions. The operational difficulty of each set of ten was designated as either Easy (e.g. 2 + 3), Hard (e.g. 4 + 5) or Carry (e.g. 6 + 7). The differentiation between Easy and Hard integer pairs was based on the solution latencies for children reported by Groen and Parkman (1972). Of the 35 integer pairs summing to less than 10, (obtained by excluding the pair 1 + 1 and pairs involving zero), 19 were classified as Easy and 16 as Hard. The Carry additions were all the 32 integer pairs (excluding ties) with sums between 11 and 17 inclusive. Two sets of additions were constructed by random sampling from each of the three item pools. One set was used for oral presentation, the other for visual presentation.

Materials for the addition span task were lists of addition problems of increasing complexity (see Table 7.1). For each level of complexity there were two problems. Problems for the Easy and Hard operations lists were constructed by randomly selecting integer pairs from the relevant item pools, with any unpaired integers selected at random from the integers 1 and 2. The Carry lists contained one integer pair involving a carry operation per problem, chosen randomly from the relevant item pool, with all other integer pairs taken from the Easy pool, and unpaired integers as before. The position of the carry was varied randomly so that subjects could not anticipate in advance where it would occur. Two sets of additions were constructed by random sampling from each of the three item pools. One set was presented orally, the other visually.

Children first completed the speed tasks under instructions that emphasized speed and accuracy. The 10 integer additions in each set were presented in turn, at a rate determined by the child's answers. The order of presenting the three sets was rotated across subjects. Half the subjects were presented with the oral tasks first, half began with the visual tasks. In the oral presentation condition the experimenter read aloud each addition, in the visual condition each card was presented and remained visible until the child answered. The total time to answer all 10 sums (correctly or incorrectly) from the start to the end of the task was determined, and childrens' answers were recorded.

The addition span tasks involved presenting increasingly complex addition problems to find the limit at which performance accuracy broke down. In the oral condition, problems were read aloud by the experimenter using natural expression (e.g. "one-hundred-and-twenty-seven add four"). In the visual condition, the card showing the problem remained in view until the child had given an answer. Half the children were presented with the oral task first, half began with the visual task.

The procedure for determining addition spans for Easy, Hard, and Carry problems can be illustrated as follows. If a child correctly answered the Level 1 Easy operations problem 8 + 1 = (see Table 7.1) he or she would progress to Level 2 the next time an Easy operations problem was presented (e.g. 21 + 7 =). If, however, the Level 1 Easy operations problem was incorrectly answered on the first attempt, a second problem of the same type was presented (e.g. 2 + 3 =). A correct response on the second attempt allowed the child to progress to Level 2 problems involving Easy operations. However, a second error terminated the span procedure for problems with Easy operations. Performance at each level of complexity was explored in this way for Easy, then Hard, then Carry problems before progressing to the next level. On termination of the overall procedure, a span was determined for each type of operation by awarding one point for each level of complexity at which the child gave a correct answer (e.g. correct solution of Hard problems up to and including the level typified by 233 + 45 = was given a span score of 5; see Table 7.1). Spans could therefore range from 0 (failed Level 1) to 8 (passed Level 8).

Results and discussion

The results of the study, shown in Fig. 7.1, were remarkably clear. Mental addition spans were generally higher for visual than for oral presentation, they decreased with increasing difficulty of the component addition operations, and they increased with children's age. A three-way (age × operational difficulty × presentation mode) ANOVA showed all the main effects were significant; age [$F(3,76) = 13.6$, $P < .0001$]; operational difficulty [$F(2,152) = 94.1$, $P < .0001$]; and presentation mode [$F(1,76) = 163, P < .0001$]. There was a significant interaction between age and mode of presentation [$F(3,76) = 9.19, P < .0001$], reflecting a larger benefit from visual presentation for older children. There was also a significant interaction between mode of presentation and

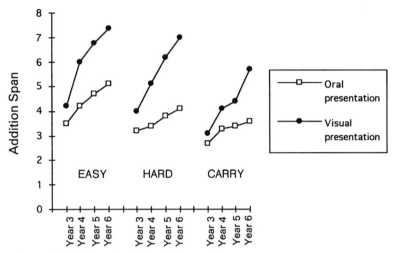

FIG. 7.1. Graph of group mean addition spans by age, operational difficulty, and presentation mode.

operational difficulty [$F(2,152) = 12.5$, $P < .0001$], corresponding to a larger advantage for visual presentation for problems with lower operational difficulty. The remaining interactions were nonsignificant.

Planned comparisons were used to examine the effect of presentation modality in greater detail. These showed that spans were significantly higher ($P < .05$) in the visual modality at all three levels of operational difficulty and for all age groups except the youngest (Year 3) children for Carry problems (see Fig. 7.1). In general, therefore, providing external storage for the addends was beneficial to childrens' performance, consistent with the hypothesis that working memory (and not arithmetical competence) constrains their mental addition spans. However, some caution is needed in accepting this conclusion. Thus, if children used very different calculation strategies when problems were presented either orally or visually this would complicate interpretation. As there was no significant benefit from visual presentation when the youngest children were given additions involving a carry, it seems likely that poor mastery of the carry operation rather than working memory was limiting their performance. Their very low spans for carry problems are consistent with such an interpretation. Clearly, working memory can only constrain performance when competence is not at issue.

It is interesting to note that the interaction effects involving presentation mode are consistent with the role of working memory. Thus, older children's ability to benefit more than younger children from visual presentation can be explained by noting that older children had higher spans than younger children for oral problems. Therefore, in relation to the limit set by oral span, visual presentation supplemented working memory with more information (i.e. problem digits) for older than younger children. Similarly, the greater advantage of visual over oral presentation for additions involving easier integer-pair operations can be interpreted by noting that oral spans were higher for problems involving easier operations. Thus once again, at the limit set by oral span, visual presentation would have supplemented working memory with a greater amount of problem information.

Given the assumption that differences between visual and oral addition spans reflect the need to store orally presented addends in working memory, the question of what limits children's visual addition spans needs to be addressed. It is clear that merely making the numbers to be added permanently visible does not obviate the need to keep track of partial results or to combine memory for partial results with ongoing mental operations. Both of these functions should involve working memory. Therefore, children's spans for visual as well as oral additions may be limited by working memory, even though this limit is reached by a different combination of demands in the two cases (except of course for the youngest children's spans for additions involving carrying, where, as already noted, above a working memory limitation seems unlikely). The question of whether visual addition spans are limited by working memory can be addressed by examining data on the relationship between addition span and addition speed, as will now be described.

First it is necessary to describe the results of the speed task. Briefly, these were as follows (see Adams & Hitch, 1997, for details). Errors were relatively few (less than 10% overall) and provided useful confirmation of the manipulation of operational difficulty. Thus, errors typically increased going from Easy, to Hard to Carry integer pairs. In terms of time taken, the speed of addition was monotonically related to children's age and to the difficulty of the addition operations, consistent with previous research on age differences (e.g. Ashcraft & Fierman, 1982; Geary et al., 1991) and the problem-size effect (Ashcraft, 1992, 1995; see also Groen & Parkman, 1972). Addition times were higher for oral than for visual presentation, but this probably reflects a constant error associated with differences between the two measurement procedures.

The relationship between addition speed and addition span across age groups and operational difficulties was examined by plotting mean mental addition span as a function of mean integer addition time for both oral and visual presentation (see Fig. 7.2). The plots indicate relatively good fits to separate linear functions for the two data sets. Regression analyses showed that oral span = 5.13 − 0.03C (where C = calculation time; and $r = .85$), and that visual span = 8.05 − 0.07C ($r = .83$). The robustness of these findings is reinforced by a replication carried out with German-speaking children of the same ages. The replication produced virtually identical results, with remarkably similar parameters for the two linear functions (see Adams & Hitch, 1997).

Thus it is clear that the relationship between addition span and addition speed is of just the same type as that between counting span and counting speed (Case

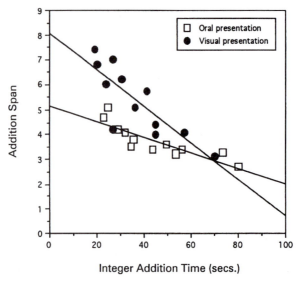

FIG. 7.2. Correlation of mean addition speed and span scores for all three levels of operational difficulty (oral and visual presentation).

et al., 1982), in that an approximately linear function describes variation with both age and difficulty of processing operations. This suggests that visual and oral mental addition spans reflect a common performance constraint that operates according to the same principles as the limit on counting span. Such an interpretation would be strengthened if the different functions for auditory and visual spans could be related to the assumed difference in the pattern of load on working memory in these two situations. The data indicate that for a given decrease in the time taken to execute elementary operations, visual addition span increases more than oral addition span. This is intuitively plausible if one assumes that oral span is limited by the need to remember addends and partial results whereas visual span is limited only by the need to remember partial results. However, explanation of results at this level of detail goes beyond the aims and scope of the study.

At first sight it might be considered remarkable that the plots of span against speed approximate a linear function, given that they cover a period of education and development in which marked qualitative changes are thought to occur in the way arithmetical operations are performed (e.g. Ashcraft, 1990; Ashcraft & Fierman, 1982; Hamann & Ashcraft, 1985). This suggests that the relationship between addition speed and addition span is indifferent to the precise manner in which addition operations are executed. However, far from being surprising, such a lack of sensitivity is consistent with the idea of working memory as a high-level system in which the important variable is not the content of operations but their general characteristics such as how long they occupy the workspace. Indeed, a similar kind of insensitivity was implicitly assumed in initially predicting that addition span and counting span would show similar speed/span characteristics, despite obvious differences in the content of their processing component.

At a practical level, the observation that mental addition reflects the dynamics of working memory in the same way as counting span (Case et al., 1982) is important in generalizing results from a relatively artificial task to a natural skill with direct applicability and obvious educational significance. Note, however, that although the present study was designed to see whether the speed/span relationship for counting span generalizes to mental arithmetic, it did not aim to distinguish between different theoretical accounts of this relationship. Thus, the question of whether addition span is constrained by a trade-off between limited capacity resources (c.f. Case et al., 1982) or by trace decay (c.f. Towse & Hitch, 1995) was not addressed. Nor, moreover, was the present study designed to investigate the way in which children's arithmetic draws on the specialized subsystems proposed in the Baddeley & Hitch (1974) model of working memory. These questions remain to be answered. The remainder of this chapter describes work that has begun to address the second question, with particular reference to the role of the phonological loop in mental calculation.

EXPERIMENT 2: THE PHONOLOGICAL LOOP AND CHILDREN'S MENTAL ADDITION

The investigation of addition span demonstrated the importance of working memory as a general resource for combining temporary information storage with ongoing processing operations in supporting children's mental arithmetic. However, from its inception Baddeley and Hitch (1974) proposed a multicomponent model of working memory, in which a limited capacity central executive controls two slave systems. The most well-specified and documented component of this model is undoubtedly the slave system known as the phonological loop. Recent research (e.g. Baddeley, 1986, 1992) supports the view that the loop comprises two components, a passive store for phonologically based information, and an active subvocal rehearsal process. Material held within the loop is subject to rapid decay, but can be maintained by rehearsal, which acts to refresh the memory traces. The idea that material stored within the loop undergoes decay is supported by the word-length effect, the observation that immediate recall is poorer for longer words than shorter words (Baddeley, Thomson, & Buchanan, 1975). Evidence for this account of rehearsal comes from studies where subjects are asked to suppress subvocal rehearsal by articulating aloud irrelevant speech sounds such as "blah, blah, blah" during the presentation and immediate recall lists of letters or digits. Typically recall is severely impaired by articulatory suppression and is no longer sensitive to word length (e.g. Baddeley, Lewis, & Vallar, 1984).

The role of the phonological loop has been examined in adult counting (Logie & Baddeley, 1987) and arithmetic (Ashcraft et al., 1992; Lemaire et al., 1996; Logie et al., 1994), though not extensively. Logie et al. (1994) employed a dual-task methodology and looked at performance deficits in mental arithmetic in adults. The primary arithmetic task involved two-digit additions that were presented in strings of three to six items over a 20-second period, (e.g. 13 + 18 + 13 + 21 + 13 + 25 [= 103]). A number of secondary tasks were examined, each being assumed to interfere selectively with the different components of working memory. Thus, in one experiment auditorily presented mental additions were accompanied by concurrent tasks of random letter generation (assumed to disrupt the central executive; Baddeley, 1992), articulatory suppression (phonological loop), irrelevant pictures, and hand movement (visuospatial sketchpad; Logie, 1995).

There was little interference from the visuospatial tasks, suggesting that the sketchpad was unimportant for calculation. The secondary task that had the most disruptive effect was random generation (38.5% errors). This result supports the view that the central executive is heavily involved in performing mental arithmetic, a view shared by Lemaire et al. (1996) on the basis of a similar study using verification tasks. It is not surprising, given that the central executive is argued to be responsible for monitoring and coordinating the processing of information in complex tasks. On the other hand, the disruptive effect of articulatory suppression (20.5% errors) is more difficult to account for, especially if it is assumed that adults solve mental arithmetic by algorithms that involve direct retrieval of basic number facts from long-term memory (e.g. Ashcraft, 1992; Campbell & Graham, 1985). One possibility is that adults use other processes besides direct retrieval (Baroody, 1994), and that these involve subvocalization. Another possibility is that verbal rehearsal plays an important role in maintaining temporary information during calculation. However, in Logie et al.'s (1994) study the method of presentating one addend at a time removed the necessity to maintain addends presented early in the sequence. Hence, the amount of information that had to be maintained was relatively small (i.e. only the most recent "running" total). Clearly, the nature of the disruptive effect of articulatory suppression on mental addition remains open to debate.

One hypothesis proposed by Logie and Baddeley (1987; see also Hitch et al., 1987) is that the phonological loop is involved in maintaining the accuracy of count totals, whereas the central executive deploys approximation or estimation strategies based on heuristics and background knowledge. For example, 28 + 19 = can be readily recognized as being close to 30 + 20, an addition that can probably be retrieved from long-term memory. Consequently Logie et al. (1994) interpreted their disruptive effect of articulatory suppression as follows: When an adult is presented with a problem such as 44 + 23 = he or she may or may not be able to retrieve the answer from long-term memory. This depends on previous arithmetic experience. If retrieval is not possible, then a close approximation will be sought (e.g. $40 + 20 = 60$). However, disruption of the phonological loop by articulatory suppression prevents the accurate "adjustment" of this arithmetic fact to the target problem so that errors may accrue. This two-tier model of reasoning supported by Logie et al. fits well with the account of "fuzzy" or "gist"-based reasoning proposed by Brainerd (1987; see also Brainerd & Reyna, 1988).

Surprisingly the most significant factor inherent in the research reviewed so far is the absence of studies involving children. One reason for this may be the difficulty perceived by researchers in getting young children to carry out concurrent secondary tasks, while performing a task they patently find problematic. However, one notable exception to this observation was a study conducted by Maeve Haughey (in Hitch et al., 1987). In a very simple design, 14 school children (mean age 7; 10) were visually presented via computer with 23 simple additions (e.g. $4 + 3 =$) and were asked to give the correct answer by key press responses. One block of trials was performed with concurrent articulation as a secondary task, the other served as a control. The results were very clear. Concurrent articulation increased children's mean error rate from 5.3% to 26.1%, and their mean solution latency from 4.64 seconds to 5.71 seconds. As in previous research, solution latencies increased as a function of the smaller of the two integers (the minimum addend) consistent with children's use of a "counting-on" strategy (see e.g. Groen & Parkman, 1972). However, there was no interaction between problem size (difficulty) and the interference task. This contradicts Lemaire et al.'s (1996) results with adults, although Lemaire et al. used a verification procedure, and not a production task. However, some caution is necessary in assessing the reliability of the Hitch et al. (1987) report, as it is based on children from a single age group and a relatively small pool of arithmetic problems.

Further evidence consistent with the importance of the phonological loop in arithmetic comes from studies that investigated links between speed of articulation, digit span, and mathematical ability. Hoosain and Salili (1987) in comparing adults speaking English and Chinese (Cantonese) found the latter to have faster pronunciation speeds for the numbers 1 to 9. This correlated with the Chinese recording a significantly larger digit span, which in turn was correlated with higher mathematics attainment. Geary, Brown, and Samaranayake (1991) found that normal children had digit spans about one point higher than mathematically disabled children, and that this measure of memory span was negatively correlated with the frequency of calculation errors. Along with Ellis (1992; see also Ellis & Hennelly, 1980; Hitch & McAuley, 1991) these studies indicate that speed of articulating the number sequence, digit span, and arithmetical ability are related.

According to the Baddeley and Hitch (1974) model of working memory, speed of articulation is related to span because it reflects the speed of subvocal rehearsal of information stored in the phonological loop (Baddeley et al., 1975;

Baddeley, 1986). Correlations with arithmetic are therefore consistent with the involvement of the phonological loop in calculation. However, as the earlier discussion of Case et al.'s (1982) model and Experiment 1 in this chapter make clear, speed/span relationships are also consistent with explanations in terms of general working memory resources. Therefore, more powerful evidence is required. Accordingly, a further study looked again a the effects of concurrent articulatory suppression on children's calculation, but did so more extensively than in previous work (Hitch et al., 1987).

As already indicated, it is commonly thought that adults use arithmetic fact retrieval in adding integers (e.g. Ashcraft, 1982, 1992). However, in the early stages of formal education young children have only a small repertoire of arithmetic facts on which to draw, (e.g. ties such as $2 + 2$, $3 + 3$, etc.). The overwhelming majority of integer additions have to be solved by adopting an appropriate procedural algorithm. In the case of addition, this is often counting-on or some other counting based strategy (e.g. Groen & Parkman, 1972; Siegler & Shrager, 1984; see also Siegler & Jenkins, 1989). Given that counting involves articulation, it is likely to involve the phonological loop. Therefore, introducing articulatory suppression to disrupt the phonological loop in children using counting strategies would be expected to have particularly severe effects. Without access to heuristics and derived facts based on past experience, one might even expect performing arithmetic problems to become impossible.

The experiment also explored whether multidigit additions with a carry operation are more likely to be affected by articulatory suppression than those with no carry. In Experiment 1, problems with a carry operation appeared to place more demand on working memory resources. If the extra demand imposed by carrying is placed on the phonological loop subsystem of working memory, concurrent articulatory suppression will have a greater impact on carry problems than on no-carry problems.

The investigation (reported fully in Adams, 1997) employed a variation of the addition span task used in Experiment 1. In doing so, some improvements to Logie et al.'s (1994) study were introduced. Logie et al. (1994) examined all their subjects on addition sequences preset to their level of arithmetic performance (i.e. from 3 to 6 addends) and used a between-subjects design to assess dual-task interference, with only six subjects in each group. This is a somewhat insensitive procedure. Use of the addition span task negated the requirement to predetermine difficulty levels and enabled a more sensitive within-subjects design involving larger numbers of participants to be adopted.

In summary, the aim of Experiment 2 was to investigate whether the disruption of children's subvocalization by articulatory suppression would impair their ability to perform mental addition. Positive results would confirm previous findings (Hitch et al., 1987) and would confirm the involvement of the phonological loop in children's calculation. The hypothesis that young children are more reliant on subvocal counting algorithms led to the prediction that disruption would be greater for younger children. The hypothesis that carry information is stored in the phonological loop led to the prediction that interference would be greater for additions involving carrying.

Method

The study was carried out at a suburban primary school in the Lancaster area. In a within-subjects design, 48 children, 24 from each of two age groups, Year 3 (approximately 8 years old) and Year 6 (approximately 11 years old), were presented with two versions of an addition span task involving either Easy or Carry operations (see Experiment 1) under three experimental conditions. A control condition was presented along with two dual-task conditions involving either articulatory suppression or nonspatial tapping. The latter is commonly used (e.g. Logie & Baddeley, 1987) to control for a general disruption effect caused by simply carrying out two tasks. Order of presentation of the span tasks was counterbalanced across both operational difficulty and experimental conditions in a mixed design with age as the only between-subjects factor. Materials for the addition span task were two lists of problems of increasing complexity (as described in Experiment 1, see Table 7.1). For both levels of operational difficulty, three different versions of the span task were used, with each list containing different addition problems. The problems were constructed by randomly selecting integer pairs from the relevant item pools. Any repetitions across lists were rejected.

The general procedure for administering the span task and the method used to calculate addition span were as described in Experiment 1. The chief modifications were that only oral presentation of the addition span tasks was used, children answered the calculations in writing on a plain sheet of paper, and problems involving Hard operations were omitted from the span procedure. For the suppression condition the children were asked to repeat the word "rhubarb" at the rate of approximately one per second from immediately before presentation of each addition problem until after their response was reported. For the tapping condition subjects were instructed to tap the desk with a pen using their nondominant hand at a rate of one per second, again from immediately preceeding presentation of each addition problem to after their response was reported. A short practice was given to ensure that the child understood the procedure. During the two interference conditions subjects were occasionally prompted to maintain the desired response rate.

Results and discussion

The clear result from the study was that articulatory suppression significantly disrupted children's ability to perform mental arithmetic. For both age groups addition spans were significantly lower in the suppression condition than in either the control or tapping conditions (see Table 7.2). There was little evidence for a simple dual-task effect because addition span scores were not significantly impaired when accompanied by the secondary task of tapping. This is particularly striking as most of the children reported the tapping condition to be very difficult. (This impression probably arose because of interference at the response output stage, during which children had to write the answer with their dominant hand while tapping simultaneously with their nondominant hand.)

A three-way analysis of variance (age × interference condition × operational difficulty) revealed significant effects of age [$F(1,46) = 14.3, P < .0005$]; interference condition [$F(2,92) = 75.2, P < .0001$]; and operational difficulty [$F(1,46) = 137, P < .0001$]. Across both age groups children obtained higher span scores for the Easy problems than those with a Carry operation, consistent with the findings of Experiment 1. Overall, the Year 6 children performed significantly better than the Year 3 children at both levels of operational difficulty. However, there was no significant interaction between operational difficulty and age [$F(1,46) < 1$] and no suggestion of a three-way interaction [$F(2,92) < 1$]. As in Experiment 1, age differences in addition span did not vary with the difficulty of the addition operations.

Of particular interest was any possible interaction between age and interference condition. Would the younger age group be disrupted by articulatory suppression more than the older children? No evidence was found to support the hypothesis that concurrent articulatory suppression had more effect on Year 3 than Year 6 children [$F(2,92) < 1$]. This suggests that the demands placed on the phonological loop by calculation are independent of the child's arithmetic knowledge and ability. A possible post hoc interpretation is that the phonological loop was heavily engaged in retaining problem information in both age groups—and this may have masked any effect due to younger children greater reliance on the loop for calculation operations. One way of testing this would

TABLE 7.2
Mean addition span scores for each
interference condition and degree of
operational difficulty for each age group

Condition	Operational Difficulty	Year 3	Year 6
Control	Easy	3.8	4.9
	Carry	2.3	3.7
Suppression	Easy	2.6	3.6
	Carry	0.9	2.0
Tapping	Easy	3.7	4.6
	Carry	2.1	3.5

be to explore the effect of suppression on span for visually presented additions, where the need to retain the addends in working memory is greatly reduced.

The interaction between operational difficulty and interference condition was also found to be nonsignificant [$F(2,92) = 1.50$]. This result is consistent with that reported by Logie et al. (1994) with adult subjects. One explanation offered by Logie and colleagues was that keeping track of carries relies on a different part of working memory than the phonological loop. For example, while the phonological loop maintains accuracy, the central executive may be involved in keeping track of carry operations. However, in order to demonstrate this, more powerful evidence is required.

One interesting and potentially important incidental observation is that concurrent articulatory suppression can have a catastrophic impact on individual children. Thus, when presented with carry problems Jill, a Year 6 pupil, obtained spans of 5 and 6 in the control and tapping conditions respectively, but zero when the sums were accompanied by concurrent articulatory suppression. Jill's answers under suppression were interesting. For example, she made $7 + 4 = 10$, and $5 + 7 = 11$, both responses being a one-digit under-count. At the same level of complexity Jill successfully solved $9 + 8$ and $4 + 7$ in the control and tapping condition, and she went on to solve additions up to $119 + 378$. Clearly articulatory suppression was having a significant effect on the accuracy of her proposed answer. However, other children showed only minor impairment when performing concurrent articulatory suppression. These children were able to maintain respectable measures of performance even when their phonological loop was being disrupted. This is consistent with Logie et al.'s view that the central executive is involved in the calculation process, with some children being more able to make use of procedural rules and heuristics. However, it is unclear whether young children's use of the central executive to perform calculations is similar to that observed in adults (e.g. Lemaire et al., 1996), who are less likely to use counting-based strategies. Clearly the hypothesis that articulatory suppression has more of a disruptive effect on children than adults is one that needs further investigation.

A follow-up experiment (Adams, 1997) found that concurrent articulatory suppression impaired children's memory for the addition problems themselves (i.e when there was no requirement to perform the calculations). This is consistent with a large body of evidence showing that suppression disrupts simple short-term retention tasks. Surprisingly, however, the level of disruption was similar to that observed when children had to compute the answer of the sum as well as maintain the addends throughout the solution process. One possible explanation of this result is that the phonological loop is involved in the storage of problem information but does not contribute to the calculation process *per se*. This fits in with the speculation that it is the central executive which plays the major role in calculation operations, with the phonological loop playing the role of holding the original addends.

SUMMARY AND CONCLUSIONS

The aim of the two studies reported here was to extend previous research on working memory and arithmetic in primary school children, aged 7 to 11 years. Experiment 1 dealt with the issue of the involvement of working memory (in its general sense), using a methodology adopted from Case et al. (1982), which had established a linear relationship between processing speed and recall in a counting span. A novel mental addition span task was employed to see if the ability to perform mental arithmetic obeys the same kind of relationship. Experiment 1 also manipulated working memory load by using presentation modality (oral vs. visual) to vary whether or not information about the addition problems was present during calculation. Experiment 2 concentrated on the role of the phonological loop in arithmetic using a dual-task technique in which articulatory suppression was used to interfere selectively with this specific subsystem of working memory.

The overarching conclusion to emerge from these two studies is that working memory is a major factor limiting children's mental arithmetic. Converging evidence from Experiment 1 found that addition span was systematically related to the speed of performing simple addition operations and that visual addition spans were higher than oral addition spans. The existence of a quantitative relationship between addition span and the speed of addition operations suggests that mental arithmetic is subject to the same constraints as those limiting counting span, a task that was devised in order to measure working memory capacity. However, it is not clear how this relationship is to be interpreted. Case et al. (1982) and Case (1985, 1995) have argued for a resource-sharing interpretation in which some central (executive?) capacity is shared between processing operations and temporary information storage. However, it was noted that the speed/span relationship can be interpreted differently from the way Case has proposed, in terms of the greater forgetting of temporary information during slower processing operations due to trace decay (Towse & Hitch, 1995). The finding that visual addition span was generally higher than oral addition span was consistent with previous research on adults showing that mental arithmetic is more accurate when working memory is supplemented by the availability of an external record of the calculation (Hitch, 1978a). This difference was used to argue against the possibility that childrens' oral addition span is limited by their arithmetical competence. However, as an exception to this, there was some evidence for a competence limitation when very young children were given additions involving carrying.

Experiment 1 did not address the question of what types of working memory resources were involved in limiting addition span (i.e. in the Baddeley & Hitch model of working memory, the central executive, the phonological loop, or the visuospatial sketchpad). Strong evidence to support the involvement of the phonological loop in children's performance of oral mental additions was found in Experiment 2. Compared with a control and a neutral tapping condition, children's addition spans were significantly impaired when they were required to perform concurrent articulation. However, the importance of articulation as a control process must not be overstated. Although a minority of children were unable to answer a single sum correctly when they articulated aloud, the majority of children retained some level of performance. In other words, subvocal articulation did not prevent most children from solving the addition problems some of the time. More evidence is clearly needed to identify the contribution of other working memory subsystems, most obviously the central executive, to addition span.

Although not described here, the novel addition span task developed for the present investigations proved to be a simple and effective procedure for measuring individual differences (see Adams & Hitch, 1997). Subject to satisfactory evidence about its reliability, it may prove to be a useful complement to existing tasks for assessing working memory such as counting span (Case et al., 1982), reading span (Daneman & Carpenter, 1980) and complex word span (La Pointe & Engle, 1990). These well-established tasks are designed to measure the ability to combine concurrent demands of processing and temporary information storage, but differ from mental addition in that they involve novel combinations. The potential benefits of these complex tasks for educational assessment include the fact that they are quick and easy to administer. Turner and Engle (1989) demonstrated that a span measure of simple arithmetic in adults predicted reading comprehension and Scholastic Aptitude (SAT) scores. This, they argued, supported the generality of working memory span as a predictor of performance in a range of cognitive activities.

In conclusion, the results from Experiments 1 and 2 confirm the crucial role working memory plays in supporting children's mental arithmetic. They have extended the results already published on adult performance (e.g. Hitch, 1978a; b; Lemaire et al., 1996; Logie et al., 1994) and have shown that despite probable differences in children's calculation procedures, the involvement of working memory appears to conform to a similar general pattern. It follows that an impairment to the working memory system or congenitally slow operations will have an adverse effect on children's performance of mental arithmetic, and this possibility provides an obvious motivation for future research.

ACKNOWLEDGEMENTS

Experiments 1 and 2 were conducted at Lancaster University while John Adams was supported by an ESRC research studentship. We are grateful to Arthur Baroody for helpful criticisms of an earlier draft of the chapter.

CHAPTER EIGHT

On the cognitive consequences of mathematics anxiety

Mark H. Ashcraft, Elizabeth P. Kirk, & Derek Hopko
Cleveland State University, Cleveland, Ohio, USA

Affect is the least investigated aspect of human problem solving, yet it is probably the aspect most often mentioned as deserving further investigation. (Mandler, 1989, p. 3)

Two rather different research traditions have coexisted over the past 25 years: the study of mathematics anxiety and the study of mathematical cognition. Although a good deal is known about each of these areas in its own right, it is only quite recently that the two areas have begun to converge in research and theory (e.g. Ashcraft & Faust, 1988, 1994; Faust, Ashcraft, & Fleck, 1996). That is, only recently has anyone asked if maths anxious individuals actually do anything differently in mathematical problem solving because of their anxiety. This question forms the focus of the present chapter. Putting it somewhat more formally, we are interested in determining if there are specific cognitive consequences of mathematics anxiety, either at the level of mental processing or at the level of representation of mathematical knowledge.

In this chapter, we first present a brief overview of the mathematics anxiety literature, discussing in turn the normative and psychometric evidence on maths anxiety, the effects of attitudes and gender, and the consequences of maths anxiety in terms of maths competence. We then discuss the mathematical cognition area in terms of basic empirical effects, the importance of procedural knowledge, and the role of working memory in maths performance. We then turn to the combination of the two areas, and discuss how maths anxiety and competence together influence cognitive processes and structures. We include in this discussion some of our recent work, showing that a particularly important consequence of maths anxiety is on the functioning of the working memory system.

MATHEMATICS ANXIETY

Mathematics anxiety is usually defined as a feeling of tension, apprehension, or fear that interferes with maths performance (Richardson & Suinn, 1972). Maths anxious individuals report disruption in everyday activities involving number and maths, such as balancing a cheque book or figuring out a restaurant bill, as well as in school-related activities, such as taking a standardized maths achievement test or in-class exams. Early reports (e.g. Dreger & Aiken, 1957; Gough, 1954) suggested that maths anxiety is a nonintellectual factor, in the sense that it was observed even in otherwise successful students, which nonetheless had serious consequences for educational and career-related choices.

Normative and psychometric evidence

These speculations, based at the time on clinical or anecdotal evidence, have since been confirmed and extended, with more acceptable methodologies. The most important improvement in methodology appeared with the publication of a standardized assessment instrument for measuring maths anxiety, the Mathematics Anxiety Rating Scale (hereafter MARS; Richardson & Suinn, 1972; Suinn, Edie, Nicoletti, & Spinelli, 1972; see also Alexander & Martray, 1989, for a short version of the scale, which we term the sMARS). The test presents 98 items that the subject rates on a 1 to 5 scale, with 5 indicating that the item arouses a great deal of anxiety. Scores range from 98 to 490, with a mean of approximately 215, and a SD of about 65. On the sMARS, a 25-item test with a 1 to 100 score range, the mean of a large sample is about 36, with a SD of 16.

The reliability and validity of the test have been demonstrated several times. For the former, the test-retest correlations on the MARS after a two-week interval are in the .70 to .85 range (e.g. Richardson & Suinn, 1972). In our study (Faust, Ashcraft, & Fleck, 1996a, Experiment 2), the eight-week reliability of the sMARS was .71. Correlations of the MARS or sMARS with other measures of maths anxiety are in the .50 to .70 range, substantially higher as a group than correlations with other forms of anxiety. Because of these demonstrations, the MARS or the sMARS have become the standard assessment for the maths anxiety construct.

Since the appearance of the MARS, a good number of psychometric studies have been published, and a good deal is known about the personality and academic characteristics of high maths anxious individuals. Table 8.1 presents correlations particularly important to our argument here, taken from Hembree's (1990) meta-analysis and our own work. In brief, mathematics anxiety is a

TABLE 8.1
Selected correlations with math anxiety (adapted
from Hembree, 1990)

Correlation between:	r
Pre- and post-tests	
MARS two-week reliability	.85
sMARS eight-week reliability	.71
Measures of anxiety	
MARS and test anxiety	.52
MARS and general anxiety	.35
MARS and trait anxiety	.38
MARS and state anxiety	.42
Performance measures	
MARS and IQ	− .17
MARS and verbal aptitude/achievement	− .06
MARS and maths aptitude/achievement: pre-college	− .34
MARS and maths aptitude/achievement: college	− .31
MARS and high school maths grades	− .30
MARS and college maths grades	− .27
Avoidance	
MARS and extent of high school maths	− .31
MARS and intent to enrol in more maths, college	− .32

genuine anxiety reaction, separate from although moderately correlated with other forms of anxiety. The strongest intercorrelation is with test anxiety, $r =$ .52; correlations with other forms of anxiety range from .35 to .46 (Hunsley, 1987; Levitt & Hutton, 1983; Wigfield & Meece, 1988; see Hembree, Table 5, for a summary). The small but significant correlation between maths anxiety and IQ, $r = -.17$, is almost surely due to poor performance on the quantitative sections of the IQ test; the correlation between maths anxiety and verbal aptitude or achievement tests is − .06, but is − .31 (− .34 for pre-college ages) between maths anxiety and maths aptitude or achievement.

Avoidance of maths

Enrollment and achievement in maths courses are significantly influenced by one's maths anxiety, both at the high school and college levels. Across a number of studies, highly maths anxious students report lower intentions to enroll in more maths courses, take fewer elective maths courses, and earn lower grades in the maths coursework in which they do enroll (see Table 8.1).

Not surprisingly, maths anxiety is also related to students' choices of a college major, with those majoring in mathematics and the physical sciences scoring considerably lower in maths anxiety than those, for example, in the humanities (e.g. Chipman, Krantz, & Silver, 1992; Dick & Rallis, 1991). From an educational standpoint, one of the most distressing findings has been that students preparing for careers in elementary education had a higher mean level of maths anxiety than any other assessed group (Hembree, 1990, Table 7). In a particularly informative illustration of the importance of maths anxiety, LeFevre, Kulak, and Heymans (1992) constructed a regression model to predict student's choices of a university major. Whereas age, fluency in maths, and experience with maths contributed significantly to the prediction, a "maths affect" factor, composed of maths anxiety and avoidance measures, more than doubled the variance accounted for by the model. Even so, "fear of maths," in the form of maths anxiety, is problematic for a large portion of college students, even those whose majors and careers require a considerable maths background (Betz, 1978; Levitt & Hutton, 1983).

Attitudes toward maths

Several investigators have examined attitudes toward maths among samples whose maths anxiety was also assessed. Probably the most popular of the attitude tests are the Fennema–Sherman Mathematics Attitude Scales (Fennema & Sherman, 1976). These scales examine attitudes regarding confidence in learning maths, parent's and teacher's attitudes and support, motivation toward maths, and perception of maths as a stereotypically male domain. Not surprisingly, maths anxiety and attitudes towards maths are correlated, often quite strongly, with more acceptable or positive attitudes associated with lower maths anxiety. As an example, the correlation between maths anxiety and enjoyment of maths is – .75 among pre-college students, and – .71 between maths anxiety and self-confidence in maths (Hembree, 1990).

A plausible synthesis of the attitude and maths anxiety research has been proposed by Fennema (1989), in her "autonomous learning behaviour" model. Fennema argues that three factors be considered precursors or antecedants, these being maths attitudes, maths anxiety, and external sources such as parents', teachers', and peers' attitudes. If internal and external attitudes are negative, and maths anxiety high, this combination then depresses a student's "autonomous learning behaviours"; these are the activities that lead to mastery and competence, such as paying attention in class, doing homework, or enrolling in elective maths courses. This results in lowered maths competence, of course, which dooms the student to lower scores on aptitude and achievement tests, lower grades, etc.

We note in passing that, however plausible Fennema's model is, there are several deficiencies with the formulation, most stemming from the obvious limitations of correlational data. Of course, it is completely reasonable that one's poor attitudes and experienced maths anxiety would reduce the effort spent in learning and mastering maths. In other words, Fennema's proposed causal pathway from attitudes and anxiety to lower competence is entirely plausible.

It is also possible, however, that difficulties or substandard performance in the maths class (or other factors) might induce poor attitudes and learned maths anxiety. Geary (1990; Geary & Brown, 1991), for example, has documented several performance consequences of mathematics disabilities, with the disability diagnosed as early as first grade. Because it is unlikely that such early difficulties are anxiety driven, we must acknowledge that at least for some individuals, maths deficiencies and difficulties can exist early on, and could be precursors to maths anxiety and poor attitudes. Stodolsky (1985) claims there is in fact a very close link between educational conditions and attitudes towards maths, such that classroom instructional issues, rather than aptitude or socialization factors, are more important explanations of maths attitudes and anxiety.

This is in line with anecdotal and self-report evidence, in which many "recall" unpleasant, embarrassing experiences in maths class, and claim that those led to their maths anxiety (e.g. Tobias, 1979). Such reports suggest that sociocultural and emotional factors may also play a role in the development of maths anxiety (see McLeod, 1992; for an account of cultural influences on maths learning, see Stigler & Fernandez, 1995). Unfortunately, there are only a few studies that have examined maths anxiety or attitudes earlier than about sixth grade (e.g. Gierl & Bisanz, 1995), so we know very little about the onset of maths anxiety (for tests suitable for children, see Chiu & Henry, 1990, and Suinn, Taylor, & Edwards, 1988). And one simply cannot determine the order of influence with presently available correlational data (see discussions in Armstrong & Price, 1982, and McLeod, 1992).

Given this state of affairs, we merely accept the correlational data, and acknowledge that there may be many different causes of maths anxiety, poor attitudes, and lower maths competence. For the work presented later in this chapter, an important implication is that studies of the cognitive consequences of maths anxiety must carefully assess the possibility that competence is an ever-present, potentially confounding variable in the study of maths performance.

Gender effects

Finally, there is indeed evidence of gender-related effects in maths anxiety, although generally at more modest levels than conventional wisdom would hold. Several studies have found that females score somewhat higher on maths anxiety tests than males (Dew, Galassi, & Galassi, 1983; LeFevre et al., 1992; Levitt & Hutton, 1983). This appears even at the youngest age level for which sufficient data have been collected, grade 6, and persists through to college level. In support of the notion that the gender difference is reliable yet small,

Hembree's (1990) meta-analysis revealed a mean effect size (in standard deviation units) of .19 for pre-college and .31 for college students.

It is possible, however, that this gender effect is not distributed uniformly across the entire range of maths anxiety. For example, the gender effect reported in Ashcraft and Faust (1994) seemed limited to the high maths anxious group, defined as those in the top quartile of scores on the MARS. In this group, a somewhat disproportionate number of subjects were female (14 out of 20), and their group mean was significantly higher the males'. This is consistent with the conclusion offered by Hyde, Fennema, Ryan, Frost, and Hopp (1990), that gender effects are typically stronger in restricted or more highly selected samples (e.g. college students, gifted children) than in broadly sampled groups (see Hyde, Fennema, & Lamon, 1990, for evidence on gender effects in maths performance).

The evidence on attitudes toward maths adds an important component to understanding the gender-maths anxiety relationship. Generally, women report somewhat poorer attitudes toward maths than men, for example in self-confidence in maths (Hyde et al., 1990). This is the case even when achievement and parental attitudes are controlled (Tocci & Engelhard, 1991). It may be that women are more influenced by surrounding negative attitudes towards maths, or merely that women are more likely to report negative affect towards maths than men. (Interestingly, in our work in the past two years we have found no evidence in *expressed* attitudes that maths continues to be viewed as a stereotypically male domain, either for males or females.)

Effects on competence

Because attitudes and motivations are likely to have an important effect on choice of elective courses and major field of study, gender effects are assumed to provide at least a partial account for the relatively low number of women in scientific and technical fields (Armstrong & Price, 1982). More generally, it is probably safe to assume that for both men and women the combination of maths anxiety and attitudes toward maths exerts at least an indirect influence on competence (e.g. McLeod, 1989). That is, individuals with higher maths anxiety and poorer attitudes towards maths display a general avoidance of maths; they take fewer courses, earn lower grades, and tend to select career paths in nonquantitative areas. In such a situation, the individual would derive less conceptual understanding and lower skill from the maths class, hence would be at a disadvantage when competence or mastery are assessed with standardized tests (Reynolds & Walberg, 1992). This is the negative effect on maths competence predicted by Fennema (1989), the negative correlation between maths anxiety and maths aptitude/ achievement scores interpreted as due to avoidance. (But as noted earlier, these possible causal pathways are subject to several qualifications.)

What has yet to be determined, however, is the extent of this negative relationship between maths anxiety and maths competence. That is, the correlational approach in the existing literature has led to the assumption that maths competence is uniformly lower among high anxious individuals, regardless of maths content. In a later section, we report evidence that this is not always the case, in other words, that the competence-anxiety relationship does not uniformly confound comparisons of performance at different levels of maths anxiety.

MATHEMATICAL COGNITION

The area of mathematical cognition investigates the underlying mental processes used in solving arithmetic and maths problems, as well as the nature of the mental representation of numerical knowledge. Because several recent papers and collections are available, we provide only a brief and selective review of the area here; see Ashcraft (1992; 1995) for general reviews, and Geary (1994), Seigler and Jenkins (1989), and several chapters in this current volume for reviews focused on developmental issues.

Unlike most of the research discussed earlier, based on correlational methods, and also unlike considerable developmental work, (e.g. Piagetian tasks concerning number), the research considered here is from the framework of mainstream cognitive psychology. As such, evidence about mental processing and structure relies heavily on reaction time (RT) or accuracy data as the primary measures of performance (e.g. Lachman, Lachman, & Butterfield, 1979). As discussed in Ashcraft and Christy (1995), a common misconception is that the cognitive approach, with its emphasis on speeded performance and accuracy, is interested only in speed, in rapid responses based on "rote" learning, and not interested in conceptual relationships and understanding (e.g. Baroody, 1987). Such a reading of the cognitive literature misses the point—by assessing speeded responding and accuracy, we develop an understanding of the underlying mental processes of arithmetic and maths.

Basic effects

Probably the most pervasive empirical effect in the mental arithmetic literature is the *problem-size* or *problem-difficulty* effect; subjects are both slower and more error prone when processing a larger problem like $7 + 9$ or 8×7 than a smaller problem like $2 + 3$ or 4×2. This is true for adults (e.g. Ashcraft & Battaglia, 1978; Campbell, 1987), including the elderly (Allen, Ashcraft, & Weber, 1992; Geary & Wiley, 1991), as well as for children at all stages of education (e.g. Ashcraft, Fierman, & Bartolotta, 1984; Groen & Parkman,

1972; Siegler, 1987; Woods, Resnick, & Groen, 1975). It is equally true for all four arithmetic operations, including division, only recently addressed in the cognitive laboratory (Campbell, 1996; Rickard & Bourne, 1996).

Analysis of the patterns of RT across problem size, e.g. across sum or product, is the general method for inferring the mental processes involved in problem solving. This is especially the case when the processing model can be specified and tested within a multiple regression framework, such that slope estimates can be used to rule out or support different hypothetical processes (e.g. Ashcraft & Stazyk, 1981; LeFevre, Sadesky, & Bisanz, 1996).

Early evidence was originally taken to show that children rely on a "counting up" process (known widely as "counting on" in educational circles) for simple addition (Groen & Parkman, 1972). That is, Groen and Parkman suggested that on viewing a problem like 4 + 3, a mental counter was set to the larger value in a simple addition problem (4), then incremented (3 times) by ones to yield the correct sum. More current results, however, indicate that even first-graders rely on a mix of strategies, including memory retrieval and a variety of counting methods or strategies, for addition (Hamann & Ashcraft, 1985; Siegler, 1987; Siegler & Jenkins, 1989) and, later, multiplication (Cooney, Swanson, & Ladd, 1988; Koshmider & Ashcraft, 1991). Even though it appears that adults continue to resort to strategies on some nontrivial proportion of their trials (e.g. Geary & Wiley, 1991; LeFevre et al., 1996), the bulk of an adult's performance to the "basic facts" of addition or multiplication (single-digit operands from 0 through 9) appears to reflect retrieval from an organized, associative network in long-term memory (e.g. Ashcraft, 1992; Campbell & Oliphant, 1992; Siegler & Jenkins, 1989).

Knowledge of facts and procedures

Considerable theoretical work now exists on aspects of performance beyond the basic arithmetic facts (e.g. Dehaene & Cohen, 1995; McCloskey, Harley, & Sokol, 1991). This work generally acknowledges the importance of at least two discrete classes of knowledge concerning number, fact knowledge (or "declarative" knowledge; e.g. Anderson, 1982) subject to retrieval as already discussed, and procedural knowledge invoked during more complex problem solving. The latter is assumed to consist of processes such as carrying and borrowing, as well as more loosely defined functions such as keeping track of place in a multistep problem, rule application, and the like. Beyond the considerable cognitive evidence for this distinction (e.g. Ashcraft, 1982; Siegler, 1987), there is now strong converging evidence that the two classes of knowledge are separate contributors to performance. As an example, Sokol, McCloskey, Cohen, and Aliminosa (1991) report a case study in which retrieval of simple multiplication facts was severely disrupted by brain damage, whereas procedural knowledge of the multiplication algorithm was preserved (see Dehaene & Cohen, 1995, and McCloskey, 1992, for reviews of cognitive neuropsychological evidence).

An important dimension to consider with respect to these two classes of knowledge is the automaticity of the processes (e.g. Posner & Snyder, 1975; Zbrodoff & Logan, 1986) that access the two classes of knowledge. That is, it is generally agreed that retrieval of the basic arithmetic facts becomes increasingly automatic across development (e.g. Ashcraft & Fierman, 1982; Cooney, Swanson, & Ladd, 1988; Koshmider & Ashcraft, 1991; LeFevre, Bisanz, & Mrkonjic, 1988). The advantage to automaticity, of course, is that mental operations can be performed with only minimal demands on the attentional or working memory systems. Performance based on procedural knowledge, however, has been assumed—and demonstrated (LeFevre et al., 1996)—to be slower. As such, procedures are thought to be more dependent on conscious processing, and less likely to receive sufficient practice to become relatively automatic (note, however, that in theory procedural knowledge can become automatized just as retrieval is assumed to be; e.g. Anderson, 1982). Thus, a common assumption is that performance based on procedural knowledge will be slower than performance based on more automatic processes such as retrieval, and more demanding of the capacity limited attentional and working memory system. In other words, procedural knowledge is executed at a relatively conscious, resource-consuming level.

If we consider carrying in complex addition to be a prototype of procedural knowledge, then the evidence certainly suggests that procedural knowledge is slower to instantiate and execute than declarative knowledge. Several studies have found such processes, especially those that must be interleaved or sequenced in multistep procedures, to be slow in comparison with declarative fact retrieval. Ashcraft and Stazyk (1981), for example, provided an early demonstration that carrying requires an extra increment of time, an increment that is conceptually and statistically separate from the time necessary for retrieval of basic facts (see also Widaman, Geary, Cormier, & Little, 1989). Evidence we consider later confirms this result, especially in the case where maths anxious individuals are asked to perform in the task.

The role of working memory

We assume that the procedures used in multistep maths problems are indeed reliant on the working memory system, in that they place heavier demands on the resources of working memory than the more automatic process of fact retrieval. Further development of this assumption requires a consideration of the working memory system itself, in particular Baddeley's influential model (e.g. Baddeley & Hitch, 1974). Because excellent descriptions of the model are available, and well known (e.g. Baddeley, 1986; 1992), we present only a bare sketch of the model here before considering a version of the model that addresses issues in mathematical cognition.

Baddeley's model claims that there are three separate components to the working memory system. First there is a central executive component, responsible for initiating and controlling processes, making decisions, and retrieving information from long-term memory. Two subsidiary systems, the articulatory loop and the visuospatial sketchpad, perform more limited, modality-specific tasks; for the former, such activities as maintaining and rehearsing articulatory information, and for the latter, maintaining and manipulating information in a visual or spatial code (e.g. mental rotation). When a demanding task is given to one of the subsidiary systems, it can drain processing resources or capacity from the executive, thereby degrading the efficiency or accuracy of current activity in the executive. From the standpoint of our later discussion on mathematics anxiety, this is the most important aspect of Baddeley's model, the draining of central executive resources by a secondary process. Note that this prediction of interference is most clearly tested in a dual-task setting, when subjects perform two tasks simultaneously.

Ashcraft (1995) has offered an elaboration of Baddeley's working memory model, suggesting the locus of several mathematical effects within the three-component working memory system. In this elaboration, all basic retrieval effects should have their largest impact on the central executive component. This specifically includes retrieval of basic fact knowledge (e.g. $6 + 7 = 13$), retrieval of more global knowledge (e.g. addition and multiplication are commutative), and retrieval of procedural and strategy information. Importantly, the central executive was also predicted to be the component responsible for executing the retrieved procedural knowledge, that is applying the retrieved procedures to the current problem. Thus, the central executive would keep track of the current step in a multistep sequence, hold intermediate quantities, trigger the carry/borrow operation, and the like.

The articulatory loop, it was further hypothesized, is the locus of the actual carry operation. That is, when the problem $27 + 16$ is encountered, the central executive retrieves the general procedures for doing multicolumn addition, including the carry operation, and then retrieves the sums for $7 + 6$ and $2 + 1$. But it would be the articulatory loop that actually increments the tens value for the carry operation (and likewise decrements an operand in the borrow operation). The elaboration of the visuo-spatial sketchpad, however, mentions only possible visual characteristics and positional information, because research on the contribution of this modality to mathematical cognition is essentially nonexistent (but see Logie, 1995, for a current treatment of other research on the visuo-spatial system).

Working memory and maths performance

An early paper by Hitch (1978a) considered the applicability of this working memory system to the topic of maths performance. Hitch's results suggested strongly that processes such as carrying in addition place a heavy load on the working memory system. In his paper, subjects solved multi-column addition problems after only brief visual presentation, and were sometimes required to report the answers in reverse order, (i.e. units, then tens, then hundreds). The performance he observed, both in terms of solution speed and errors, was clearly related to the predictions of the limited-capacity, working memory system. That is, the available capacity of working memory was consumed by three types of activities: maintaining greater amounts of information in temporary storage, maintaining the information for a longer period of time, and performing more steps or operations within working memory. The latter point, of course, reflected the presence of a carry operation in the problem being solved. In other words, the carry process places an extra load on the capacity of working memory.

Several more recent papers have confirmed and extended these conclusions, showing the important role of working memory for the carry process specifically (e.g. Ashcraft et al., 1992; Lemaire et al., 1996; Logie et al.,1994). In our recent work (Ashcraft, Copeland, Vavro, & Falk, 1998), one- and two-column addition problems with a carry were answered with only 75% accuracy when subjects simultaneously had to remember six random letters for subsequent recall. Incorrect answers given to basic fact problems were generally close in magnitude to the correct answer, usually wrong by only ± 1, 2, or 3; this is the standard error effect in addition. But fully 43% of the incorrect answers to two-column problems reflected an error in the carry process, that is the subject's answers were incorrect by 10 (e.g. 17 + 9 = 36; 18 + 16 = 24).

Logie and Baddeley (1987) found disruption of simple counting processes in a dual-task experiment that involved simultaneous articulation. Because of the specific interference from the articulatory task, they concluded that important elements of mental counting depend on the articulatory loop in the working memory system (see also Logie et al., 1994). Our results suggest an extension of this conclusion, in which the process of carrying in addition is viewed as a counting-like process, probably the "counting on" procedure. As such, it would be no surprise that carrying is disrupted by a simultaneous task that involves either overt articulation, as did Logie and Baddeley's, or covert articulation and rehearsal, as our memory load manipulation did.

Another connection is important to note here as well. Ashcraft et al. (1998) found that even single-digit basic fact problems were performed quite inaccurately under the six-letter memory load condition, nearly 25% errors versus 4.6% errors in the single-task control condition. On the face of it, this would appear to show significant working memory involvement in responding to basic fact problems, despite the common view that basic addition facts are uniformly retrieved from long-term memory in a largely automatic fashion (e.g. Ashcraft, 1982; 1992).

On the other hand, LeFevre et al.'s (1996) recent evidence suggests that a nontrivial portion of performance to basic facts is due to procedural, that is nonretrieval processing. These investigators presented the basic facts of addition for timed performance, but also asked subjects to indicate whether the problem had been solved via memory retrieval or some strategy. Subjects indicated that a significant portion of trials on the larger basic facts, (i.e. those with two-column answers), had been answered by means of strategies or procedures other than retrieval. The standard problem-size effect, according to LeFevre et al., is largely—though not completely—due to slower, procedural solutions on the larger facts.

If this is the case, then it would seem quite natural that procedural solutions would depend on access to the processing resources of the working memory system. That is, procedural solutions can be assumed to be less automatic than retrieval, hence more reliant on conscious involvement of working memory. This would explain the pattern of results reported by LeFevre et al. (1996), as well as the error pattern on basic facts in Ashcraft et al.'s (1998) report.

Note finally that the involvement of strategies and procedures, even on basic addition facts, is a straightforward prediction of Siegler and Jenkins's (1989) developmental theory of mental arithmetic. In that approach, children not only form associations between problem operands and answers (including incorrect answers), but also between problems and strategies. Imagine, for example, that a larger basic fact like 7 + 6 is repeatedly solved by a particular child with the same reconstructive strategy, a "solve from known facts" strategy. Here, because the child can retrieve the answer to 6 + 6 directly, the original problem is transformed to 6 + 6 + 1, and the easily retrieved intermediate answer 12 is then incremented by one.

In Siegler and Jenkins' model, the particular strategy used on a problem acquires associative strength in memory along with associations between operands and answers. This accumulated strength renders it more likely that the same strategy will be invoked on subsequent encounters with the same problem. Thus, the model predicts that the history of solutions, both retrieval and strategy-based, will be reflected in subsequent performance, even for adults. Consistent with the implication of LeFevre et al.'s (1996) results, we suggest a minor elaboration of the Siegler and Jenkins model, such that the resources of working memory are still needed for the actual execution of the solution strategy, even though the strategy itself is stored in long-term memory.

ANXIETY EFFECTS IN MATHEMATICS

Having discussed the two separate areas of maths anxiety and mathematical cognition, we turn now to a consideration of their joint implications, to the possibility that maths anxiety has specific cognitive consequences on mental processing and representation. This is a relatively recent and novel focus; our report (Ashcraft & Faust, 1988; 1994) appears to have been the first paper that considered this possibility in any direct way. This is not to say that the general consequences of maths anxiety had never been considered until then, of course. The bulk of that research, on the negative relationship between maths anxiety and maths aptitude and achievement, was conducted in the 1970s and 1980s. But there had been no consideration of the possibility that mental processing might differ as a function of maths anxiety level. Indeed, as we noted at the outset (Ashcraft & Faust, 1994), it seemed entirely possible that the experience of maths anxiety might be irrelevant to mathematical processing, for example if maths performance were substantially faster than conscious awareness of anxiety.

We begin by ruling out maths competence as an overall, confounding difference among individuals at different levels of maths anxiety. We then discuss some of the on-line effects of maths anxiety that have been observed on laboratory tasks, and present Eysenck's (1992) important model of generalized anxiety effects on cognitive processing. It is from this viewpoint that we derive our current hypothesis, the working memory-mathematics anxiety hypothesis. We conclude with some preliminary tests of this hypothesis, and then discuss some of its implications for developmental and educational issues.

Maths anxiety and maths competence

The typical correlational study investigating maths anxiety and maths competence merely reported the negative correlation (– .31 in Hembree's meta-analysis; see Table 8.1), and implied that there is a pervasive, uniform reduction in maths competence as a function of maths anxiety. We present three lines of evidence to argue that this is not the case.

Effects of anxiety interventions

Hembree (1990) reports an interesting finding in the literature on the effectiveness of various treatments for mathematics anxiety. Competence in maths, as assessed with standardized tests, displays a significant discrepancy for high versus low maths anxious individuals, a mean effect size of – 0.61 (in standard deviation units). Effective treatments, especially "behavioural (except relaxation) and cognitive-behavioural methods produced a collective mean improvement of 0.57 in test performance" in Hembree's meta-analysis (1990, p. 43).

That is to say, standardized test scores improved + 0.57 (again in SD units) for previously high maths anxious individuals after successful treatment. Thus, on post-test, subject's scores approached the level of maths achievement and aptitude found for low maths anxious individuals. This effect makes no sense if we insist on a normal interpretation of achievement and aptitude scores. That is, the effect would assert that therapeutic relief from maths anxiety improves one's competence. Instead, we propose a more suitable interpretation of the findings, obvious yet apparently not suggested elsewhere. Original, pre-therapeutic assessment of maths achievement and aptitude yields a significant *underestimate* of the individual's true competence. The source of the underestimate is clear—the high maths anxious individual is experiencing an on-line maths anxiety reaction while taking the standardized maths test, thus depressing the test score. If the anxiety is overcome through therapeutic treatment, then this source of disruption during standardized testing is removed, allowing the individual's true competence to be reflected more accurately in the test score.

A somewhat less obvious conclusion also follows from this interpretation. The − .31 correlation between maths anxiety and competence very probably exaggerates the extent of the true relationship between these constructs. It seems likely, in other words, that more specifically targeted research might find areas of maths in which there is no significant competence difference between high and low maths anxious individuals, and others in which there is a strong relationship. Such research cannot merely administer a global maths achievement or aptitude test in order to isolate such areas of maths content. Instead, it should examine performance at graded levels of maths difficulty, to obtain a clearer view of competence.

Content specific-competence and maths anxiety

In one of our efforts to disentagle maths anxiety and competence (Ashcraft & Kirk, 1998), we administered both the sMARS assessment and the Wide Range Achievement Test (WRAT; Jastak Associates, 1993), a widely used test of maths achievement. The correlation of the two scores in our sample of 91 subjects was − .35, remarkably close to the overall correlation reported in Hembree (1990).

More informatively, however, we examined the structure of the WRAT itself. The test is composed of 40 maths problems, eight lines with five problems each. The first three lines consist entirely of whole-number problems in the four arithmetic operations; the next three lines begin testing fractions, decimal arithmetic, and long division with a remainder; and the final two include algebraic problems with one and two unknowns. We took advantage of this clear progression of difficulty, by scoring our subjects' tests line-by-line then analyzing the scores as a function of maths anxiety.

The analysis demonstrated convincingly that there were no systematic differences in competence for simple, whole-number arithmetic. Performance for all three anxiety groups (low, medium, high) exceeded 95% correct on the first three lines of the test, and correlations between the sMARS and these line scores were essentially zero. Systematic group differences began to appear in lines 5 and 6, and were largest on the final line of the test, where low anxious subjects averaged 1.9 correct out of 5, versus 0.5 correct out of 5 for high anxious subjects. All correlations between sMARS and WRAT lines 5 through 8 were significant, averaging – 0.30.

Results on paper-and-pencil tests of addition and maths, reported in Faust et al., 1996a; Experiment 3) also documented the same effects as Ashcraft & Kirk (1998) results with the WRAT. In short, when simple whole-number arithmetic is considered, there appear to be no competence differences at all for individuals differing in maths anxiety.

On-line analysis of simple arithmetic

These conclusions suggest that the effects of maths anxiety on performance are not uniformly contaminated by a confounding with maths competence. Instead, performance on simple arithmetic seems amenable to analysis of anxiety effects independent of any initial differences in competence. We have thus tested such performance in the laboratory, using RT and accuracy as dependent measures, to determine if any on-line anxiety effects are present.

The results on simple arithmetic now seem quite consistent. Across three large experiments, we have only occasionally found even minor differences in processing speed and accuracy when testing the basic facts of addition and multiplication (Ashcraft & Faust, 1994; Faust et al., 1996a). For example, in a test of the basic facts in addition and multiplication (Ashcraft & Faust, 1994, Experiment 2), no anxiety effects, either on RT or errors, even approached significance when performance on true problems was assessed. That is to say, when the problem-size effect is examined separately for groups differing in maths anxiety, no noticeable differences have been found on measures of cognitive processing (but see Faust, Johnson, & Ashcraft, 1996b, for evidence of physiological reactivity to these problems). The few anxiety group differences that were significant involved false problems, tested in the true/false verification task, and seemed to involve not straightforward arithmetic fact knowledge but procedures dealing with magnitude estimation (for a similar report on estimation strategies, see LeFevre, Greenham, & Waheed, 1993).

Thus, we find no important differences in performance characteristics among the different levels of maths anxiety when the simple, basic facts of addition and multiplication are studied in the lab; there may, however, be some anxiety-related differences in mental processing of magnitude information. On the other hand, as described next, we have found prominent anxiety effects on more difficult arithmetic, especially when the carry operation is involved.

On-line maths anxiety effects in procedural processing

Performance on multicolumn addition problems and sets of difficult mixed operation problems has shown marked effects of maths anxiety, with highly anxious subjects either considerably slower, dramatically less accurate, or both. The clearest example we have seen to date is when subjects are asked to solve two-column addition problems with carrying, e.g. 57 + 16 (Faust et al., 1996a). In this work, high maths anxious subjects were considerably slower and/or less accurate on problems that included the carry operation (e.g. Fig. 3 and Table 4 of Faust et al., 1996a). Specifically, estimated time for the carry operation was three times longer (764msec) for high maths anxious subjects than for the low maths anxious group (253msec). Carry problems were also frequently more error prone for high than for low anxious subjects.

We return to this finding in a moment, because of its relationship to the role of working memory. For now, note that the stimulus set that yielded this anxiety effect was the same set Faust et al. (1996a, Experiment 3) tested in a paper-and-pencil format. In that untimed, hence more relaxed setting, no differences were obtained. Probably just as important, however, is the impact that paper-and-pencil format has on mental processing, in particular on working memory processes. Unlike our computer-based testing format, written format on a paper-and-pencil test shifts the carry operation from a mental to a physical task—the need to carry is written on the paper versus held in working memory. As such, the demands placed on working memory by the carry operation appear to be minimized in written format.

The working memory-maths anxiety hypothesis

We argued earlier that there now appears to be clear evidence that mental arithmetic performance relies on the resources of working memory (Ashcraft et al., 1998). This seems particularly true in two circumstances, when relatively large basic fact problems are processed, and when procedural knowledge is important to processing, as in the carry operation in addition. Not that this statement is in fact somewhat of a revision of earlier conclusions in the literature. In those, the problem-size or problem-difficulty effect was attributed to lower overall strength of problem representation in memory, akin, for example, to slower lexical decision performance on less frequent words in the language. It now appears possible, based on the LeFevre et al. (1996) results, that the problem-size effect may be due in part to the use of strategy-based, procedural processes other than retrieval. Such procedural solutions would be called for, note, when the strength of a problem in memory falls below some criterion for retrieval.

This explanation overlaps considerably with the scheme proposed by Siegler and Jenkins (1989), as discussed earlier. Further, and most important for the present discussion, such procedural solutions would be expected to place a significant drain on the capacity of the working memory system. That is, problems solved via strategies rather than retrieval should be the same problems that show decrements in performance under dual-task conditions, as performing a secondary task concurrent with applying a strategy should result in serious depletion of working memory resources.

Consider now the impact that generalized anxiety has on information processing. Eysenck (1992; Eysenck & Calvo, 1992) has provided an extensive discussion of the ways in which generalized anxiety reactions affect concurrent cognitive processing. The basic notion is that anxiety acts like a secondary task in dual-task settings. That is, Eysenck proposes that an anxiety reaction is composed of intrusive thoughts and worry, to which the anxious individual pays attention. These thoughts are disruptive in Eysenck's model because they consume resources in the working memory system, resources often needed for other mental processing. When an anxious individual performs a cognitive task, therefore, performance on the task will be degraded to the extent that it relies on working memory. The reason is that essential working memory resources are being devoted to disruptive thoughts rather than the task at hand.

Eysenck's processing efficiency theory was intended to account for the effects that generalized anxiety has on cognitive processing. Although he did not discuss maths anxiety specifically, we have argued elsewhere (Ashcraft & Faust, 1994) that the theory should apply equally to the maths anxiety phenomenon, but only when the setting arouses the individual's maths anxiety. In other words, what Eysenck has proposed to be true of generalized anxiety, observable in any task that depends on working memory, we have proposed should be true of maths anxiety, in any context that induces a maths anxiety reaction.

Thus, the hypothesis we are proposing, based on an extension of Eysenck and Calvo's (1992) theory, is as follows. In mathematical tasks that rely on the working memory system, high maths anxious subjects will show degraded performance, either in speed or accuracy measures. This deterioration of performance is hypothesized to be due to the dual-task nature of maths anxiety itself. That is, the on-line experience of maths anxiety is one of intrusive thoughts and worry, with attention devoted to those thoughts. Directing attentional resources in such a fashion robs the working memory system of the resources needed for efficient performance of the primary task.

What is not yet clear is the precise mechanism by which this working memory is disrupted. For example, we do not know if the maths anxiety reaction should be considered a constant drain on working memory, or whether the intermittent nature of intrusive thoughts predicts only intermittent interference with ongoing mental activity. Although the mere presence of such intrusive thoughts in working memory might be sufficient to disrupt processing, it might also be argued that the real difficulty involves failure to inhibit attention to those thoughts. In any case, the predicted effect is distinguishable from the more general consequence of maths anxiety, in which one's level of maths competence is compromised because of long-term avoidance and failure to master maths content. As discussed, this difference in competence is not uniform throughout all maths content, but begins to be observable in multistep arithmetic and maths problems, especially beyond the whole-number problem stage.

Preliminary results

We have recently conducted several studies to test this hypothesis, with encouraging results. One major result that is consistent with the hypothesis has already been discussed, the difficulties high anxious subjects had in processing two-column addition with carrying (Ashcraft & Faust, 1994; Faust et al., 1996a). We briefly discuss two further investigations here.

In one series of studies (Ashcraft & Kirk, 1998, Experiments 1 and 5), subjects at low, medium, and high maths anxiety levels were given standard assessments of working memory capacity, the Salthouse and Babcock (1990) language- and computation-span tasks. High maths anxious subjects scored significantly lower on both assessments than did medium subjects, who in turn scored lower than subjects at the low maths anxiety level. At a general level, then, high maths anxious subjects demonstrated a lower working memory capacity when tested with the demanding span tasks.

In Experiment 5, subjects were also given a processing task that places even greater demands on working memory, Eysenck's (1985) letter transformation task. In this task, the subject sees either two or four randomly selected letters, one at a time, and must perform a two- or four-step alphabetic transformation on each letter (e.g. transform F by moving four steps forward in the alphabet, yielding the letter J). Each transformation result must then be held in working memory while subsequent transformations are performed, in order to name all the transformed values at the end of the trial. We recorded two measures of on-line processing, time to transform the letters, and accuracy in recalling the transformed values.

Both measures of performance showed significant interactions between task difficulty and maths anxiety level. In particular, the anxiety groups showed comparable transformation times and recall accuracy in the simplest conditions, two-letter sets with a two-step transformation. But in the four-letter, four-step transformation condition, high maths anxious subjects spent significantly more time performing the transformations than either the low or medium anxious subjects. And despite this seemingly greater effort, the high anxious group's recall of the transformations was significantly worse than that of the low and medium groups.

Because of the nature of these interactions, we concluded that the transformation task places increasingly strenuous demands on the working memory system. In combination with the on-line maths anxiety reaction, the net effect is increasingly compromised functioning in working memory, due to insufficient available resources. In short, the results were in agreement with the working memory-maths anxiety hypothesis described earlier.

A second series of studies examined the hypothesis one step further, using a very different task. As noted, Eysenck (1992) suggests that it is the anxious individual's preoccupation with intrusive thoughts and worry that drains working memory of sufficient processing resources. We reasoned that the specific mechanism here could be one of inhibition, in particular failure to inhibit attention to intrusive thoughts. Although there are both anecdotal and verbal reports showing that high maths anxious subjects report more such intrusive thoughts during processing (e.g. Faust, 1992), there appears to be no direct empirical evidence that demonstrates the particular explanation we are offering, disruption because of failure to inhibit attention.

Such a hypothesis has recently been supported in a very different line of work, however, in Zacks and Hasher's (1994) investigation of attentional allocation among the elderly. These investigators presented a reading task to their subjects, in which subjects read a paragraph orally and then were tested on comprehension. The manipulation of interest involved embedded distractor information; distractor words, printed in a different font, appear periodically throughout the paragraph. Subjects are instructed to ignore the distractor words as they read the paragraph. Interestingly, in Zacks and Hasher's report, the elderly exhibited significantly higher reading times on the paragraphs, that is, greater devotion of attention to the distractor words. The elderly were apparently unable to inhibit attention to the distractor words as effectively as the young adults.

We have adopted this task in our study of maths anxiety because it mimics experimentally the hypothesized mental operation of anxiety, preoccupation with and attention to intrusive, distracting information. Thus, Hopko (1996) presented paragraphs for oral reading to subjects classified as low, medium, or high maths anxious. All three groups read control paragraphs, in which strings of x's are used instead of distractor words, in about 40sec. Reading times for the experimental paragraphs were slower overall for all groups, but especially at higher levels of anxiety; mean reading time was approximately 66sec for the low group, but 95sec for the high maths anxious group (Hopko, 1996, Experiment 1). Furthermore, it was clear that the additional reading time was not spent on improving memory for the paragraphs, because the groups scored quite similarly on the comprehension tests that followed each paragraph (80.3%, 80.3%, and 80.5% correct, respectively for low, medium, and high anxious groups; Experiment 1). In other words, we infer that the higher anxiety groups' additional reading time was spent in attending to the distractors, or more accurately, in failing to inhibit attention to the distractors. This was the case in all three of Hopko's experiments, whether or not the paragraphs were related to maths topics, and whether or not the distractor words named maths concepts.

We interpret the results as supporting the hypothesized relationship between maths anxiety and working memory. As research on the basic question of working memory's role in mathematical cognition is pursued, we expect to find additional aspects of cognitive processing that distinguish high and low maths anxious individuals.

CONCLUSION

Traditional accounts of maths anxiety have focused on rather global consequences, such as lower standardized scores on maths achievement tests, or large-scale consequences, such as influences on chosen university majors and career choices. Work on the cognitive processes involved in maths, however, has revealed some of the underlying detail about relevant mental operations and knowledge of maths. By studying these operations and knowledge structures within the context of maths anxiety, we have begun to answer questions about the possible cognitive consequences of maths anxiety. For the most part, our initial research suggests that maths anxiety disrupts the efficient operation of the working memory system, and hence any mathematical processing that relies on working memory.

Implications for developmental and educational issues are as yet few, given that the relevant questions are only now coming into focus. We conclude by juxtaposing some ideas and possible relationships that appear to deserve further investigation.

As noted earlier, there is only a small body of work in the literature on the onset of maths anxiety (e.g. Gierl & Bisanz, 1995; Suinn et al., 1988). If maths anxiety compromises ongoing acquisition and mastery regardless of age, then one might expect genuine, competence-based disadvantages beginning about the same time as maths anxiety itself. The literature suggests that maths anxiety is observable prior to sixth grade, and grows stronger up through the ninth grade level. If this effect is genuine, then it might be more than a coincidence that maths anxious adults often mention anxiety difficulties with topics commonly introduced at about this age, for example algebra. On the other hand, the effect may only be an artifact, for example of the age groups that have been tested. In any event, systematic research on the development of maths anxiety is sorely needed.

Another possibility worth mentioning involves the developmental progression observed in maths problem solving methods. Several influential reports indicate that children rely heavily on counting and other reconstructive strategies early in grade school, and that these strategies are slowly replaced across development—although not completely—with retrieval from long-term memory (e.g. Ashcraft & Fierman, 1982; Cooney et al., 1988; Siegler, 1987). It is presumed, though perhaps not yet thoroughly documented, that counting and reconstructive methods place heavy demands on the working memory system, such demands being lessened as performance shifts more and more toward retrieval. If so, then early arithmetic learning is made more difficult because of the load on working memory imposed by strategy-based solutions.

Whereas the developmental change from strategies to retrieval seems to be the case for normally progressing school children, mathematically disabled children seem not to develop the same rich mixture of strategies, and tend to cling to less efficient strategies instead of shifting toward memory retrieval (Geary et al., 1991). Interestingly, Geary et al. (1991) also report that their maths disabled students scored significantly lower on working memory span tests. Thus, reduced working memory capacity is implicated in maths disability.

We speculate that maths anxiety effects may parallel those of maths disability at the level of cognitive processing. That is, the reduced working memory capacity of maths-disabled children seems to be an important component of their failure to develop normal processing operations in arithmetic and maths. Given that maths anxiety at the adult level has the same effect on working memory capacity, it is not unreasonable to expect similar effects on the development of maths skills due to maths anxiety. In a sense, the mature repertoire of strategies characteristic of mathematically normal children would not develop because of an anxiety-induced drain on working memory resources. It might be, for instance, that the pupil who is already dividing working memory resources between problem solving and maths anxiety is so overloaded that learning and mastery of more complex arithmetic cannot proceed successfully. Preoccupation with intrusive thoughts would thereby compromise the entire educational process.

Such explanations assume that working memory plays a critical role in arithmetic and mathematics learning at all stages, including higher-level achievements such as inventing more efficient strategies and understanding underlying relations and concepts. Although these are entirely plausible assumptions, they have received little direct empirical attention. On the other hand, considerable work confirms the importance of working memory to other domains, for example reading and comprehension (e.g. Gernsbacher, 1990; King & Just, 1991), reasoning (Baddeley & Hitch, 1974), and retrieval from long-term memory (Conway & Engle, 1994). From that perspective, it would be surprising if working memory were not central to acquisition and mastery of mathematical knowledge.

To summarize, maths anxiety indeed appears to have specific cognitive consequences for performance, not merely global consequences in terms of maths competence, but specific consequences involving the functioning of working memory. It is important to pursue this avenue of research for at least two reasons. First, given the unfortunate global consequences of maths anxiety in terms of mastery of maths, career choices, and the like, it is obviously important to understand the phenomenon at a much more detailed level. And second, the same logic applies in studies of mathematical cognition as in many other domains; we may glean new insights about mathematical cognition by studying how mental processing is disrupted or altered in certain groups or settings.

Sources of individual difference in mathematical development

INTRODUCTION

Studying the cognitive performance of patients who have suffered brain damage as a result of stroke or some other neurological insult has for some time now been considered an important method for increasing our understanding of the structure of the undamaged cognitive system (Ellis & Young, 1988). Cognitive neuropsychological studies of patterns of deficit and of spared function may help to identify the dependencies of the normal system and, for example, the extent to which its architecture is modular. Work in this area has made a substantial contribution to our understanding of mathematical cognition in adulthood (e.g. Dehaene & Cohen, 1995, McCloskey, 1992). Paul Macaruso and Scott Sokol, in Chapter 9, draw on their experience in this area to address developmental studies in similar fashion.

There is an important issue concerning the application of cognitive neuro-psychological principles to developmental issues: Children with developmental disorders (as those studied by Macaruso and Sokol) are, by definition, not showing *acquired* deficits. Their condition is a developmental one for which causal factors are unlikely to be specified in any detail. The question arises then, how far do these exceptional cases allow conclusions to be drawn about normal development? No simple answer can be given. What is clear is that any such conclusions must be cautious. There is no limitation, however, on the clinical application of studies of this sort; any evidence that may lead to closer specification of individual patterns of cognitive function may also assist in clinical and educational management.

Macaruso and Sokol acknowledge both goals: They seek information for both theoretical and clinical purposes. The cases they present are of individuals with dyslexia who are also known to have problems with maths. The assessments carried out are based on a model of adult numerical cognition. The authors acknowledge the limitations which this imposes. Nonetheless, their systematic investigations provide important preliminary evidence of dissociations, for example between Arabic and verbal numeral processing (see Chapter 11), and set a wide agenda for future detailed individual case studies.

Chapters 10 and 11 report group studies of mathematical skills in children with hearing and language impairments respectively. This approach is in conflict with the detailed single-case method strongly advocated by the previous authors. The reader is invited to form his or her own opinion on this important issue. To some extent the question revolves around the nature and extent of individual differences between the special participants in each study reported, and the experimental questions and types of analyses used.

Terezinha Nunes and Constanza Moreno, in Chapter 10, explore a specific hypothesis, that hearing impairment is a risk factor, rather than a causal factor, in mathematical learning difficulties. Their sample is large (85 participants) and the regression procedures used to analyse the data are sensitive to individual difference. It is the combined pattern of individuals' performance across a range of measures that is the focus of these analyses. The conclusions are positive in the sense that hearing impairment is not found to impose qualitative restrictions on children's mathematical learning. Though delayed, problem-solving skills appear to develop in the same way in hearing-impaired as they do in hearing children.

Nunes and Moreno lay emphasis on "action-schemas" whereby children learn to represent numerical concepts. They particularly focus on a shopping task in which children are required to use coins of different values to make purchases. Performance in this task has been shown to be highly predictive of a variety of arithmetical skills including place value knowledge. The action schemas underlying these concepts, it is argued, develop in the same way whether a child's hearing is impaired or not.

Some corroborative findings are reported by Chris Donlan in Chapter 11. A number of studies have explored the mathematical skills of children with specific language impairments (the nonverbal abilities of these children are generally considered intact). A consistent pattern emerges within which verbal numerical skills are in deficit. Rote-counting is poor (the sequences are short and unreliable compared to controls) and knowledge of arithmetic facts develops extremely slowly. However, there is relatively unimpaired development in other areas. In one study, knowledge of Arabic numerals, in particular basic place value knowledge, appeared to develop normally in the majority of children with language impairments. Note that this finding emerged from a study of simple magnitude comparison, not of multidigit arithmetic. The possibility arises that verbal and nonverbal skills may be separable in development; hints of this have already been noted in Chapters 9 and 10. Important individual differences are reported by Donlan, and it may be that individual case studies are needed in this area.

The final chapter, by Ann Dowker, lays to rest any suspicion that the "normal" population, defined as those children for whom no particular special need is identified, demonstrates a unitary coherent pattern of mathematical development. Dowker's study derives considerable strength from its dual approach: On the one hand she uses a large sample (213 children aged 5–9 years) to explore, through covariance analyses, the extent of consistency of performance across a range of arithmetical and estimation tasks. Note the subtlety with which Dowker assesses arithmetical reasoning in contrast to general arithmetical performance. Findings here are taken to indicate a multi-component model of mathematical skills. Dowker goes on to present a number of individual cases who show marked performance discrepancies between one or other component of mathematical skill. She concludes that individual differences in the "normal" population are substantial and that risk attaches to any assumption that a child "does not understand maths" based on performance on one specific calculation task.

Dowker's findings are salutary. In sampling from clinical populations we often jump to the conclusion that the patterns of performance we find are never found in normally developing children. Sometimes they are. Perhaps mathematics is a domain in which the diversity of component skills is such as to allow dramatic individual differences to occur with some frequency.

The possibility that intra-individual variation in the levels of component skills indicates the relative strength of "separable" components of the cognitive system is suggested by a number of findings in this section of the book. A general distinction between verbal and visual representation seems possible and may offer a developmental parallell to findings in adult neuropsychology (e.g. Dehaene & Cohen, 1995). Careful further research into individual differences in clinical and normally developing populations is needed to explore not only the possible dissociation of verbal and visual representations of numerical information, but also their possible interaction in the formation of mathematical concepts.

CHAPTER NINE

Cognitive neuropsychology and developmental dyscalculia

Paul Macaruso* & Scott M. Sokol**
*Massachusetts General Hospital, Boston, USA
**Massachusetts General Hospital and Harvard Medical School,
Boston, USA

INTRODUCTION

In this chapter, we discuss a somewhat different source of data that can be brought to bear on the study of mathematical development, namely patterns of impaired performance seen in individuals with arithmetic learning disability (also referred to as developmental dyscalculia). In general, the use of perform-ance data from neuropsychological populations is predicated on the assumption that such data are not merely aberrational, but rather reveal something about the ways in which cognition ordinarily takes place (see Caramazza, 1986). In the developmental case, the implication is that neuropsychological data reflect interruption in normal processes of knowledge or skill acquisition (e.g. Mar-shall, 1989). For instance, the discovery that individuals with developmental dyscalculia may suffer from selective disturbances in numeric abilities (e.g. reading or understanding numbers, retrieving arithmetic facts) would suggest that in normal development these skills are subserved by relatively distinct cognitive components.

In the following sections, we first review some of the major findings from group studies and single-case descriptions of arithmetic learning disability. We then highlight a relatively new approach to the study of developmental dyscal-culia—rooted in cognitive neuropsychology—and some preliminary findings stemming from this approach. We conclude with a discussion of research areas in which data from developmental dyscalculia may further enhance our under-standing of normal mathematical development.

Group studies

Most studies of developmental dyscalculia have employed group designs (see Gordon, 1992, for review). For example, Kosc (1974) utilized screening tests to identify three groups of children with mathematical disabilities. One group performed poorly on numeric tests (e.g. basic addition, subtraction, and multiplication), a second group had difficulty with performance tests (e.g. dividing geometric figures into specific shapes), and a third had difficulty on both sets of tests. Kosc then showed that the three groups of children display different performance patterns on psychological tests. For example, the lowest scores on a test of word reading and writing were obtained by the two groups with poor numeric skills.

Group studies have been used extensively by Rourke and his associates in their neuropsychological investigations of subtypes of arithmetic learning disability (e.g. Ozols & Rourke, 1988; Rourke & Finlayson, 1978; Strang & Rourke, 1983, 1985; see Rourke, 1993, for review). They compared two main subgroups of arithmetic learning disability: Group A includes children with low arithmetic scores and average reading/spelling scores, whereas Group R-S includes children with low arithmetic scores and even lower reading/spelling scores. The two subgroups were found to differ on various measures of auditory-perceptual, visual-spatial, psychomotor, and reasoning skills. In general, children in Group A displayed right-hemisphere dysfunction (i.e. poor performance on visual-spatial, psychomotor, and nonverbal reasoning tasks, and arithmetic errors attributed to difficulty in spatial organization and graphomotor output). In contrast, students in Group R-S showed left-hemisphere dysfunction (i.e. low scores on auditory-perceptual tasks, and difficulty with arithmetic facts and printed word problems).

In a recent study Shalev, Manor, Amir, Wertman-Elad, and Gross-Tsur (1995) used criteria similar to Rourke to identify two groups of children with developmental dyscalculia—one with right-hemisphere dysfunction and the other with left-hemisphere dysfunction. The two groups were administered a battery of arithmetic tasks constructed on the basis of a cognitive model of number processing developed by McCloskey, Caramazza, and Basili (1985; for details of this model, see later). Significant group differences were obtained in just three areas (mastery of addition/subtraction, complex multiplication and division, visual-spatial errors), and in all cases performance favoured the right-hemisphere group. Shalev et al. concluded that for the most part they were unable to identify patterns of arithmetic errors consistent with Rourke's notion of right- versus left-hemisphere dysfunction and that, in general, left-hemisphere dysfunction may be more detrimental to acquisition of arithmetic skills. Other results inconsistent with the right-hemisphere/left-hemisphere dichotomy have been reported elsewhere (see, for example, Nolan, Hammeke, & Barkley, 1983; Rosenberger, 1989; Share, Moffitt, & Silva, 1988).

A number of group studies have focused on the performance of learning-disabled children in solving basic arithmetic problems. A commonly reported finding is that learning-disabled children have difficulty in recall of basic arithmetic facts. For example, Russell and Ginsburg (1984) found that fourth-graders experiencing "mathematics difficulty" fell well behind normal achievers in rapid recall of addition facts, but displayed adequate performance in other areas of mathematics such as estimation, relative magnitude judgements, knowledge of base-10 concepts, and enumeration skills. Similarly, Fleischner, Garnett, and Shepherd (1982) and Garnett and Fleischner (1983) found that learning-disabled children produce fewer correct responses than nondisabled children on speeded tests of single-digit addition, subtraction, and multiplication (see also Pritchard, Miles, Chinn, & Taggart, 1989). Based on similar findings, Ackerman, Anhalt, and Dykman (1986) concluded that learning-disabled children have difficulty in automatization of basic skills like number facts, and argued that these difficulties may stem from poor sequential-memory abilities.

Some researchers have employed group studies to examine the memory skills of children with arithmetic learning disability (e.g. Shafrir & Siegel, 1994; Siegel & Linder, 1984; Webster, 1979). In one study Siegel and Ryan (1989) tested reading-disabled and specific arithmetic-disabled children on two working memory tasks, one which requires supplying the final word to a series of sentences and then recalling the set of final words, and the other which requires counting the number of yellow dots in random patterns containing blue and yellow dots and then recalling how many yellow dots there were in each pattern. They found that reading-disabled children had difficulty on both verbal (sentences) and nonverbal (dots) memory tasks, whereas specific arithmetic-disabled children displayed below normal performance only on the nonverbal task (see also Fein, Davenport, Yingling, & Galin, 1988; Fletcher, 1985). A follow-up study by Hitch and McAuley (1991) suggests that the difficulties experienced by specific arithmetic-disabled children on the nonverbal counting span task may stem more from its counting requirements than the fact that nonverbal stimuli were employed. Specific arithmetic-disabled children scored below normal on a counting-span task with auditory stimuli (sequences of taps) and showed subpar performance on tests of basic counting skills (e.g. counting speed). Finally, in a recent study, Swanson (1993) failed to find differences between learning disabled subgroups (reading impaired versus arithmetic impaired) on a variety of working memory tasks contrasting verbal and nonverbal materials.

Single-case descriptions

In contrast to group studies, some researchers have explored developmental dyscalculia through descriptions of individual cases. For instance, in an early study Guttman (1937) presented a number of case histories of children with numeric processing difficulties. One child was described as having a "constructional disturbance of figure writing (p. 21)". The child produced errors in writing numbers (e.g. "three thousand two hundred twenty-eight" → 302028) and in solving written arithmetic problems (e.g. 68 – 29 = 30).

Single-case descriptions of developmental dyscalculia are also seen in Cohn (1968, 1971) and Slade and Russell (1971). Cohn's work is informative in that it demonstrates the range of disturbances that may arise in developmental dyscalculia, including malformed number symbols, failure to discriminate specific order characteristics of multidigit numbers, inability to remember multiplication facts, and errors in carrying. Slade and Russell discussed four cases of developmental dyscalculia in which poor multiplication skill was the core deficit. Three of the children had a "faulty grasp of basic multiplication tables". In a qualitative analysis of performance, Slade and Russell uncovered a number of compensatory methods used by the children to overcome their lack of factual knowledge. For example, one child solved 8 × 7 by multiplying 2 × 7 = 14 and adding four 14s.

Badian (1983) described numerous cases of developmental dyscalculia using a classification scheme devised by Hecaen, Angelergues, and Houillier (1961) to study acquired dyscalculia. Three classes of dyscalculia are included in Hecaen et al.'s scheme: *alexia and agraphia for numbers*, deficits in reading and writing numbers; *spatial acalculia*, impaired calculation due to spatial processing deficits; and *anarithmetia*, disruption of calculation ability *per se*. Badian found many cases of spatial dyscalculia and anarithmetia in the developmental population, but little evidence of alexia and agraphia for numbers. Most of Badian's cases were placed in a fourth category called *attentional-sequential* dyscalculia. These children make careless errors in carrying out procedures and have great difficulty learning and recalling multiplication facts.

In a more recent study O'Hare, Brown, and Aitken (1991) contrasted two cases of childhood dyscalculia, one showed signs of right-hemisphere dysfunction and the other displayed left-hemisphere dysfunction. The child with right-hemisphere dysfunction had problems understanding abstract values of numbers and showed constructional dyspraxia. Disturbances seen in the child with left-hemisphere dysfunction include poor naming of number symbols, inability to write numbers or letters to dictation, and difficulty distinguishing right from left. O'Hare et al. note that the cluster of symptoms seen in the left hemisphere case is consistent with a profile of Developmental Gerstmann Syndrome (e.g. Kinsbourne & Warrington, 1963; PeBenito, Fisch, & Fisch, 1988).

Evaluation

Although the group and single-case studies reviewed earlier have heightened our awareness of the range of disorders associated with developmental dyscalculia, these studies suffer from both theoretical and methodological shortcomings. In the single-case studies, for instance, few attempts have been made to determine the locus/loci of impairment through a systematic evaluation of various numeric and arithmetic processes captured in a well-specified cognitive model. Identification of locus/loci of impairment is given even less attention in group studies. In a typical study children are first assigned to groups on the basis of performance on a cursory standardized test, and then administered one or more tasks designed to tap global processing abilities (e.g. visual-spatial skills, nonverbal memory). Without attempting to evaluate numeric processing skills in any detail, there is no way to determine what sorts of numeric processing deficiencies the children suffer from, nor how these deficiencies relate to a global processing disorder (see Sokol, Macaruso, & Gollan, 1994, for further discussion).

COGNITIVE NEUROPSYCHOLOGY AND NUMERIC PROCESSING

We believe that the study of developmental dyscalculia can benefit greatly from the methods employed in cognitive neuropsychology. Over the past two decades cognitive neuropsychology has received growing acceptance as a useful tool in building models of normal cognitive systems and in understanding acquired cognitive disorders (for reviews, see Ellis & Young, 1988; McCarthy & Warrington, 1990; Parkin, 1996). In this approach individuals with cognitive impairments are investigated on a single-case basis to determine the locus of breakdown within an information-processing model of the normal cognitive system. The approach assumes that a cognitive skill (e.g. arithmetic) can be conceptually decomposed into a number of separate processing components, and that brain damage may selectively disrupt one or more of these components without modifying other components. A cognitive deficit is described in terms of functional damage to either the representations or processes implicated in normal performance.

A model of numeric processing

In 1985, McCloskey, Caramazza and Basili proposed a cognitive model of numeric processing and reported data from several brain-damaged patients in support of the model's componential architecture (see Fig. 9.1). Since that

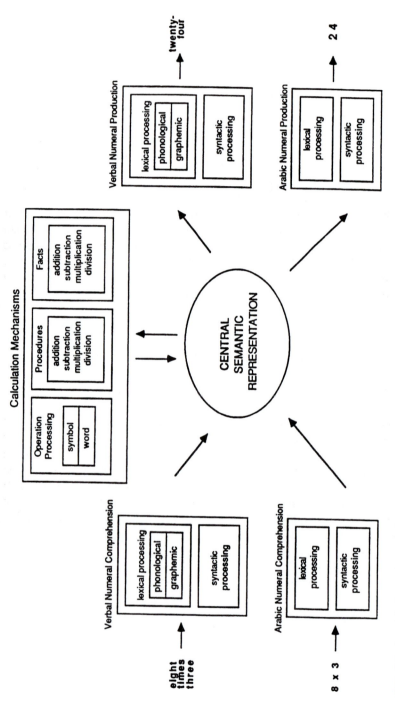

FIG. 9.1. A model of numeric processing.

time, we have made extensive use of this model and more generally the cognitive neuropsychological approach to study acquired dyscalculia (e.g. Macaruso, Harley, & McCloskey, 1992; Macaruso, McCloskey, & Aliminosa, 1993; McCloskey, Aliminosa, & Sokol, 1991; McCloskey & Macaruso, 1995; McCloskey, Sokol, & Goodman, 1986; McCloskey, Sokol, Goodman-Schulman, & Caramazza, 1990; Sokol & McCloskey, 1988; 1991; Sokol, McCloskey, & Cohen, 1989; Sokol, McCloskey, Cohen, & Aliminosa, 1991).

At the most general level, the McCloskey et al. (1985) model draws a distinction between numeral processing mechanisms and calculation mechanisms. Within numeral processing, the model separates numeral comprehension and numeral production mechanisms. Numeral comprehension mechanisms are used to convert numeric inputs into central semantic representations for use in subsequent processing, such as calculation, and numeral production mechanisms translate central semantic representations of numbers into specific forms for output. The numeral comprehension and numeral production systems are further subdivided into components for processing Arabic numerals (e.g. 328) and components for processing verbal numerals (e.g. three hundred twenty-eight). Arabic numeral comprehension is required to read a price tag, whereas writing a cheque makes use of both Arabic and verbal numeral production.

Within each of the numeral comprehension and numeral production components, a distinction is drawn between lexical and syntactic processing. Lexical processing refers to comprehension or production of the individual elements in a numeral (e.g. 7 or seven), whereas syntactic processing involves processing of relations among elements (e.g. digit or word order) to comprehend or produce a numeral as a whole. A final distinction is made in lexical processing for both verbal numeral comprehension and production. Namely, phonological processing mechanisms are postulated for processing spoken number words and graphemic processing mechanisms for written number words. For example, production of the spoken number word "ninety" requires retrieval of a phonological representation from a phonological output lexicon, whereas written production of *ninety* requires retrieval of a graphemic representation from a graphemic output lexicon.

To perform calculations, special mechanisms are required in addition to numeral comprehension and numeral production. The model posits three distinct types of mechanisms: comprehension of operation symbols (e.g. +, −, ×) and words (e.g. plus, minus, times), retrieval of arithmetic facts (e.g. $4 \times 9 = 36$), and execution of calculation procedures (e.g. in multidigit addition, start at the right-most column, compute the sum of the digits in the column, write the ones digit of the sum at the bottom of the column, carry the tens digit, if any, and so forth).

Evidence

A substantial amount of data has been accumulated from studies of acquired dyscalculia showing that cognitive numeric processing may be selectively disrupted by brain damage, and that in many cases the observed performance patterns conform to those expected by the McCloskey et al. model (see McCloskey, 1992, for review). As an example, consider patient JS studied by Sokol and McCloskey (1988). JS produced syntactic errors in reading aloud Arabic numerals (e.g, 146,359 → "one hundred thousand forty-six, three hundred fifty-nine"). JS's comprehension of Arabic numerals was shown to be unimpaired, so errors were attributed to verbal numeral production. The McCloskey et al. model assumes that syntactic processes in verbal numeral production are shared for spoken and written output. Support for this assumption comes from the finding that JS produced syntactic errors of the same type on both spoken and written verbal numeral production tasks. It was further shown that JS produced lexical errors in spoken verbal production (e.g. 407 → "four hundred *eight*") but *not* in written verbal production. This is also consistent with the McCloskey et al. model, which claims that lexical processes (and specifically the phonological and graphemic lexicons) are separate for spoken and written number words.

Other reported outcomes consistent with McCloskey et al.'s model include dissociations between numeral processing and calculation (e.g. Grewel, 1969; McCloskey et al., 1985), between numeral comprehension and numeral production (e.g. Benson & Denckla, 1969; McCloskey et al. 1986; Singer & Low, 1933), and between Arabic and verbal numeral processing (e.g. Grafman, Kampen, Rosenberg, Salazar, & Boller, 1989; Macaruso et al., 1993; Noel & Seron, 1993). Within the domain of calculation, dissociations have been reported between operation symbol comprehension and other calculation abilities (Ferro & Botelho, 1980), between retrieval of arithmetic facts and execution of calculation procedures (e.g. Cohen & Dehaene, 1994; Sokol et al., 1991; Warrington, 1982), and between retrieval of arithmetic facts associated with different operations (e.g. Dagenbach & McCloskey, 1992; Lampl, Eshel, Gilad, & Sarova-Pinhas, 1994).

Cognitive neuropsychology and developmental dyscalculia

We believe cognitive neuropsychology can provide a valuable framework on which to study developmental dyscalculia. First, cognitive models built to account for patterns of impaired performance in acquired cases may prove to be good first approximations to models of arrested cognitive development within the same domain. Furthermore, we believe that the basic approach of cognitive neuropsychology, which views behavioural deficits as resulting from specific impairments to an otherwise normal cognitive system, may be as useful in understanding developmental disorders as it has been in understanding acquired ones. Such an approach not only holds much theoretical promise in informing models of cognitive development, but also allows for more precise assessment of cognitive impairments (see Margolin, 1992, on this point, and in particular the chapter by Macaruso, Harley, and McCloskey (1992) on assessment of dyscalculia).

The use of cognitive neuropsychology to investigate developmental disorders has burgeoned in recent years, particularly in the areas of developmental dyslexia and dysgraphia (e.g. Campbell & Butterworth, 1985; Goulandris & Snowling, 1991; Hanley & Gard, 1995; Hulme & Snowling, 1992; Stuart & Howard, 1995; Temple, 1986; Temple & Marshall, 1983). There have also been a limited number of studies in which developmental dyscalculia has been explored from a cognitive neuropsychology perspective (e.g. Sokol et al., 1994; Temple, 1989; 1991). Selected findings from the Sokol et al. study are presently described.

RECENT FINDINGS

These results are based on administration of a modified version of the Johns Hopkins University Dyscalculia Battery to 20 students attending a private school. Students attending the school have a diagnosis of developmental dyslexia. Students were selected for this study on the basis of teacher referrals and test scores indicating weaknesses in basic maths skills. The students ranged in age from 12 to 20 years.

The JHU Dyscalculia Battery consists of tasks designed to probe systematically the numeral processing and calculation mechanisms specified in the McCloskey et al. (1985) model. Magnitude comparison tasks (e.g. Which is larger, *twenty* or *thirteen?*, 83,497 or 84,398?) are used to probe numeral comprehension. Transcoding tasks (e.g. "eighteen" → 18, 4,601 → *four thousand six hundred one*) are used to probe both numeral comprehension and numeral production. The battery also includes single-digit arithmetic problems (e.g. $4 + 7$, 8×5) which are used to probe arithmetic fact retrieval, and multidigit problems (e.g. $617 - 328$, 23×86) which probe both fact retrieval and execution of calculation procedures. (See Macaruso et al., 1992, for further description of the original battery.) In addition to completing the battery, some of the students were administered follow-up tasks. These tasks were selected on an individual basis to obtain more information about the status of particular processing mechanisms.

Overall, the students displayed a wide range of performance levels on the battery. A few students had difficulty on only one or two tasks (e.g. transcoding written verbal numerals into Arabic form), whereas others produced errors on nearly every task. Here we discuss the performance of students who displayed relatively circumscribed forms of impairments in numeric processing.

Numeral processing versus calculation

At the broadest level, the McCloskey et al. model proposes that the cognitive mechanisms involved in numeral comprehension and numeral production are functionally distinct from the mechanisms used to perform calculations. Support for this distinction can be seen in the performance patterns of Rob and Tom. Rob produced errors at a rate of 33% (13/40) in transcoding numerals in the range 101 to 99,999 across four transcoding tasks (spoken-verbal-to-Arabic, spoken-verbal-to-written-verbal, Arabic-to-spoken-verbal, Arabic-to-written-verbal). Examples of his errors include 372 → *three seven hundred two*, and "eight thousand two hundred seventeen" → 8,2017. Rob's poor performance on transcoding tasks suggests a general impairment in numeral processing. In contrast, Rob performed extremely well on arithmetic tasks, responding correctly to 92% (110/120) of the single- and multidigit problems on the battery. His only errors occurred in multidigit division, a source of difficulty for virtually every student in the study. Thus, Rob's calculation mechanisms appeared relatively intact.

According to the McCloskey et al. model, solving arithmetic problems implicates both numeral comprehension and numeral production processes as well as calculation mechanisms. Thus, one might have expected Rob's poor numeral processing skills to affect his arithmetic performance. However, Rob's difficulties in numeral processing occurred mainly for numerals greater than 100. He made just one error in transcoding numerals less than 100 across the four transcoding tasks. Because the component processes involved in calculation (e.g. arithmetic fact retrieval) typically manipulate numerals smaller than 100 (indeed, typically the numbers 0–9), Rob's impaired ability to process large numerals did not affect his arithmetic performance. Thus, Rob shows relatively intact calculation in the face of impaired numeral processing.

The opposite pattern was displayed by Tom. Tom produced just one error in transcoding numerals smaller than 100 across the four transcoding tasks, and his error rate for numerals in the range 101 to 99,999 was only 10% (4/40). These results suggest at most only minor difficulties in numeral comprehension and numeral production. In contrast, Tom erred on 27% (32/120) of the single- and multidigit arithmetic problems on the battery. Of his 32 errors, 28 occurred in multiplication and division. For example, Tom wrote 50 in response to 4 × 5, and responded "six" to "fifty-six divided by seven". On follow-up tests of single-digit multiplication and division, Tom erred on 28% (140/495) of the multiplication problems, and 44% (115/259) of the division problems. In sum, Tom displayed poor calculation skills in the face of basically intact numeral processing abilities.

Arabic versus verbal numeral processing

According to the McCloskey et al. (1985) model, the processing of Arabic numerals is subserved by separate mechanisms from the processing of verbal numerals. Evidence for this distinction can be seen in Chuck's numeral transcoding performance. Chuck had much more difficulty on transcoding tasks requiring the production of Arabic numerals than on transcoding tasks involving verbal numeral production. For instance, he produced errors at a rate of 44% (29/66) in spoken-verbal-to-Arabic transcoding for numerals in the range 101 to 999,999. Examples of his errors include "five hundred six thousand one" → 5,061, and "nine thousand nine hundred thirty" → 9,9030. The fact that Chuck showed excellent performance in magnitude comparison for spoken verbal numerals in the same range (28/30 correct) suggests that his errors in spoken-verbal-to-Arabic transcoding were not due to faulty comprehension of spoken verbal numerals but to an impairment in production of Arabic numerals. Chuck's 52% (34/66) error rate in written-verbal-to-Arabic transcoding of numerals in the same range (e.g. *one hundred three thousand five hundred* → 100,305) provides further evidence for an impairment in Arabic numeral production. In comparison to his poor performance on transcoding tasks requiring the production of Arabic numerals, Chuck had more success on transcoding tasks involving the production of verbal numerals. For example, his error rate was only 18% (12/66) in Arabic-to-spoken-verbal transcoding for numerals in the range 101 to 999,999. These results support a distinction between Arabic and verbal numeral production.

Additional support for this distinction can be seen in Joe's performance pattern. Whereas Chuck was impaired in Arabic numeral production, Joe had difficulty in verbal numeral production. Joe made no errors on the battery in spoken-verbal-to-Arabic transcoding of numerals in the range 101 to 99,999, which suggests intact comprehension of spoken verbal numerals and intact production of Arabic numerals. In contrast, he responded incorrectly to 40% (4/10) of the items in spoken-verbal-to-written-verbal transcoding for numerals in the same range. For example, in response to "eighteen thousand one hundred forty-five", Joe wrote *eight thosd seven hundd forty five*. (Spelling errors were overlooked in scoring written verbal responses.) Because Joe's comprehension of spoken verbal numerals appears intact, his poor performance in spoken-verbal-to-written-verbal transcoding suggests an impairment in written verbal numeral production. Converging evidence for this claim is seen in the Arabic-to-written-verbal task. On this task, Joe made 50% (5/10) errors on numerals in the same range as above, despite apparently intact Arabic comprehension. Given a rather limited amount of data, however, our conclusions concerning Joe's performance pattern must remain tentative.

Lexical versus syntactic processing

The distinction between lexical and syntactic processing is readily apparent in the errors produced by Robyn on transcoding tasks requiring the production of Arabic numerals. For numerals in the range 101 to 999,999, her error rate was 40% (21/52) in spoken-verbal-to-Arabic transcoding and 48% (25/52) in written-verbal-to-Arabic transcoding. As illustrated in Table 9.1, Robyn's errors nearly always preserved the lexical identity of the nonzero digits, but were syntactically ill-formed (e.g. "one hundred ninety-four thousand five" → 19405). Ninety-six per cent (44/46) of her errors were pure syntactic errors in which the nonzero digits were correct but the response was of the wrong order of magnitude. Only two responses contained a lexical error (e.g. "sixty-*seven* thousand three hundred four" → *60*,304). In contrast to the error pattern displayed by Robyn, Temple (1989) described an 11-year-old boy with developmental dyscalculia who produced predominately lexical errors on numeral transcoding tasks (e.g. *"seven* hundred eleven" → *5*11; *85* → "eighty-*two*").

Analysis of syntactic errors

Recent studies have examined the syntactic errors produced by young children in writing Arabic numerals to dictation (e.g. Power & Dal Martello, 1990; Seron, Deloche, & Noel, 1992). Most of the errors reported in these papers show a consistent pattern, as seen in the following examples from Power and Dal Martello: "due cento cinque" (205) → 2005; "tre mila cinque cento otto" (3508) → 30005008. Power and Dal Martello claim that children produce errors of this sort because they fail to apply "overwrite rules". For instance, transcoding "due cento cinque" requires application of a rule in which 5 is written over the final 0 of 200 to produce 205. Instead, children apply concatenation rules

TABLE 9.1
Examples of Robyn's errors on numeral transcoding tasks

Stimulus	*Response*
Spoken-verbal-to-arabic	
"five hundred eleven"	5011
"eight thousand sixty-seven"	867
"one hundred ninety-four thousand five"	19,405
"eight hundred seven thousand three hundred twenty-three"	87,323
Written-verbal-to-arabic	
nine thousand six	906
five hundred four thousand	54,000
three hundred thousand four	304
eight hundred five thousand nine hundred forty	85,940

in which 5 is appended to 200 to produce 2005. A related explanation based on literal transcoding is given by Seron et al. (1992).

As discussed earlier, Chuck produced numerous errors on transcoding tasks involving the production of Arabic numerals and, like Robyn, most of his errors were syntactic (e.g. "sixty-six thousand one hundred five" → 66,15). Sullivan, Macaruso, and Sokol (1996) conducted a detailed analysis of Chuck's syntactic errors and found that they were extremely inconsistent. Whereas some of his errors were longer than the correct response (e.g. "fourteen thousand four hundred ninety" → 14,400,90), most of his errors were shorter than or the same length as the correct response (e.g. "five hundred six thousand one" → 5,061; *two hundred thirty thousand five hundred seven* → 200,357). The inconsistent nature of Chuck's errors does not conform to what would be expected if he were applying concatenation rules to construct Arabic numerals (see Power & Dal Martello, 1990).

Sullivan et al. also tested normal third- and fourth-graders on a subset of items given to Chuck and discovered that the children's error patterns resembled Chuck's. That is, highly inconsistent errors were seen both across and within individuals. Any model of the development of numeral transcoding skills needs to take into account the diversity of errors displayed by Chuck and other children tested in Sullivan et al. (1996).

Arithmetic facts versus execution of calculation procedures

In the domain of calculation, the McCloskey et al. model separates the processes involved in retrieval of arithmetic facts from those involved in the execution of calculation procedures. Support for this distinction is evident when we compare the arithmetic performance of Matt and Robyn. Matt made many errors in fact retrieval but had few problems in executing calculation procedures. Robyn, on the other hand, showed excellent knowledge of arithmetic facts, but made numerous procedural errors in solving multidigit problems.

The double dissociation is most evident when we compare Matt and Robyn's multiplication performance. Matt's success rate in solving single-digit multiplication problems was only 66% (342/518). For problems in the range 6 × 6 through 9 × 9, his success rate dropped to 17% (14/82). Examples of his errors include "forty-six" in response to "seven times seven" and 65 to 8 × 9.

In contrast to his poor fact retrieval performance, Matt was quite successful in carrying out the procedures required to solve multidigit problems. For instance, he responded correctly to 60% (6/10) of the multidigit multiplication problems on the battery. Only one of his error responses was clearly due to a problem in executing the multiplication procedure. When Matt was provided with a "cheat sheet" containing the 100 multiplication facts with answers, his success rate in solving multidigit problems rose to 83% (15/18). Of his three errors, none could be clearly attributed to a procedural difficulty. Two of his errors were due to faulty fact retrieval, and one was ambiguous. The fact retrieval errors occurred because Matt sometimes forgot to consult his facts sheet.

The left column of Fig. 9.2 shows examples of Matt's fact retrieval errors in the context of accurately carrying out the multiplication procedure. In the first problem, Matt retrieved the incorrect answer 35 to 6×7 (correctly carrying the 1); in the second problem he again incorrectly retrieved 35, this time as the product of 5×6; finally, in the third example, he retrieved 27 as the product of 7×3. These results show that Matt's difficulties in solving multiplication problems arose from an impairment in fact retrieval and not from difficulties in execution of the multiplication procedure.

The opposite pattern is seen in the multiplication performance of Robyn. In response to 120 single-digit multiplication problems, Robyn's success rate was 93%. All of her errors except one were instances in which Robyn responded N to a $0 \times N$ problem (e.g. $0 \times 6 = 6$). Answers to problems like $0 \times N$ are presumably solved by rule (i.e. $0 \times N = 0$), and thus errors like $0 \times N = N$ appear to reflect the application of the wrong rule rather than a problem in fact retrieval *per se*. (The distinction between arithmetic fact retrieval and application of rules is discussed in a later section.)

Although Robyn displayed excellent fact retrieval abilities, she had a great deal of difficulty solving multidigit multiplication problems. Her success rate in solving the same problems presented to Matt was only 39% (11/28). Of her 17 error responses, 12 contained at least one mistake in applying the multiplication procedure. Only one contained a clear multiplication fact error, and four were ambiguous.

Examples of Robyn's errors in executing the multiplication procedure are shown in the right column of Fig. 9.2. In the first problem, although she retrieves the correct answers to 6×2 and 6×7, she makes several procedural errors, which include neglecting to carry the 1 from the partial product 12, failing to shift the second row of partial products, and omitting the required final addition procedure. In the second problem, regardless of the product obtained she apparently carries a 1; then she neglects the 3×0 product, carrying the 1 to the 3×8 product; also, she misaligns her partial products, thus leaving out the left-most zero in the first row's partial product during the addition procedure. In the final example, she inappropriately adds the carry digit 6 from the first row of partial products to the second (i.e. to the product of 1×1).

In summary, the contrast between Matt and Robyn's multiplication performance provides strong support for the processing distinction between arithmetic fact retrieval and execution of calculation procedures proposed in the McCloskey et al. model. A similar double dissociation seen in developmental dyscalculia has been reported in Temple (1991).

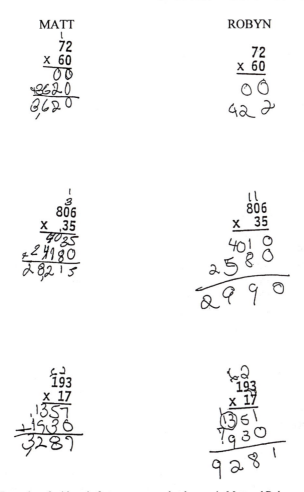

FIG. 9.2. Examples of arithmetic fact versus procedural errors in Matt and Robyn.

Calculation versus approximation

Although not made explicit in the McCloskey et al. model, a distinction between calculation and approximation has been included in other models of numeric processing (e.g. Dehaene, 1992). One task commonly used to assess approximation is computational estimation (e.g. Is 2000 a reasonable estimate of 43 × 52?). According to Sowder (1992b), success in computational estimation requires strong number sense, that is a well-organized conceptual understanding of numerical magnitudes and how they relate to properties of arithmetic operations.

Evidence in support of a distinction between calculation and approximation can be found in both acquired and developmental dyscalculia. For example,

Dehaene and Cohen (1991) discuss a patient with acquired dyscalculia who produced numerous errors in solving simple calculations (e.g. $2 + 2 = 3$) but quickly rejected implausible answers on an estimation task (e.g. Is $2 + 2 = 9$ correct?). Dehaene and Cohen concluded that the patient lost the ability to carry out precise arithmetic operations while retaining the ability to activate approximate quantity information (see also Warrington, 1982). Russell and Ginsburg (1984) reported that children with "mathematics difficulty" who show subpar performance on single- and multidigit calculations are able to judge whether an answer is close in magnitude to the correct answer on an estimation task (e.g. Is 926 close to or far away from the real answer to $53 + 28$?).

The opposite dissociation—excellent calculation in the face of poor approximation abilities—can be seen in the performance of our subject Doug. In solving single-digit addition, subtraction, multiplication, and division problems, Doug responded with 97% (551/570) accuracy. Doug also solved 90% (27/30) of the multidigit addition, subtraction, and multiplication problems on the battery, and answered an additional set of multidigit multiplication problems with 89% (16/18) accuracy. Overall, Doug's calculation performance was superior to that of nearly all of the students in our study.

In contrast to his excellent calculation skills, Doug had a great deal of difficulty with computational estimation. Doug was asked to select the correct answer (out of four) to arithmetic problems without performing any calculations (e.g. $40 \times 20 = 80\ 800\ 8000\ 80,000$; $5 \times 52 = 110\ 2,500\ 260\ 560$). He was presented with 54 multiplication, 10 division, 5 addition, and 5 subtraction problems. His success rate was 41% (22/54) for multiplication, and 50% (10/20) across the other operations. To gauge how poorly Doug performed on this task, we compared his performance with Tom's on the same task. Recall that Tom produced numerous errors in single- and multidigit calculations. Despite his poor calculation skills, Tom outperformed Doug on the approximation task. Tom's success rate of 63% (34/54) for multiplication was significantly higher than Doug's 41% success rate. Tom also scored higher than Doug across the other operations (14/20 correct). When Doug was given the four choice task a second time with scrap paper to help him derive the correct answer, his performance improved dramatically. He responded correctly to 91% (49/54) of the multiplication problems, and 90% (18/20) of the other problems.

In Dehaene's model (1992), approximation includes not only computational estimation but also quantitative estimation. In quantitative estimation subjects are asked to provide numerical estimates to real-world objects or events (Brown & Siegler, 1993). An example of a quantitative estimation question would be: "About how many miles is it from Boston to Los Angeles?". As in the case of computational estimation, Doug performed poorly in quantitative estimation. When asked to answer 10 quantitative estimation questions, Doug's responses fell completely outside of the range of answers given by 38 age-matched control subjects on three of the 10 questions. For example, Doug responded "ninety-six" to the Boston-Los Angeles distance question.

Doug was not alone in his problems with quantitative estimation. Indeed, on the first eight questions involving relatively small quantities, our dyscalculic subjects gave deviant responses (i.e. greater than two standard deviations from the control mean) 24% of the time (38/160 responses). On the two remaining questions that involved large quantities, both dyscalculic and control subjects gave a wide range of responses, leading to very large standard deviations. Therefore, the dyscalculic subjects were considered to give a deviant response if it fell entirely outside the control range. Here, such responses accounted for virtually the same proportion: 25% (10/40). These data are illustrated in Table 9.2 along with the mode response(s) of normal control subjects. (See Sokol, Macaruso, & Gollan, 1991 for further discussion.)

In summary, these results show that approximation skills may dissociate from calculation abilities, and more generally that approximation is an area of difficulty for many students with developmental dyscalculia. Further research is needed to systematically explore the extent to which successful acquisition of approximation is dependent on or may occur independent of calculation skills (see Macaruso & Albertson, 1996), and whether different forms of approximation (i.e. computational and quantitative estimation) tap into dissociable or common underlying mechanisms.

FUTURE DIRECTIONS

In this final section we discuss a number of directions in which future research in developmental dyscalculia may enhance our understanding of normal mathematical development. First we consider other research findings in the domains of cognitive arithmetic and developmental dyscalculia not specifically targeted in the McCloskey et al. (1985) model. Second, we introduce current issues in

TABLE 9.2
Examples of quantitative estimation errors of dyscalculic students

Question	Control mode	% Deviant	Example of response	
Length of a bus	20 (ft)	20	300 (ft)	(Joe)
Slices of bread in a loaf	15, 20	30	50	(Heather)
Sections in an orange	8	30	20	(Dana)
Height of (quart) milk carton	12 (in)	25	2 (in)	(Rob)
Spokes on a bicycle wheel	20, 30	15	100	(Sean)
Weight of a brick	5 (lbs)	25	100	(Robyn)
Grapes in a bunch	25	30	100	(Chris)
Height of a giraffe	20	15	48 (ft)	(Tim)
Population of the US	250,000,000	30	32,000	(Doug)
Distance from Boston to LA	3000	20	72 miles	(Matt)

acquired dyscalculia research and how studies in developmental dyscalculia could potentially address these issues.

Efficiency in basic processes

One area that has received relatively little attention concerns efficiency of basic numeric processes in individuals with developmental dyscalculia. For instance, given specific numeric stimuli (e.g. the Arabic digit 4, the spoken numeral "nine") how rapidly can quantity representations associated with these stimuli become activated and how precise are these representations? Koontz and Berch (1996) have recently begun to explore questions of this sort by comparing the response times of students with arithmetic learning disabilities (ALD) and age-matched controls on physical and name (quantity) matching tasks using the digits 2 and 3 and corresponding dot patterns (e.g. 2 – 2 is a physical match and a name match, whereas 2 – •• is a name match only). They report that the ALD group is no slower than the control group in speed of access to quantity representations, but that the ALD students show more interference than controls from irrelevant physical information in name-match judgements, and, unlike controls, are slower with 3-dot patterns than 2-dot patterns. This latter finding suggests that the ALD students suffer from inefficiency in subitizing (i.e. fast and accurate reporting of quantities associated with small arrays of elements), such that on occasion they must rely on dot counting to derive quantities.

Although interesting, the initial findings of Koontz and Berch are quite limited. Further exploration into speed of access to quantity information should encompass a broader range of quantities and would benefit from tasks, such as magnitude comparisons, that look at relationships between quantities (see Holender & Peereman, 1987). More fundamentally, research in developmental dyscalculia should consider how processing inefficiencies at these basic levels impact on more complex tasks that depend on them (e.g. arithmetic fact retrieval, calculation procedures, estimation). We suspect that the depth of experimentation and analyses required to uncover these relationships will be best suited to single-case investigations (e.g. Weddell & Davidoff, 1991).

Working memory and mental arithmetic

As reviewed earlier, a number of group studies have reported that children with arithmetic learning disabilities suffer from deficiencies in working memory (e.g. Fletcher, 1985; Shafrir & Siegel, 1994; Siegel & Ryan, 1989). However, a major shortcoming of these studies is that they fail to look at working memory functioning as it relates directly to arithmetic performance.

Such an approach has been taken in the literature on normal cognitive functioning. For example, Hitch (1978a) conducted a seminal study on working memory in mental arithmetic in which subjects heard orally presented multi-digit addition problems and were asked to write answers in the conventional right-to-left manner or in reverse order. Hitch found that performance declined as a function of number of operands in the problem, the number of embedded carry operations, and the order of writing answers. Hitch concluded that each of these manipulations affected different facets of working memory.

Ashcraft (1995) has recently proposed how components of Baddeley's (1986) working memory model may be employed in mental arithmetic. The central executive component of working memory would be responsible for carrying out calculation procedures including retrieval of arithmetic facts. The articulatory loop, a slave system of the central executive, would be involved in counting and holding intermediate values in working memory. A second slave system of the central executive, the visuospatial sketchpad would be used to maintain column-wise position information required for operations such as carrying.

This above model could serve as a basis for investigating how limitations in working memory may contribute to poor arithmetic performance. Tasks could be constructed that target the involvement of each system (e.g. one could systematically manipulate the number of intermediate values to be held in working memory to assess functioning of the articulatory loop). Performance on these tasks may then reveal the specific types of working memory disturbances which impact on the arithmetic abilities of students with developmental dyscalculia.

Counting and arithmetic fact retrieval

Earlier we pointed out the robust finding that automatic recall of basic arithmetic facts is problematic for many students with arithmetic learning disabilities (e.g. Garnett & Fleischner, 1983; Russell & Ginsburg, 1984). Studies in mathematics education show that basic arithmetic facts are first solved via counting routines and eventually these routines are replaced by direct retrieval of answers from long-term memory (Fuson, 1992).

A series of studies by Geary and his associates have explored single-digit addition performance in children with arithmetic learning disabilities (for review, see Geary, 1993). For instance, Geary, Widaman, Little, and Cormier (1987) found that whereas normal children typically shift from counting in grade 2 to direct memory retrieval in grades 4 and 6, most arithmetic-disabled children rely on counting strategies in all three grades (see also Geary et al., 1991), and that arithmetic-disabled second-graders count more slowly, produce more errors, and are more variable in their application of counting strategies than normal second-graders. In a subsequent study, Geary (1990) showed that when memory retrieval is used instead of counting, arithmetic-disabled first and second-graders produce a higher proportion of retrieval errors and less systematic solution times than normal children (see also Geary & Brown, 1991).

These above findings suggest a relationship between poor counting skills and subsequent difficulties in direct retrieval of arithmetic facts (Geary, 1993). In Siegler's (1988) distribution of associations model of arithmetic fact retrieval, erroneous answers to arithmetic problems based on faulty application of counting routines become associated with the problems in long-term memory and contribute to difficulties in direct retrieval of correct answers.

Our own studies suggest, however, that for some individuals with developmental dyscalculia, poor arithmetic fact retrieval may not be tied to inefficient counting. For instance, Macaruso and Buchman (1996) discuss a well-educated adult female with developmental dyscalculia who has difficulty in direct retrieval of basic addition and subtraction facts (but, incidentally, has no trouble recalling other types of factual information from long-term memory). She relies heavily on counting strategies to arrive at fact answers, and applies these strategies very efficiently. Extensive training in rote memorization of addition facts led to improved recall of addition (and subtraction) facts in the short term, but performance declined once training ended. These findings hint at the selective and perhaps irreparable nature of arithmetic fact retrieval impairments in some cases of developmental dyscalculia, and suggest that the relationship between counting skills and subsequent retrieval of facts is not as straightforward as one might assume.

Dyscalculia and dyslexia

Following the work of Rourke (1993) and others (see Gordon, 1992, for review) we might expect to find distinct types of arithmetic disturbances in individuals who have concomitant difficulties in reading/spelling (i.e. left-hemisphere dysfunction) and those who do not (i.e. right-hemisphere dysfunction). In this chapter, we presented data on the numeric processing performance of dyslexic students who had difficulty in arithmetic, and discovered even in this rather homogenous group a variety of circumscribed disturbances; some students had problems one might expect to be associated with reading/spelling impairments (e.g. reading aloud Arabic numerals; retrieval of arithmetic facts), whereas others had quite different disturbances (e.g. carrying out arithmetic procedures in multidigit multiplication). In this regard our results corroborate the findings of Shalev et al. (1995) in that apparently little is gained from a left hemisphere/right hemisphere dichotomy when examining numeric processing errors.

Perhaps, though, we should not be surprised by the apparent mismatch between our data (and others) and the expectations of group results based on a rather impoverished understanding of cognitive specialization in the cerebral hemispheres. Indeed, even when empirical expectations stem from cognitive considerations (as opposed to mainly neuroanatomical ones), the theoretical links proposed are often rather superficial. One excerpt from Geary (1993,

p. 356) underscores some of these points. Geary is speaking here about the co-occurrence of mathematical disability and reading disability.

> For many children, MD and RD co-occur because of a common underlying neuro-psychological deficit, perhaps involving the posterior regions of the left hemisphere. At the cognitive level, this deficit manifests itself as difficulties in the representation and retrieval of semantic information from long-term memory. This would include fact-retrieval problems in simple arithmetic and, for instance, word-recognition and phonological-awareness difficulties in reading.

A basic problem with this type of proposal is its lack of specificity. Difficulties in "the representation and retrieval of semantic information from long-term memory" could account for a broad range of cognitive impairments, in an equally broad range of cognitive domains (including but certainly not limited to arithmetic or reading). Geary extends this locus of impairment even further when he encapsulates phonological-awareness difficulties within semantic memory. This is far from an obvious inclusion; application of phonological knowledge (such as reading or spelling through use of letter-to-sound correspondences) would not normally be considered a part of semantic memory. Thus, the implied model of reading to which the mathematical domain (i.e. fact retrieval) is being compared is too broad to support any useful generalizations.

This criticism noted, the co-occurrence of cognitive impairments in students with learning disabilities should not be ignored. Furthermore, it may be possible to limit the purview of a theory such as Geary's to render it more empirically useful. For example, rather than assuming a gross impairment in the representation and retrieval of semantic information *in toto*, perhaps the problem lies more specifically in transitioning from the application of early acquired procedures (counting skills, grapheme-phoneme conversion) to more direct memory retrieval. Targeting the theory at this stage of development may permit more careful empirical observation, as well as better informed remedial efforts.

In conclusion of this section, two additional points should be made. Although we agree that it may be useful to attempt to understand symptom comorbidity in learning-disabled students, it may ultimately turn out that the highly modular nature of cognition (let alone its complexity) renders such an attempt unproductive. Furthermore, as we have stated previously (Sokol et al., 1994), it seems more important at the present time to try to understand the numeric (or any other specific cognitive) impairments themselves in affected individuals than it is to speculate about their co-morbidity with other cognitive impairments (see Marshall, 1989 on this same point).

Arithmetic facts versus application of rules

Most cognitive models assume that answers to basic arithmetic facts (e.g. 6 × 7 = 42; 6 × 8 = 48) are stored as individual fact representations (see Ashcraft,

1992). Some arithmetic facts, however, may be stored in the form of general rules. For example, given that the product of any multiplication with zero is zero, it would seem more parsimonious to assume that retrieval of an answer to a zero product would be done via such a rule. Indeed, many researchers have either implicitly or explicitly assumed this to be the case (e.g. Baroody, 1983; Campbell & Graham, 1985; Miller, Perlmutter, & Keating, 1984). Other examples of potential rule-based retrieval include addition by zero ($N + 0 = N$) and multiplication by one ($N \times 1 = N$).

In the acquired dyscalculia literature there has been a fair amount of evidence supporting a rule-based account, at least for multiplication by zero (see Sokol & McCloskey, 1991, for review). For example, Sokol & McCloskey discuss patient AT, who had a severe impairment in arithmetic fact retrieval, including an inability to solve correctly any single-digit problem involving zero. AT participated in a remediation program in which several multiplication facts were selected for retraining, including two involving zero ($0 \times 6 = 0$ and $3 \times 0 = 0$). After training, AT responded correctly to all $0 \times N$ problems, not only those on which she was explicitly trained. This suggests that AT had reacquired a general rule $0 \times N = 0$ that she applied to all zero problems. Recovery of nonstudied facts was observed only for the zero problems; no recovery was observed for nonstudied nonzero facts. For example, before training AT was 0% correct for the problem 3×4. She remained completely impaired on this fact after training even though a number of different facts with operands 3 and 4 were trained (i.e. other than 3×4). These results suggest that a single rule underlies retrieval of zero products in contrast to nonzero facts.

Although the data in the acquired literature are fairly strong in this regard, we are not aware of any systematic investigation of rule-based fact retrieval in developmental dyscalculia. Given the difficulties that these students have in learning individual arithmetic facts, it might be the case that they have less difficulty solving facts that require application of simple rules. Alternatively, we might discover that acquiring any type of number-related declarative information (facts or rules) is problematic for students with arithmetic learning disabilities.

Multiple numeral transcoding routes

A number of recent findings from acquired dyscalculia have suggested modifications to the McCloskey et al. model. One area of interest concerns the internal processes employed in transcoding numerals from one form to another. According to the McCloskey et al. model, numeral transcoding is a semantically mediated process. The stimulus numeral is first converted into a semantic (magnitude) representation, which is then transformed into a specific response format (see Macaruso et al., 1993, for evidence of semantic mediation in numeral transcoding).

An alternative approach to modelling numeral transcoding is presented in Deloche and Seron (1987). They describe numeral transcoding in terms of asemantic transcoding processes that convert stimulus-related representations (e.g. lexical primitives for verbal numerals) into response-related representations (e.g. Arabic digit forms) without computing an internal semantic representation. As pointed out by McCloskey (1992), however, these asemantic transcoding routes would have to be posited *in addition to* semantic routes. In many instances when people process numerals, the meaning of the numeral is of central importance (e.g. reading a price tag to determine whether to purchase an item). Indeed, recent models of numeral transcoding have included both semantic and asemantic routes (e.g. Dehaene, 1992).

Evidence presented in support of multiple transcoding routes comes from the work of Cipolotti (1995; Cipolotti & Butterworth, 1995) and others (e.g. Cohen, Dehaene, & Verstichel, 1994; see Seron & Noel, 1995, for a review and critique of the evidence). For instance, Cipolotti (1995) discusses patient SF who had difficulty reading aloud Arabic numerals (e.g. 15,702) but not reading aloud verbal numerals (e.g. *fifteen thousand seven hundred two*). According to the McCloskey et al. model, SF's poor Arabic-to-spoken-verbal transcoding performance should reflect impairments to a semantically mediated transcoding process—either in comprehension of Arabic numerals, production of spoken verbal numerals, or both. However, SF performed well on tasks assessing comprehension of Arabic numerals (e.g. magnitude comparisons) and on tasks requiring the production of spoken verbal numerals (e.g. saying aloud the answers to number fact questions). To account for these findings, Cipolotti argues that SF suffers from damage to an asemantic transcoding route used to convert Arabic numerals into verbal form. To explain why SF did not make use of a semantic transcoding route, Cipolotti suggests that the specific task of "reading aloud Arabic numerals" activates the asemantic route, which in turn inhibits the semantic route.

Detailed investigations of numeral transcoding performance in developmental dyscalculia could shed light on the issue of multiple routes in numeral transcoding. For instance, studies of children who show poor understanding of magnitude for verbal numerals yet have no difficulty transcoding verbal numerals into Arabic form would provide support for asemantic routes in numeral transcoding.

Representational form for arithmetic facts

Another area in which modifications to the McCloskey et al. model have been suggested concerns the representational form in which basic arithmetic facts are stored in long-term memory. According to the McCloskey et al. model, regardless of the format in which a stimulus problem is presented, the problem is first converted into an internal semantic representation and this representation is then used to access a semantic representation of the answer. Sokol et al. (1991) provide support for this proposal in their study of patient PS, who had an acquired impairment in retrieval of multiplication facts. PS was asked to solve sets of 100 multiplication facts (0 × 0 through 9 × 9) in which the input and output formats were systematically varied among Arabic numbers, written verbal numbers, and numbers presented as columns of dots. PS's overall error rate, error rates on individual problems, and pattern of errors were extremely similar across tasks. These results suggest that PS's performance was mediated by a common representational form for arithmetic facts independent of stimulus and response formats.

The claim that arithmetic fact retrieval is based on a unitary form of representation has also been proposed by Dehaene (1992). However, in Dehaene's model the unitary representation is not semantic, but verbal in nature. Arithmetic facts are initially transcoded into a verbal word frame, which is then used to trigger retrieval of the answer in the same representational form. More recently, Dehaene and Cohen (1995) suggest that verbal word frame representations are localized in the left hemisphere.

Another possibility is that there are multiple forms of representation for arithmetic facts and the particular one employed depends on the format in which problems are presented (Campbell, 1994). Neuropsychological evidence in support of this proposal comes from a study by McNeil and Warrington (1994). Their patient HAR had difficulty with basic addition facts when problems were presented in Arabic format but not when problems were presented in spoken format. According to the McCloskey et al. model, this performance pattern might suggest a comprehension impairment for Arabic numerals. However, HAR had no trouble with subtraction facts presented in Arabic format which argues against an Arabic comprehension impairment. McNeil and Warrington provide an interpretation of HAR's performance pattern in terms of separate verbal and visual calculators. In the case of addition, the verbal calculator is preferred and so HAR must convert Arabic input into verbal number names prior to fact retrieval. The fact that HAR makes errors in reading aloud Arabic digits implies that this conversion process is faulty. Addition errors that occur with Arabic input are attributed to the conversion process. In the case of subtraction, no conversion is necessary because Arabic input is processed directly by the visual calculator, which, like the verbal calculator, is not impaired (see Dehaene & Cohen, 1995, for a different interpretation of these results).

Studies of developmental dyscalculia may be conducted to address these representational issues. For instance, do children who have difficulty in arithmetic fact retrieval show similar or dissimilar performance patterns (e.g. error rates, error types) across stimulus and response formats? Do the effects of training arithmetic facts in one stimulus format generalize across formats (see Macaruso & Buchman, 1996) or are they restricted to the trained format? Do errors made by children suggest activation of semantic representations or verbal word forms? Answers to these questions should help decide between competing proposals regarding representational forms for arithmetic facts.

CONCLUDING REMARKS

In this chapter, we have attempted to show how data from individuals with arithmetic learning disability can help inform our understanding of the normal processing components required of arithmetic computation, and the ways in which they develop. We began by reviewing how previous group and single-case studies have investigated arithmetic learning disabilities, and pointed out some of the theoretical and methodological problems associated with these approaches. In our own investigations of arithmetic learning disability, we turned to the cognitive neuropsychological paradigm, and specifically to a body of scientific work in acquired dyscalculia, which helped us model the disordered development seen in our experimental subjects. Although no approach is free of shortcomings, we believe strongly that when viewed from the proper theoretical perspective, neuropsychological data offer one of the most unique and informative windows on cognitive development. We hope that this brief foray into arithmetic learning disability will encourage others to pursue issues in the field, and in so doing provide greater opportunity for scientific and clinical progress.

ACKNOWLEDGMENTS

We are grateful to the students, teachers and administrators at the Landmark School, Prides Crossings, Massachusetts, for their cooperation. We also thank Tamar Gollan and Kara Sullivan for their valuable contributions to our research.

CHAPTER TEN

Is hearing impairment a cause of difficulties in learning mathematics?

Terezinha Nunes & Constanza Moreno
Institute of Education, University of London, UK

Research has consistently shown that deaf children lag substantially behind hearing children of the same age in mathematics achievement tests. The aim of this chapter is to consider evidence on and the explanations for this delay. We first review evidence that goes against a causal link betwen hearing loss and difficulties in learning mathematics. We then suggest an alternative hypothesis and attempt to show that hearing and hearing-impaired children deal with the obstacles in the development of basic mathematical concepts in essentially the same manner.

HEARING-IMPAIRED CHILDREN'S MATHEMATICS ACHIEVEMENT

A report by the National Council of Teachers of the Deaf (1957) on a study carried out in four schools in England and using the Schonell Arithmetic Test (Essential Mechanical Arithmetic and Diagnostic Mechanical Arithmetic) showed an average difference of 2.5 years between deaf children ($n = 246$) and the standardized norms. About a decade later, Wollman (1965) tested approximately one-third of the pupils from 13 schools for the deaf in the United Kingdom and a comparison group of 162 pupils in secondary modern schools.[1] Hearing-impaired pupils were once again found to perform significantly lower: their average was about one standard deviation below the norms. In this study, a large proportion of pupils "showed a skill in simple arithmetical processes (four rules) ... Far more errors were attributable to lack of understanding than to mistakes in calculation" (Wollman, 1965, p. 126). Unfortunately, the situation was much the same two decades later. Wood, Wood, and Howarth (1983) carried out a survey including 80 schools in England and Wales on a similar population of hearing-impaired (n = 414) and secondary modern hearing pupils (n = 465). They used the Vernon and Miller (1976) Graded Arithmetic Test, which they describe as containing little written instruction, in an attempt to avoid confounding with reading comprehension. The hearing-impaired youngsters were on the average 3.4 years behind their hearing counterparts.

Research using nonstandardized tests has also found poor results in problem solving among hearing-impaired youngsters. Their performance on conservation tasks (Watts, 1981; 1982), the Tower of Hanoi (Luckner & McNeill, 1994), and arithmetic problems presented in writing (Pau, 1995) is significantly poorer than the performance of hearing youngster of the same age level.

Despite the consistency in the results of comparisons between hearing and hearing-impaired youngsters' mathematical abilities, the reasons for the poor performance of the latter group remain unclear. When the mathematics assessment involves a considerable amount of reading, the results correlate with reading comprehension (Pau, 1995); reading comprehension is also correlated with vocabulary and the mathematical vocabulary of deaf pupils has been found wanting at least in residential pupils (Kidd, Madsen, & Lamb, 1991). In these cases, reading comprehension could be a cause of poor performance in mathematics tests. In a study in England and Wales, Conrad (1979) found that school leavers (15 to 16 years of age) were reading on the average about 6 years behind their age level. Thus, their reading difficulty would be a cause of their poor performance in mathematics achievement tests. However, the explanation in terms of reading comprehension cannot account for poor performance in tasks that do not involve reading—for example, in studies using the Tower of Hanoi or conservation tasks.

Another possibility is that, in tests where reading is involved, reading comprehension acts as a mediator of poor performance but the real cause is hearing loss: Because reading comprehension relates to degree of hearing loss (Wollman, 1965), hearing loss might be the underlying cause of poor mathematical achievement whereas reading comprehension mediates the relationship. In other, oral mathematical tasks, hearing loss is directly related to poor performance.

This hypothesis would lead to the prediction that hearing loss is related to poor performance in mathematics tests. It is consistent with the fact that pupils attending mainstream schools with units for the hearing impaired showed a smaller delay in the Vernon and Miller test than those from special schools for the deaf (Wood et al., 1983). If the children in mainstream schools with units for the hearing impaired are those who have a lower level of hearing loss, then the level of hearing loss might be a direct explanation for the poor performance in mathematics tests. However, results in mathematics assessments are weakly related to degree of hearing loss in some studies (Wood et al., 1983, found a correlation of $-.13$) and in others not at all (Wollman, 1965).

Considering the negative results regarding a straightforward relationship between hearing loss and mathematics achievement and the important difference observed between the performance of youngsters attending special schools for the deaf and those attending mainstream schools, Wood, Wood, Kingsmill, French, and Howarth (1984) then hypothesized that special educational provision for the deaf might be deficient in mathematics teaching because teachers of the deaf focus much of their effort on teaching oral and written language. They reasoned that those pupils attending schools with units for the hearing impaired might actually be receiving better mathematics instruction when working in the regular classrooms—and this would account for their better performance in comparison with youngsters attending schools for the deaf. They tested this hypothesis by fitting a series of regression models to the prediction of mathematics achievement in the hearing impaired, including degree of hearing loss, school background, and sex as possible predictors. They tested both linear and nonlinear models. The best-fitting model with these three variables was a linear model, where result from the audiogram was the strongest predictor; however, only 8% of the variance in mathematics performance was accounted for. If type of school provision was dropped from the model, there was no significant decrease in the amount of variance explained. This result is inconsistent with the hypothesis that type of school provision might explain the difference in performance between youngsters in schools for the deaf and those in mainstream schools. The low level of success of their models led Wood and colleagues to conclude that "the major determinants of mathematical ability in hearing-impaired children must lie outside the factors explored here" (Wood, Wood, Kingsmill, French, & Howarth, 1984, p. 258)—namely, sex, level of hearing loss, and type of school provision.

Research on number processing has not led to better insights into the reasons for the differences between hearing and hearing-impaired children in mathematics. Hitch, Arnold, and Phillips (1983) hypothesized that deaf children's poor performance in arithmetic would be explained by their lack of subvocal, covert strategies that mediate hearing children's superior performance in arithmetic tasks. The method used in their study was a response time analysis of decisions about whether a sum of the form $m + n = p$ was correct. Their prediction was that hearing-impaired and hearing children should be found to differ in their number processing strategies: The hearing-impaired would depend more on recall than on covert, subvocal counting than hearing children of comparable knowledge of arithmetic. Thus, there should be no response time difference for the hearing-impaired children between sums that are usually recalled (e.g. $2 + 3 = 5$) and those that are usually not recalled: The hearing-impaired, lacking covert, subvocal strategies, would always rely on recall and would not show an increase in response time for the usually nonrecalled sums. This pattern would differ from the response times of hearing children, who should show an increase in response time in the nonrecalled sums.

The size of the increase in response time among hearing children depends on the type of counting strategy that the children use. If the children count from one up to the value of one addend and then continue counting until they have reached the value of the second addend, the increase in response time will be related to the total value of the sum; this way of using counting to solve sums is known as the *count all* model. If the children count on from the value of the first addend—the *count on* model—the increase in response time is related to the value of the second addend. The third counting model is the *min* model, which assumes that the children count on from the largest addend regardless of whether it is the first or the second in the sum: that is, if the sum is either $8 + 5$ or $5 + 8$, the response time is expected to be the same, and is predicted by the value 5, because children would count on from 8 in both cases.

Hitch et al. (1983) expected that one of these models would be the best-fitting model for response times of hearing children when sums are not memorized but that these models would not show a good fit to the response times of hearing-impaired children, who would rely more on memorization. Contrary to their prediction, Hitch et al. observed that the pattern of response times for eight of the ten hearing-impaired and nine of the ten hearing subjects was best described by the same model of number processing, namely the *min* model. They concluded that the response times of both hearing and deaf children were consistent with the same counting model and that differences in mathematical performance could not be accounted for by differences in the processing of sums.

Epstein, Hillegeist, and Grafman (1994) also studied number processing in deaf and hearing subjects. Their study included secondary school and college students and the deaf participants were all users of American Sign Language. They analysed patterns of response time to judgements of magnitude, correctness of addition, subtraction, multiplication and division sums, and short-term memory for digits from one to six digits. The level of accuracy and patterns of response time in judgement of magnitude and correctness of sums were the same for hearing and deaf participants, suggesting that processing is carried out in the same way by both groups. The deaf participants were, however, significantly slower in both tasks. For short-term memory tasks, the accuracy of deaf subjects decreased significantly when compared to hearing subjects when six digits were presented. The pattern of response times thus suggests the same form of processing, although at a slower rate (with differences of the order of 200msec); short-term memory seems significantly less accurate when the number of digits in the trial is equal to six (accuracy drops from 90% in the hearing subjects to 82% in the deaf subjects). Despite the two significant differences, it is difficult to see how these predominantly negative results can be of use in explaining why hearing-impaired children lag behind in mathematics achievement tests. In particular, there is no evidence connecting absolute level of response time rather than response time pattern to skill in arithmetic and there are no theoretical reasons why there should be a connection either. There is also no evidence or theory that would explain why remembering six digits might make a difference for understanding mathematical problems, which is the domain where hearing-impaired pupils seem to fall behind rather than calculation skill (Wollman, 1965).

Thus no clear framework has been found to explain why hearing-impaired children lag behind hearing children in mathematics achievement and to suggest whether anything can be done to change their current low achievement. Yet changing their low achievement in mathematics would greatly enhance their educational and vocational perspectives in today's world, where mathematics plays such an important role.

We suggest that previous analyses of why hearing-impaired children have difficulties with mathematics have been hindered because the implicit assumption was that hearing impairment is a cause of problems in learning. We propose that hearing impairment is a risk factor rather than a cause of difficulties in learning mathematics. A cause is internal to the learning process and should result in flaws in that very learning process: Hearing and hearing-impaired children should differ qualitatively in the development of mathematical concepts. A risk factor is external to the learning process: The process of numerical development should be very similar for hearing and hearing-impaired children. Even if certain mathematical activities are more difficult for hearing-impaired children to carry out, alternatives to oral language can be found and learning can be accomplished.

Some evidence for the risk factor hypothesis can be found in the literature, albeit weak. The first indication that hearing impairment is not a cause of difficulties in learning mathematics is negative: The fact that hearing loss explains so little variance in mathematics achievement tests goes against a causal model. The second sort of result that suggests that hearing loss is not a cause of difficulties in learning mathematics is the performance of profoundly deaf children, for whom acquisition of oral language is particularly difficult. A causal hypothesis leads to the prediction that profoundly deaf children should be at serious disadvantage in terms of their mathematics learning and cannot be expected to achieve average scores in mathematics tests. However, Wollman (1965) and Wood et al. (1983) did not find evidence to support this prediction: in the study by Wood and colleagues, 15% of the profoundly deaf performed at average or above average levels in mathematics achievement tests.

The risk factor hypothesis has not been explicitly put forth in the literature, although some analyses imply a similar view. Furth (1966) and Rapin (1986), for example, suggest that deaf children's poor results in logical reasoning tasks and educational assessments may be related to an "information deprivation" (Rapin, 1986, p. 214). This information deprivation is a consequence of their exclusion from certain activities (e.g. watching television, listening to the radio) or the difficulty in participating in other activities where much incidental learning may be accomplished by hearing children (e.g. conversations around the dinner table). The information deprivation is likely to be related also to their reading difficulties because much information is acquired by school children through reading and the hearing-impaired are considerably hindered in reading acquisition.

However, in order to find direct support for the risk factor hypothesis, the hypothesis must be more clearly specified through an analysis of the obstacles and processes involved in the development of mathematical concepts. This analysis must show that oral language does not play a central role as a process in the development of mathematics concepts: that it plays a peripheral role in providing information, and that this informational function can be accomplished in other ways. We present here a very brief summary of some central issues in children's development of numerical concepts in primary school, indicate sources of difficulties for hearing-impaired children, and report the findings of an empirical study that provides direct evidence for the risk factor hypothesis.

THE DEVELOPMENT OF NUMERICAL CONCEPTS

Children start to reason about situations that involve number quite early and by about age 5 or 6 they can solve a variety of simple problems. The majority of children at this age can use counting to find the answer to simple addition, subtraction, multiplication, and division problems if they are allowed to act out the situations with objects: They have action schemas—that is, generalized ways of organizing their actions—that they can use to solve the problems. These action schemas, *not language*, form the basis of children's numerical reasoning later on, as they become coordinated with counting and other mathematical representations, such as the signs for operations (Nunes & Bryant, 1996; Riley, Greeno, & Heller, 1983). However, there is not a simple match between action schemas and arithmetic operations: Children have to learn the particular ways in which the informal mathematical knowledge contained in action schemas relates to formal arithmetic concepts in school. Two key difficulties for young children in this developmental process are: To understand the numeration system (that is, the particular conventions for representing number in their culture) and to coordinate their schemas of action with the concepts of arithmetic operations.

Understanding number

Some very simple problems present children with difficulties that relate to the representation of number rather than to the problem situation itself. For example, the problem: "Mary had 5 sweets; her mother gave her 4 sweets; how many sweets does she have now?" is very easy if the children can use blocks to represent each of the sweets and then count all of them. But if the problem is presented with a hidden addend; for example, by saying that "Mary has 5 sweets inside this box and her mother gave her these 4 sweets here; how many does she have altogether?", the problem becomes significantly more difficult because the children would have to count on from the number of sweets in the box.

Research has shown that many 5- and 6-year-old children have difficulty with this type of hidden addend problem (Steffe, Thompson, & Richards, 1982). It has also been shown that they do not master these problems without going through an intermediary phase, where the sweets in the box are externally represented—by pointing gestures accompanied by counting, by using fingers to represent the hidden sweets, or by counting up to the number of sweets without any gestures. Finally, it has also been found that solving hidden addend problems is a necessary step on the way to understanding numerical relations (Kornilaki, 1994; Wang, 1995) that are essential to the mastery of our numeration system. Children who can count, for example, up to 12, may nevertheless be unable to combine a 10p with two 1p coins to make 12p. In order to add the two 1p coins with the 10p coin the children need to realize that all the values up to 10 are contained or embedded in that single representation: an understanding of counting based simply on a linear, one-to-one correspondence reasoning does not suffice. The ability to combine coins of different denominations is an index of children's understanding of additive composition, that is, the property of numeration systems that indicates that any number can be composed by two other numbers by a process of addition. This ability, which can be tested in a Shop Task (designed by Nunes Carraher, & Schliemann, 1990), where children buy objects and pay for them with coins of different denominations, is the best specific predictor that we have identified in past research with hearing children of their learning of place value, addition and subtraction concepts (tested through problem solving), and mastery of sums (Nunes, Miranda, & Silva, 1991).

Although the Shop Task is more difficult than hidden addend problems (Kornilaki, 1994; Wang, 1995), the process involved in its mastery is very similar to that observed in hidden addend problems: Children construct intermediary solutions, which involve the external representation of the values implicitly contained in a coin and count on their fingers, for example, up to 10 when the value of the coin is 10.

These findings suggest one starting point for the description of hearing-impaired children's learning: the analysis of how they come to master the Shop Task. Hearing children rely on gestures to represent the sweets inside the box or the numbers embedded in the value of a 10p coin: How do hearing impaired children cope with the situation? Do these tasks play the same role as predictors of their learning of addition/subtraction?

Understanding operations with numbers

Another central aspect of the development of basic mathematical concepts relates to children's understanding of the relationships between arithmetic operations and their schemas of action. In some problems, there is a clear match between the situation and the arithmetic operation used to solve it (as in the example described earlier on). In other problems, there is not. For example, in the problem "Mary had some sweets; her mother gave her 4 and now she has 9; how many did she have before?", the situation involves adding sweets but the arithmetic operation that leads from the information in the problem to solution is subtraction. This means that children need to build several types of connections between their action schemas and arithmetic operations: direct connections do not suffice.

We suggest that the process by which these connections are developed must be a social process because the boundaries of arithmetic operations defined in the course of history are cultural and conventional. To learn these historically and culturally defined concepts, instruction is necessary. We have previously shown (Nunes, 1992) that unschooled adults, who know how to solve many arithmetic problems using their own methods, have difficulty in solving arithmetic problems with a calculator when the operation required is the inverse of the action described in the problem. The reason for this difficulty is that the use of the calculator requires that solution be accomplished through the conventional representation in terms of the arithmetic operation that leads to solution: The informal reasoning based on the action schema leads to the choice of the wrong operation in inverse problems. In contrast to the unschooled subjects, adults from the same social background who were attending adult education programmes performed significantly better after three years of instruction (following a curriculum equivalent to grade 5 in primary school). The majority of the schooled adults had learned the connection between the action schemas and arithmetic operations and chose the correct operation in inverse problems. However, the two groups of adults, schooled and unschooled, did not differ significantly in their ability to solve arithmetic problems where there was a direct connection between action schema and operation, a result that indicates that the difference between the two groups was not a global but rather a specific one.

In short, young children are able to make some logical moves and solve problems when they can use their action schemas but they may not be able to connect this logic in action to the conventional mathematical systems of signs. These systems, including the numeration system, have to be learned and connected to their action schemas. Because communication is involved in this learning, hearing-impaired children will be at risk. However, the basis for learning mathematical concepts is not language, but the schemas of action; therefore, hearing-impaired children's processes are not expected to differ qualitatively from those of hearing children. Once they master the conventional difficulties, the organization of their concepts should be very similar to that of hearing children's concepts, and the predictors of performance in both groups should be the same.

CHALLENGES FOR HEARING-IMPAIRED CHILDREN: SPECIFYING THE RISK FACTOR HYPOTHESIS

If hearing-impaired children are at risk in respect to the development of mathematical knowledge, where would the risks come from? In this section, we consider the mathematical activities that are particularly difficult for children and how they might influence their learning of numerical concepts.

Counting

Learning the counting string is not as simple for hearing-impaired children as it is for hearing children. Oral counting in English is difficult for them. We observed confusions between teen words and decades, most likely because of phonological similarity; the children would jump, for example, from 18 to 81, 82, etc. It also takes hearing-impaired children longer to learn the counting string than it takes hearing children, even if the hearing-impaired are learning sign language (Secada, 1984). The difficulty of acquiring the counting string is likely to be one of the reasons for their delay in the development of numerical concepts. However, the risk factor hypothesis leads to the prediction that, once the counting string is mastered, they can use it as efficiently as hearing children to solve problems.

As far as we know, only one study has been carried out to assess this hypothesis. Secada (1984) compared hearing-impaired primary school children with a control group of hearing children *with the same level of knowledge of the counting string* in a series of counting tasks. There was no difference between the two groups in tasks such as counting objects and counting on; in two tasks, namely counting backwards and saying what comes after *x*, the hearing-impaired performed better. Thus, when they solve the difficulty of learning the counting string, they can use it as well as hearing children with a comparable counting ability.

Another difficulty for deaf children that is related to counting is the use of counting to solve problems. Hearing children can easily count orally and use their fingers as "objects to be counted" or "counters". In contrast, hearing-impaired children who count in sign language will find that their fingers are "busy with signing" and therefore cannot be used as counters. Young hearing-impaired children can become confused during problem solving and make mistakes even if they understand the problem and could well solve it if they had counters to represent the objects.

In a previous study, we (Nunes & Moreno, 1998) observed that some, although not all, children solve this difficulty by developing a signed algorithm, where signed numbers are used in addition and subtraction. This algorithm, which was as far as we could ascertain developed by the children themselves, was also taught by a teacher to her six profoundly deaf Year 2 pupils (age range 6 to 8 years; mean age 7.23), users of Sign Supported English, attending a London primary school for the deaf. The algorithm involves simultaneously signing each of the numbers in an addition or subtraction sum with a different hand—for example, one hand signs 8 while the other signs 7 when the pupil wants to solve $8 + 7$. Increments of one are then added to 8 (the value to be operated on) at the same time as 7 (the value of the transformation) is progressively decreased by one. The result is achieved when the hand signing the transformation reaches 0; it will be read on the other hand, which works as the notepad. In a subtraction problem, the minuend is signed with one hand, the subtrahend with the other, and they are both decreased by one until the subtrahend reaches 0. The procedure is extremely ingenious because it solves the "hand overload" problem: The children can figure out the sums using their fingers and do not have to rely on retrieval from verbally encoded addition and subtraction facts. But this is not the only solution; the availability of other types of counters rather than fingers should do as well (for more details, see Nunes & Moreno, 1997).

In the study reported here, we use knowledge of the counting string and the hidden addend task as a predictors of children's performance in the Shop Task, which was our main focus. According to our analysis of the development of numerical concepts and the risk factor hypothesis, we expect that:

- success in the Shop Task will be delayed among the hearing-impaired children in comparison to hearing children because of their delay in learning the counting string; knowledge of the counting string should be a significant predictor of hearing-impaired children's performance in the Shop Task;
- similarly to hearing children, hearing-impaired children's success in the Shop Task will be related to their ability to solve the hidden addend task even after controlling for knowledge of the counting string;
- intermediary solutions will be observed in the Shop Task based on gestures and fingers;

- similarly to the results for hearing children, the Shop Task will be a significant predictor of the performance of hearing-impaired children in mathematics achievement tests.

If our analysis is correct, we expect to be able to explain a much larger proportion of the variance in hearing-impaired children's performance in mathematics tests than that explained in previous studies.

Connecting schemas of action with concepts of operations

A second challenge that hearing-impaired children face is in the building of connections between action schemas and numerical concepts. These connections depend on communication and much can be lost in the communication with a hearing-impaired child. But, as with counting, this is a risk factor only, a problem external to the numerical concepts. Therefore, we expect that:

- inverse tasks will be significantly more difficult than direct tasks for the hearing impaired, as they are for hearing children;
- children will perform differently when different mediators are used as signs to represent the situation: in a testing situation where the schemas of action can be easily called into play, performance will be better than in a situation that is more similar to the mathematics classroom, where the resources used in problem solving might not be as easily connected to the children's action schemas.

THE EMPIRICAL STUDY

The study we report here was designed to observe closely the problem-solving processes used by hearing-impaired children in an individual testing situation, to identify predictors of their performance in mathematical tests, to analyse the impact of the mediators of problem solving that support children's use of action schemas on their performance, and to compare the order of acquisition of concepts with that observed among hearing children. We found it necessary to document first the resources used in the classroom to support children's problem solving strategies. This information was used in setting up two testing conditions, one in which the children used as support for problem solving the same materials normally available in the classroom and another situation where we provided them with cut-out shapes, representing the objects in the problems, to instigate the use of their action schemas.

Method

Participants

The project was carried out in eight different schools (two special schools for the deaf and six mainstream schools with units for hearing-impaired children) in London and involved 85 children (approximately 20 in each of the Year groups between 2 and 5). All the children with hearing loss in the participating schools were included in the sample with the exception of six, who had multiple impairments and were unable to respond to the testing situation. The degree of hearing loss was classified by adapting the classification recommended Katz (1978) to yield seven categories: mild (27 to 35dB of loss); mild/moderate (36 to 45); moderate (46 to 55); moderate/severe (56 to 70); severe (71 to 85); severe/profound (86 to 95); profound (96 and above). Children with mixed results across ears were classified according to the average for the purposes of statistical analysis. The degree of hearing loss in our sample was: mild to moderate in 11 children; moderate/severe in 18; severe in 10; severe/profound in 14; profound in 25; 7 children had mixed results.

The cause of hearing loss was not known in 42 children; 7 suffered from a genetic syndrome including other characteristics; in 18 deafness was hereditary; in 4 cases it was due to congenital infections; in 14 deafness was a consequence of a variety of environmental factors (meningitis, birth trauma, etc.; see Table 10.1.) Approximately 30% of the children used British Sign Language (BSL) at home. There was no significant association between cause of deafness and use of BSL at home (chi-square = 8.85648; $df = 7$; $P = .263$).

TABLE 10.1
Frequency of children by cause of hearing loss and
use of BSL

Cause of hearing loss	Use of BSL at home		
	No	Yes	Total
Not known	33	9	42
Meningitis	1	2	3
Hydrocephaly	1	–	1
Birth trauma	6	2	8
Ear infection	2	–	2
Genetic syndrome	5	2	7
Genetic	9	9	18
Congenital infection	2	2	4
Total F	59	26	85
Total (%)	69	31	100

There was also no association between a family history of deafness and use of BSL in the home (chi-square = 4.20; df = 4; P = .379; see Table 10.2). This lack of association was replicated even if a simplified yes/no categorization for history of deafness in the family was used (chi-square = 2.05; df = 1; P = .152). This lack of association, as far as we could ascertain from interviews with the teachers, is a consequence of the fact that many of the hearing-impaired parents were educated mostly through oral methods when young and some did not know BSL themselves.

In contrast, parents with different histories seem to be sensitive to their children's characteristics: The children's degree of hearing loss was significantly associated with the use of BSL at home (chi-square = 31.18739; df = 2; P < .001; see Table 10.3).

Procedure

During the first phase of the project, we interviewed teachers and consulted school records to obtain information about the children. Following each school's procedure, we obtained consent for the children's participation; in the mainstream schools, we obtained consent for video-recording lessons from parents of hearing children who were in the same classroom as our target children. In order to describe the resources used by the teachers with each child, we video-taped mathematics lessons and interviewed the teacher about other resources normally used. A total of 47 mathematics lessons was described during this phase.[2]

During the second phase, the children solved a series of 33 arithmetic problems (presented in random order) involving addition, subtraction, multiplication, division, simple fraction questions, and the Shop Task. We also obtained a measure of the children's knowledge of the counting string by asking them to count as far as they could; we stopped them at 50, if they had reached this number without help or with only one clue from the interviewer. In addition, the children also answered a standardized mathematics achievement test

TABLE 10.2
Frequency of children by family history of deafness
by use of BSL

	Use of BSL at home		
Family history	*No*	*Yes*	*Total*
Not known	2	1	3
Deaf parents	5	5	10
Deaf siblings only	10	7	17
Deaf aunts/uncles	1	–	1
No previous history	41	13	54

TABLE 10.3
Frequency of children by degree of hearing loss and
use of BSL

	Use of BSL at home		
Degree of hearing loss	No	Yes	Total
Mild to moderate	11	–	11
Mod./severe or severe	27	1	28
Severe/profound or profound	15	24	39
Total	53	25	78

Note: Children with mixed results in the audiogram were excluded from this analysis. A simplified categorization of the degree of hearing loss was used to avoid having a large number of cells with expected frequency below 5.

(NFER-Nelson, 1994, year-graded tests) on another occasion, which contains questions covering both numerical and non numerical (e.g. geometry, graphs) concepts.

The children were tested individually in English, Sign Supported English, or BSL by one of the researchers. The translation of the problems from English to BSL was carried out by one of the researchers; the problems were then presented to a BSL teacher, who back-translated them into English and made suggestions for improvement, when appropriate.

To test for the effect of different types of external representations on children's problem solving, the arithmetic problems were presented under two conditions: In *condition 1*, the children were given cut-out shapes of the objects mentioned in the problems (e.g. flowers, marbles); in *condition 2*, the children were provided with the resources used by their teachers in mathematics lessons. The order of conditions of testing was constant: Sessions with cut-out shapes were always given first because we had observed that little emphasis on problem solving was placed in the classrooms. Although this procedure might make it more difficult to observe the facilitating effects of the use of cut-out shapes on children's performance, because they will have had some practice when tested in the second condition, we considered that some positive experience with problem solving might be necessary to engage the children in the tasks.

The problems were presented over four or five sessions to avoid tiring the children. The children in Year 2 answered a reduced set of problems, which excluded the most difficult multiplication problems; we report here only the results of the problems presented to all the children.

The problems were designed to allow us to answer a series of questions about the development of the children's understanding of numerical concepts. Three groups of problems were constructed: (1) the Shop Task, which assesses children's understanding of relative value and additive composition in a practical situation (i.e. the children are asked to count money using combinations of 5p and 1p, 10p and 1p, and 10p only; play money is used); (2) addition/subtraction problems (including situations involving change, part-whole relations, and comparisons); and (3) multiplication and division (including ordering and calculation). The two last groups were presented in condition 1 and 2; the Shop Task was only presented in condition 1 (Table 10.4 contains the list of problems).

Results

The results will be presented in three sections. The first section contains a brief description of the teaching of mathematics to hearing-impaired children. The second section describes general quantitative results; in particular, we will look at predictors of children's performance in the standardized mathematics test and in the series of problems designed for this study. In the third section, the more specific questions about the children's developing understanding of numerical concepts will be analysed.

Lesson content and resources used in the mathematics classroom

Little emphasis was observed on arithmetic problem solving during the lessons we observed: of the 47 lessons observed, only three included arithmetic problem solving. Other activities related to numerical concepts and skills were observed: teaching children to find patterns in number series; discriminating odd and even numbers; practice in solving written sums; using Dienes blocks to analyse numbers in tens and ones (but in one class only); decomposing written numbers into tens and ones in writing (in one class only); solving series of related sums (e.g. 8 + 9; 8 + 19; 8 + 29; etc.) or different sums with the same result (e.g. 13 + 5 = 18; 12 + 6 = 18; etc.); solving multidigit sums. A variety of other activities, not directly related to the development of numerical understanding, was observed: reading clocks, identifying points in a system of coordinates; learning shape vocabulary; and reading information from tables are some of the examples.

The absence of activities related to arithmetic problem solving can be viewed as a source of concern. This lack of instruction in problem solving means that children's coordination of their action schemas with the mathematical concepts of arithmetic operations is dependent on what they can learn informally, outside school.

When interviewed, most of the teachers indicated that they use unifix blocks as mediators for children to solve sums in the classroom; we only observed this use in about half of the lessons because not all lessons observed were about

TABLE 10.4

Example: Yesterday boy had 4 flowers. Mummy gave the boy 6 flowers. How many flowers does the boy have now? (Given as a warm-up at the beginning of each session)

1. Yesterday a girl had 5 flowers. Mummy gave the girl 8 flowers. How many flowers does the girl have now?

2. Yesterday a boy had 4 balloons. Daddy gave him some balloons. Now the boy has 7 balloons. How many balloons did Daddy give the boy?

3. Yesterday a girl had some sweets, she played a game and won 2 sweets. Now she has 12 sweets. How many sweets did the girl have yesterday?

4. Yesterday a boy had 12 flowers, he gave Mummy 2 flowers. How many flowers does the boy have now?

5. A boy had 13 paperclips, he put them in his pocket, but he lost some paperclips. Now he has 6 paperclips. How many paperclips did the boy lose?

6. Yesterday, a girl had some marbles. The girl gave 5 marbles to her friend. Now she has 8 marbles. How many marbles did the girl have yesterday?

7. There is a pond with fish in it. There are 6 red fish and 7 orange fish. How many fish are there in the pond?

8. A girl has 5 balloons, 1 is a red balloon and all the others are orange. How many orange balloons does the girl have?

9. In a classroom there are 9 children. There are 4 chairs. How many sad children do not have a chair?

10. A girl has 5 sweets in a box. Mummy gives her 4 sweets. How many sweets does the girl have altogether?

11. I have some paperclips under paper. I know there are 9 paperclips altogether. You can see 3. How many paperclips are hiding under the paper?

12. A girl has 5 marbles, a boy has 3 marbles. Who has more? How many more?

13. A girl has 6 marbles, a boy has 4 marbles. Who has less marbles? How many less?

14. A girl has 5 balloons. A boy has 2 more than girl. How many balloons does the boy have?

15. A girl has 7 balloons. A boy has balloons. The girl has 3 more than boy. How many does the boy have?

16. I have two mugs of tea. In this one I am putting 3 spoonfuls of sugar [large spoon], and in this one I am putting 3 spoonfuls of sugar [small spoon]. Do the mugs have the same amount of sugar? [If child answers "no"] Which has more sugar?

17. I have put all the 5p in a line, and the 1p in a line. I want to buy some sweets, the money in which line will buy more sweets?

18. There are two groups of lorries. The first group, with green lorries, they carry 2 bags each inside. The Second group, with blue lorries, they carry 3 bags each inside. Which group has more bags? Can you make green lorries carry the same number as blue. How many bags does each group have?

19. There are 2 parties: At the first party, 6 blue rabbits have 12 sweets. At the second party 6 pink rabbits have 18 sweets. Will the rabbits eat same number of sweets? Which rabbits eat more sweets, the pink or blue rabbits? Show me how many sweets each rabbit has.

20. There are 2 parties: At the first party, 5 pink rabbits have 10 sweets. At the second party, 2 blue rabbits have 10 sweets. All the rabbits want sweets. Will the rabbits eat the same number of sweets? Which rabbits will eat more, the pink or blue rabbits? Show me how many sweets each rabbit has.

21. There are two parties: At the first party: for the blue rabbits, we have 12 sweets and we're going to give each rabbit 4 sweets. At the second party for the pink rabbits, we have 12 sweets and we're going to give 3 sweets each. Can we ask same number of rabbits to each party? How many rabbits can we ask? Show me.

22. There are 2 parties: At the first party, for blue rabbits, have 20 sweets and we're going to give each rabbit 5 sweets each. At the second party, for the pink rabbits, we have 10 sweets and we're going to give each rabbit 5 sweets each. Can we ask same number of rabbits to each party? How many can come to parties? Show me.

23. We are going to make a party for the rabbits while they are sleeping. I want to give each rabbit 4 sweets each, we have 20 sweets. How many rabbits can come to the party?

24. We have 24 sweets, and there are 6 rabbits. How many sweets can we give each rabbit?

25. There are two groups of children: In the first group, 5 children have 2 chocolate bars. In the second group 5 children have 3 chocolate bars. All children want some chocolate. Do you think one group will have more chocolate to eat? Which group? Why?

26. There are two groups of children: In the first group 6 children have 3 chocolate bars. In the second group 4 children have 2 chocolate bars. All the children want some chocolate. Do you think one group has more chocolate to eat? Which group? Why?

27. There are two groups of children: In the first group 5 children have 3 chocolate bars. In the second group 6 children have 3 chocolate bars. All children want some chocolate. Do you think you one group have more chocolate to eat? Which one? Why?

28. There are two groups of children: In the first group 6 children have 4 chocolate bars. In the second group 10 children have 5 chocolate bars. All the children want some chocolate. Do you think you one group will have more chocolate to eat? Which one? Why?

29. If you squeeze 6 oranges it makes 2 cups of orange juice. How many oranges do you need if you want to make 4 cups of juice?

30. If you squeeze 6 oranges it makes 2 cups of orange juice. How many oranges do you need if you want 5 cups of juice?

31. I buy ½ m ribbon at 30p. How much would 1½m of the same ribbon cost?

32. I buy 3m ribbon at 60p. I only want 1m of ribbon. How much do I pay?

33. I buy 2m of ribbon at 80p. I only want ½m. How much do I pay?

34–42. *Shop Task items:* Child is asked to choose items to buy from shop. Values to be presented in random order: With 5p and 1p coins: 5, 7, 9; with 10p and 1p coins: 13, 17, 21, 23; with 10p: 20p; 30p (5p is not scored: to be treated as example; child must pay with 5p coin).

solving sums. In only a few classes the teachers used Dienes blocks; in one, these resources were combined with the use of a number line.

The reliance on unifix cubes had a marked disadvantage in respect to the development of the understanding of the numeration system: The children typically counted in ones when solving problems, even when asked to represent the numbers in tens and ones (but note that this request was only observed in one classroom; in others, children simply made one row with the unifix blocks to represent any number, including those above ten). In one classroom where Dienes blocks were available, the children most of the time treated the tens-bars as objects, counting for example 8 bars to represent the number 8. Thus, although the material was designed to reinforce children's understanding of the decimal numeration system, the teaching approaches did not emphasize this aspect.

An abacus with coloured beads where each colour was meant to represent a different place value was used in one class. However, the children counted all beads as ones, and simply used them as counters.

This description allowed us to choose the resources to be used in condition 2: All children had unifix blocks at their disposal; those whose teachers used other resources, namely Dienes blocks and a number line, also had these materials.

General quantitative results

The children's performance in the standardized test was well below that of the hearing cohorts. The mean standard score for the sample was 64.8, which is more than two standard deviations below the mean for the test (namely, 100). If we exclude the 16 children whose score was very low, the mean goes up to 83.4, which corresponds to the 13th percentile; it is still rather low. The range of performance, with the exclusion of the outliers, was between 70 and 120 (percentiles 2 and 91, respectively).

For further analysis, we grouped the children's standardized scores into four bands: below 50, from 51 to 70, from 71 to 90, and above 90. The scores of the children with severe/profound and profound loss of hearing were spread in all of these levels: 10 were in the lowest band, 3 in the next, 12 in the next, and 14 in the upper band. As in other studies, severe hearing loss did not preclude mathematics learning. This result supports the hypothesis that hearing impairment works as a risk factor rather than a cause for difficulty in learning mathematics.

Overall quantitative analyses: The predictors of performance

The purpose of analysing the predictors of performance was to seek further confirmation for the risk factor hypothesis. There are two aspects to be considered. The first one is how hearing loss relates to the measures of numerical competence used in our study. On the basis of the risk factor hypothesis discussed earlier on, we expect hearing loss to make at best a small contribution to the prediction of children's performance in measures of numerical knowledge; the use of BSL at home may act as a compensatory factor and make a contribution to the prediction of children's performance in numerical tasks. However, because hearing loss is simply a risk factor, our predictions are mostly negative and the support that they can bring to the risk factor hypothesis is consequently rather weak.

The second aspect to be considered is whether hearing-impaired children's numerical knowledge has the same organization as that of hearing children's. If there is no qualitative difference between hearing-impaired and hearing children's learning, the same predictors that work well for hearing children should explain significant amounts of the variance in hearing-impaired children's mathematical performance.

Before any further analysis, we tested for the effects of school: If these were significant, schools would have to be entered as a control in all subsequent analyses. We carried out an analysis of covariance with scores in the standardized test as the dependent variable and degree of hearing loss and Year group as covariates. This analysis did not show a significant effect of school. For this reason, subsequent analyses did not contain school as one of the predictors. We then ran a series of regression analyses where we tested different predictors and different outcome measures.

The first analysis had knowledge of the counting string as the outcome variable and Year group, degree of hearing loss, and use of BSL in the home as predictors. We used a fixed-order regression to control for Year group before entering degree of hearing loss; hearing loss was entered before use of BSL in the home because we had found that these two variables are related and therefore degree of hearing loss had to be controlled for before entering use of BSL in the equation. Table 10.5 shows the results of this analysis. The only significant predictor was Year group, a variable where the contributions of age and schooling are combined; these cannot be separated in studies of children attending school in England. This predictor accounted for 15% of the variance. Level of hearing loss is not a significant predictor, a result that is understandable when one considers that children were allowed to count orally or in sign because our interest was not in which counting string they knew but whether they knew a counting string up to a high number.

The second set of analyses had the Shop Task and the score in the standardized test as the outcome measure. We know that, for hearing children, performance in a hidden addend task predicts performance in the Shop Task (Kornilaki, 1994; Wang, 1995) and that performance in the Shop Task predicts performance in mathematics achievement tests (Nunes, Miranda, & Silva, 1991). Thus, we wanted to test whether the same relationships are observed

TABLE 10.5
Fixed-order multiple regression with knowledge of the counting
string as the predicted variable

Predictor	Mult. R	R sq change	F change	Sig. F change
Year group	.39098	.15287	13.17239	0.0005
Hearing loss	.41131	.01631	1.41355	0.2384
Use of BSL	.41157	.00022	0.01845	0.8923

Summary:

Predictor	Mult. R	R sq	F(Eqn)	Sig. F	Beta In
Year group	.3910	.1529	13.173	0.001	.3910
Hearing loss	.4113	.1692	7.331	0.001	− .1283
Use of BSL	.4116	.1694	4.827	0.004	.0192

among hearing-impaired children; if this is the case, the results can be interpreted as supporting the risk factor hypothesis, which assumes that there are no qualitative differences between the numerical knowledge of hearing and hearing-impaired children. The regression analyses followed a fixed-order model. It was necessary to control first for Year group to test whether degree of hearing loss was a significant predictor of performance. Next, hearing loss was controlled for to test the impact of use of BSL in the home. Finally, the specific predictors were entered: knowledge of the counting string and performance in the hidden-addend task used as predictors of performance in the Shop Task; this order of steps controls for knowledge of the counting string before entering the results from the hidden addend task and therefore introduce very stringent controls. If the hidden addend task still proves to make a significant contribution to the prediction of results in the Shop Task, very strong evidence in favour of a similar structure of numerical knowledge between hearing and hearing-impaired children will have been found. In the analysis of the Standardized Test, the first three steps were the same, Year group, degree of hearing loss and use of BSL in the home; the Shop Task was used as the specific predictor.

Performance in the Shop Task was significantly related to Year group, as expected. It was neither related to degree of hearing loss nor to use of BSL in the home. Knowledge of the counting string made a significant contribution to the prediction of performance in the Shop Task (accounting for 28% of the variance) and so did the hidden-addend task, which explained 5% extra variance even after the stringent controls of Year group and knowledge of counting were entered in the equation (Table 10.6). The results support the hypothesis that impaired hearing children's learning processes are qualitatively similar to those of hearing children. It is worth noting that almost 46% of the variance in this task is accounted for by the regression equation, which is a very important finding.

TABLE 10.6
Fixed-order multiple regression with the Shop Task as the predicted variable

Predictor	Mult. R	R sq change	F change	Sig. F change
Year group	.3337	.11134	7.2669	0.009
Hearing loss	.3385	.00323	0.2079	0.650
Use of BSL	.3609	.01569	1.0101	0.319
Knowledge of counting string	.6419	.28180	26.3615	0.0001
Hidden addend. task	.6814	.05222	5.2633	0.026

Summary:

Predictors	Mult. R	R sq	F(Eqn)	Sig. F	Beta In
Year group	.3337	.1113	7.267	.009	.3337
Hearing loss	.3385	.1146	3.688	.031	– .0576
Use of BSL	.3609	.1303	2.796	.048	.1760
Knowledge of counting string	.6419	.4121	9.637	.0001	.5628
Hidden addend. task	.6814	.4643	9.360	.0001	.2625

The analysis of scores in the Standardized Test showed that neither degree of hearing loss nor use of BSL in the home were significant predictors of this outcome measure (Table 10.7). The regression analysis also shows that children neither fall further behind their hearing counterparts nor catch up as they progress through school: Year group is not significantly related to scores in the standardized test. Finally, the analysis shows that performance in the Shop Task is a significant predictor of the children's standardized scores even after controls for their Year group, degree of hearing loss, and use of BSL in the

TABLE 10.7
Fixed-order multiple regression with Standardized test scores as the predicted variable

Predictor	Mult. R	R sq change	F change	Sig. F change
Year group	.0065	.00004	0.0020	0.964
Hearing loss	.0704	.00491	0.2321	0.632
Use of BSL	.1320	.01247	0.5840	0.449
Shop Task	.5079	.24058	14.5908	0.001

Summary:

Predictor	Mult. R	R sq	F(Eqn)	Sig. F	Beta In
Year group	.0065	.0000	0.002	0.964	– .0065
Hearing loss	.0704	.0050	0.117	0.890	– .0702
Use of BSL	.1320	.0174	0.272	0.845	.1460
Shop Task	.5080	.2717	3.912	0.008	.5305

home have been entered in the equation. The amount of extra variance explained by performance in the Shop Task is quite high: 24%. The total amount of variance explained, although still a modest 27%, represents a substantial increase in comparison to previous studies.

The last set of analyses used our arithmetic problems as the outcome variables. Four subtotals were used, two for addition/subtraction and two for multiplication/division; each one of these pertained to a different testing condition, with cut-out objects (condition 1) or with systems of signs used in the classroom (condition 2). Performance in the hidden addend task was not included in the addition/subtraction scores because this would inflate the amount of variance related to the Shop Task. All of these analyses were carried out by entering the predictors in a fixed order. The general predictors were Year group, hearing loss, and use of BSL in the home; the specific predictor was performance in the Shop Task.

These regression analyses with the different groups of scores in the problem-solving tasks as outcome variables gave mostly negative results in respect to hearing loss: It was significantly and negatively related to only one group of scores, multiplication/division problems in condition 2. The results for the use of BSL in the home were nonsignificant.

Performance in the Shop Task was a significant predictor of scores in addition/subtraction in both testing conditions and added considerably to the amount of variance predicted in the regression equations (24% in condition 1 and 31% in condition 2) even after controlling for Year Group. It was also a significant predictor of children's performance in the multiplication/division tasks in condition 1 but not in condition 2 (see Tables 10.8 to 10.11).

We consider these findings rather significant. First, they indicate that children's knowledge of the counting string, which is difficult for hearing impaired-children to learn, is a significant predictor of the development of numerical concepts as assessed in the Shop Task. This indicates that greater stress in teaching young hearing-impaired children to count in school is likely to have a positive impact on their numerical knowledge. Second, the evidence strongly supports the risk factor hypothesis: Hearing-impaired and hearing children's numerical concepts seem to develop along the same path. Finally, informal learning, as assessed by the Shop Task, is an important predictor of their performance in a standardized test, and again this is a concept that is amenable to instruction.

The impact of mediators on performance

The impact of mediators on performance was analysed quantitatively and qualitatively. The quantitative analysis showed that the overall mean number of correct responses (out of 19 items that involved calculation) was 10.3 when the children had the cut-out objects as support and 8.8 when they had the

TABLE 10.8
Fixed-order multiple regression with addition/subtraction in
condition 1 as the predicted variable

Predictor	Mult. R	R sq change	F change	Sig. F change
Year group	.2479	.06147	3.99520	0.050
Hearing loss	.3005	.02882	1.90064	0.173
Use of BSL	.3243	.01488	0.98134	0.326
Shop Task	.6120	.26911	24.81233	0.0001

Summary:

Step	Mult. R	R sq	F(Eqn)	Sig. F	Beta In
Year group	.2479	.0615	3.995	0.050	.2479
Hearing loss	.3005	.0903	2.977	0.058	−.1709
Use of BSL	.3243	.1052	2.311	0.085	−.1684
Shop Task	.6110	.3733	8.636	0.0001	.5596

mediators from the classroom. This difference was significant according to an analysis of variance with Year group as a between subjects factor and condition of testing as a within-subjects variable; the dependent variable was the children's score. This analysis showed a significant effect of condition of testing ($F = 8.54$; $P = .006$), a significant effect of Year group and no significant interaction. The children in all Year Groups performed significantly better when they could use the cut-out objects and their action schemas to solve the problem than when they had to rely on the mediators that they normally use in their classroom (in all but five cases, the children used unifix blocks; two children used Dienes blocks but treated the tens as objects, counting each ten-bar as one object, and three children used a number line for some problems).

TABLE 10.9
Fixed-order multiple regression with addition/subtraction scores in
condition 2 as the predicted variable

Predictor	Mult. R	R sq change	F change	Sig. F change
Year group	.1910	.03647	2.1956	0.144
Hearing loss	.0365	.00003	0.0019	0.965
Use of BSL	.2050	.00551	0.3221	0.573
Shop Task	.6116	.33201	29.1721	0.0001

Summary:

Step	Mult. R	R sq	F(Eqn)	Sig. F	Beta In
Year group	.1910	.0365	2.196	0.144	.1910
Hearing loss	.1911	.0365	1.080	0.346	.0058
Use of BSL	.2050	.0420	0.819	0.489	−.1033
Shop Task	.6116	.3740	8.612	0.0001	.6153

TABLE 10.10
Fixed-order multiple regression with multiplication/division in
condition 1 as the predicted variable

Predictor	Mult. R	R sq change	F change	Sig. F change
Year group	.3011	.09066	5.4831	0.023
Hearing loss	.3350	.02155	1.31091	0.257
Use of BSL	.3352	.00014	0.00841	0.928
Shop Task	.4874	.12522	8.54065	0.005

Summary:

Step	Mult. R	R sq	F(Eqn)	Sig.F	Beta In
Year group	.3011	.0907	5.483	0.023	.3011
Hearing loss	.3350	.1122	3.413	0.040	– .1470
Use of BSL	.3352	.1123	2.236	0.095	.0167
Shop Task	.4874	.2376	4.051	0.006	.3883

Some children seemed to lose grasp of what to do in this testing condition and, instead of trying to reason about the problem rigorously, attempted guessing rather than calculating a solution. This could be observed even in problems that the child had correctly solved with cut-out objects.

These results indicate that the children's informal knowledge of arithmetic, as characterized by their ability to solve problems using action schemas, is significantly better than the knowledge that they use in school settings with the materials normally available to them. The results are consistent with the hypothesis that both hearing and hearing-impaired children develop their numerical understanding from their action schemas, which at a later stage needs to be coordinated with formal representations in school. They are also consis-

TABLE 10.11
Fixed-order multiple regression with multiplication/division in
condition 2 as the predicted variable

Predictor	Mult. R	R sq Change	F change	Sig. F change
Year group	.1449	.02100	1.09413	0.300
Hearing loss	.3195	.08109	4.51548	0.039
Use of BSL	.3612	.02840	1.60026	0.212
Shop Task	.3614	.00010	0.00571	0.940

Summary:

Step	Mult.R	R sq	F(Eqn)	Sig. F	Beta In
Year group	.1449	.0210	1.094	0.300	– .1449
Hearing loss	.3195	.1021	2.843	0.068	.2896
Use of BSL	.3612	.1305	2.451	0.074	– .2344
Shop Task	.3614	.1306	1.803	0.144	– .0105

tent with the risk factor hypothesis: The hearing-impaired children display understanding when they can rely on their action schemas but these schemas have not been coordinated with their school learning.

Our final analysis of mediators of reasoning was a qualitative investigation of the processes used by the hearing-impaired children to solve the logical moves in the Shop Task. We observed that the same intermediary strategies observed in hearing children were used by the hearing-impaired children: To figure out, for example, the total amount if one 5p and four 1p coins are put together, children using the externally represented solution did not count on from five, but counted up to five on their fingers and then went on to count the remaining four coins. As the task progressed, these children often abbreviated the process and counted on.

In a case study of an older participant (Year 5, severe/profoundly deaf) who initially did not succeed in the Shop Task, we instigated the use of the strategy of representing the value of the 5p coin with fingers; the child succeeded in solving the problem at hand and used the strategy to solve subsequent items on his own initiative. This suggests that the logical move of using one object to represent several at the same time seems to be solved by hearing and deaf children through the same process of external, gestural representation that makes explicit the numbers implicitly contained in the total.

Inverting relationships is another difficult move for hearing children and proved equally difficult for the hearing-impaired participants. Success in direct addition/subtraction tasks was significantly higher than in inverse tasks according to an analysis of variance with type of task as repeated measures ($F = 29.7$; $P < .001$); no significant interaction was observed between type of task and Year group.

A more detailed analysis of patterns of correct responses was carried out by comparing the results in our group of hearing-impaired children with the pattern observed among hearing children at younger age levels; younger age levels were used both because the children in our sample performed below their age in the standardized test and because ceiling effects are observed around ages 9 or 10 in the addition/subtraction problems we used. We used as a comparison a simplified version of Riley et al.'s (1983) classification of change problems, that is, those where the story describes a situation in which someone had a set and then a transformation in the value of the set takes place. Six problem types are defined by the type of transformation, increase or decrease in amount, and location of the unknown in the problem, the initial value of the set, the transformation, or the result. In the simplified version, we considered only the location of the unknown, which affects patterns of response more consistently. Riley and colleagues ordered the problems in terms of percentage of correct responses and observed that problems with the result unknown were the easiest, followed by those where the value of the transformation is unknown. The most difficult ones where those where the start was unknown: for example, "Yesterday a girl had some sweets; she played a game and won 2; now she has 12. How many sweets did she have yesterday?". Even hearing children at the age of 9 do not yet master this problem. The children have to solve two difficulties. First, it is an inverse problem. Second, the first number mentioned in the problem, 2, is actually contained in the second one, 12, if the situation is correctly represented. That means that even the reconstruction of the situation is difficult: if the children simply take two sweets and then twelve, these actions will not help solve the problem correctly. We examined the order of difficulty of these problems in our sample by looking at the percentages of correct responses. Like hearing children, the children in our sample also had the greatest difficulty with problems where the start was unknown; problems with result unknown were easiest and those with unknown transformation were of an intermediary level of difficulty. Thus, this analysis of level of difficulty does not give any reason to suspect that the development of hearing and hearing-impaired children differs in quality in respect to addition and subtraction problem solving.

We also considered children's strategies and errors in the more difficult problems to see whether there might be any indication of qualitative differences. The few children who successfully solved the start-unknown problem described earlier on and used an observable strategy first built a set of 2, then counted on to 12 sweets, and then designated the last two—the 11th and 12th—as the ones the girl had won; to find the answer, they searched for the number that comes before 11. This is the same strategy described for hearing children solving problems with objects (Carpenter & Moser, 1982). The most common mistake in this problem type according to Riley et al. is to offer as the answer the value of the transformation—"two" in our example. The pattern of results observed among the hearing-impaired children fits this description: 25% of the children gave this wrong solution, which was more than twice as frequent as either of the other frequent errors (12 and 14).

In short, both quantitative and qualitative analyses of children's success patterns and errors in solving addition and subtraction problems indicate that hearing-impaired and hearing children progress along the same developmental path; there is no sign of qualitative differences. Success in the more difficult problems is initially accomplished through action schemas and external representations rather than by means of language. These results are compatible with the risk factor hypothesis but less so with the hypothesis of hearing impairment as a cause for difficulties in mathematics learning due to the absence of a supposedly essential process in development.

CONCLUSIONS AND DISCUSSION

Our results suggest that it is more appropriate to consider hearing impairment a risk factor than a cause of children's difficulties in learning numerical concepts. Hearing impairment did not make a significant contribution to predicting children's mathematical scores, replicating previous studies of a weak or nonsignificant relationship between these two measures. The results also indicate that the nowadays common belief that the use of BSL in the home has compensatory effects on children's learning cannot be accepted without further investigation; in this project, there is no support for such a belief.

The results also show that Year Group is not a significant predictor of the standard scores in the mathematics achievement test. This result would be expected in the general population because standard scores are adjusted by age level. However, in this context, they have to be considered from a different perspective: They indicate that hearing-impaired children do not catch up with the hearing cohorts as they receive more instruction, nor do they fall further behind. A catching-up effect would indicate a truly successful educational programme and should be the aim of schools in this case, but it is already encouraging that there is not a growing gap between hearing-impaired and hearing children's performance, at least in primary school.

We also found positive support for the risk factor hypothesis. Hearing-impaired children seem to learn numerical concepts in the same way as hearing children: using their schemas of action, including counting, to analyse numerical situations. However, they have to face extra hurdles: It is difficult for them to learn the counting string and to use it to solve problems.

The moderate success we obtained in predicting children's mathematics learning from their informal learning as described in the Shop Task and the identification of possible mechanisms involved in its mastery have important implications. Theoretically, these results suggest that hearing-impaired children have to deal with the same conceptual obstacles in understanding numerical concepts as hearing children and that they deal with these obstacles in the same way. From the practical viewpoint, they show ways in which one might develop intervention programmes to support hearing-impaired children's development more effectively. However, it is important to be cautious until research that investigates this issue through intervention methodologies has been carried out. Correlational studies can only be considered exploratory in this case.

ACKNOWLEDGEMENTS

We are very grateful to the Nuffield Foundation for funding this project (Grant No. AT/259). We also thank the children and teachers of the participating schools for their generous cooperation.

NOTES

1. At the time of Wollman's study school children in the United Kingdom were placed within a three-tier segregated school system on the basis of their performance on aptitude tests at age eleven. The lowest performers attended "secondary modern" schools.

2. In a few cases, the lessons were observed rather than video-taped because some of the hearing children had not returned their consent letter by the date scheduled for observation. Because they were not the target children in our study and we were not registering their behaviour, we decided to proceed with observations but did not-video-tape the lessons, in which case the hearing children might have been unwittingly filmed.

CHAPTER ELEVEN

Number without language? Studies of children with specific language impairments

Chris Donlan
University College London, UK

INTRODUCTION

Harry is aged 1;11, He is developing normally. In his parents' bedroom, one morning, he looks at the display on the digital alarm clock. It reads 8:14. He points to the 8 and says "That two". His mother points to each digit in turn and says "Eight, one, four". Harry points at the 1 and says "That eight", then points at the colon (separating the hours and minutes) and says "And that..?"

A few days later Harry is having lunch. He is still hungry after his bowl of baked beans and toast. He says "More", and Daddy agrees to make more. As the beans are being warmed Harry says proudly "Daddy, two beans. Two beans".

That afternoon, in a car park, Harry goes up to an unfamiliar car number plate, rubs his hands over the symbols and says "Four six". He has recently used this phrase in other contexts where Arabic or alphabetic symbols occur, e.g. when the credits are shown at the end of a television programme.

A couple of days later Harry shows Mummy two pictures of tractors that he has found in different books. He says "Mummy, two tractors. One, two." (Donlan, 1997)

Much of our knowledge of the way children learn about numbers is derived from what they say to us. Parent-toddler conversations frequently refer to numbers (Durkin et al., 1986). The diary quoted above suggests that normally developing children as young as 2 years of age are developing the skills to allow them to share with others both their awareness of numerical attributes of objects or events in the world and their grasp of written numeric symbols. These records of verbal interaction are forceful reminders of the power of language as a tool for negotiating numerical meaning. Harry uses number words in such a way as to invite the adult to share his point of view and to extend his knowledge in specific ways.

The importance of socially constructed knowledge in the development of mathematical skills is a major theme of current research (see Chapters 2, 3, and 10). This general model lays emphasis on children's social experience and, by implication, their skills in verbal interaction. Elsewhere, Nunes and colleagues have been powerful advocates of the importance of language as a tool for mathematical learning (Nunes et al., 1993; Nunes & Bryant, 1996). Within this framework of research, it appears that the development of functional linguistic skills is a prerequisite for mathematical learning. If verbal deficits restrict the social context within which the child develops, then mathematical skills may be fundamentally compromised.

However, there is an alternative view. Wynn (1992a and Chapter 1) has presented cogent experimental evidence to support her view that number awareness precedes the development of language. Specifically, Wynn is arguing that innate cognitive mechanisms specialized for numerical information processing operate during the first six months of life, in advance of linguistic communication about number. Consistent with this claim, Gallistel and Gelman (1992) have proposed that nonverbal cognitive processes present at birth continue to subserve numerical thought throughout the lifespan. Gallistel and Gelman cite the classic study of numerical comparison carried out by Moyer and Landauer (1967), which suggested that numerical information is represented in our minds as "analogue magnitudes" that have more in common with representations of sense-data such as light and heat than they do with representations of verbal symbols.

These contrasting viewpoints, in which numerical thought is seen as innate on the one hand and socially constructed on the other, seem hardly reconcilable. However, as a close reading of the first two chapters in this volume reveals, there is some degree of complementarity. Findings from yet a third area of research offer a valuable prespective. Recent studies of numerical cognition in subjects with acquired or developmental disorders (Dehaene & Cohen, 1995; Macaruso & Sokol, Chapter 9; McCloskey, 1992) have started to examine the interaction of verbal and nonverbal skills. Dehaene and Cohen (1995) have combined evidence from imaging studies of normal subjects and from brain-damaged patients to support a localized model of number processing. Within this account a broad distinction is drawn between different sorts of numerical cognition: Activities requiring rapid generation of approximate value (e.g. comparison of two prices) are generally subserved by the right hemisphere, in contrast to other more complex sorts of numerical processing (e.g. arithmetic fact retrieval), which are generally dependent on left-hemisphere function. Part of the evidence for this functional and anatomical distinction comes from the finding that aphasic patients (whose language problems are traceable to left-hemisphere damage) may show a variety of impairments of complex number processing but are generally unimpaired in their ability to make simple comparisons of number magnitudes.

An important characteristic of Dehaene and Cohen's model (and this characteristic is shared by competing models, e.g. McCloskey, 1992; Campbell, 1994) is that they differentiate between types of numerical material according to its notation, so that, for example, spoken numerals and Arabic numerals are processed by different systems. Thus there is general acknowledgement that numerical information processing, in the adult at least, involves verbal and nonverbal systems that may operate independently.

How far might this independence of verbal and nonverbal numerical skills hold also for children? Might it be a feature of development? An important source of evidence lies in the developmental progress of children known to have specific deficits in language despite normal nonverbal skills. This chapter examines this evidence, evaluating the general hypothesis that nonverbal numerical skills may develop normally despite severely restricted language development.

SPECIFIC LANGUAGE IMPAIRMENTS IN CHILDREN

Children with specific language impairments (SLI) show average or above average scores on standardized tests of nonverbal ability despite significant deficits in language development for which there is no obvious cause. The nature of the language deficits varies considerably between individuals but is most often characterized by speech problems (not traceable to anatomical defects), expressive language limited in lexical and grammatical development and comprehension deficits that may not be obvious but are still significant (Bishop, 1979; Haynes & Naidoo, 1992).

Conflicting accounts of the underlying causes of these deficits have been proposed (see Bishop, 1994, for a full review). There is broad and unequivocal evidence that poor auditory short-term memory is associated with SLI (Haynes & Naidoo, 1992), though the interpretation of this finding in terms of cause and effect is uncertain (see Gathercole & Baddeley, 1993, and Van der Lely & Howard, 1993, for conflicting views). Of particular relevance to the concerns of this chapter is the debate about the language-specific nature of the deficits. Many researchers accept the view that nonverbal processes are unimpaired in these children, and many indeed use SLI as evidence for an independent language module in cognitive development (e.g. Gopnik & Crago, 1991). On the other hand, some (e.g. Connell & Stone, 1992; Morehead & Ingram, 1976; Stone & Connell, 1993) have suggested that SLI entails an underlying representational deficit, affecting the processing of symbolic information generally, even where this information is not explicitly linguistic. Johnston and Smith (1989) concluded from studies of verbal and nonverbal problem solving that "language-impaired children are also thought-impaired" (Johnston & Smith, 1989, p. 38).

Investigation of the development of mathematical skills in children with SLI promises to clarify the nature of their difficulties, while at the same time offering insights into the normal pattern of interaction between linguistic and mathematical development. Note that the breadth of this undertaking imposes some restriction on the interpretation of findings. If generally depressed mathematical development is found in SLI, then this could be the result of *either* general cognitive deficits in SLI *or* the pervasive influence of language in mathematical development. Much clearer conclusions may be drawn if some or all of SLI children's mathematical learning is unimpaired. This would confirm the specificity of SLI and indicate the extent of linguistic influence in mathematical development.

This chapter will examine evidence concerning the general hypothesis that children with specific language impairments may develop normal nonverbal mathematical skills. Within this general framework three particular hypotheses are proposed:

1. That limitations on the rate of acquisition and efficiency of use of spoken numerals will impose commensurate restrictions on the acquisition of counting skills.
2. That poor counting skills, combined with restrictions in short term verbal memory will impede the development of arithmetical knowledge and skills.
3. That nonverbal numerical skills will develop at the rate expected for age and show corresponding efficiency of operation.

GENERAL MATHEMATICAL ATTAINMENT IN CHILDREN WITH SLI

Intuitively, many of us might draw a clear distinction between verbal skills and mathematical skills: Our stereotypes of people who show special aptitude in one or other area might be substantially different. An extension of this view would predict that children with SLI should show substantially better attainments in numeracy than literacy. Such evidence as is available, however, absolutely contradicts this prediction. Aram and Nation (1980) examined academic success in 20 adolescents, all of whom had an early history of clinically diagnosed language impairments. Some of this group had low nonverbal ability as well as poor verbal skills. Standardized testing of general attainments in reading, spelling, and mathematics showed that academic achievements in the group were generally poor. More than half the group had reading and spelling scores below the 25th centile, but maths scores were substantially lower, with 80% scoring below the 25th centile. What is more, these proportions were maintained when subjects with generally low ability were excluded from the analysis.

The outcomes of Aram and Nation's study, so far from showing any special advantage in mathematics for children with a history of specific language impairments, suggest that maths skills are even more vulnerable than literacy skills in this population. However, tests of overall attainment are necessarily gross measures. They make demands on a range of skills; it would be hard to construct a comprehensive mathematics tests that did not to make substantial demands on verbal skills (e.g. presenting verbal problems for solution). To understand the impact of language impairments on mathematical development we need to look more closely at the components of mathematical skill and their evolution in the child.

STUDIES OF PRE-SCHOOLERS WITH SLI

Seminal work examining early stages in the the relationship between language and mathematical thinking was carried out by Linda Siegel and colleagues in a series of studies conducted in the 1970s (see Siegel, 1982, for a full summary). Then, as now, different theories made different predictions about the role of language in cognitive development. Piagetian theory, on the one hand, proposes that cognitive structures develop independent of language; both language and thought are considered to depend on the same underlying mechanism of symbolic functioning (e.g. Inhelder & Piaget, 1964). Other approaches, especially that of Vygotsky (1962), assigned a primary role to language in the development of thought.

Siegel succeeded in operationalizing these theoretical issues within a experimental framework designed to separate the effects of perceptual and linguistic factors on the development of number and quantity concepts. She used a nonverbal discrimination learning paradigm to explore young children's awareness of numerical and quantitative relations. In one particular study large groups of 4- and 5-year-olds were reinforced for choosing numerically greater, smaller, or equivalent sets from various arrays of dots. The stimuli offered clear perceptual cues consistent with the numerical relations being tested (see Siegel, 1982, for full details). No quantitative language was used in the instructions. The same stimuli were also used for verbal tasks in which the children were asked "Which is bigger?" or "Which has the same number?". Siegel found that substantial percentages of children in both age groups passed the nonverbal task but failed the verbal equivalent. The reverse pattern was found in only three out of 102 cases. Siegel concluded that relatively simple quantitative problems can be solved by pre-schoolers using nonverbal skills based on direct perceptual information.

For Siegel the opportunity to study children with specific language impairments offered an important new perspective. These children, unlike normally developing subjects, had nonverbal skills significantly in advance of their level of language. If quantitative reasoning develops independent of language, then these children should perform at their age level on Siegel's nonverbal tasks. On the other hand, if linguistic mediation is entailed in solving the problems, then children with SLI should fail to perform at their age level, despite the exclusion of overt verbal demands from the test procedure. This paradigm offered an opportunity to test the general independence of quantitative reasoning and language. Siegel's nonverbal test procedure afforded an excellent tool for investigating number and quantity concepts without making demands on verbal input and output processes.

Siegel, Lees, Allan, and Bolton (1981) compared number and quantity concepts in 26 SLI children aged 3–5 years with those of a group of unimpaired children matched for age, sex, social class, and nonverbal ability. The SLI group was clinically diagnosed, and showed significant deficits relative to controls on the both the expressive and the receptive language measures. Nine experimental tasks were used. The range of difficulty was substantially greater than in the study previously described. The first three tasks involved binary choices based on perceptual discrimination. The remaining tasks were more complex, including a "conservation" test requiring identification of numerical equivalence between random arrays of up to nine items, as well as a "seriation" task requiring selection of the second longest of four bars of different lengths. All tasks were presented within a discrimination learning paradigm without explicit verbal instructions.

The results were extremely clear-cut. There was no significant difference between groups on the perceptual tasks. On five of the six complex tasks controls significantly outperformed the SLI children. Siegel et al. (1981, p. 157) explained their findings as follows:

> ... the language-impaired children had difficulty with concepts such as one-to-one correspondence, conservation, spatial ordering, and seriation that may involve some kind of sequential processing. Language may be important in these situations ... because it helps in the storage of information and/or place marking in a sequence. Language may facilitate the cognitive processes that are involved in these tasks and for this reason children with impaired language development may experience difficulty with this task.

Reviewing the findings from this and other studies Siegel (1982) concluded that the involvement of language in numerical and quantitative reasoning is age-dependent. Early perceptually based judgements, she argues, precede linguistic skills. However, the involvement of language increases as more complex reasoning is achieved. Siegel suggests that counting, even at a subvocal level, is language-based and that the involvement of count skills in quantitative reasoning marks a distinctive developmental advance.

The counting skills of pre-school children with specific language impairments were examined in detail by Barbara Fazio (1994). Fazio identified subcomponents of the count process, distinguishing between rote-counting skills (simple recitation of the number word sequence) and conceptual understanding (e.g. knowing that the last number spoken represents the set size). In a group of children with SLI aged around 5 years Fazio found that most subjects could rote-count up to six or so, similar to the levels reached by younger controls matched for expressive language level, and dramatically less than unimpaired age-peers (most of whom were counting up to 20 and beyond).

The SLI children in Fazio's study also failed to count objects as accurately as age peers. The proportion of sequence errors (i.e. the production of number words out of order) was especially high in the SLI group. However, detailed analysis of the nature of children's responses suggested that SLI children's conceptual understanding was close to that expected for their age and significantly better than would be predicted by their language level. By answering "How many?" questions with an immediate number word response (instead of a recount) the SLI children showed significantly better understanding of the function of counting (in particular, the "cardinality principle" discussed in Chapter 2) than younger controls who were their peers in both rote counting and expressive language ability.

An ingenious technique was used by Fazio to examine nonverbal count skills further. She used video-taped lessons to teach her subjects a gestural counting system based on touching body parts. The children were then asked to use the gestural system to perform rote and quantity counts. SLI children were able to learn and use this system better than language-matched controls, but not as well as unimpaired age peers. Using the gestural system, SLI children made proportionately fewer sequence errors. However, this did not represent an absolute improvement in performance. All the groups found the gestural system difficult to learn and use; SLI children simply found it less difficult than younger controls.

Fazio concluded that the SLI children's difficulty with counting originated in specific deficits in auditory-sequential processing. The severe restrictions this had imposed on their acquisition of the number word sequence did not extend to the gestural sequence, nor did it interfere with their knowledge of basic count principles. However, Fazio predicted that this pattern of learning was likely to produce cumulative deficits over time, and that poor rote counting would eventually provide a substantial obstacle to the development of arithmetical skills.

Taken together, these important studies carried out by Fazio and by Siegel and colleagues paint a somewhat negative picture. In the pre-school years normally developing children are able to extend their conceptual understanding of number; many start to understand the function of written numerical symbols (see Chapter 3). The findings of Siegel and Fazio are convergent insofar as they propose that specific language impairments and the auditory-sequential deficit which they entail present obstacles to numeracy acquisition that are likely to have increased impact as children with SLI enter school and are exposed to formal numerical instruction.

STUDIES OF SLI CHILDREN IN MID-CHILDHOOD: COUNTING AND ARITHMETIC SKILLS

Fazio (1996) followed up her original pre-school sample after a two-year interval. Fourteen of the original twenty children with SLI were tested; these were children, now aged 6 or 7, who were still receiving speech and language therapy. Fifteen of the original age-matched controls and sixteen of the younger language-matched controls were seen. Recall that Fazio (1994) had predicted that the obstacles that specific language impairments present to the acquisition of the verbal number sequence would have a cumulative negative impact on the acquisition of arithmetical skills.

Deficits in rote-counting skills had been especially marked in the SLI group at pre-school age. There was substantial improvement over the two-year interval. The mean highest number reached in correct order had increased from 6.3 to 42. However, the deficit in comparison to controls was still severe (mean highest number for age controls was now 85), and the level reached by the SLI group continued to shadow closely the level reached by the younger language-matched group.

By contrast the SLI children's accuracy in object counting had improved relative to controls. High accuracy was achieved by both SLI and age controls in counting small (2–9) and large (10–30) sets of toys. Language-matched controls were very substantially poorer.

SLI children also surpassed the performance level predicted by their language skills in an important new task, numeral reading. In the relatively demanding task of reading numerals in the range 11–50 the SLI group performed similarly to age controls (around 70% correct), far better than the younger language-matched group. SLI performance in writing numerals within this range was poorer, but still exceeded language-control level. These findings are important. The rate of acquisition of Arabic numeral knowledge shown by the SLI group is apparently close to the level expected for their age and therefore differs substantially from the rate of acquisition of verbal number knowledge (as indicated by rote counting).

Considerable emphasis was given by Fazio to investigation of the development of arithmetic skills. A variety of tasks was used. First, two sets of items (e.g. raisins) were presented and the child was asked to tell how many there were on the table all together. SLI children understood the task and were able to perform with very high accuracy (age-control level) for small totals (3–9). For higher totals (up to 20) they performed worse than age controls but still exceeded language-control level. Again, when presented with formal addition sums (totals 3–9) and asked to respond verbally, the SLI group performed worse than age controls but better than language controls. It was noted that all children tended to use their fingers and count in this task, but that age controls used the "count on" rather that "count all" strategy more often than both other groups. These observations are especially important since the move to "count on" is a significant development in strategy use, and one which appears to entail conceptual as well as procedural knowledge (see Johnson and Siegler, this volume).

Three further arithmetical tasks were included, each of which was simply too difficult for the language-controls, whose scores showed floor effects. The first was a "Say it quick" game in which single-digit addition sums were presented in traditional vertical format. Children were asked to respond quickly without using their fingers. Responses were accepted up to three seconds after presentation. SLI children were poorer on this task than age-controls (though still not at floor level). The same pattern of results was found for tasks involving written calculation, i.e. providing written responses to formal single-digit addition and subtraction sums.

Cognitive deficits underlying SLI performance

Fazio summarizes the deficit in SLI children's mathematical learning as a weakness in two types of declarative knowledge: the production of number words in correct order, and the recall of stored facts. Underlying deficits in short-term verbal memory (Gathercole & Baddeley, 1990) are cited as possible causal factors; these are held to restrict the acquisition of vocabulary and language skills generally. The verbal number sequence constitutes a special set of lexical items whose serial nature and phonological characteristics, in English at least, present special problems for a learner with limited capacity for processing new information. Consistent with this view is a descriptive account of number-word learning difficulties in a child with SLI presented by Hutt and Donlan (1991).

Fazio argues that the count-based strategies of the SLI children in her study, although affording reasonable levels of success in concrete addition tasks, are so demanding on cognitive resources as to restrict progress towards rapid problem-solving. Other studies have shown that children with specific language impairments have difficulties with counting that persist at least into mid-childhood. Conti-Ramsden, Donlan, and Grove (1992) gave a speeded count task to a group of 15 7-year-olds with SLI and a group of age-matched controls. Random arrays of dots (totals 2–9) were presented. Subjects were required to touch each dot and count aloud. Accuracy was high for both SLI and control groups, but the SLI group were significantly slower to perform the task. Donlan (1993a) gave the same task to a further group of eight 8-year-olds with SLI ; once again accuracy was as high as that of age-matched controls, but the count speed of the SLI group approximated that of unimpaired 5-year-olds. Finally, Donlan (1993b) gave two count tasks to 13 SLI 7-year-olds and 17 unimpaired 6-year-olds. Both groups performed at ceiling level when presented with random arrays of dots (totals 2–6). But with sets of 6–9 items comprising more complex perceptual material (e.g. cutlery, pens, toys, all of varied size and shape, cut from sales catalogues) the accuracy of the SLI group fell significantly below that of controls.

These convergent findings of reduced efficiency in counting demonstrate the appeal of a "limited resource" account of SLI children's difficulties. Within the working memory framework (Baddeley & Hitch, 1974; Baddeley, 1986) the severe deficits in immediate verbal memory typically associated with SLI are traceable to a "slave" subsystem dedicated to short-term storage of phonological information. On the other hand, tasks that require the simultaneous processing of novel information and maintenance of previously registered traces tax the efficiency and capacity of a central executive system operating in conjunction with slave system(s). This framework has appeal not only as an account of the cognitive processes serving mental arithmetic (see Chapter 8), but also of counting itself (Logie & Baddeley, 1987). In order to perform a successful count it is necessary not only to apply knowledge of general principles (Gelman & Gallistel, 1978) but also to operate and coordinate the appropriate information processing system(s) (Wilkinson, 1984). Satisfying these demands (e.g. recall of the verbal sequence, place-holding in the sequence, memory for items counted versus those remaining) makes substantial demands on working memory capacity, especially for the unskilled counter. The simultaneous requirement to store (items counted) and process (new items) is liable to be especially "costly" where recall and production of the verbal sequence is compromised; under these circumstances any increase in demand, even an increase in visual complexity, is liable to produce a substantial reduction in efficiency (Donlan, 1993b).

As Fazio (1996) proposes, this "limited resource" account predicts special problems for SLI children in the development of mental arithmetic skills. Fazio observed that her SLI subjects were less likely than controls to apply a "count on" rather than a "count all" strategy in simple addition, and were also less likely to achieve rapid retrieval of simple facts. According to Ashcraft (1995) both of these skills are traceable to the operation of the working memory system, and we know that deficits in short-term verbal memory are almost always found in children with SLI (Haynes & Naidoo, 1992). Might it be the case that limited capacity in working memory causes delay in acquisition of the "count-on" strategy, and that this delay itself inhibits storage of arithmetic facts? The account has obvious appeal (see Geary et al., 1991, for a discussion of related issues). However, evidence for the co-occurrence of working memory deficits and immature arithmetic strategies in SLI children is as yet conjectural; no single study has examined both tasks.

Nunes and Bryant (1996) suggest that the development of the "count on" strategy is a product of the child's developing ability to "expand" the representation of an addend and treat it as both a cardinal value and as the start point of a count procedure. This account, then, emphasizes the importance of the development of rich representations of numerical information in long-term memory, rather than the development of short-term memory capacity. To date no studies have been undertaken that explore Nunes and Bryant's proposal using children with SLI, but our own research has examined other aspects of SLI children's long-term representation of number. This will be summarized in the next section.

STUDIES OF MID-CHILDHOOD: NUMBER SYSTEM KNOWLEDGE IN CHILDREN WITH SLI

Nunes and Bryant (1996) draw an important distinction between the mastery of simple counting skills, based on one-to-one correspondence, and the mastery of additive composition, whereby a single item can stand for a set. The latter is evidenced by the child's ability to understand composite units (e.g. of money) and to be able to treat a single "composite" item (e.g. a 10p piece) as a representation of many units. Furthermore, "counting on" is itself seen as an important precursor of understanding the additive composition of the Arabic number system, within which the face value of symbols is systematically multiplied according to their position or place of occurrence. This place value rule whereby 1, 10, and 100, for example, are understood to represent cumulative powers of ten, is clearly a pivotal achievement in numeracy development. If, as Nunes and Bryant propose, this knowledge does not depend on simple count skills, might SLI children be able to acquire number system knowledge relatively easily, despite their deficits in number word knowledge?

SLI children's knowledge of single-digit numerals

Donlan, Bishop, and Hitch (1998) investigated SLI children's single-digit knowledge using the classic judgement task introduced by Moyer and Landauer (1967). The procedure tests subjects' ability to choose the greater of two simultaneously presented Arabic numerals. Moyer and Landauer showed that adults' reaction time (RT) in judging which of two single digits is larger is an inverse function of the numeric difference between the two digits; the greater the difference between the numbers, the faster the judgement. Moyer and Landauer observed that this pattern of RT for number judgements is very similar to the function known to hold for judgements of physical difference.

Thus, it seems that, within the judgement task, we treat differences in number in the same way that we treat, for example, differences in length or differences in temperature. Moyer and Landauer proposed that number judgements are based on mental representations characterized as "analogue magnitudes"; the comparison process involving these representations became known as the Symbolic Distance Effect (SDE).

Similar results are found in studies with children. Sekuler and Mierkiewicz (1977) gave the single-digit number judgement task to groups of 6-,7-,10-, and 13-year-old children. Overall reaction time decreased with age. All groups showed significant effects of symbolic distance, these effects being steeper for the younger children. The findings were discussed in relation to the analogue representation model. Sekuler and Mierkiewicz suggested that increased RT and steep SDE in the youngest children reflect "noisier" mental representations, but argued that the same basic process of comparison of mental analogues underlies digit comparison at all ages.

The judgement task, and the RT function it yields, provide a sensitive measure, then, not just of subjects' ability to discriminate between stimuli according to size or value, but also of the cognitive processes involved. It suited our purposes especially well because it made no explicit verbal demands, and, according to the accounts of Moyer and Landauer (1967) and Sekuler and Mierkiewicz (1977), draws on nonverbal mental representations of stimuli stored in long-term memory.

We examined SLI children's numeral judgement skills in comparison with their ability to judge other sorts of stimuli, using four different SDE tasks. Each task used a different sort of visual stimulus: houses (picture size systematically varied), animals (picture size held constant), dots, and numerals. Houses were depicted with graded increase in picture size, so that direct judgements of picture size were required. In constructing the animal stimuli picture size was held constant, so that comparative judgement required access to semantic information about real-life size stored in long-term memory. Each stimulus set included five items. In this way we were able to compare processing of symbolic versus perceptual material (animals and numerals versus houses and dots) as well as processing of numeric versus non-numeric material (numerals and dots versus animals and houses). We were confident that SLI children would be unimpaired on judgements of visual perceptual material. If these expectations were borne out, then our experimental design would allow us to any deficits specific to symbolic processing or to symbolic-numeric processing in particular.

In order to test the specific contribution of language skills to judgement ability a control group matched with the SLI subjects for language comprehension abililty was recruited. Subjects were selected on the basis of grammatical comprehension ability, as measured by the Test for the Reception of Grammar (Bishop, 1983).

We anticipated that children with SLI might show a reduced symbolic distance effect. In that case, it would be unclear whether the problem was a failure to use verbal mediation (e.g. covert naming or counting) to do the task, or some more general difficulty. As a further specific test of verbal mediation in the task we included an experimental manipulation involving concurrent articulation.

Subjects were required to repeat an irrelevant sound ("ice-cream, ice-cream, ice-cream") during task performance. If this requirement for concurrent articulation was found to interfere with size comparisons involving written numbers, this would suggest that processing written numbers involves verbal recoding (for discussion of this issue in relation to reading and spelling see Kimura & Bryant, 1983).

Twelve children with SLI aged around 6;6 and 19 normally developing controls aged around 5;0 were tested. Two of the SLI children showed high overall error rates (above the criterion level, which was set at 15% of trials). All of the controls were accurate. RT data were analysed for the 10 accurate SLI subjects and the 19 controls. The pattern of results was extremely clear-cut:

1.   There was significant group effect whereby SLI subjects were significantly faster than controls for each type of material.
2.   There was a significant distance effect whereby "closer" items took longer to judge than more "distant" items. The pattern was consistent across subject groups.
3.   There was a significant effect of stimulus type: houses were judged faster than all other stimuli; RT for numerals and dots did not differ; animals were judged more slowly than all other stimuli). The pattern was consistent across subject groups.
4.   There was no effect of concurrent articulation on performance.

A pre-test screening procedure had established that the nonverbal skills of each child in the SLI group (tested on Raven's Coloured Progressive Matrices, Raven, 1985) were age-appropriate. It is unsurprising, therefore, that this group should perform judgements based on visual perceptual information more efficiently than a group some 18 months younger whose raw scores on nonverbal testing were substantially lower. What is surprising is that symbolic stimuli, especially such highly abstract stimuli as Arabic numerals should be treated in the same way. Note that the pattern of RT for the SLI group did not suggest the involvement of any abnormal processes; the classic SDE was observed throughout. Furthermore, there was no effect of concurrent articulation on SLI performance, despite their obvious speech and language difficulties. The combined force of these findings is to suggest (in support of the original proposal of Moyer & Landauer, 1967) that symbolic judgements generally and numeral judgements in particular draw on nonverbal representations in long-term memory that are processed without verbal recoding. Furthermore, these long-term stored representations are early acquired, appearing to be well established by mid-childhood.

Before drawing strong conclusions from this study, however, we must acknowledge the following limitations.

1. The study is based on a relatively small sample; there is a risk that its findings may not generalize.
2. The range covered by each stimulus set is extremely small. The findings for numerals 1–5 may not extend to the full range of single-digits, or to multidigit numbers.
3. Even within the small sample studied individual differences between the SLI subjects emerged. Two out of 12 SLI children tested for the current study failed to reach accuracy criterion on the judgement task, though all 19 control 5-year-olds were accurate.

In order to clarify these issues a further study was made.

SLI children's knowledge of double-digit numerals

Donlan and Gourlay (in press) set out to extend earlier findings by testing children's ability to make judgements of the complete range of single digits, as well as double-digit pairs. Performance in the latter task was taken as a direct indicator of implicit knowledge of place value. By carefully controlling the stimulus items over a substantial number of trials and by setting stringent criteria for passing the test we believed it was possible to state confidently that those subjects reaching the criterion level had demonstrated knowledge of the place-value rule.

This approach to exploring the development of place-value knowledge was innovative. Many studies have attempted to evaluate the success of different pedagogical approaches to place-value rules. Attention has frequently focused on the use of concrete materials that represent composite base-10 units and aim to clarify the procedures of multidigit addition and subtraction (Fuson, 1986, 1990). The use of these materials is clearly intended to facilitate students' access to the semantic information (i.e. power of ten increase) encoded by place-value notation. Special emphasis has been given to the optimal location of these methods within an ordered and meaningful curricular framework (Hiebert & Wearne, 1992). Outcomes are most frequently evaluated via measures of attainment in multidigit arithmetic.

An alternative approach has been outlined by Becker and Varelas (1993). They point out that place value in Arabic notation uses the same set of characters to denote differing values, for example, the statement 11 uses the same symbol to denote values ten and one. This contrast between place value and face value is deliberately avoided in base-10 teaching materials that use, for example, stick and cube to denote values ten and one. Becker and Varelas constructed a modified notation system in which the relation between face-value and place-value is explicitly represented (i.e. special coloured "tens" cards have face-value on on side and full place-value on the other). They found that training in this system improved children's performance on a direct test of place-value knowledge more than training with base-10 materials. Understanding the relation between symbols in place-value notation, then, appears to be just as important as understanding the groupings of items to which the symbols refer.

Of central concern to us was the possible relation, or independence, of verbal and nonverbal representations of place-value. Towse and Saxton (Chapter 6) present a full review of cross-linguistic studies that have attempted to evaluate the effects of varying levels of correspondence between verbal realizations of number and the Arabic symbols on mathematical knowledge in general and place-value knowledge in particular. Such studies frequently show differences between groups, but it is unclear whether these reflect cognitive gains determined by linguistic advantages, or simply the combined effects of complex cultural differences.

The possible independence of verbal and nonverbal systems of enumeration has been extensively explored by Terezinha Nunes (Nunes et al., 1993). In one particular study Nunes used evidence from unschooled Brazilian adults to demonstrate that the central skill of understanding composite units does not depend on a written number system, but can be mastered using oral numeration, at least in coordination with composite monetary units (Carraher, 1985). This despite the fact that the Portuguese language, like English, fails to represent place value consistently. Relatively sophisticated number skills may develop without knowledge of written notation.

But what of the other alternative? Might place-value knowledge develop despite severe and persistent deficits in the acquisition of the verbal number sequence? Some surprising support for this view has already been reported. Fazio (1996) found that the rate of acquisition of double-digit naming skills in 6- and 7-year-olds with SLI was disproportionately rapid in comparison with the same children's persistently slow progress in rote counting. From this evidence it appears that the expected developmental pattern (Bialystok, 1992), whereby "pure" verbal skills (in this case rote counting) precede Arabic system knowledge (in this case numeral naming), might be reversed in SLI learners. Their verbal skills might be enhanced by exposure to the visually explicit Arabic system.

We tested the hypothesis that nonverbal and verbal routes to place-value knowledge may be independent in two ways. First, a within-subjects comparison was made of nonverbal and verbal skills. Nonverbal skills were tested using the judgement task outlined earlier for the full range of single-digits and for a representative set of double-digit numbers. Note that this task cannot be performed accurately without access to the meaning or value represented by each symbol. Verbal skills were tested using a simple "transcoding" task in which the experimenter presented numbers in spoken form and subjects were required to indicate Arabic equivalents on a visual display. Note that it is theoretically possible to perform this task accurately without knowledge of the relative values of the symbols involved. The distinction between tasks in respect of their requirement for semantic knowledge allows the following interpetation of possible outcomes for double-digit tasks. If children show mastery of the judgement task (A) but fail the transcoding task (B) this would suggest that place-value knowledge does not require spoken number knowledge. If children pass (B) but fail (A) then this would suggest that knowledge of verbal numerals is not sufficient to support place-value knowledge, though it may still be a necessary precondition. If children pass both (A) and (B) or fail both (A) and (B) then definite conclusions cannot be reached.

The second perspective from which the experimental hypothesis was explored involved a between-subjects comparison of the patterns of performance of three groups of children. A group of 8-year-olds with specific language impairments (SLI group), was compared to a group of 8-year-olds matched for age and nonverbal IQ (age-control or AC group) and to a younger group matched for language-comprehension level (LC group).

If the experimental tasks make primary demands on verbal processing then the SLI group should perform at the level of younger children matched for language ability (LC). If nonverbal processing predominates then SLI performance should match that of the AC group.

The pattern of correspondences between the SLI and control groups was of central importance to the experimental design. Nonverbal ability (as indicated by standards scores on Raven's Coloured Progressive Matrices, Raven, 1985) was closely matched betwen groups. Age-matching between SLI and AC groups was near perfect. Some considerable thought was given to the question of language matching for the SLI and LC groups. Matching on the basis of language comprehension scores was considered appropriate, as the experimental tasks on which group comparisons were to be made were primarily tests of numeral comprehension. This technique had the further advantage of offering a conservative comparison. It is a general characteristic of SLI populations that expressive language deficits are measurably greater than receptive deficits (Bishop & Edmundson, 1987; Haynes & Naidoo, 1992). This proved to be true of the current sample, and therefore selection of LC subjects on the basis of comprehension levels entailed selection of older subjects than would have been chosen if an expressive language match were made. The narrower age gap between SLI and LC that comprehension matching produces reduces the probability of distinguishing between the groups on experimental testing. This conservative matching procedure strengthens the force of any inter-group differences which may emerge. Language matching was carried out using raw scores on the Test for Reception of Grammar (TROG) (Bishop, 1983), a picture selection test in which the subject is required to comprehend sentences of increasing grammatical complexity. Mean raw scores for SLI and LC groups differed by less than one point. The LC subjects were around 2 years younger than their SLI counterparts.

The first experiment compared single-digit judgements (range 1–9) with a control condition requiring judgement of direct perceptual information (blocks graded in size from 1–9). Accuracy was perfect for all groups for the block comparisons. Latency data was analysed for all subjects. SLI and AC groups showed similar speed of response; both were faster that the LC group. All groups showed uniform distance effects (SDE) as expected.

These findings confirmed the validity of the experimental design insofar as perceptual (nonverbal) judgements were performed with equal skill by the SLI and AC groups, with the younger LC group showing less efficiency than both older groups.

Accuracy for single-digit judgements was achieved by 100% of AC subjects, 92% of SLI subjects, and 69% LC subjects. Latencies were analysed for all subjects who reached the accuracy criterion. The pattern of latencies exactly matched that found for block judgements (SLI = AC < LC) with uniform distance effects for all groups.

Verbal comprehension of numbers 1–9 was presented using a printed number line. The experimenter placed the number line in front of the subjects and instructed them to point to the numbers as they were spoken. Performance on this task was perfect for all subjects.

At single-digit level, then, with the exception of one subject, the number-system knowledge of the SLI group appears to be age-appropriate. The five subjects (one SLI and four LC) who failed to reach accuracy criterion on single-digit judgement all showed perfect comprehension of the corresponding spoken numerals, conforming to the generally expected pattern of whereby spoken number knowledge precedes Arabic system knowledge.

The second experiment examined double-digit judgements (range 10–99). As the LC group had no formal school experience of double-digit numbers, only the AC and LC groups were tested. Three different judgement types were used. "Transparent" trials involved simple decade comparisons, comparisons in which a unit value lower than either decade value is shared by both numerals (e.g. 70 vs. 50; 21 vs. 71), and comparisons in which both numerals contain repeated digits (e.g. 33 vs. 88). "Reversible" pairs included 19 versus 91 and 12 versus 21. "Misleading" pairs involved numerals in which the nontarget item contains a unit value greater than the sum of digits in the target numeral (e.g. 18 vs. 21; 32 vs. 29).

Accuracy was achieved by 61% of SLI children and 83% of AC children. Latency data was analysed for all subjects reaching the accuracy criterion. SLI and AC groups showed similar speed of response. Analysis of the effect of judgement types on response times showed that transparent trials were judged faster than both reversible and misleading pairs, and that this pattern was consistent across groups.

Comprehension of double-digit numbers was presented using a printed 100 square. The subject was asked to point to twenty double-digit numbers spoken by the experimenter. The numbers were selected at random from those included in the judgement task. 69% of SLI subjects and 83% of AC subjects reached this criterion.

Recall that the comparison of judgement and transcoding skills within each subject was a central concern of the study. If children can judge double-digit Arabic numerals without comprehension of their spoken forms (Pattern 1) this is taken to indicate that place-value knowledge does not require spoken number knowledge. If the reverse is found, and children fail to judge double-digit Arabic numerals but succeed in comprehending spoken numbers (Pattern 2), then spoken number knowledge is not sufficient to support place-value knowledge, but it may still be a necessary precondition.

The performance of the control group was extremely clear-cut. Most subjects were successful on both tasks, but two individuals showed Pattern 2. This pattern shows general consistency with the consensus view articulated by Bialystok (1992) that verbal number knowledge is a necessary precursor of Arabic numeral knowledge.

Within the SLI group performance was more varied. Most subjects passed both tasks. Three subjects failed both tasks. Two subjects conformed to Pattern 2 (as had two AC subjects). However, one SLI subject showed Pattern 1, demonstrating, albeit in a single case, that spoken number knowledge is not a necessary prerequisite for knowledge of place value within the Arabic numeral system.

Our findings in the place-value study need careful interpretation. First, it is clear that specific language impairments in children do not necessarily preclude the acquisition of place-value knowledge. More than half of our group were successful in judging double-digit numbers, and were therefore employed the place-value rule in deriving values from the symbols. The efficiency and processing strategies of these children were not distinguished from those of the control group who were sucessful in the judgement task. Furthermore, one of the successful SLI subjects, perhaps surprisingly, was not able to match Arabic numerals to spoken double digits satisfactorily. This is rather strong evidence, we believe, of the possible independence of verbal and nonverbal representations in development.

However, the problem of individual differences remains; one 8-year-old with SLI was unable to judge single digits and five were unable to judge double digits. A full theoretical account of the developmental pattern must include an explanation of these differences. Further work is needed to identify the source of this variation.

SUMMARY OF FINDINGS

Research into the development of mathematical skill in children with specific language impairments is in its infancy. As yet few studies have been devoted to comprehensive or detailed investigation of mathematical skills in this group, despite the strong theoretical interest of the issues raised.

In theory it is likely that the impact of specific language impairments on mathematical development will reflect an interaction in normal development between verbal and nonverbal components of mathematical skill. The few pieces of experimental evidence currently available support this view.

The 3- to 5-year-olds with SLI studied by Siegel et al. (1981) provide us with our earliest snapshot of the special developmental progress of these children; their success in making perceptually based quantitative judgements is qualified by poorer performance on more complex tasks where place-holding in a sequence and other count-based skills are required. This is consistent with Fazio's (1994) findings in which 5-year-olds with SLI had special problems with rote counting, which apparently affected accuracy in object counting tasks. However, Fazio also found that these SLI 5-year-olds had relatively good functional knowledge of counting; it was as if their verbal deficits provided a methodological obstacle that had not, at this stage at least, undermined their conceptual grasp of the uses of number.

The picture in mid-childhood is also mixed. On the one hand it is clear from a number of studies that SLI children tend to show persistent deficits in count skills. The range of rote counting is slow to extend (Fazio, 1996), the rate of counting for small sets is slow (Conti-Ramsden et al., 1992, Donlan, 1993a), and the accuracy of counting can be compromised if the material is perceptually complex (Donlan, 1993b). Observed deficits in simple arithmetic and slow arithmetical strategy development (Fazio, 1996) may be understood in relation to the slow and effortful counting strategies on which SLI children appear to depend.

On the other hand, evidence is emerging that the majority of SLI children are able to acquire knowledge of the Arabic number system at a rate that is close to that expected for their age. Transcoding tasks involving double-digit numerals and their spoken forms are far better performed by SLI 7- to 8-year-olds than their language level or their rote-counting skill would predict (Donlan &

Gourlay, in press; Fazio, 1996). Furthermore, early indications are that knowl-edge of double-digit numeral meanings (as demonstrated in Donlan and Gour-lay's comparative judgement task) is at an age-appropriate level in most SLI children, and may be present, exceptionally, when spoken number names are poorly understood.

CONCLUSIONS

Studies carried out so far suggest that impairments in children's language development affect their mathematical learning significantly, but not in a global fashion. Substantial individual differences are found, but still a developmental pattern is emerging that distinguishes children with SLI from their normally developing peers. The expectation that the most explicitly verbal of numerical skills, rote-counting, will be impaired, is amply borne out. This deficit extends to object counting by reducing overall efficiency, but seems not to prevent the development of conceptual principles underlying purposeful counting.

Somewhat surprisingly, we have suggestive evidence that number-system knowledge, and place-value knowledge in particular, develop at the normal rate in many children with SLI. If the results of our studies in this area are extended and replicated then they will carry important implications: First, that some children at least show modular language impairments in so far as they acquire the central principles of symbolic representation of number in a way that is indistinguishable from unimpaired age peers; second that normal pathways to place-value knowledge depend in part at least on nonverbal skills that may be dissociated from simple rote-counting ability.

Further work is needed to relate SLI children's number-system knowledge to their developing arithmetical skills. At present such evidence as we have suggests a possible further dissociation between number-system knowledge and arithmetical skill. We urgently need to explore this relationship. By doing so we may be able to throw further light not only on the intricate effects of SLI on mathematical learning but also on the subtle interdependence of verbal and nonverbal skills in the normal development of mathematical skills.

CHAPTER TWELVE

Individual differences in normal arithmetical development

Ann Dowker
University of Oxford, UK

INTRODUCTION

It is well known that individual differences in arithmetical performance are very marked in both children and adults. For example, Cockcroft (1982) reported that an average class of 11-year-olds is likely to contain the equivalent of a seven-year range in arithmetical ability. Such individual differences often appear to persist through life.

Admittedly, individual differences are also marked in other educational domains, such as reading. Many children have specific learning difficulties in reading (e.g. Bryant & Bradley, 1985; Frith, 1986; Snowling, 1991), and some adults experience persistent literacy difficulties, despite seemingly adequate educational opportunities. Moreover, there are noticeable individual differences between normal individuals, regarding the *strategies* that they favour in reading (Bryant & Impey, 1986). Nevertheless, most normal adults who have received adequate instruction do read well, whatever their preferred strategy. By contrast, many adults show pronounced persisting difficulties in arithmetic (Cornelius, 1992; Hitch, 1978c; Sewell, 1981).

Although arithmetical ability is sometimes treated as a single entity, it has been occasionally argued over many years (e.g. Weaver, 1954) that it is made up of a number of components and there is increasing evidence for that view. A central argument of this chapter is that there is no such thing as arithmetical ability: only arithmetical abilities. The corollary is that arithmetical development is not a single process, but several processes, involving the development of the different components. There are some virtually universal discrepancies between the developmental patterns of different components. For example, the recognition of quantities up to 3 is probably innate (Starkey & Cooper, 1980; Wynn, 1992a), whereas manipulation and possibly even comprehension of very large multidigit numbers is difficult even for most adults (Hofstadter, 1982).

In addition to these universal discrepancies, there are also individual differences in performance on a variety of specific components or arithmetic, leading to individual differences in the nature, extent, and direction of discrepancies between these components. Evidence for these comes from (1) studies of specific aspects of arithmetical functioning in normal individuals; (2) neuropsychological studies of dyscalculic patients; (3) factor analytic studies; and (4) studies of children with developmental disabilities in arithmetic.

(1) Studies of normal children and adults demonstrate that a single individual can show marked discrepancies between different components of arithmetical ability. For example, studies of pre-schoolers' counting (Greeno et al., 1984) have given rise to the idea of a distinction between conceptual competence (understanding basic number concepts and counting principles) and procedural competence (being able to count accurately).

Distinctions between procedural and conceptual competence are also relevant to the arithmetical development of primary and secondary school children (cf. Baroody & Ginsburg, 1986). Children may carry out arithmetical procedures accurately without understanding the concepts behind them or being able to reason effectively about numbers (Bidwell, 1983; Bryant, 1985; Erlwanger, 1973). It is being increasingly recognised that they may also show discrepancies in the opposite direction, with better conceptual than procedural knowledge (Baroody, 1987; Dowker, 1995; Jordan & Montani, 1996a, b; Ginsburg, 1977; Russell & Ginsburg, 1984). Discrepancies in both directions can also be found in normal adults (Hitch, 1978c). Moreover, both conceptual and procedural competence can be further divided into numerous components, and individual differences regarding the different components are easily observed in both children and adults.

Indeed, it seems that, when investigated, almost no component is so simple as to fail to evoke individual differences in normal adults. Deloche et al. (1994) gave 180 normal adult subjects the EC301, a standardized testing battery for the evaluation of brain-damaged adults in the area of calculation and number processing. Although most of the normal subjects performed well, there were significant individual differences even in such components as written and oral counting, and transcoding between digits and written and spoken number words. Normal adults also show significant individual differences both in reaction times and in strategy choice for single-digit addition (Geary & Wiley, 1991; Lefevre and Kulak, 1994) and multiplication (Lefevre et al., 1996).

(2) There have been several factor analytic studies of arithmetic, involving identification of tests that cluster together. Such studies have led to the distinction between two mathematical domains: numerical facility and mathematical reasoning (e.g. Geary & Widaman, 1987, 1992; Thurstone & Thurstone, 1941). These may correspond to the general domains of procedural and conceptual competence described earlier. It should be remembered that factor analysis is more a means of investigating *associations* than *dissociations*, and so would not normally aim to examine whether the main factors can be further subdivided into potentially dissociable components. Also, factor analysis depends on the number and nature of tests that are introduced into the study in the first place; and a few studies that have incorporated additional tests have appeared to uncover additional factors, for example, the Dot Counting factor proposed by Thurstone & Thurstone (1941). However, whatever the limitations of such studies, they do agree with other types of study in providing support for componential theories of individual differences in arithmetic (Geary & Widaman, 1992).

(3) Some of the most striking evidence for the componential nature of arithmetic, and the possibility of individual differences in the relative levels of functioning of the different components, comes from studies of patients who have become dyscalculic as the result of brain damage. Such patients may demonstrate single and double dissociations between different arithmetical operations (Cipolotti & Delacycostello, 1995; Dagenbach & McCloskey, 1992; McNeil & Warrington, 1994); between oral and written presentation modes (Campbell, 1994; McNeil & Warrington, 1993); and between number comprehension and production (Campbell, 1994). On a more abstract level, double dissociations are found between factual and procedural knowledge (McCloskey, 1992; Warrington, 1982); between factual/procedural and conceptual knowledge (Girelli & Delazer, 1996; Hittmair-Delazer, Sailer, & Berke, 1995; Hittmair-Delazer, Semenza, & Denes, 1994; Luchelli & DeRenzi, 1993) and between exact calculation and estimation (Dehaene & Cohen, 1991; Warrington, 1982).

(4) Results of studies of children with arithmetical disabilities (Geary, 1993; Rourke, 1993; Jordan & Montani, 1996a, b; Russell & Ginsburg, 1984; Shalev, Wiertman, & Amir, 1988; Temple, 1991) also suggest that arithmetic is componential. For example, double dissociations have been reported between factual and procedural knowledge of arithmetic in children (Temple, 1991). Such studies also indicate the possibility of discrepancies between different aspects of arithmetical reasoning: For example, children with arithmetical disabilities are often impaired at arithmetical word-problem solving, but not at

other aspects of arithmetical reasoning such as derived fact strategy use and estimation (Russell & Ginsburg, 1984).

Thus, there is overwhelming evidence that arithmetical ability is not unitary. Its components include basic number knowledge, memory for arithmetical facts, the understanding of concepts, and the ability to follow procedures. Each of these components has, in turn, a number of subcomponents. Number knowledge involves the ability to recognize numbers in different forms (numerals, number words, and concrete quantities) and to place them in order. Factual knowledge involves memory for different *categories* of facts (e.g. addition, multiplication, subtraction, division). Conceptual understanding involves, for example, understanding of the properties of and relationships between arithmetical operations; and also the ability to use them in the derivation of unknown arithmetical facts, especially where standard calculation procedures are also unknown, or are cumbersome and time-consuming. Unknown fact derivation includes both the derivation of new *exact* arithmetical answers from known facts by means of arithmetical principles such as commutativity and associativity (cf. Baroody, Ginsburg, & Waxman, 1983; Renton, 1992; Webb, 1995), and the derivation of *approximate* answers, that is estimation (cf. Sowder, 1992). Another aspect of conceptual knowledge is the semantic understanding of an arithmetical word problem or real-world arithmetical problem, and the ability to select the arithmetical operations and strategies appropriate to the problem in question (De Corte & Verschaffel, 1987). The latter subcomponent interacts with procedural knowledge, which involves, for example, memory for learned procedures; ability to carry them out in an appropriate sequence without losing track; and, in the case of written calculation, correct spatial alignment of numerals. Moreover, procedural knowledge and possibly other components may vary with the format of presentation (auditory versus visual; concrete versus numerical); and indeed, one important subcomponent of arithmetical ability may be the ability to *translate* from one format to another (cf. Hughes 1986).

Moreover, situation and context have a very great influence on the performance of arithmetical, or, indeed, any tasks. Several studies (Carraher, Carraher, & Schliemann, 1985; Carraher & Schliemann, 1985; Hughes, 1986; Lave, 1988; Pettito & Ginsburg, 1981) have shown that both children and adults may perform very differently, both in terms of accuracy level and of strategies, when mathematically equivalent problems are presented as a formal task and when they are embedded in a context that makes "human sense" to them. This is especially true for people with relatively limited formal schooling (Carraher et al., 1985), but it is certainly not confined to such people.

In addition, research either on individual differences or on the componential nature of a cognitive domain must take into account that *within*-individual variability in responses to very similar problems seems to be an important human cognitive characteristic. The same person may use a wide variety of arithmetical strategies for apparently very similar problems, or even for the same problem (Cowan & Renton, 1989; Dowker, 1992a; Dowker et al., 1996; Hennessy, 1992; Lefevre et al., 1996; Siegler & Engle, 1994; Siegler & Jenkins, 1989).

Despite all the converging evidence for the componential nature of arithmetical ability, there are still issues that need to be explored further. In particular, studies of normal subjects have tended to involve groups rather than individuals, which means that where separable components are identified, it may not be clear whether these components may be further divisible. If two abilities (for example, mental calculation for addition and mental calculation for subtraction) are closely related, and thus describable as a single component, does this mean that they must *always* be associated, or are there some individuals in whom they are discrepant? By contrast, studies of people with acquired dyscalculia usually involve individuals rather than groups, and, moreover, involve individuals whose functioning is highly atypical. These studies have the advantages of making it possible to study dissociations in a very marked form, and to facilitate our understanding of the neurological bases of cognition. However, individual case studies of *normal* subjects are important if we are to gain some idea of the level of encapsulation of different components of arithmetical ability and the nature of individual differences in specific components (cf. also Ginsburg, 1977). The *combination* of such studies with larger-scale, statistically analysable group studies seems desirable if we are to explore both associations and discrepancies adequately.

The issue is not only of theoretical importance but also of educational importance. Educational implications include the possibility of developing suitable means of assessing children's individual strengths and weaknesses and of adapting teaching techniques to these strengths and weaknesses. The importance of both between- and within-individual variability in arithmetical functioning is indeed being increasingly emphasized by educators (Department of Education and Science and the Welsh Office, 1989; Keating, 1993).

Other questions that need to be answered include the issue of whether the different arithmetical components have other cognitive correlates (e.g. psychometric or memory components)? Some studies (e.g. Hitch & McCauley, 1991) have suggested that poor working memory for numbers plays an important part in specific arithmetical difficulties (see Chapter 7). There have also been suggestions (Deluka, Deldotto, & Rourke, 1987; Rourke, 1993) that there are two main subtypes of arithmetic disabilities. In the first, reading is unimpaired; verbal IQ is superior to nonverbal IQ, and there may even be "nonverbal learning disabilities" involving spatial and social learning deficits and indications of right-hemisphere dysfunction; and the arithmetical disabilities involve predominantly conceptual deficits. In the second, reading is also impaired; nonverbal IQ is superior to verbal IQ; and the arithmetical disabilities are mostly memory-related. However, Jordan and Montani (1996b) found the opposite distinction between the types of arithmetical deficit shown by children with specific arithmetical disabilities and those with combined reading/arithmetic disabilities (their study did not investigate verbal and nonverbal IQ). Also, findings concerning groups selected for having disabilities may not necessarily generalize to individual differences in unselected groups.

The research to be reported in this chapter involves a group study of normal primary school children, investigating individual differences in, and relationships between, measures of calculation performance in addition and subtraction. Two different types of arithmetical reasoning involving unknown fact derivation are explored: (1) derived fact strategy use to obtain exact answers; and (2) estimation; some psychometric measures are also taken. The study includes some individual case studies of children within the group.

In addition, effects of gender and social class were examined. Gender differences in mathematics have been investigated and discussed extensively (cf. Geary, 1994). In fact, such gender differences are usually not great in the age group under study here; however, it seemed desirable to investigate whether they would be noticeable in a study where different arithmetical components were being analysed separately. Social class is associated with performance in many academic domains, and on psychometric tests. With regard to arithmetic, it is sometimes found (Ginsburg, 1977; Jordan, Levine & Huttenlocher, 1994) that children from lower-income families perform worse in formal arithmetic, but are not greatly delayed in the development of informal arithmetical concepts. The present study included social class as a measure in order to investigate whether it would have different degrees of influence on calculation and arithmetical reasoning measures.

The term "normal" is always an ambiguous one. It is here used only to mean that all the subjects were attending mainstream schools and were not selected for having any specific arithmetical or other disabilities. It does *not* mean that none of them had any such disabilities, nor does it imply any value judgement.

PART 1: RELATIONSHIPS BETWEEN ARITHMETICAL CALCULATION, ARITHMETICAL REASONING, AND SOME PSYCHOMETRIC TEST PERFORMANCE

The central foci of this part of the study are the relationships between *calculation performance* and *derived fact strategy use* in addition and subtraction. We also examine relationships between these measures and performance on other tasks that were given to some of the children in the study, including another arithmetical reasoning task (estimation) and different parts of the Wechsler Intelligence Scale for Children (Wechsler, 1991).

A total of 213 children in age ranging from 5;2 to 9;10 were tested individually. A very few came from a private school, but over 200 were drawn from three state schools. Six-year-olds were represented more than other age-groups (12 five-year-olds; 101 six-year-olds; 30 seven-year-olds; 42 eight-year-olds; and 28 nine-year-olds). Of the children tested 95 were boys and 118 were girls; 58 came from working-class backgrounds, 117 from middle-class backgrounds, and the social class background of the rest was not known.

Method and techniques

In order to evaluate the children's competence in addition calculations, a mental calculation task was given to each child. This was the test previously devised to assess children's mental addition performance prior to an estimation task (Dowker, 1997). It consisted of a list of 20 addition sums graduated in difficulty from 6 + 3, 4 + 5, etc. to 349 + 235. These sums were simultaneously presented orally and visually in a horizontal format. The children's answers were oral.

The sums were as follows:

(1)	6 + 3	(11)	31 + 57
(2)	4 + 5	(12)	68 + 21
(3)	8 + 2	(13)	52 + 39
(4)	7 + 1	(14)	45 + 28
(5)	4 + 9	(15)	33 + 49
(6)	7 + 5	(16)	26 + 67
(7)	8 + 6	(17)	235 + 142
(8)	9 + 8	(18)	613 + 324
(9)	26 + 72	(19)	523 + 168
(10)	23 + 44	(20)	349 + 234

Testing continued with each child until he or she had failed to give a correct response to six successive items.

The children were then divided into five levels according to their performance on the mental calculation task.

Table 12.1 gives brief descriptions of the levels, with numbers and children at each level, means and standard deviations for their ages, and examples of the problems that could and could not be solved at these levels.

The children were then given an arithmetical reasoning test involving *use of arithmetical principles in derived fact strategies*. The technique was used in giving children the answer to a problem and then asking them to solve another problem that could be solved quickly by using this answer, together with the principle under consideration. Problems preceded by answers to numerically unrelated problems were given as controls. The exact arithmetic problems given varied according to the previously assessed calculation ability of the

TABLE 12.1
Age and levels of arithmetical performance in addition

Level	No. of children	Mean age (yrs;mths)	SD for age (mths)	Prob. just within range	Prob. outside range
Beginning arithmetic	27	6;4	(5.10)	2 + 2	6 + 3
Facts to 10	51	6;9	(11.85)	6 + 3	8 + 6
Simple facts	67	7;21	(4.70)	8 + 6	23 + 44
2-digit (no carry)	19	7;11	(13.24)	23 + 44	52 + 39
2-digit (carry)	31	8;3	(8.67)	52 + 39	523 + 168
3-digit	18	8;6	(9.23)	523 + 168	–
Total	213				

child, and were selected to be just a little too difficult for the child to solve unaided. Such a set of problems is referred to here, as in earlier studies (Dowker, 1989; Dowker, 1997), as the child's *base corresponding set*. Children of the highest (3-digit Addition) level had no base corresponding set. They were given the same set as the next highest (2-digit Addition; No Carrying Level). These were problems that they might have been able to solve by calculation, and this fact must be taken into account when considering the results obtained from children at this level. These children's results are, however, included for the sake of completeness.

Each child was shown the arithmetic problems, while the experimenter simultaneously read them to him or her. Children were asked to respond orally. The children received three arithmetical problems per principle; on rare occasions, when there was serious ambiguity about the interpretation of their responses, they received a fourth problem.

The principles investigated were as follows, in order of their difficulty for the children:

1 The *identity principle* (e.g. if one is told that $8 + 6 = 14$, then one can automatically give the answer "14", without calculating, if asked "What is $8 + 6$?").
2 The *commutativity principle* (e.g. if $9 + 4 = 13$, $4 + 9$ must also be 13).
3 The *n + 1 principle* (e.g. if $23 + 44 = 67$, $23 + 45$ must be 68).
4 The *n – 1 principle* (e.g. if $9 + 8 = 17$, $9 + 7$ must be $17 – 1$ or 16).
5 The *n × 10 principle* (e.g. if $26 + 72 = 98$, then $260 + 720 = 980$).
6 The *addition/subtraction inverse principle* (e.g. if $46 + 27 = 73$, then $73 – 27$ must be 46).

A child was deemed to be able to use a principle if he or she could explain it and/or used it to derive at least 2 out of 3 unknown arithmetical facts, while being unable to calculate *any* sums of similar difficulty when there was no opportunity to use the principle. For children at the 3-digit addition level, only the first criterion was taken into account.

Table 12.2 gives the means and ranges of the numbers (out of 6) of the arithmetical principles used by the children at each level.

A very similar test for subtraction was given to 143 of the children. Once again, the children were given a calculation pretest, this time consisting of a list of 20 subtraction problems, as follows:

(1)	6 – 2	(11)	68 – 42
(2)	8 – 4	(12)	86 – 44
(3)	10 – 3	(13)	62 – 14
(4)	9 – 5	(14)	43 – 17
(5)	15 – 7	(15)	75 – 38
(6)	13 – 6	(16)	84 – 59
(7)	12 – 4	(17)	326 – 125
(8)	15 – 7	(18)	894 – 513
(9)	37 – 23	(19)	681 – 214
(10)	55 – 32	(20)	572 – 348

Testing continued with each child until he or she had failed to give a correct response to six successive items. The children were then divided into five levels according to their performance on the mental calculation task.

Table 12.3 give brief descriptions of the levels, with numbers and children at each level, means and standard deviations for their ages, and examples of the problems that could and could not be solved at these levels.

The principles investigated for *subtraction* were as follows, in order of their difficulty for the children:

TABLE 12.2
Numbers of arithmetical principles (out of 6) used for derived fact strategies in addition

Level	No. of children	No. of principles			
		Range	*Median*	*Mean*	*SD*
Beginning arithmetic	27	0–4	0	0.72	(1.18)
Facts to 10	51	0–4	1	1.82	(1.56)
Simple facts	67	0–6	3.5	3.01	(1.90)
2-digit (no carry)	19	1–6	4	3.89	(0.98)
2-digit (carry)	31	0–6	3	3.55	(1.63)
3-digit	18	1–6	5	3.92	(1.79)
Total	213				

TABLE 12.3
Age and levels of arithmetical performance in subtraction

Level	No. of children	Mean age (yrs;mths)	SD for age (mths)	Prob. just within range	Prob. outside range
Beginning arithmetic	17	6;6	8.75	–	6–2
Facts to 10	37	6;6	8.35	6–2	12–5
Simple facts	45	7;3	12.71	15–7	55–32
2-digit (no borrow)	18	7;10	10.90	55–32	62–14
2-digit (borrow)	22	8;5	10.06	62–14	894–513
3-digit	4	8;6	4.65	894–513	–
Total	143				

1   The *identity principle* (e.g. if one is told that $12 - 5 = 7$, then one can automatically give the answer "7" without calculating, if asked "What is 12 – 5?").
2   The *minuend + 1 principle* (e.g. if $67 - 45 = 22$, $68 - 45$ must be 23).
3   The *minuend – 1 principle* (e.g. if $572 - 348 = 224$, $571 - 348$ must be 223).
4   The *subtrahend + 1 principle* (e.g. if $9 - 6 = 3$, $9 - 7$ must be 2).
5   The *subtrahend – 1 principle* (e.g. if $37 - 23 = 14$, $37 - 22$ must be 15).
6   The *addition/subtraction inverse principle* (e.g. if $681 - 214 = 467$, then $214 + 467$ must be 681.
7   The *reversal* principle (e.g. if $11 - 3 = 8$, $11 - 8$ must be 3).

Table 12.4 give the means and ranges of the numbers (out of 6) of the arithmetical principles used by the children at each level.

Seventy of the children were also given an addition estimation task, which was also the subject of a larger-scale study in its own right (Dowker, 1989, 1992b; Dowker, 1997). In this study, each child was presented with an set of

TABLE 12.4
Numbers of arithmetical principles (out of 7) used for derived fact strategies in subtraction

Level	No. of children	No. of principles			
		Range	Median	Mean	SD
Beginning arithmetic	17	0–5	0	0.59	1.28
Facts to 10	37	0–5	2	1.65	1.47
Simple facts	45	0–5	4	2.42	1.31
2-digit (no borrow)	18	0–7	3.5	2.81	1.14
2-digit (borrow)	22	0–6	5	3.60	1.73
3-digit	4	4–5	5	4.75	1.50
Total	14				

addition problems within their base correspondence as defined earlier. (They were also asked to estimate answers to sums outside the base correspondence, but the results of that part of the task will not be included in the present analysis.) Each set included a group of nine sums to which a pair of imaginary characters ("Tom and Mary") estimated answers. Each set of "Tom and Mary's" estimates included three good estimates (e.g. "7 + 2 = 10" "71 + 18 = 90"); three that were too small; and three that were too large. The children were asked to evaluate each guess on a five-point scale from "very good" to "very silly", represented by a set of schematic faces ranging from very smiling to very frowning, and were themselves asked to suggest "good guesses to the sums".

There were also other tests that many children received, which are not included in the present analysis. Some of these will be mentioned later with regard to Part 2 of this study: the individual case studies.

Analyses of relationships between calculation, reasoning, background, and psychometric measures

The relationships between the arithmetical calculation and reasoning measures and between these and certain background and psychometric measures were analysed.

The particular arithmetical performance measures included in the analysis were: (1) addition level; (2) use of addition principles for derived fact strategies; (3) subtraction level; (4) use of subtraction principles for derived fact strategies; and (e) addition estimation.

For the purpose of the analysis, these were defined in a simplified way by single numerical values: (2) and (4) were defined as the *numbers* of the principles (out of 6 for addition, and out of 7 for subtraction) that were accepted and used in derived fact strategies; (5) was defined as the number of estimates, within the base correspondence, that were reasonable. Reasonable estimates were defined (Dowker, 1989) as those that were within 30% of the correct answer, and that were also less than the larger addend.

Of course, there are many important aspects of estimation performance and derived fact strategy use that are not taken into account in these measures. However, for the purposes of the present study, it seemed desirable to use measures that were as simple as possible.

The background and psychometric measures that were investigated were: (1) gender; (2) social class; (3) age (in months); (4) WISC Verbal IQ; (5) WISC Performance IQ; (6) WISC Arithmetic scaled score; and (7) WISC Digit Span scaled score. The Arithmetic and Digit Span measures were Verbal IQ subtests, but were also included separately, because they may be thought to have particular relevance to arithmetical calculation and reasoning. The Arithmetic subtest may indeed be regarded as another arithmetical performance measure, predominantly assessing the ability to solve arithmetical word problems. Digit

Span would be expected to be of particular importance to calculation if one accepts theories of the importance of working memory for numbers (but see Introduction to Section 3, this volume, for an alternative view).

Table 12.5. gives Spearman Rank Correlation Coefficients between all the variables. As can be seen, most correlations were significant.

Further analyses appeared desirable, to gain a more detailed understanding of the interrelationships, and the extent to which different factors might influence another *independently*.

A stepwise multiple regression or a multiway analysis of variance incorporating all the variables might have been the most economical and powerful way of achieving this knowledge. However, such procedures would have been limited by the fact that at the time of the analyses only 38 children in the sample had been subjected to *all* the possible measures. This means that a great deal of potentially informative data would have needed to be omitted, and the analyses would have been subject to all the disadvantages of small samples. Therefore, the more cumbersome but more flexible technique was adopted of using multiple analyses of variance, with several different measures used as dependent variables, and with and without certain key measures included as covariates. The results of these analyses are shown in Table 12.6, and are *summarized* in the next section.

In some of the analyses, the number of levels was reduced from six to four by grouping the three most advanced levels together. This simplified the analyses, and reduced the possibility of anomalous results occurring because of certain groups being too small: simplification was particularly important for subtraction, where the highest calculation level accounted for only four subjects. This form of grouping appeared appropriate because it divided children who had achieved some degree of competence in multidigit arithmetic from the groups who had not. Also, as can be seen from Tables 12.2 and 12.4, increases in Number of Principles with Level became much less marked once the fourth (2-digit; No Carry) level had been reached.

Table 12.6 gives the results of the analyses of variance that were carried out.

Summary and discussion of results

In brief, the results show strong associations between calculation and estimation; between calculation and derived fact strategy use; and, most of all, between estimation and derived fact strategy use. The strongest associations were between addition and subtraction, in regard to both calculation and derived fact strategy use. However, individuals could show marked discrepancies between any and all of these tasks. Gender had no effect on performance; social class had only modest effects; and IQ measures had rather larger effects.

The results of the analyses will now be summarized in greater detail:

TABLE 12.5
Spearman rank correlations between the variables

	No. tested	Addition performance level	No. of principles for addition	Subtraction performance level	No. of principles for subtraction	Estimation (No. of reasonable estimates in base correspondence)	Age	Verbal IQ	Performance IQ	Verbal/performance discrepancy	Arithmetic scaled score	Digit span scaled score
Addition performance level	213	—	0.522**	0.838**	0.509**	0.406**	0.559**	0.92**	0.346**	0.052	0.424**	0.305**
Number of principles for addition	213	—	—	0.557**	0.773**	0.583**	0.379**	0.555**	0.453**	0.274*	0.394**	0.353*
Subtraction performance level	137	—	—	—	0.52**	0.276*	0.54**	0.313**	0.347**	0.15	0.479**	0.332**
No. of principles for subtraction	137	—	—	—	—	0.615**	0.36**	0.471**	0.497**	0.084	0.12	0.211
Estimation (No. of reasonable estimates for base correspondence)	70	—	—	—	—	—	0.288**	0.471**	0.373**	0.006	0.185	0.11
Age	213	—	—	—	—	—	—	0.126	0.019	-0.03	-0.007	-0.013
Verbal IQ	132	—	—	—	—	—	—	—	0.52**	0.207*	0.58**	0.52
Performance IQ	102	—	—	—	—	—	—	—	—	0.208*	0.512**	0.407
Verbal performance discrepancy	99	—	—	—	—	—	—	—	—	—	0.12	0.211*
Arithmetic scaled score	165	—	—	—	—	—	—	—	—	—	—	0.398**
Digit span scaled score	133	—	—	—	—	—	—	—	—	—	—	—

$*P < .05; **P < .01.$

287

TABLE 12.6
Analyses of variance

Dependent variable	Grouping factor(s)	Covariate(s)
1. Addition performance level	Gender $F_{(1,212)}=0.06$ Class $F_{(1,212)}=10.51**$ Interaction: $F_{(1,212)}=2.55$	Age $F_{(1,168)}=9.92**$
2. Addition performance level	Gender $F_{(1,78)}=1.33$ Class $F_{(1,78)}=0.36$ Interaction: $F_{(1,83)}=0.23$	Verbal IQ $F_{(1,78)}=4.13*$ Performance IQ $F_{(1,78)}=5.87*$ Verbal/Performance discrepancy $F_{(1,78)}=0.08$
3. No. of addition principles	Gender $F_{(1,168)}=0$ Class $F_{(1,168)}=5.92*$ Interaction: $F_{(1,168)}=0.17$	Age $F_{(1,83)}=53.65**$ Addition performance level $F_{(1,168)}=33.96**$
4. No. of addition principles	Level (last 3 levels collapsed) $F_{(3,89)}=7.39*$ Verbal/Performance discrepancy (<11 points vs. > 11 points) $F_{(1,98)}=5.91*$ Interaction: $F_{(3,98)}=0.63$	Verbal IQ $F_{(1,98)}=16.79**$ Performance IQ $F_{(1,89)}=1.48$
5. No. of addition principles	Level (last 3 levels collapsed) $F_{(3,81)}=5.63**$ Class $F_{(1,81)}=0.01$ Interaction: $F_{(1,81)}=0.18$	Verbal IQ $F_{(1,81)}=18.98**$ Performance IQ $F_{(1,91)}=0.35$ Verbal/Performance discrepancy $F_{(1,81)}=3.86(*)$
6. No. of addition principles	Verbal/Performance discrepancy (<11 points vs. ≥11 points) $F_{(1,98)}=9.09**$ Direction of discrepancy (Verbal higher vs. performance higher) $F_{(1,98)}=0.57$ Interaction: $F_{(1,98)}=0.36$	Addition performance level $F_{(1,98)}=46.68**$
7. Subtraction performance level	Gender $F_{(1,56)}=0.46$ Class $F_{(1,56)}=0$ Interaction: $F_{(1,56)}=0.46$	Performance IQ $F_{(1,46)}=0.14$ Verbal IQ $F_{(1,46)}=4.71*$ No. of addition principles $F_{(1,46)}=0.92$
8. No. of subtraction principles	Level (last 3 levels collapsed) $F_{(1,131)}=1.72$ No. of addition principles $F_{(1,131)}=116.24**$	
9. No. of subtraction principles	Gender $F_{(1,100)}=1.46$ Class $F_{(1,100)}=6.41*$ Interaction: $F_{(1,100)}=0.37$	Subtraction performance level $F_{(1,100)}=33.14**$ Age $F_{(1,100)}=1.67$
10. No. of subtraction principles	Level (last 3 levels collapsed) $F_{(3,62)}=3.76*$ Verbal/Performance (<11 points vs. > 11 points) $F_{(1,62)}=0.02$ Interaction: $F_{(3,62)}=0.07$	Verbal IQ $F_{(1,62)}=9.19**$ Performance IQ $F_{(1,62)}=6.39*$

11. No. of subtraction principles	Level (last 3 levels collapsed) $F(3,58) = 1.96$	Verbal/Performance discrepancy (< 11 points vs. > 11 points)	Verbal IQ $F(1,.58) = 8.07$**	Performance IQ $F(1.58) = 5.84$*	Verbal/Performance discrepancy $F(1.58) = 0.01$	Age $F(1.58) = 4.26$*
12. Estimation (No. of reasonable responses)	Gender $F(1,55) = 3.29$(*) Interaction: $F(1,55) = 2.14$	Class $F(1,55) = -0.04$	Age $F(1,55) = 5.55$*	Addition performance level $F(1,55) = 1.65$	No. of addition principle $F(1,55) = 23.87$**	
13. Estimation	Addition performance level (last 3 levels collapsed) $F(3,46) = 0.4$	Verbal/Performance discrepancy (< 11 points vs. > 11 points) $F(1,46) = 0.19$	Verbal IQ $F(1,46) = 4.71$*	Performance IQ $F(1,46) = 0.14$	No. of addition principles $F(1,46) = 0.92$	
14. Estimation	Addition performance level (last 3 levels collapsed) $F(3,67) = 7.67$**					
15. Estimation	Addition performance level (last 3 levels collapsed) $F(3,66) = 0.68$			No. of Addition Principles $F(1,66) = 12.22$**		
16. No. of addition principles	Level (last 3 levels collapsed) $F(3,80) = 5.18$** Interaction: $F(3,80) = 0.92$	Verbal/Performance discrepancy (< 11 points vs. > 11 points) $F(1,80) = 3.81$(*)	Verbal IQ $F(1,80) = 18.95$**	Performance IQ $F(1,80) = 1.95$	Arithmetic scaled score $F(1,80) = 0.01$	Digit span scaled score $F(1,80) = 0.41$
17. Estimation	Level (last 3 levels collapsed) $F(3,46) = 2.55$(*)		Verbal IQ $F(1,46) = 12.8$**	Performance IQ $F(1,46) = 0.7$	Arithmetic scaled score $F(1,46) = 1.33$	Digit span scaled score $F(1,46) = 5.88$*
18. Addition performance level	Gender $F(1,78) = 0.01$ Interaction: $F(1,78) = 0.05$	Class $F(1,78) = 0.52$	Verbal IQ $F(1,78) = 3.89$(*)	Performance IQ $F(1,78) = 1.35$	Arithmetic scaled score $F(1,78) = 2.76$	Digit span scaled score $F(1,78) = 0.01$
19. Subtraction performance level	Gender $F(1,55) = 1.46$	Class $F(1,55) = 0.02$	Verbal IQ $F(1,55) = 0.77$	Performance IQ $F(1,55) = 0.26$	Arithmetic scaled score $F(1,55) = 8.91$**	Digit span scaled score $F(1,55) = 1.57$
20. No. of subtraction principles	Level (last 3 levels collapsed) $F(3,58) = 4.8$**	Interaction: $F(1,55) = 2.71$	Verbal IQ $F(1,58) = 10.47$**	Performance IQ $F(1,58) = 6.1$*	Arithmetic scaled score $F(1,58) = 0$	Digit span scaled score $F(1,58) = 2.4$

* $P < .05$; ** $P < .01$; (*) borderline: $0.05 < P < 0.07$

The analyses in Table 12.6 indicate no significant *gender* differences for any of the arithmetical calculation or reasoning measures used in the study. At least in this age range, it appears that boys and girls are performing very similarly.

Social class does have a significant effect on some of the measures, but this is greatly reduced when Verbal and Performance IQ are introduced as covariates. Thus, at least in the sample described here, it is *not* a strongly significant independent factor. It is also not clear that it affects any specific arithmetical components more than others.

Not surprisingly, Tables 12.5 and 12.6 show that calculation performance level is strongly influenced by age and by IQ measures. *Older children tend to be much better than younger children at addition and subtraction* (Table 12.6, Analyses 1, 2, and 7), although Tables 12.1 and 12.3 demonstrate that there are wide age ranges at any given calculation level. *Children with higher IQs calculate better than children with lower IQs* (Table 12.6, Analysis 2). Social class is also associated with calculation performance, though it ceases to have a significant effect when IQ is controlled (Table 12.6, Analyses 1, 2, 7, and 9).

From Tables 12.5 and 12.6 (Analyses 3 and 9), we can also see that, in both addition and subtraction, *calculation performance level is very significantly associated with derived fact strategy use.* This may be either because children with "expertise" in numerical facts and procedures have more access to arithmetical strategies of various sorts; or because the ability to use derived fact strategies contributes to success in calculation; or because both are affected by some common factor(s). However, Tables 12.2 and 12.4 demonstrate strikingly that children at quite low levels of arithmetical performance can have access to a wide variety of derived fact strategies.

Older children tend to use more derived fact strategies than younger children for subtraction (Table 12.6, Analysis 11), *although the effect is not significant when calculation performance level is controlled* (Analysis 9). *IQ makes an important independent contribution to derived fact strategy use*, with Verbal IQ being more important for addition (Analyses 4 and 5), whereas both Verbal and Performance IQ are important for subtraction (Analyses 10 and 11).

There are close links between performance measures for the two operations. Table 12.5 shows *very high correlations between calculation performance in addition and in subtraction, and between derived fact strategy use for addition and for subtraction.*

Indeed Table 12.6 (Analysis 8) shows *an overwhelming association between derived fact strategy use in addition and subtraction*, which completely overrides the effect of subtraction performance level on derived fact strategy use for subtraction. Although it is certainly possible for addition and subtraction abilities to dissociate (see, for example, the case study of Ben to be described later), most children perform quite similarly on both, and, in particular, use of derived fact strategies for one operation strongly predicts their use for the other.

Contrary to what might have been predicted by the theories of Rourke and others, there was little evidence in this study for any pattern whereby children with superior Verbal to Performance IQs demonstrated good calculation with poor derived fact strategy use, and vice versa. Rather, *both calculation and derived fact strategy use appeared to be strongly related to both Verbal and Performance IQ, but rather more so to Verbal IQ.*

Verbal/Performance IQ discrepancies in *either* direction appeared to be modestly but significantly related to extent of use of derived fact strategy use in addition, but not in subtraction. They were not related to calculation performance level in either addition or subtraction. At an earlier stage of the study (Dowker, 1995), it was suggested that this may reflect the fact that teaching, especially in a highly structured subject such as arithmetic, tends to be geared to children who have a relatively uniform range of abilities. Those who do not may fall behind, and this is likely to affect calculation more than the various forms of arithmetical reasoning, which may be less dependent on instruction.

Although this explanation goes some way toward accounting for the significant number of children whose calculation performance level had failed to keep pace with their use of derived fact strategies, it cannot be the whole story. If it were, then one would expect that Verbal/Performance discrepancies would actually correlate *negatively* with calculation performance level. In fact, it does not correlate at all with calculation performance level, while showing some positive correlation with derived fact strategy use. One possible explanation is that children with uneven patterns of abilities learn to seek and adopt alternative strategies when "standard" procedures do not work; and this may stand them in good stead for the use of derived fact strategies in arithmetic.

Estimation in addition (Table 12.5; Table 12.6, Analyses 12, 13, 14, and 15) is associated with Verbal IQ and Age, and also very strongly with use of principles in derived fact strategies for addition. Although addition performance level has a significant effect on estimation (Analysis 14), this is completely overridden when derived fact strategy use is taken into account (Analysis 15). *Thus, returning to componential theories of arithmetical ability, it may be fair to speak of a single (but sometimes further divisible) component of unknown fact derivation through arithmetical reasoning. This typically comprises both exact unknown fact derivation ("derived fact strategy use") and approximate unknown fact derivation ("estimation").*

When we include the scores on specific number-related WISC subtests as covariates (Table 12.6, Analyses 16 to 20), it is interesting to note that *Arithmetic* was independently associated with *subtraction* calculation performance but not with any of the other measures, whereas *Digit Span* was independently associated with *estimation*, but not with any of the calculation measures. The latter may suggest that working memory for numbers is particularly important in the mental manipulations involved in *estimation*. Further research is needed to investigate why this should be so.

Findings of strong correlations between different tests should not be interpreted as indicating that they do not represent potentially discrepant subcomponents. For example, although there was a very strong association between addition estimation and derived fact strategy use, there were some children—e.g. Stephanie (Dowker, 1995) and Katie to be described later—who performed well at the latter but not the former, and others who showed discrepancies in the reverse direction.

PART 2: INDIVIDUAL CASE STUDIES

The second part of the study includes brief descriptions of the arithmetical performance of ten children, which may shed some further light on the componential nature of individual differences in arithmetic.

It is here appropriate to reiterate that many of the children in the study were given tests other than those used in the analyses in the first part of the study. These included the British Abilities Scales Basic Number Skills test; Warrington's (1982) Magnitude Comparison Test, involving comparisons of 2- and 3-digit numbers; and a few of Russell and Ginsburg's (1984) tests. Where relevant, results of these will be mentioned in the case studies.

Of the children now to be described, Meg and Tony were examples of children who seemed to have general difficulties in arithmetic; Martin, Julie, Katie, and John are examples of children who, to varying degrees, performed much better on tasks involving derived fact strategy use than on calculation; James showed the reverse pattern; and Zoe and Jose performed well on both types of task. Ben demonstrated good calculation and limited use of derived fact strategies for addition, and the reverse pattern for subtraction.

Their calculation levels and performance on the Use of Principles Task are shown in Table 12.7, and their performance on the WISC subtests is shown in Table 12.8. (It may be noticed that in this group the boys tended to have higher Performance IQs than Verbal IQs and the girls higher Verbal IQs than Performance IQs. In fact, this is coincidental. In the sample as a whole, gender was not significantly related to Verbal IQ, Performance IQ or to either the extent or the direction of the difference between them.)

Although many of the children in the sample, including some described in the case studies, showed striking discrepancies between different arithmetical (and, as far as this type of study could demonstrate it, nonarithmetical) abilities, few if any of the children appeared to have a selective and specific disruption of a global arithmetical "module", in the sense that *all* arithmetical abilities and *only* arithmetical abilities were affected. Rather, most children who had some arithmetical difficulties appeared to have deficits in *some* but not all components of arithmetic. The affected components varied from child to child. When numerous components were simultaneously disrupted, this was usually

TABLE 12.7
Individual subjects' use of principles in derived fact strategies for addition and subtraction

Age	Tony 8;9	Meg 6;10	Martin 6;9	John 8;8	Katie 9;1	Julie 8;7	James 6;6	Ben 9;8	Zoe 8;2	Jose 6;6
Addition										
Level[a]	C	A	A	C	B	C	C	E	F	D
Identity	Y	N	Y	Y	Y	Y	N	N	Y	Y
Commutativity	Y	N	Y	Y	Y	Y	N	N	Y	Y
N + 1	N	N	Y	Y	Y	Y	N	N	Y	Y
N − 1	N	N	N	Y	Y	Y	N	N	Y	Y
Inverse	N	N	N	Y	N	N	N	N	Y	Y
N × 10	N	N	N	N	N	Y	N	N	Y	N
No. of principles used (out of 6)	2	0	3	5	4	5	0	0	6	5
Subtraction										
Level	A	A		B	C	A	A	A	D	D
Identity	N	N		Y	Y	Y	Y	Y	Y	Y
Minuend + 1	N	N		Y	a	Y	Y	Y	Y	Y
Minuend − 1	N	N		Y	Y	Y	Y	Y	a	Y
Subtrahend + 1	N	N		a	a	a	Y	Y	Y	Y
Subtrahend − 1	N	N		a	a	a	Y	Y	Y	Y
Complement	N	N		N	N	N	N	N	Y	Y
Inverse number	N	N		Y	N	N	N	N	Y	Y
Number of principles used (out of 7)	0	0		4	2	3	0	5	6	7

[a]*For addition:* A, beginning arithmetic; B, facts to 10; C, simple facts; D, 2-digit addition (no carrying); E, 2-digit addition (carrying); F, 3-digit addition.
For subtraction: A, beginning arithmetic; B, facts to 10; C, simple facts; D, 2-digit subtraction (no borrowing); E, 2-digit addition (borrowing); F, 3-digit subtraction.
a, consistent error as to direction of change (e.g. if $12 - 5 = 7$, then $12 - 6$ must be one more than 7, i.e. 8; or if $12 - 5 = 7$, then $12 - 4$ must be one less than 7, i.e. 6).

associated with difficulties that extended beyond the domain of arithmetic; for example, Tony had problems with a wide variety of verbal skills. Conversely, most children who performed consistently well on a variety of arithmetical tasks, performed well on many other tasks as well; for instance, both Zoe and José obtained high scores on most WISC subtests, and were considered to be of generally high ability.

TABLE 12.8
WISC test scores of individual subjects

	Tony	Meg	Martin	John	Katie	Julie	James	Zoe	Jose	Ben
Verbal										
Information	3	11	8	11	4	15	9	14	13	11
Comprehension	4	9	8	8	13	12	4	14	10	8
Vocabulary	6	13	8	9	9	14	10	19	9	10
Similarities	3	2	5	8	8	13	10	19	10	8
Arithmetic	2	7	1	7	7	7	4	18	17	4
Digit span	2	12	4	10	12	10	8	14	16	13
Verbal IQ	66	90	77	93	89	113	84	141	110	87
Performance										
Block design	10	10	9	12	11	3	5	12	16	3
Object assembly	11	10	5	16	9	6	11	10	13	12
Picture arrangement	10	11	10	12	4	17	6	11	16	10
Picture completion	8	11	15	14	4	7	13	16	14	10
Coding	7	5	1	11	7	11	9	16	11	8
Performance IQ	94	95	83	123	78	91	91	123	131	90

1. Meg

Of all the children in the sample, Meg probably came closest to the notion of a selectively but globally disrupted arithmetical module. She was initially tested at the age of 6 years 10 months. Her teachers described her as a good reader (at the age of 7;2, her reading age on the Schonell Reading Test was 10 years 5 months) but poor at mathematics. She was still at the Beginning Arithmetic level for both addition and subtraction, and did not use any of the principles assessed in the Use of Principles task for either operation. She also had difficulty with computational estimation. She provided reasonable estimates to only three out of nine items in the base correspondence, and her evaluations of "Tom and Mary's" estimates did not correlate at all with their actual discrepancies from the correct answers. Her estimates of numerosities of dots were also highly inaccurate (e.g. 15 dots were estimated as "8"; 70 as "1000" and 100 as "13"). Her performance on Magnitude Comparison task was at chance level. She could read and write numbers up to 10, but made many reversals with larger numbers. On the British Abilities Scale Basic Number Skills test, she scored at the 20th centile for her age.

This was a rare case of a child performing poorly across a wide variety of arithmetical calculation, reasoning, and estimation tasks, but performing well in other academic domains. Yet even here we do not see a clear-cut case of total incapacity in the arithmetical area, and good performance in every other area. Meg was able to carry out simple sums with concrete objects, and, when shown a simple sum written on a page, could demonstrate it with counters. She was also able to retrieve some arithmetical facts, obtaining a score of 5 out of 12 on Russell and Ginsburg's (1984) Memory for Number Facts test. Nor did she perform uniformly well on all nonarithmetical tasks. As can be seen from Table 12.8, her overall WISC IQ scores were somewhat lower than would be expected from her reading age, reflecting large discrepancies between different subtests. Her scaled scores for the Similarities and Coding subtests were *worse* than for the Arithmetic subtest.

2. Tony

This another example of a child who was weak in a variety of aspects of arithmetic, but, once again, not uniformly in all. In contrast with Meg's case, Tony's poor arithmetical performance was consistent with his poor performance in many academic areas. He was 8 years 9 months at the time of testing. He was considered to be one of the least able children in his school, both in arithmetic and in other subjects. In particular, he was a virtual nonreader despite a considerable amount of remedial teaching. Psychometric testing (see Table 12.8) revealed very poor performance on most verbal subtests, and average performance on most nonverbal subtests.

He was unable to cope with the word problems of the Arithmetic subtest. However, he had reached the Simple Facts level for addition, and used the Identity and Commutativity principles, though he could not explain them. Not only did he show no calculation ability or use of principles for subtraction, but he did not demonstrate a concept of subtraction at all: When presented with a subtraction problem (whether in numerical or word-problem format) he invariably attempted to add the numbers.

Tony showed an unusual discrepancy between responses to 2-and 3-digit numbers; on the Magnitude Comparison task he scored only 25 out of 40 for 2-digit numbers, but 18 out of 20 for 3-digit numbers. This was despite having great difficulty in reading large numbers. He could read numbers up to 30 correctly. Beyond 30, he made reversals (e.g. reading 69 as 96); and beyond 100 his responses were erratic, so that 125 was read as 22; 200 as 203; 213 as 85; and some other numbers, such as 357, were not read at all.

3. Martin

Martin will be described in some detail, as he showed extremely marked discrepancies between different components of arithmetic. He initially appeared to have very limited arithmetical ability indeed; for example, his WISC Arithmetic scaled score was the lowest in the entire sample. Yet further testing revealed considerable strengths in some areas of both concrete and (eventually) numerical arithmetic.

He was seen several times between the ages of 6 years 0 months and 6 years 9 months. He was reported to be highly distractible and to have language and communication difficulties and poor motor skills. He obtained a Verbal IQ of 77 (Verbal Comprehension Index 83; Freedom from Distractibility Index 58), and a Performance IQ of 85 (but the Perceptual Organization Index was 98). It is probable that these are considerable underestimates of his "true" abilities, due to a combination of attentional failures and problems in understanding what is expected of him in a test. (His teacher also considered that he underperformed on standardized tests such as the SATs.) He was totally unable to solve the arithmetical word problems of the Arithmetic subtest. For example, when told "John had four pence; his mother gave him two more; how many pence did he have altogether?", he replied "Four".

At 6 years 0 months, Martin was at the Beginning Arithmetic level. had some procedural difficulties in counting, but had relatively good understanding of counting principles: He could conserve number, understood the order irrelevance principle, and could carry out simple concrete sums, giving the correct answer when asked what one would get if one added or took away one or two counters from a set that had been counted. On one occasion, he counted 4 counters as 5. Then when one counter was added he recounted correctly, getting 5 but "corrected" himself: "No, it's one more, it's 6". This seems to show his arithmetical reasoning outrunning his counting. His ability to read and write numbers was surprisingly good: He could read and write numbers up to 100, and seemed, at least for numbers up to 10, to know what they meant: He could look at the numeral and count out the correct number of counters. (This could not be tested for larger numbers because of his difficulty with counting procedures.) He could also read 0 (as "zero") and seemed to know what it meant. However, he could not do formal written arithmetic.

At 6 years 9 months, his counting was very much more accurate. He counted to over 40, missing out only the number 25. He was accurate at giving the next number after, or number before, any number up to 100. However, he was still very hesitant at formal arithmetic, saying "I don't know" even to many sums with single-digit addends. He occasionally gave the correct answer when the addends added up to less than 10, but was still classified at the Beginning Arithmetic level. Despite his limited formal arithmetic, on the Use of Principles Task he demonstrated the ability to use the Identity, Commutativity, and $N + 1$ principles for addition. He has not yet been tested on Use of Principles for subtraction. Attempts to assess his estimation abilities were unsuccessful, due to his failure to understand what was expected of him.

4.   Katie and Julie

These two resembled one another in regard to their considerable use of derived fact strategies relative to their calculation performance levels, and also in that they both had considerably higher Verbal than Performance IQ scores. Julie performed rather better than Katie, both in arithmetic and in other areas. At the age of 8 years 7 months, Julie had a Schonell reading age of 9 years 9 months but had some difficulty in arithmetic, being at the Simple Facts level for both addition and subtraction. At one point she commented: "I'm terrible at maths, I'm thinking". Katie was behind at reading, with a Schonell reading age of 7 years 9 months at the age of 9 years 1 month: but her weakness in arithmetic was particularly striking. She was at the Facts to 10 level for addition, but only two weeks later was at the Simple Facts level for subtraction. In both cases, the difficulties were with both written and oral arithmetic. Despite these arithmetical weaknesses, both children were able to use and explain their use of the identity, commutativity, $N + 1$, and $N - 1$ principles consistently and correctly in deriving unknown arithmetical facts from known facts, and Julie was also able to use the $N \times 10$ principle. Examples of their responses and justifications can be seen in Fig 12.1. These examples concern base correspondence problems, that is those just a bit too difficult for these children to calculate mentally. But they were also able to use these principles to derive unknown arithmetical facts from known facts, even when the problems were very much too difficult for them, involving 3-digit numbers.

Both girls performed poorly on Russell and Ginsburg's (1984) test of retrieval of arithmetical facts, even though these involved single-digit numbers. This was slightly surprising in Julie's case, as in calculation tasks she was able to add single-digit numbers correctly. It is possible that she was using some calculation strategy other than retrieval, though she did not use any overt strategy such as finger counting.

As regards estimation, Julie was very good at estimating the answers to arithmetical problems that she could not calculate (all responses reasonable within the base correspondence) but was poor at estimating quantities of dots shown on a page (e.g. 9 dots were estimated as "6", 15 as "8", 70 as "12" and 100 as "25"). Katie showed a contrasting pattern, being very accurate at estimating quantities of dots, but erratic at arithmetical estimation (6 out of 9 responses reasonable within the base correspondence).

6.   John (Tony's brother)

John was tested at the age of 8 years 8 months. He was regarded by his teachers as average or slightly below average in general scholastic ability. Psychometric testing (see Table 12.8) indicated a Performance IQ of 123, compared with a Verbal IQ of only 93. He was at the Simple Facts level for addition and the Facts to 10 level for subtraction. He consistently used five "derived fact" principles for addition, and four for subtraction, though he could not describe them. His computational estimation performance was exceptionally good: Not only were all his responses reasonable within the base correspondence, but, most untypically, they were also all reasonable one level above the base correspondence.

KATIE (8 years, 10 months):

General question: "If you know that 9 + 8 = 17, does that help you to do ...":

17 – 8? (Addition/subtraction inverse principle): "No"

9 + 9? ('n + 1' principle): "It shows you add them together, because that (first sum) is 9 + 8, and you can just add 1 on, and that is the new number: 18"

8 + 8? ('n – 1' principle): "Yes, because you just take 1 away from 17, and then it will be 16"

90 + 80? ('× 10' principle): "No"

8 + 6? (Unrelated sum): "No"

8 + 9? (Commutativity principle): "Yes, because that's the same one. 17"

9 + 8? (Identity principle): "Yes, because that's the same one. 17"

JULIE (8 years, 11 months):

General question: If you know that 23 + 44 = 67, does that help you to do ..."

67 – 23? (Addition/subtraction inverse principle): "I don't really know. 27?"

24 + 44? ('n + 1' principle): "Yes. 'cause that's the one number higher. 68"

23 + 43? ('n – 1' principle): "Yes. That's (43) just one number less than that (44), so it will equal just one number less than the answer. 66"

230 + 440? ('× 10' principle): "Yes. 'Cause 44 is just the same there (pointing to first two digits of 440) (Julie wrote '670', but could not read it aloud.)

31 + 58? (Unrelated sum): "Not very much"

44 + 23? (Commutativity principle): "Yes, because 23 is just in a different place, but you're adding on the same numbers. It's the same sum, but the numbers are in different places."

23 + 44? (Identity principle): "44 is in the same place as the other 44, and 23 in the same place as the other 23. They're the same."

FIG. 12.1.   Some responses by Katie and Julie to Arithmetical Principles Test.

7.   James

James was tested at the age of 6 years 6 months. He was at the Simple Facts level for addition, but, unlike Julie, John, and even Tony, used no principles at all in the Use of Principles task. He was much less proficient at subtraction than addition: He was at the Beginning Arithmetic level for subtraction, and here again used no principles. As can be seen from Table 12.8, his overall perform-ance on the WISC was somewhat below average with wide scatter between subtests, and a particularly low score on the Arithmetic subtest. James moved to another class before some other tests could be completed; but his arithmetical reasoning (both as regards word problem solving, and derived fact strategy use) seems to be much less good than that of many children at the same addition performance level.

8.   Zoe

Zoe was regarded by her teachers as generally extremely able. Table 12.8 shows her very high scores on the WISC, especially the verbal subtests, at the age of 8 years 1 month. We may note that when presented with the WISC Information item "What do you have to do with water to make it boil?", she responded, "Make it over 100 degrees".

She was at the 3-Digit Addition level for addition and the 2-Digit Addition (No Carrying) level for subtraction. Table 12.7 demonstrates use of almost all the available principles for both addition and subtraction, with some confusion between adding and subtracting 1 for the Minuend – 1 principle. She was not given the addition estimation task, as all items would have been below the base correspondence.

9.   José

José was considered by his teachers to be very able, especially in arithmetic. As can be seen from Table 12.8, he performed well on most of the WISC subtests, and very well indeed on some. The apparent discrepancy between Verbal and Performance IQ must be seen in the context of José's having lived in England for less than a year, and having previously spoken no English.

He was first tested at the age of 6 years 6 months, and was at the 2-digit (No Carry) level for both addition and subtraction. As can be seen from Table 12.7, he used every possible principle correctly in the Use of Principles task, except the $N \times 10$ principle for addition. His high WISC Arithmetic subtest score demonstrates extremely good word problem-solving ability. A few months later, he was at the 2-digit (Carry) level for addition. At that time, he performed well on the Computational Estimation test, providing 8 reasonable responses to the nine items within the base correspondence.

10. Ben

Ben showed a very unusual pattern of responses. Ben was at the 2-digit (No Carry) level for addition at the age of 7 years 8 months, but, when tested three months later, only at the Beginning Arithmetic level for subtraction. By contrast, he made no use of derived fact strategies involving addition principles, but used *five* subtraction principles. This contrasts with the general findings that addition performance level was strongly correlated with subtraction performance level, and that use of principles for addition was strongly correlated with use of principles for subtraction. Admittedly, the greater-than-usual gap in time between administration of the addition and of the subtraction tasks may have made discrepancies more likely; however, this cannot explain why Ben's performance level was so much *lower* for subtraction than for addition.

Thus we see discrepancies between calculation and derived fact strategy use (Martin, John, Katie and Julie in one direction; James in the other; Ben in both for different operations); between derived fact strategy use and arithmetical estimation (Katie); between numerosity estimation and arithmetical estimation (Katie and Julie in opposite directions); between magnitude judgements for 2- and 3-digit numbers, in a counter-intuitive direction (Tony); between the ability to read 3-digit numbers and to compare their magnitudes (Tony); between concrete and numerical arithmetic (Meg). Some children show much better calculation for addition than subtraction (Zoe, James and especially Ben and Tony); others (Meg, Julie, Katie and José) do not.

CONCLUSIONS

We may thus conclude, from both parts of the study, that (1) individual differences in arithmetic are marked; (2) that arithmetic is indeed not unitary and that it is relatively easy to find children with marked discrepancies between different components; and that (3) in particular it is risky to assume that a child "does not understand maths" because he or she performs poorly in some calculation tasks. We may also conclude that not only is it inappropriate to think of arithmetic as just one aspect of general intelligence, but it is also inappropriate to think of it as a single module. Indeed, even models of arithmetic and arithmetical development that involve two or three different components (e.g. of factual, procedural, and conceptual knowledge) are unlikely to tell the whole story; such components appear to be further divisible. Finally, we may conclude that the componential nature of at least some domains is readily observable, not only in patients, but in subjects taken from the general population. This is most likely to be the case for domains that do typically elicit large individual differences between "normal" subjects, for example, arithmetic as here, and very possibly such domains as music and drawing.

The fact that the domain of arithmetic is made up of many components and subcomponents does not mean that they need all have neurological substrates. Some may have, and functional brain imaging studies may help to elucidate this issue (Dehaene et al., 1996). However, educational, cultural, and other environmental factors will also play an important role. The argument in this chapter is merely for the existence and functional autonomy of different components in normal arithmetical development and functioning: nothing is here being said about their innateness.

What research remains to be done? Clearly it is desirable to carry out studies focusing directly on individual differences in the developmental process itself, whether using longitudinal techniques or the "microgenetic" techniques pioneered by Siegler and Engle (1994). It has already been shown (Dowker, 1994) that between- and within-individual differences in arithmetical abilities, similar to those described here, are also easily found in normal adults. This finding must be emphasized, because, if associations and/or especially discrepancies were observed in only one age group, then it would be difficult to determine the extent to which these were an intrinsic feature of cognitive functioning, rather than an artifact of differences in the rate of development of different processes (Lynch, Vincent, Mitchell, & Trueman, 1982) or even of schools emphasizing particular skills at particular times. The fact that they are found in widely disparate age groups means that they are more likely to involve fundamental cognitive characteristics. However, we still do not know whether a particular pattern of strengths and weaknesses in a particular young child predicts a similar pattern when that child becomes an adult, or even in the child a year later. It is of particular theoretical and practical importance to discover whether environmental factors (e.g. teaching) and affective factors (e.g. attitudes to mathematics) may reinforce or alter the longitudinal stability of such patterns.

Task performance does not only depend on the individual's ability level, or on task difficulty, but on the interaction between the two. Therefore, it is desirable not only to observe the effects of varying an individual's ability level (e.g. through the types of longitudinal study described earlier) but also the effects of varying problem difficulty. Thus, more extensive investigations should be carried out as to whether the same child, at the same time, will show similar patterns of strengths and weaknesses for problems of greater and lesser difficulty.

ACKNOWLEDGEMENTS

I have chosen not to name the schools where the study was carried out, so as to maximize the children's confidentiality. However, I would like to express my enormous gratitude to the staff and children at these schools for their help and cooperation. Financial support was provided by the Economic and Social Research Council (award number R000234392).

References

Ackerman, P. T., Anhalt, J. M., & Dykman, R. A. (1986). Arithmetic automatization failure in children with attention and reading disorders: Associations and sequela. *Journal of Learning Disabilities, 19*, 222–232.

Adams, J. W. (1997). *Phonological working memory and children's mental arithmetic.* Unpublished Ph D thesis, University of Lancaster.

Adams, J. W., & Hitch, G. J. (1997). Working memory and children's mental addition. *Journal of Experimental Child Psychology, 67,* 21–38.

Ahl, V. A., Moore, C. F., Dixon, J. A. (1992). Development of intuitive and numerical proportional reasoning. *Cognitive Development, 7*, 81–108.

Alexander, L., & Martray, C. (1989). The development of an abbreviated version of the Mathematics Anxiety Rating Scale. *Measurement and Evaluation in Counseling and Development, 22*, 143–150.

Allen, P. A., Ashcraft, M. H., & Weber, T. A. (1992). On mental multiplication and age. *Psychology and Aging, 7*, 536–545.

Anderson, J. R. (1982). Acquisition of cognitive skill. *Psychological Review, 89*, 369–406.

Antell, S., & Keating, D. P. (1983). Perception of numerical invariance in neonates. *Child Development, 54*, 695–701.

Aram, D., & Nation, J. (1980). Pre-school language disorders and subsequent academic difficulties. *Journal of Communication Disorders, 13*, 159–98.

Arimoto, N. (1991). A computer tool designed to change children's concept of school math. *Educational Technology Research, 14*, 11–16.

Armstrong, J. M., & Price, R. A. (1982). Correlates and predictors of women's mathematics participation. *Journal for Research in Mathematics Education, 13*, 99–109.

Ashcraft, M. H. (1982). The development of mental arithmetic: A chronometric approach. *Developmental Review, 2*, 213–236.

Ashcraft, M. H. (1990). Strategic processing in children's mental arithmetic: A review and a proposal. In D. F. Bjorklund (Ed.), *Children's strategies: Contemporary views of cognitive development* (pp. 185–212). Hillsdale, NJ: Erlbaum.

Ashcraft, M. H. (1992). Cognitive arithmetic: A review of data and theory. *Cognition, 44*, 75–106.

Ashcraft, M. H. (1995). Cognitive psychology and simple arithmetic: a review and summary of new directions. *Mathematical Cognition, 1*, 3–34.

Ashcraft, M. H., & Battaglia, J. (1978). Cognitive arithmetic: Evidence for retrieval and decision processes in mental addition. *Journal of Experimental Psychology: Human Learning and Memory, 4,* 527–538.

Ashcraft, M. H., & Christy, K. S. (1995). The frequency of arithmetic facts in elementary texts: Addition and multiplication in grades 1–6. *Journal for Research in Mathematics Education, 26,* 396–421.

Ashcraft, M. H., Donley, R. D., Halas, M. A., & Vakali, M. (1992). Working memory, automaticity, and problem difficulty. In J. I. D. Campbell (Ed.), *The nature and origins of mathematical skills* (pp. 301–329). Amsterdam: Elsevier.

Ashcraft, M. H., & Faust, M. W. (1988, May). *Mathematics anxiety and mental arithmetic performance.* Paper presented at the meetings of the Midwestern Psychological Association, Chicago, IL.

Ashcraft, M. H., & Faust, M. W. (1994). Mathematics anxiety and mental arithmetic performance: An exploratory investigation. *Cognition and Emotion, 8,* 97–125.

Ashcraft, M. H., & Fierman, B. A. (1982). Mental addition in third, fourth, and sixth graders. *Journal of Experimental Child Psychology, 33,* 216–234.

Ashcraft, M. H., Fierman, B. A., & Bartolotta, R. (1984). The production and verification tasks in mental addition: An empirical comparison. *Developmental Review, 4,* 157–170.

Ashcraft, M. H., & Kirk, E. P. (1998). The relationships among working memory, math anxiety, math competence, and attitudes toward math. Manuscript submitted for publication.

Ashcraft, M. H., & Stazyk, E. H. (1981). Mental addition: A test of three verification models. *Memory and Cognition, 9,* 185–196.

Ashcraft, M. H., Copeland, D., Vavro, C., Falk, R. (1998). Working memory and mental addition. Manuscript submitted for publication.

Atkinson, S. (1992). *Mathematics with Reason: The Emergent Approach to Primary Maths.* London: Hodder & Stoughton.

Baddeley, A. (1986). *Working memory.* Oxford: Oxford University Press.

Baddeley, A. (1992). Is working memory working? The Fifteenth Bartlett Lecture. *Quarterly Journal of Experimental Psychology, 44A,* 1 31.

Baddeley, A. D. (1996). Exploring the central executive. *The Quarterly Journal of Experimental Psychology, 49A ,* 5–28.

Baddeley, A. D., & Hitch, G. J. (1974). Working memory. In G. H. Bower (Ed.), *The psychology of learning and motivation* (Vol. 8, pp. 47–89). New York: Academic Press.

Baddeley, A. D., Lewis, V. J., & Vallar, G. (1984). Exploring the articulatory loop. *The Quarterly Journal of Experimental Psychology, 36A,* 233–252.

Baddeley, A. D., Thomson, N., & Buchanan, M. (1975). Word length and the structure of short-term memory. *Journal of Verbal Learning and Verbal Behavior, 14,* 575–589.

Badian, N. A. (1983). Dyscalculia and nonverbal disorders of learning. In H. R. Myklebust (Ed.), *Progress in Learning Disabilities* (Vol. 5). New York: Grune & Stratton.

Baillargeon, R. (1994). Physical reasoning in young infants: Seeking explanations for impossible events. *British Journal of Developmental Psychology, 12,* 9–33

Baron-Cohen, S. (1995). *Mind-blindness: An essay on autism and theory of mind. Cambridge, MA: MIT Press.*

Baroody, A. J. (1983). The development of procedural knowledge: An alternative explanation for chronometric trends of mental arithmetic. *Developmental Review, 3,* 225–230.

Baroody, A. J. (1984). More precisely defining and measuring the order-irrelevance principle. *Journal of Experimental Child Psychology, 38,* 33–41.

Baroody, A. J. (1987). *Children's mathematical thinking: A developmental framework for preschool, primary and special education teachers.* New York: Teachers College.

Baroody, A. J. (1990). How and when should place-value concepts and skill be taught? *Journal for Research in Mathematics Education, 4,* 281–286.

Baroody, A. J. (1992). The development of preschoolers. counting skills and principles. In *Pathways to number: Children's developing numerical abilities* J. Bideaud, C. Meljac, J-P. Fischer (Eds.), (pp. 99–126). Hillsdale, NJ: Erlbaum.

Baroody, A. J. (1993). The relationship between the order-irrelevance principle and counting skill. *Journal for Research in Mathematics Education, 24,* 415–427.

Baroody, A. J. (1994). An evaluation of evidence supporting fact-retrieval models. *Learning and Individual Differences, 6,* 1–36.

Baroody, A. J., & Gannon, K. E. (1984). The development of the commutativity principle and economical addition strategies. *Cognition and Instruction, 1,* 321–339.

Baroody, A. J., & Ginsburg, H. P. (1986). The relationship between initial and mechanical knowledge of arithmetic. In J. Hiebert (Ed.) *Conceptual and procedural knowledge: the case of arithmetic.* Hillsdale, NJ: Erlbaum.

Baroody, A. J., Ginsburg, H. P., & Waxman, B. (1983). Children's use of mathematical structure. *Journal for Research in Mathematics Education, 14,* 156–168.

Bateson, G. (1979). *Mind and nature: A necessary unity.* New York, NY: Bantam Books.

Becker, J., & Varelas, M. (1993). Semiotic aspects of cognitive development: Illustrations from mathematical cognition. *Psychological Review, 100,* 420–431.

Benson, D. F., & Denckla, M. B. (1969). Verbal paraphasia as a source of calculation disturbance. *Archives of Neurology, 21,* 96–102.

Bermejo, V. (1996). Cardinality development and counting. *Developmental Psychology, 32,* 263–268.

Betz, N. E. (1978). Prevalence, distribution, and correlates of math anxiety in college students. *Journal of Counseling Psychology, 25,* 441–448.

Bialystok, E. (1992). Symbolic representation of letters and numbers. *Cognitive Development, 7,* 301–316.

Bidwell, J. K. (1983). Calculation skills versus problem-solving: Scotland vs. Michigan. *School Sciences and Mathematics, 83,* 682–693.

Bishop, D. V. M. (1979). Comprehension in developmental language disorders. *Developmental Medicine and Child Neurology, 21,* 225–238.

Bishop, D. V. M. (1983). *Test for the reception of grammar.* Published by the author and available from Age and Cognitive Performance Research Centre, University of Manchester, UK

Bishop, D. V. M. (1994). Developmental disorders of speech and language. In M. Rutter & L. Hersov (Eds.) *Child and adolescent psychiatry,* (3rd edn., pp. 546–568). Oxford: Blackwell Scientific Publications pp. 546–568.

Bishop, D. V. M., & Edmundson, A. (1987). Language-impaired 4-year-olds: Distinguishing transient from persistent impairment. *Journal of Speech and Hearing Disorders, 52,* 156–173.

Blevins-Knabe, B., & Musun-Miller, L. (1996). Number use at home by children and their parents and its relationship to early mathematical performance. *Early development and parenting, 5,* 35–45.

Bloom, A. H. (1981). *The linguistic shaping of thought: a study in the impact of language on thinking in China and the West.* Hillsdale, NJ: Erlbaum.

Bloom, P. (1994). Generativity within language and other cognitive domains. *Cognition, 51,* 177–189.

Bloom, P., & Kelemen, D. (1995). Syntactic cues in the acquisition of collective nouns. *Cognition, 56,* 1–30.

Boysen, S. T., & Berntson, G. G. (1989). Numerical competence in a chimpanzee *Pan troglodytes. Journal of Comparative Psychology, 103,* 23–31.

Brainerd, C. J. (1983). Young children's mental arithmetic errors: A working memory analysis. *Child Development, 54,* 812–830.

Brainerd, C. J. (1987). Sources of working-memory error in children's mental arithmetic. In G. Deloche & X. Seron (Eds.), *Mathematical disabilities: A cognitive neuropsychological perspective* (pp. 87–109). Hillsdale, NJ: Erlbaum.

Brainerd, C. J., & Reyna, V. F. (1988). Generic resources, reconstructive processing, and children's mental arithmetic. *Developmental Psychology, 24*, 324–334.

Briars, D., & Siegler, R. S. (1984). A featural analysis of preschoolers' counting knowledge. *Developmental Psychology, 20*, 607–618.

Brown, J. S., & Burton, R. B. (1978). Diagnostic models for procedural bugs in basic mathematical skills. *Cognitive Science, 2*, 155–192.

Brown, M. (1996). FIMS and SIMS: the first two IEA International mathematics surveys. *Assessment in Education, 3*, 181–200.

Brown, N. R., & Siegler, R. S. (1993). Metrics and mappings: A framework for understanding real-world quantitative estimation. *Psychological Review, 100*, 511–534.

Brown, R. (1976). In memorial tribute to Eric Lenneberg. *Cognition, 4*, 125–153.

Brown, R., & Lenneberg, E. (1954). A study in language and cognition. *Journal of Abnormal and Social Psychology, 49*, 454–462.

Bryant, P. E. (1985). The distinction between knowing when to do a sum and knowing how to do it. *Educational Psychology, 5*, 207–215.

Bryant, P. E., & Impey, L. (1986). The similarities between normal readers and developmental and acquired dyslexics. *Cognition, 24*, 121–137.

Bryant, P. (1993). Reading and development. In C. Pratt & A. Garton (Eds.), *Systems of representation in children.* (pp. 235–250). Chichester, UK: Wiley.

Bryant, P. E., & Bradley, L. (1985). *Children's reading problems: Psychology and education.* Oxford: Blackwell.

Butterworth, B., Cipolotti, L., & Warrington, E. K. (1996). Short-term memory impairment and arithmetic ability. *The Quarterly Journal of Experimental Psychology, 49A*, 251–262.

Byrnes, J. P., & Wasik, B. A. (1991). Role of conceptual knowledge in mathematical procedural learning. *Developmental Psychology, 27*, 777–786.

Campbell, J. I. D. (1987). Network interference and mental multiplication. *Journal of Experimental Psychology: Learning, Memory, and Cognition, 13*, 109–123.

Campbell, J. I. D. (1994). Architectures for numerical cognition. *Cognition, 53*, 1–44.

Campbell, J. I. D. (1996). On the relation between skilled performance of simple division and multiplication. Manuscript submitted for publication.

Campbell, J. I. D., & Graham, D.J. (1985). Mental multiplication skill: Structure, process, and acquisition. *Canadian Journal of Psychology, 39*, 338–366.

Campbell, J. I. D., & Oliphant, M. (1992). Representation and retrieval of arithmetic facts: A network-interference model and simulation. In J. I. D. Campbell (Ed.), *The nature and origins mathematical skills* (pp. 331–364). Amsterdam: Elsevier.

Campbell, R., & Butterworth, B. (1985). Phonological dyslexia and dysgraphia in a highly literate subject: A developmental case with associated deficits of phonemic processing and awareness. *Quarterly Journal of Experimental Psychology, 37A*, 435–475.

Caramazza, A. (1986). On drawing inferences about the structure of normal cognitive systems from the analysis of patterns of impaired performance: The case for single-patient studies. *Brain and Cognition, 5*, 41–66.

Carey, S. (1985). Conceptual change in childhood. Cambridge, MA: MIT Press.

Carpenter, T. P., & Moser, J. M. (1982). The development of addition and subtraction problem solving. In T. P. Carpenter, J. M. Moser and T. A. Romberg (Eds.) *Addition and subtraction: a cognitive perspective.* (pp. 10–24). New York: Erlbaum.

Carraher, T. N. (1985). The decimal system: understanding and notation. In Streefland (Ed.) *Proceedings of the International Conference for the Psychology of Mathematics in Education,*

(Vol. 1, pp. 288–303). Utrecht, Netherlands: Research Group on Mathematics Education and Educational Computer Centre, State University of Utrecht.

Carraher, T. N., Carraher, D. W., & Schliemann, A. D. (1985). Mathematics in the streets and in the schools. *British Journal of Developmental Psychology, 3,* 21–29.

Carraher, T. N., & Schliemann, A. D. (1985). Computation routines prescribed by schools: help or hindrance? *Journal for Research in Mathematics Education, 3,* 16, 37–44.

Case, R. (1985). *Intellectual development: Birth to adulthood.* New York: Academic Press.

Case, R. (1995). Capacity-based explanations of working memory growth: A brief history and reevaluation. In F. E.Weinert & W. Schneider (Eds.), *Memory performance and competencies: Issues in growth and development* (pp. 23–44). Hove, UK: Erlbaum.

Case, R., Kurland, M., & Goldberg, J. (1982). Operational efficiency and the growth of short-term memory span. *Journal of Experimental Child Psychology, 33,* 386–404.

Cauley, K. M. (1988). Construction of logical knowledge: Study of borrowing in subtraction. *Journal of Educational Psychology, 80,* 202–205.

Chi, M. T. H., Bassok, M., Lewis, M. W., Reimann, P., & Glaser, R. (1989). Self-explanations: How students study and use examples in learning to solve problems. *Cognitive Science, 13,* 145–182.

Chi, M., & Klahr, D. (1975). Span and rate of apprehension in children and adults. *Journal of Experimental Child Psychology, 19,* 434–439.

Chipman, S. F., Krantz, D. H., & Silver R. (1992). Mathematics anxiety and science careers among able college women. *Psychological Science, 3,* 292–295.

Chiu, L. H., & Henry, L. L. (1990). Development and validation of the Mathematics Anxiety Scale for Children. *Measurement and Evaluation in Counseling and Development, 23,* 121–127.

Chomsky, N. (1980). *Rules and representations.* New York: Columbia University Press.

Church, R. M., & Meck, W. H. (1984). The numerical attribute of stimuli. In H. Roitblatt, T. G. Bever, & H. S. Terrence (Eds.), *Animal cognition.* Hillsdale, NJ: Erlbaum.

Cipolotti, L. (1995). Multiple routes for reading words, why not numbers? Evidence from a case of arabic numeral dyslexia. *Cognitive Neuropsychology, 12,* 313–342.

Cipolotti, L., & Butterworth, B. (1995). Toward a multiroute model of number processing: Impaired number transcoding with preserved calculation skills. *Journal of Experimental Psychology: General, 124,* 375–390.

Cipolotti, L., & Delacycostello, A. (1995). Selective impairment for simple division. *Cortex, 31,* 433–449.

Clay, M. M. (1979). *The early detection of reading difficulties.* London: Heinemann.

Clements, D. H. (1984). Training effects on the development and generalization of Piagetian logical operations and knowledge of number. *Journal of Educational Psychology, 76,* 766–776.

Cobb, P., & Bauersfeld, H. (1995). The emergence of mathematical meaning. Hillsdale, NJ: Erlbaum.

Cockcroft, W. H. (1982). *Mathematics counts.* London: HMSO.

Cohen, L., & Dehaene, S. (1994). Amnesia for arithmetic facts: A single case study. *Brain and Language, 47,* 214–232.

Cohen, L., Dehaene, S., & Verstichel, P. (1994). Number words and number nonwords: A case of deep dyslexia extended to arabic numerals. *Brain, 117,* 267–279.

Cohn, R. (1968). Developmental dyscalculia. *Pediatric Clinics of North America, 15,* 651–668.

Cohn, R. (1971). Arithmetic and learning disabilities. In H. Myklebust (Ed.), *Progress in learning disabilities* (Vol. 2). New York: Grune & Stratton.

Cole, M. (1988). Personal communication.

Comber, L. C., & Keeves, J. (1973). *Science achievements in nineteen countries.* New York: Wiley.

Connell, P. J., & Stone, C.A. (1992). Morpheme learning of children with specific language impairment under controlled intstructional conditions. *Journal of Speech and Hearing Research*, *35*, 844–885

Conrad, R. (1979). *The deaf school child*. London: Harper & Row.

Conti-Ramsden, G., Donlan, C., & Grove, J. (1992). Children with specific language impairments; curricular opportunities and school performance. *British Journal of Special Education*, *19*, 75–80.

Conway, A. R. A., & Engle, R. W. (1994). Working memory and retrieval: A resource-dependent inhibition model. *Journal of Experimental Psychology: General*, *123*, 354–373.

Cooney, J. B., Swanson, H. L., & Ladd, S. F. (1988). Acquisition of mental multiplication skill: Evidence for the transition between counting and retrieval strategies. *Cognition and Instruction*, *5*, 323–345.

Cooper, R. G. (1984). Early number development: Discovering number space with addition and subtraction. In C. Sophian (Ed.), *Origins of cognitive skills* (pp. 157–192). Hillsdale, NJ: Erlbaum.

Cornelius, M. (1992). *The numeracy needs of graduates in employment*. University of Durham: Unpublished manuscript.

Cosmides, L., & Tooby, J. (1994). Origins of domain specificity: The evolution of functional organization. In L. A. Hirschfeld & S. A. Gelman (Eds.), *Mapping the mind: Domain specificity in cognition and culture* (pp. 86–116). New York: Cambridge University Press.

Cowan, R., Dowker, A., & Christakis, A., Bailey, S. (1996). Even more precisely assessing children's understanding of the order-irrelevance principle. *Journal of Experimental Child Psychology*, *62*, 84–101.

Cowan, R., Foster, C. M., & Al-Zubaidi, A. S. (1993). Encouraging children to count. *British Journal of Developmental Psychology*, *11*, 411–420.

Cowan, R., & Renton, M. (1989). *Primary school children's strategies for addition*. Paper presented at the British Psychological Society Annual Conference.

Cowan, R., & Renton, M. (1996). Do they know what they are doing? Children's use of economical addition strategies and knowledge of commutativity. *Educational Psychology*, *16*, 409–422.

D'Andrade, R. (1990). Some propositions about the relation between culture and human cognition. In J. Stigler, R. A. Shweder & G. Herdt (Eds.), *Cultural Psychology*. (pp. 65–129). Cambridge University Press.

Dagenbach, D., & McCloskey, M. (1992). The organization of arithmetic facts in memory: Evidence from a brain-damaged patient. *Brain and Cognition*, *20*, 345–366.

Damon, W. (1990). Social relations and children's thinking. In D.Kuhn (Ed.), *Contributions to human development* (Vol. 21, pp. 95–107). Basel: S. Karger.

Damon, W., & Hart, D. (1982). The development of self-understanding from infancy throught to adolescence. *Child Development, 53*, 841–864.

Daneman, M., & Carpenter, P. A. (1980). Individual differences in working memory and reading. *Journal of Verbal Learning and Verbal Behavior*, *19*, 450–466.

Davis, H. (1984). Discrimination of the number three by a raccoon (*Procyon lotor*). *Animal Learning and Behavior*, *12*, 409–413.

Davis, H., & Albert, M. (1986). Numerical discrimination by rats using sequential auditory stimuli. *Animal Learning and Behavior*, *14*, 57–59.

Davis, H., & Bradford, S. A. (1986). Counting behavior by rats in a simulated natural environment. *Ethology*, *73*, 265–280.

Davis, H., & Perusse, R. (1988). Numerical competence in animals: Definitional issues, current evidence, and a new research agenda. *Behavioral and Brain Sciences*, *11*, 561–615.

Davis, R. B., & McKnight, C. (1980). The influence of semantic content on algorithmic behavior. *Journal of Mathematical Behavior*, *3*, 38–87.

De Corte, E., & Verschaffel, L. (1987). The effect of semantic structure on first-graders' solution strategies of elementary addition and subtraction word problems. *Journal for Research in Mathematics Education, 18*, 363–386.

de Ribaupierre, A., & Hitch, G. (1994). *The development of working memory.* Hove, UK: Erlbaum.

Dehaene, S. (1992). Varieties of numerical abilities. *Cognition, 44*, 1–42.

Dehaene, S., & Cohen, L. (1991). Two mental calculation systems: A case study of severe acalculia with preserved approximation. *Neuropsychologia, 29*, 1045–1074.

Dehaene, S., & Cohen, L. (1995). Towards an anatomical and functional model of number processing. *Mathematical Cognition, 1*, 83–120.

Dehaene, S., Tzourio, N., Frank, V., Raynaud, L., Cohen, L., Mehler, J., & Mazoyer, B. (1996). Cerebral activations during number multiplication and comparison: a PET study. *Neuropsychologia, 34*, 1097–1116.

Deloche, G., & Seron, X. (1987). Numerical transcoding: A general production model. In G. Deloche & X. Seron (Eds.), *Mathematical disabilities: A Cognitive neuropsychological perspective.* Hillsdale, NJ: Erlbaum.

Deloche, G., Seron, X., Larroque, C., Magnien, C., Metz-Lotz, M. N. et al. (1994). Calculation and number processing assessment battery: The role of demographic factors. *Journal of Clinical and Experimental Neuropsychology, 16*, 915–208.

Deluka, J. W., Deldotto, J. E., & Rourke, B. P. (1987). Subtypes of arithmetic-disabled children: a neuropsychological taxonomic approach. *Journal of Clinical and Experimental Neuropsychology, 9*, 26.

Department of Education and Science and the Welsh Office (1989). *Mathematics in the National Curriculum: Non-statutory guidelines.* London: HMSO.

Dew, K. M., Galassi, J. P., & Galassi, M. D. (1983). Mathematics anxiety: some basic issues. *Journal of Counseling Psychology, 30*, 443–446.

Dick, T. P., & Rallis, S. F. (1991). Factors and influences on high school students' career choices. *Journal for Research in Mathematics Education, 22*, 281–292.

Dixon, J. A., & C. F. Moore (1996). The developmental role of intuitive principles in choosing mathematical strategies. *Developmental Psychology, 32*, 241–253.

Donaldson, M. (1978). Children's minds. London: Fontana.

Donlan, C. (1993a). *The development of numeracy in children with specific language impairment.* Unpublished thesis. University of Manchester, UK.

Donlan, C. (1993b). Basic numeracy in children with specific language impairment. *Child Language Teaching and Therapy, 9*, 95–104.

Donlan, C. (1997). Unpublished diary study.

Donlan, C., Bishop, D.V.M., & Hitch, G.J. (1998). Magnitude comparisons by children with specific language impairments: Evidence of unimpaired symbolic processing. *International Journal of Language and Communication Disorders, 33*, 149–160.

Donlan, C., & Gourlay, S. (in press). The importance of non-verbal skills in the acquisition of place-value knowledge; evidence from normally developing and language-impaired children. *British Journal of Developmental Psychology.*

Douglass, H. R. (1925). The development of number concept in children of pre-school and kindergarten ages. *Journal of Experimental Psychology, 8*, 443–470.

Dowker, A. D. (1989). *Computational estimation by young children.* Proceedings of the British Society for Research in Learning Mathematics, Brighton, UK.

Dowker, A. D. (1992a). Computational estimation strategies of professional mathematicians. *Journal for Research in Mathematics Education, 23*, 45–55.

Dowker, A. D. (1992b). Children's views of other people's estimates. *Proceedings of the British Society for Research in Learning Mathematics, Oxford.*

Dowker, A. D. (1995). Children with specific calculation difficulties. *Links, 2*, 7–12.

Dowker, A. D. (1997). Young children's addition estimates. *Mathematical Cognition, 3,* 141–154.

Dowker, A. D., Flood, A., Griffiths, H., Harriss, L., & Hook, L. (1996). Estimation strategies of four groups. *Mathematical Cognition, 2,* 113–135.

Dreger, R. M., & Aiken, L. R. (1957). The identification of number anxiety in a college population. *Journal of Educational Psychology, 48,* 344–351.

Durkin, K., Shire, B., Riem, R., Crowther, R. D., & Rutter, D. R. (1986). The social and linguistic context of early number word use. *British Journal of Developmental Psychology, 4,* 269–288.

Elbers, E. (1991). The development of competence and its social context. *Educational Psychology Review, 3,* 73–94.

Ellis, A. W., & Young, A. W. (1988). *Human cognitive neuropsychology.* Hove, UK: Lawrence Erlbaum.

Ellis, N. C. (1992). Linguistic relativity revisited: The bilingual word-length effect in working memory during counting, remembering numbers and mental calculation. In R. J. Harris (Ed.), *Cognitive processing in bilinguals* (pp. 137–155). Amsterdam: Elsevier.

Ellis, N. C., & Hennelly, R. A. (1980). A bilingual word-length effect: Impications for intelligence testing and the relative ease of mental calculation in Welsh and English. *British Journal of Psychology, 71,* 43–52.

Epstein, K. I., Hillegeist, E., & Grafman, J. (1994). Number processing in deaf college students. *American Annals of the Deaf, 139,* 336–347.

Erlwanger, S. H. (1973). Benny's conceptions of rules and answers in IPI mathematics. *Journal of Children's Mathematical Behaviour, 1,* 7–26.

Eysenck, M. W. (1985). Anxiety and cognitive-task performance. *Personality and Individual Differences, 6,* 579–586.

Eysenck, M. W. (1992). *Anxiety: The cognitive perspective.* Hove, UK: Lawrence Erlbaum Associates Ltd.

Eysenck, M. W., & Calvo, M. G. (1992). Anxiety and performance: The processing efficiency theory. *Cognition and Emotion, 6,* 409–434.

Faust, M. W. (1992). *Analysis of physiological reactivity in mathematics anxiety.* Unpublished doctoral dissertation, Bowling Green State University, OH.

Faust, M. W., Ashcraft, M. H., & Fleck, D. E. (1996a). Mathematics anxiety effects in simple and complex addition. *Mathematical Cognition, 2,* 25–62.

Faust, M. W., Johnson, H. J., & Ashcraft, M. H. (1996b). Analysis of physiological reactivity in mathematics phobia. Unpublished manuscript.

Fayol, M., Abdi, H., & Gombert, J.-E. (1987). Arithmetic problems formulation and working memory load. *Cognition and Instruction, 4,* 187–202.

Fazio, B. (1994). The counting abilities of children with specific language impairments: A comparison of oral and gestural tasks. *Journal of Speech and Hearing Disorders, 37,* 358–368.

Fazio, B. (1996). Mathematical abilities of children with specific language impairment: A follow-up study. *Journal of Speech and Hearing Research, 39,* 839–849.

Fein, G., Davenport, L., Yingling, C. D., & Galin, D. (1988). Verbal and nonverbal memory deficits in pure dyslexia. *Developmental Neuropsychology, 4,* 181–197.

Fennema, E. (1989). The study of affect and mathematics: A proposed generic model for research. In D. B. McLeod & V. M. Adams (Eds.), *Affect and mathematical problem solving: A new perspective.* New York: Springer-Verlag.

Fennema, E., & Sherman, J. (1976). Fennema-Sherman Mathematics Attitudes Scales. *JSAS Catalog of Selected Documents in Psychology, 6,* (Ms. No. 1225).

Ferreiro, E., & Teberosky, A. (1982). Literacy before Schooling. London: Heinemann Educational.

Ferro, J. M., & Botelho, M. A. S. (1980). Alexia for arithmetic signs: A cause of disturbed calculation. *Cortex, 16,* 175–180.

Flavell, J. H. (1970). Developmental studies of mediated memory. In H. W. Reese & L. P. Lipsitt (Eds.), *Advances in child development and behaviour* (Vol. 5, pp. 182–211). New York: Academic Press.

Flavell, J. H. (1971). Stage-related properties of cognitive development. *Cognitive Psychology*, 2, 421–453.

Fleischner, J. E., Garnett, K., & Shepherd, M. (1982). Proficiency in arithmetic basic fact computation of learning disabled and nondisabled children. *Focus on Learning Problems in Mathematics*, 4, 47–55.

Fletcher, J. M. (1985). Memory for verbal and nonverbal stimuli in learning disability subgroups: Analysis by selective reminding. *Journal of Experimental Child Psychology*, 40, 244–259.

Foxman, D. (1992). *Learning mathematics and science (The Second International Assessment of Educational Progress in England)*. Slough: National Foundation for Educational Research.

Frege, G. (1893/1980). *The foundations of arithmetic*. Evanston, IL: Northwestern University Press.

Frith, U. (1986). A developmental framework for developmental dyslexia. *Annals of Dyslexia*, 36, 69–81.

Frye, D., Braisby, N., Love, J., Maroudas, C., & Nicholls, J. (1989). Young children's understanding of counting and cardinality. *Child Development*, 60, 1158–1171.

Fuligni, A. J., & Stevenson, H. W. (1995). Time use and mathematics achievement among American, Chinese, and Japanese High school students. *Child Development*, 66, 830–842.

Furth, H. G. (1966). *Thinking without language: Psychological implications of deafness*. New York: Free Press.

Fuson, K. (1986). Roles of representation and verbalization in the teaching of multidigit addition and subtraction. *European Journal of the Psychology of Education*, 1, 35–56.

Fuson, K. C. (1988). *Children's counting and concepts of number*. New York: Springer-Verlag.

Fuson, K. C. (1990). Conceptual structures for multiunit numbers: Implications for learning and teaching multidigit addition, subtraction, and place value. *Cognition and Instruction*, 7, 343–403.

Fuson, K. C. (1992). Research on learning and teaching addition and subtraction of whole numbers. In G. Leinhardt, R. Putman, & R. A. Hattrup (Eds.), *Analysis of arithmetic for mathematics teaching*. Hillsdale, NJ: Erlbaum.

Fuson, K. C., & Briars, D. (1990). Using a base-ten blocks learning/teaching approach for first- and second-grade place-value and multidigit addition and subtraction. *Journal for Research in Mathematics Education*, 21, 180–206.

Fuson, K. C., & Kwon, Y. (1992). Korean children's understanding of multidigit addition and subtraction. *Child Development*, 63, 491–506.

Fuson, K. C., Richards, J., & Briars, D. J. (1982). The acquisition and elaboration of the number word sequence. In C. J. Brainerd (Ed.), *Children's logical and mathematical cognition: Progress in cognitive development research* (pp. 33–92). New York: Springer-Verlag.

Fuson, K. C., Smith, S. T., LoCicero, A. M. (1997). Supporting Latino first-graders' ten structured thinking in urban classrooms. *Journal of Research in Mathematics Education*, 28, 738–766.

Gallistel, C. R. (1990). *The organization of learning*. Cambridge, MA: MIT Press.

Gallistel, C. R., & Gelman, R. (1992). Preverbal and verbal counting and computation. *Cognition*, 44, 43–74.

Garden, R. A. (1987). The Second IEA Mathematics Study. *Comparative Education Review*, 31, 47–68.

Garfinkel, H., & Sacks, H. (1970). On formal structures of practical actions. In J. C. McKinney and E. A. Tiryakian (Eds.), *Theoretical sociology*. New York: Appleton Century Crofts.

Garfinkel, H., Lynch, M., & Livingston, E. (1981). The work of a discovering science construed with materials from the optically discovered pulsar. *Philosopy of the Social science, 11*, 131–158.

Garnett, K., & Fleischner, J. E. (1983). Automatization and basic fact performance of normal and learning disabled children. *Learning Disability Quarterly, 6*, 223–230.

Gathercole, S., & Baddeley, A. (1990). Phonological working memory deficits in language-disordered childlren; Is there a causal connection? *Journal of Memory and Language, 29*, 336–360.

Gathercole, S., & Baddeley, A. (1993). *Working memory and language.* Hove, UK: Erlbaum.

Geary, D. C. (1990). A componental analysis of an early learning deficit in mathematics. *Journal of Experimental Child Psychology, 49*, 363–383.

Geary, D. C. (1993). Mathematical disabilities: Cognitive, neuropsychological and genetic components. *Psychological Bulletin, 114*, 345–362.

Geary, D. C. (1994). *Children's mathematical development.* Washington, DC: American Psychological Association.

Geary, D. C. (1995). Reflections of evolution and culture in children's cognition: Implications for mathematical development and instruction. *American Psychologist, 50*, 24–37.

Geary, D. C. (1996). The problem-size effect in mental addition: Developmental and cross-national trends. *Mathematical Cognition, 2*, 63–93.

Geary, D. C., & Brown, S. C. (1991). Cognitive addition: Strategy choice and speed-of processing differences in gifted, normal and mathematically disabled children. *Developmental Psychology, 27*, 398–406.

Geary, D. C., Brown, S. C., & Samaranayake, V. A. (1991). Cognitive addition: A short longitudinal study of strategy choice and speed-of-processing differences in normal and mathematically disabled children. *Developmental Psychology, 27*, 787–797.

Geary, D. C., Salthouse, T. A., Chen, G., Fan, L. (1996). Are East Asian versus American differences in arithmetical ability a recent phenomenon? *Developmental Psychology, 32*, 254–262.

Geary, D. C., & Widaman, K. F. (1987). Individual differences in cognitive arithmetic. *Journal of Experimental Psychology: General, 116*, 154–171.

Geary, D. C., & Widaman, K. F. (1992). Numerical cognition: On the convergence of componential and psychometric models. *Intelligence, 16*, 47–80.

Geary, D. C., Widaman, K. F., Little, T. D., & Cormier, P. (1987). Cognitive addition: Comparison of learning disabled and academically normal elementary school children. *Cognitive Development, 2*, 249–269.

Geary, D. C., & Wiley, J. G. (1991). Cognitive addition: Strategy choice and speed-of-processing differences in young and elderly adults. *Psychology and Aging, 6*, 474–483.

Geis, M. F., & Hall, D. M. (1978). Encoding and congruity in children's incidental memory. *Child Development, 49*, 857–861.

Gelman, R. (1982). Assessing one-to-one correspondence: Still another paper about conservation. *British Journal of Developmental Psychology, 73*, 209–220.

Gelman, R. (1978). Counting in the preschooler: What does and does not develop. In R. S. Siegler (Ed.), *Children's thinking, what develops?* (pp. 213–241). Hillsdale, NJ: Lawrence Erlbaum.

Gelman, R. (1991). Epigenetic foundations of knowledge structures: Initial and transcendent constructions. In S. Carey & R. Gelman (Eds.), *The Epigenesis of Mind: Essays on biology and cognition* (pp. 293–322). Hillsdale, NJ: Erlbaum,

Gelman, R. (1993). A rational-constructivist account of early learning about numbers and objects. In D. Medin (Ed.), *The psychology of learning and motivation* (pp. 61–96). San Diego, CA: Academic Press.

Gelman, R., & Brenneman, K. (1994). First principles can support both universal and culture-specific learning about number and music. In L. A. Hirschfeld & S. A. Gelman (Eds.), *Mapping the mind: Domain specificity in cognition and culture* (pp. 369–390). New York: Cambridge University Press.

Gelman, R., Cohen, M., & Hartnett, P. (1989). *To know mathematics is to go beyond the belief that "Fractions are not numbers"*. Proceedings of Psychology of Mathematics Education, Vol. 11 of the North American Chapter of the International Group of Psychology.

Gelman, R., & Gallistel, C. R. (1978). *The child's understanding of number*. Cambridge, Mass.: Harvard University Press.

Gelman, R., & Meck, E. (1983). Preschoolers. counting: Principles before skill. *Cognition, 13*, 343–359.

Gelman, R., & Meck, E. (1986). The notion of principles: The case of counting. In J. Hiebert (Ed.) *Conceptual and procedural knowledge: The case of mathematics* (pp. 29–57). Hillsdale, NJ: Erlbaum.

Gelman, R., & Meck, E. (1992). Early principles aid initial but not later conceptions of number. In J. Bideaud, C. Meljac, & J-P. Fischer (Eds.) *Pathway to number: Children's developing numerical abilities* (pp. 99–126). Hillsdale, NJ: Erlbaum.

Gelman, R., Meck, E., Merkin, S. (1986). Young children's numerical competence. *Cognitive Development, 1*, 1–29.

Gentner, D. (1983). Structure-mapping: A theoretical framework for analogy. *Cognitive Science, 7*, 155–170.

Gernsbacher, M. A. (1990). *Language comprehension as structure building*. Hillsdale, NJ: Erlbaum.

Gibbon, J. (1981). On the form and location of the psychometric bisection function for time. *Journal of Mathematical Psychology, 24*, 58–87.

Gierl, M. J., & Bisanz, J. (1995). Anxieties and attitudes related to mathematics in grades 3 and 6. *Journal of Experimental Education, 63*, 139–158.

Ginsburg, H. P. (1977). *Children's arithmetic: The learning process*. New York: Van Norstrand.

Girelli, L., & Delazer, M. (1996). Subtraction bugs in an acalculic patient. *Cortex, 32*, 547–555.

Glaser, N. (1976). Social and cultural factors in economic growth. In H. Patrick & H. Rosovsky (Eds.), *Asia's new giant*. Washington, DC: Brookings Institution.

Goodwin, C. (1981). *Conversational organization: Interaction between speakers and hearers*. New York, NY: Academic Press.

Goodwin, C. (1995). *Gestures that count*. Papers presented at the Conference on Gestures and Compared Cross-Linguistically. Lingustic Institute, University of New Mexico.

Gopnik, M., & Crago, M.B. (1991). Familial aggregation of a developmental language disorder. *Cognition, 39*, 1–50.

Gordon, N. (1992). Children with developmental dyscalculia. *Developmental Medicine and Child Neurology, 34*, 459–463.

Gough, M. F. (1954). Mathemaphobia: Causes and treatments. *The Clearing House, 28*, 290–294.

Goulandris, N. K., & Snowling, M. (1991). Visual memory deficits: A plausible cause of developmental dyslexia? Evidence from a single case study. *Cognitive Neuropsychology, 8*, 127–154.

Grafman, J., Kampen, D., Rosenberg, J., Salazar, A. M., & Boller, F. (1989). The progressive breakdown of number processing and calculation ability: A case study. *Cortex, 25*, 121–133.

Greeno, T. G., Riley, M. S., & Gelman, R. (1984). Conceptual competence and children's counting. *Cognitive Psychology, 16*, 94–134.

Grewel, F. (1969). The acalculia. In P. J. Vinken & G. W. Bruyn (Eds.), *Handbook of clinical neurology*, (Vol. 4). New York: Wiley.

Groen, G. J., & Parkman, J. M. (1972). A chronometric analysis of simple addition. *Psychological Review, 79*, 329–343.

Guttman, E. (1937). Congenital arithmetic disability and acalculia (Henschen). *British Journal of Medical Psychology, 16*, 16–35.

Hamann, M. S., & Ashcraft, M. H. (1985). Simple and complex addition across development. *Journal of Experimental Child Psychology, 40*, 49–72.

Hanley, J. R., & Gard, F. (1995). A dissociation between developmental surface and phonological dyslexia in two undergraduate students. *Neuropsychologia, 33*, 909–914.

Harris, P. (1995). Children's awareness and lack of awareness of mind and emotion. In D. Cicchetti & S. L. Toth (Eds.) *Emotion, cognition and representation.* (pp. 35–57). Rochester, NY: University of Rochester Press.

Hatano, G. (1982). Learning to add and subtract: a Japanese perspective. In T. P. Carpenter, J. M. Moser, & T. A. Romberg (Eds.), *Addition and subtraction: A cognitive perspective* (pp. 211–223). Hillsdale, NJ: Erlbaum.

Hatano, G. (1990). Toward the cultural psychology of mathematical cognition. *Monographs of the Society for Research in Child Development, 55, 108–115*.

Hauser, M. D., MacNeilage, P., & Ware, M. (1995). Numerical representations in primates. *Proceedings of the National Academy of Sciences, 93*, 1514–1516.

Haynes, C., & Naidoo, S. (1992). *Children with specific speech and language impairments.* Oxford: Blackwell Scientific.

Hecaen, H., Angelergues, R., & Houillier, S. (1961). Les varietes cliniques des acalculies au cours des lésions retrolandiques: Approche statistique du probleme. *Révue Neurologique, 105*, 85–103.

Hembree, R. (1990). The nature, effects, and relief of mathematics anxiety. *Journal for Research in Mathematics Education, 21*, 33–46.

Hennessy, S. (1992). *The stability of children's mathematical behaviour: When is a bug really a bug?* Open University, Milton Keynes, UK. Unpublished manuscript.

Heritage, J. (1984). *Garfinkel and ethnomethodology.* Cambridge, MA: Polity Press.

Hess, R. D., Chang, C., & McDevitt, T. M. (1987). Cultural variations in family beliefs about children's performance in mathematics: comparisons among People's Republic of China, Chinese-American, and Caucasian American families. *Journal of Educational Psychology, 79*, 179–188.

Hiebert, J., & Wearne, D. (1996). Instruction, understanding and skill in multidigit addition and subtraction. *Cognition and Instruction, 14*, 251–283.

Hiebert, J., & Lefevre, P. (1986). Conceptual and procedural knowledge in mathematics: An introductory analysis. In J. Hiebert (Ed.), *Conceptual and procedural knowledge: The case of mathematics* (pp. 29–57). Hillsdale, NJ: Erlbaum.

Hiebert, J., & Carpenter, T. P. (1992). Learning and teaching with understanding. In D.A. Grouws (Ed.), *Handbook of research in mathematics teaching and learning* (pp. 65–97). New York: MacMillian Publishing Company.

Hiebert, J., & Wearne, D. (1992). Links between teaching and learning place value with understanding in the first grade. *Journal for Research in Mathematics Education, 23*, 68, 122.

Hitch, G. J. (1978a). The role of short-term working memory in mental arithmetic. *Cognitive Psychology, 10*, 302–323.

Hitch, G. J. (1978b). Mental arithmetic: Short-term storage and information processing in a cognitive skill. In A. M. Lesgold, J. W. Pellegrino, S. D. Fokkema, & R. Glaser (Eds.), *Cognitive psychology and instruction* (pp. 331–338). New York: Plenum.

Hitch, G. J. (1978c). The numerical ability of industrial apprentices. *Journal of Occupational Psychology, 51*, 163–176.

Hitch, G. J., Arnold, P., & Phillips, L. J. (1983). *British Journal of Psychology, 74*, 429–437.

Hitch, G. J., Cundick, J., Haughey, M., Pugh, R., & Wright, H. (1987). Aspects of counting in children's arithmetic. In J. Sloboda & D. Rogers (Eds.), *Cognitive processes in mathematics*, (pp. 26–41). Oxford: Oxford University Press.

Hitch, G. J., & Halliday, M. S. (1983). Working memory in children. *Philosophical Transactions of the Royal Society London B, 302*, 325–340.

Hitch, G. J., & McAuley, E. (1991). Working memory in children with specific arithmetical learning disabilities. *British Journal of Psychology, 82*, 375–386.

Hittmair-Delazer, M., Sailer, V., & Berke, T. (1995). Impaired arithmetical facts but intact conceptual knowledge: a single case study of dyscalculia. *Cortex, 31*, 139–147.

Hittmair-Delazer, M., Semenza, L., & Denes, G. (1994). Concepts and facts in calculation. *Brain, 117*, 715–728.

Hofstadter, D. (1982). Metamagical themas: Number numbness, or why innumeracy may be just as dangerous as illiteracy. *Scientific American, 246:5*, 16–23.

Holender, D., & Peereman, R. (1987). Differential processing of phonographic and logographic single-digit numbers by the two hemispheres. In G. Deloche & X. Seron (Eds.), *Mathematical disabilities: A cognitive neuropsychological perspective.* (pp. 43–85). Hillsdale, NJ: Erlbaum.

Hoosain, R., & Salili, F. (1987). Language differences in pronunciation speed for numbers, digit span and mathematical ability. *Psychologia, 30*, 34–38

Hopko, D. (1996). *Inhibition in working memory, implicit/explicit memory tasks, and math anxiety.* Unpublished master's thesis, Cleveland State University, Cleveland, OH.

Hughes, M. (1983/1991). What is Difficult about Learning Arithmetic? In P.Light, S. Sheldon & M. Woodhead (Eds). *Child development in social context, 2, Learning to think.* London: Routledge.

Hughes, M. (1986). *Children and number.* Oxford: Blackwell.

Hulme, C., & Snowling, M. (1992). Deficits in output phonology: An explanation of reading failure? *Cognitive Neuropsychology, 9*, 47–72.

Hunsley, J. (1987). Cognitive processes in mathematics anxiety and test anxiety: The role of appraisals, internal dialogue, and attributions. *Journal of Educational Psychology, 79*, 388–392.

Hunting, R. P., & Davis, G. E. (1991). Dimensions of young children's conceptions of the fraction one half. In R. P. Hunting & G. E. Davis (Eds.), *Early fraction learning* (pp. 27–53). New York: Springer-Verlag.

Husen, T. (1967). *International study of achievement in mathematics: a comparison of twelve countries.* New York: Wiley.

Hutchins, E. (1988). The technology of team navigation. In J. Galagegher, R. Kraut and C. Egido (Eds.), *Intellectual teamwork: Social and technological foundation of cooperative work* (pp. 191–220). Hillsdale, New Jersey: Lawrence Erlbaum Associates Inc.

Hutt, E., & Donlan, C. (1991). Teaching maths to young children with language disorders. In K. Durkin & B. Shire (Eds). *Language and Mathematical Education.* Milton Keynes, UK: Open University Press.

Hyde, J. S., Fennema, E., & Lamon, S. J. (1990). Gender differences in mathematics performance: A meta-analysis. *Psychological Bulletin, 107*, 139–155.

Hyde, J. S., Fennema, E., Ryan, M., Frost, L. A., & Hopp, C. (1990). Gender comparisons of mathematics attitudes and affect. A meta-analysis. *Psychology of Women Quarterly, 14*, 299–324.

Inhelder, B., & Piaget, J. (1964). *The early growth of logic in the child.* London: Routledge Kegan Paul.

Istomina, A. Z. (1975). The development of voluntary memory in preschool-age children. *Soviet Psychology, 13*, 5–64.

Jastak Associates (1993). Wide Range Achievement Test, Rev. 3. Wide Range Inc., Wilmington, DE.

Johnston, J. R., & Smith, L. B. (1989). Dimensional thinking in language impaired children. *Journal of Speech and Hearing Research, 32*, 33–38.

Jones, G. A., & Thornton, C. A. (1993). Children's understanding of place value: a framework for curriculum development and assessment. *Young Children, 48*, 12–18.

Jordan, K., & Lynch, M. (1993). The mainstreaming of a molecular biological tool: A case study of a new technique. In G. Button (Ed.), *Technology in working order: Studies of work, interaction, and technology* (pp. 162–178). New York, NY: Routledge.

Jordan, N. C., Levine, S. C., & Huttenlocher, J. (1994). Development of calculation abilities in middle and low income children after formal instruction in school. *Journal of Applied Developmental Psychology, 15*, 223–240.

Jordan, N. C., & Montani, T. O. (1996a). Mathematical difficulties in young children: cognitive and developmental perspectives. In M. A. Mastrapieri & J. F. Scruggs (Eds.) *Advances in learning and behavioral disabilities.* Greenwich, CT: JAI Press.

Jordan, N. C., & Montani, T. O. (1996b). *Cognitive arithmetic and problem solving: a comparison of children with specific and general mathematics difficulties.* (Unpublished manuscript).

Just, M. A., & Carpenter, P. A. (1992). A capacity theory of comprehension: Individual differences in working memory. *Psychologial Review, 99,* 122–149.

Kamii, C. (1986). Place value: an explanation of its difficulty and educational implications for the primary grades. *Journal of Research in Childhood Education, 1,* 75–85.

Kant, I. (1781/1965). *Critique of pure reason.* New York: St Martin's Press.

Katz, J. (1978). *Handbook of clinical audiology.* Baltimore, MD: William & Wilkins.

Kawatoko, Y. (1996). *Space, time, and documents in a refrigerated warehouse.* Paper prepared for the symposium for Vygotsky/Piaget Conference in Geneva.

Kawatoko, Y. (in press). Cognition and learning embedded in classroom activity. In Y. Moro (Ed.), *Ethnography of practices.* Tokyo: Kaneko-shobo.

Kaye, K. (1979). The development of skills. In G. J. Whitehurst & B. J. Zimmerman (Eds.), *The functions of language and cognition* (pp. 23–55). New York: Academic Press.

Keating, D. P. (1993). Developmental diversity in mathematical and scientific competence. In L. A. Penner, G. M. Batsche, H. M. Knoff, & D. L. Nelson (Eds.), *The challenge in mathematics and science education: psychology's response.* Washington, DC: American Psychological Association.

Kidd, D. H., Madsen, A. L., & Lamb, C. E. (1991). Mathematics vocabulary: Performance of residential deaf students. *School Science and Mathematics, 93*, 418–421.

Kimura, Y., & Bryant, P. (1983). Reading and writing in English and Japanese : A cross-cultural study of young children. *British Journal of Developmental Psychology, 1*, 143–154.

King, J., & Just, M. A. (1991). Individual differences in syntactic processing: The role of working memory. *Journal of Memory and Language, 30*, 580–602.

Kinsbourne, M., & Warrington, E. K. (1963). The developmental Gerstmann syndrome. *Archives of Neurology, 8*, 490–501.

Kitcher, P. (1984). *The nature of mathematical knowledge.* Oxford: Oxford University Press.

Koechlin, E., Dehaene, S., & Mehler, J. (in press). Numerical transformations in five-month-old human infants. *Mathematical Cognition.*

Koontz, K. L., & Berch, D. B. (1996). Identifying simple numerical stimuli: Processing inefficiencies exhibited by arithmetic learning disabled children. *Mathematical Cognition, 2,* 1–23.

Kornilaki, E. (1994). *The understanding of the numeration system among preschool children.* Unpublished MSc thesis, Department of Child Development and Primary Education, University of London.

Kosc, L. (1974). Developmental dyscalculia. *Journal of Learning Disabilities, 7,* 46–59.

Koshmider III, J. W., & Ashcraft, M. H. (1991). The development of children's mental multiplication skills. *Journal of Experimental Child Psychology, 51,* 53–89.

Kouba, V. L., Carpenter, T. P., & Swafford, J. O. (1989). Number and operations. In M. M. Lindquist (Ed.), *Results from the fourth mathematics assessment of the national assessment of educational progress*, (pp. 64–93). Reston, VA: National Council of Teachers of Mathematics, Inc.

La Pointe, L. B., & Engle, R. W. (1990). Simple and complex spans as measures of working memory capacity. *Journal of Experimental Psychology: Learning, Memory and Cognition, 16*, 1118–1133.

Labinowicz, E. (1985). *Learning from children: New beginnings for teaching numerical thinking.* Menlo Park, CA: Addison-Wesley.

Lachman, R., Lachman, J. L., & Butterfield, E. C. (1979). *Cognitive psychology and information processing: An introduction.* Hillsdale, NJ: Erlbaum.

Lakoff, G., & Nunez, R. E. (1997). The metaphorical structure of mathematics: sketching out cognitive foundations for a mind-based mathematics. In Lyn D. English (Ed.), *Mathematical reasoning: analogies, metaphor and images.* Hillsdale, NJ: Lawrence Erlbaum Associates Inc.

Lampl, Y., Eshel, Y., Gilad, R., & Sarova-Pinhas, I. (1994). Selective acalculia with sparing of the subtraction process in a patient with left parietotemporal hemorrhage. *Neurology, 44*, 1759–1761.

Lave, J. (1988). *Cognition in action.* Cambridge: Cambridge University Press.

Lave, J. (1988). *Cognition in practice: Mind, mathematics and culture in everyday life.* Cambridge: Cambridge University Press.

LeFevre, J., & Liu, J. (1997). The role of experience in numerical skill: Multiplication performance in adults from Canada and China. *Mathematical Cognition, 3*, 31–62.

LeFevre, J., Bisanz, J., & Mrkonjic, L. (1988). Cognitive arithmetic: Evidence for obligatory activation of arithmetic facts. *Memory and Cognition, 16*, 45–53.

LeFevre, J., Greenham, S. L., & Waheed, N. (1993). The development of procedural and conceptual knowledge in computational estimation. *Cognition and Instruction, 11*, 95–132.

LeFevre, J., Kulak, A. G., & Heymans, S. L. (1992). Factors influencing selection of university majors varying in mathematical content. *Canadian Journal of Psychology, 24*, 276–289.

LeFevre, J., Sadesky, G. S., & Bisanz, J. (1996). Selection of procedures in mental addition: Reassessing the problem size effect in adults. *Journal of Experimental Psychology: Learning, Memory, and Cognition, 22*, 216–230.

Lefevre, J. A., & Kulak, A. G. (1994). Individual differences in the obligatory activation of addition facts. *Memory and Cognition, 22*, 188–200.

Lefevre, J. A., Bisanz, J., Daley, K. E., Buffone, L., Greenham, S. L., & Sadesky, G.S. (1996). Multiple routes to solution of single-digit multiplication problems. *Journal of Experimental Psychology: General, 123*, 284–306.

Lemaire, P., Abdi, H., & Fayol, M. (1996). The role of working memory resources in simple cognitive arithmetic. *European Journal of Cognitive Psychology, 8 (1)*, 73–103.

Levine, D. R. (1982). Strategy use and estimation of college students. *Journal for Research in Mathematics Education, 13*, 350–359.

Levine, M. D., Lindsay, R. L., & Reed, M. S. (1992). The wrath of math: deficiencies of mathematical mastery in the school child. *Pediatric Clinics of North America, 39*, 525–536.

Levitt, E. E., & Hutton, L. A. (1983). Correlates and possible causes of mathematics anxiety. In C. D. Spielberger & J. N. Butcher (Eds.), *Advances in Personality Assessment*, (Vol. 3, pp. 129–140). Hillsdale, NJ: Erlbaum.

Logie, R. (1995). *Visuo-spatial working memory.* Hillsdale, NJ: Erlbaum.

Logie, R. H., & Baddeley, A. D. (1987). Cognitive processes in counting. *Journal of Experimental Psychology: Learning, Memory and Cognition, 13*, 310–326.

Logie, R. H., Gilhooly, K. J., & Wynn, V. (1994). Counting on working memory in arithmetic problem solving. *Memory and Cognition, 22*, 395–410.

Logie, R. H., & Baddeley, A. D. (1987). Cognitive processes in counting. *Journal of Experimental Psychology, 13*, 310–326.

Luchelli, F., & DeRenzi, E. (1993). Primary dyscalculia after a medial frontal lesion of the left hemisphere. *Journal of Neurology, Neurosurgery and Psychiatry, 56*, 304–307.

Luckner, J. L., & McNeill, J. H. (1994). Performance of a group of deaf and hard-of-hearing students and a comparison group of hearing students on a series of problem-solving tasks. *American Annals of the Deaf, 139*, 371–376.

Lynch, A., Vincent, E. M., Mitchell, L. B., & Trueman, M. (1982). How flat are normal ability profiles in 4-year-olds? *Child Care, Health and Development, 8*, 39–49.

Lynch, M. (1991). Method: Measurement-ordinary and scientific measurement as ethnomethodological phenomena. In G. Button (Ed.), *Ethnomethodology and the human science* (pp. 77–108). Cambridge: Cambridge University Press.

Lynch, M., Livingston, E., & Garfinkel, H. (1983). Temporal order in laboratory work. In K. D. Knorr-cetina and M. Mulkay (Eds.), *Science observed*. Beverly Hills: Sage.

Lynn, R. (1982). IQ in Japan and the United States shows a growing disparity. *Nature, 297*, 222–223.

Macaruso, P., & Albertson, A.-M. (1996). *Computational estimation in learning disabled and control students*. Presented at the American Psychological Society meeting, San Francisco, CA.

Macaruso, P., & Buchman, A. (1996). *Arithmetic fact retrieval in a case study of developmental dyscalculia*. Presented at the Eastern Psychological Association meeting, Philadelphia, PA.

Macaruso, P., Harley, W., & McCloskey, M. (1992). Assessment of acquired dyscalculia. In D.L. Margolin (Ed.), *Cognitive neuropsychology in clinical practice*. New York: Oxford University Press.

Macaruso, P., McCloskey, M., & Aliminosa, D. (1993). The functional architecture of the cognitive numerical-processing system: Evidence from a patient with multiple impairments. *Cognitive Neuropyschology, 10*, 341–376.

Mack, N. K. (1990). Learning fractions with understanding: Building on informal knowledge. *Journal for Research in Mathematics Education, 21*, 16–32.

Mack, N. K. (1993). Learning rational numbers with understanding: The case of informal knowledge. In *Rational numbers: An integration of research* T. P. Carpenter, T. A. Romberg, E. Fennema (Eds.), (pp. 85–105). Hillsdale, NJ: Lawrence Erlbaum.

MacLeod, C. M. (1991). Half a century of research on the Stroop effect: An integrative review. *Psychological Bulletin, 109*, 163–203.

Mandler, G. (1989). Affect and learning: Causes and consequences of emotional interactions. In D. B. McLeod & V. M. Adams (Eds.), *Affect and mathematical problem solving: A new perspective* (pp. 3–19). New York: Springer-Verlag.

Mandler, G., & Shebo, B. J. (1982). Subitizing: An analysis of its component processes. *Journal of Experimental Psychology: General, 11*, 1–22.

Margolin, D. I. (Ed). (1992). *Cognitive Neuropsychology in Clinical Practice*. New York: Oxford University Press.

Markman, E. (1979). Classes and collections: Conceptual organization and numerical abilities. *Cognitive Psychology, 11*, 395–411.

Markman, E. M. (1990). Constraints children place on word meanings. *Cognitive Science, 14*, 57–77.

Marshall, J. C. (1989). The description and interpretation of acquired and developmental reading disorders. In A.M. Galaburda (Ed.), *From reading to neurons*. Cambridge, MA: MIT Press.

Matsuzawa, T. (1985). Use of numbers by a chimpanzee. *Nature, 315*, 57–59.

Mayer, R. E., Sims, V., & Tajika, H. (1995). A comparison of how textbooks teach mathematical problem solving in Japan and the United States. *American Educational Research Journal, 32*, 443–460.

McCarthy, R. A., & Warrington, E. K. (1990). *Cognitive neuropsychology: A clinical introduction*. San Diego, CA: Academic Press.

McCloskey, M. (1992). Cognitive mechanisms in numerical processing: Evidence from acquired dyscalculia. *Cognition, 44*, 107–157.

McCloskey, M., Aliminosa, D., & Sokol, S. M. (1991). Facts, rules and procedures in calculation: Evidence from dyscalculia. *Brain and Cognition, 17*, 154–203.

McCloskey, M., Caramazza, A., & Basili, A. G. (1985). Cognitive mechanisms in number processing and calculation: Evidence from dyscalculia. *Brain & Cognition, 4*, 171–196.

McCloskey, M., Harley, W., & Sokol, S. M. (1991). Models of arithmetic fact retrieval: An evaluation in light of findings from normal and brain-damaged subjects. *Journal of Experimental Psychology: Learning, Memory, and Cognition, 17*, 377–397.

McCloskey, M., & Macaruso, P. (1995). Representing and using numerical information. *American Psychologist, 50*, 351–363.

McCloskey, M., Sokol, S. M., & Goodman, R. A., (1986). Cognitive processes in verbal number production: Inferences from the performance of brain-damaged subjects. *Journal of Experimental Psychology: General, 115*, 307–330.

McCloskey, M., Sokol, S. M., Goodman-Schulman, R., & Caramazza, A. (1990). Cognitive representations and processes in number production: Evidence from cases of acquired dyscalculia. In A. Caramazza (Ed.), *Cognitive neuropsychology and neurolinguistics: Advances in models of cognitive function and impairment.* Hillsdale, NJ: Erlbaum.

McLeish, J. (1993). *Number.* London: Bloomsbury.

McLeod, D. B. (1989). The role of affect in mathematical problem solving. In D. B. McLeod & V. M. Adams (Eds.), *Affect and mathematical problem solving: A new perspective* (pp. 245–258). New York: Springer-Verlag.

McLeod, D. B. (1992). Research on affect in mathematics education: A reconceptualization. In D. A. Grouws, & D. B. McLeod (Eds.), *Handbook of research on mathematics teaching and learning* (pp. 575–596). New York: MacMillan.

McNeil, J. E., & Warrington E. K. (1994). A dissociation between addition and subtraction with written calculation. *Neuropsychologia, 32*, 717–728.

McNeil, J. E., & Warrington, E. K. (1993). A modality-specific case of dyscalculia. *Journal of Clinical and Experimental Psychology, 15.* 415.

Mechner, F. M., & Guevrekian, L. (1962). Effects of deprivation upon counting and timing in rats. *Journal of the Experimental Analysis of Behavior, 5*, 463–466.

Meck, W. H., & Church, R. M. (1983). A mode control model of counting and timing processes. *Journal of Experimental Psychology: Animal Behavior Processes, 9*, 320–334.

Mehan, H. (1985). The structure of classroom discourse. In T. van Dijk (Ed.), *Handbook of discourse analysis. Vol. III: Discourse and dialogue* (pp. 120–132). London: Academic Press.

Menninger, K. (1958). *Number words and number symbols.* Cambridge, Mass.: M.I.T. Press.

Michie, S. (1984). Why preschoolers are reluctant to count spontaneously. *British Journal of Developmental Psychology, 2*, 347–358.

Mill, J. S. (1843/1973). A System of Logic ratiocinative and inductive, (8th edn.). In J. M. Robson (Ed.), *Collected works of John Stuart Mill* (Vols. 7 & 8). University of Toronto Press.

Miller, K., Perlmutter, M., & Keating, D. (1984). Cognitive arithmetic: Comparison of operations. *Journal of Experimental Psychology: Learning, Memory, & Cognition, 10*, 46–60.

Miller, K. F., & Stigler, J. W. (1987). Counting in Taiwanese: Cultural variation in a basic cognitive skill. *Cognitive Development, 2*, 279–305.

Miller, K. F., & Zhu, J. (1991). The trouble with teens: Accessing the structure of number names. *Journal of Memory and Language, 30*, 48–68.

Miller, K. F., Smith, C. M., Zhu, J., Zhang, H. (1995). Pre-school origins of cross-national differences in mathematical competence. *Psychological Science, 6*, 56–60.

Miura, I. T., & Okamoto, Y. (1989). Comparisons of U.S. and Japanese first graders cognitive representation of number and understanding of place value. *Journal of Educational Psychology, 81*, 109–114.

Miura, I. T. (1987). Mathematics achievement as a function of language. *Journal of Educational Psychology, 79*, 79–82.

Miura, I. T., Kim, C. C., Chang, C., & Okamoto, Y. (1988). Effects of language characteristics on children's cognitive representation of number: Cross-national comparisons. *Child Development, 59*, 1445–1450.

Miura, I. T., Okamoto, Y., Kim, C. C., Chang, C. M., Steere, M., & Fayol, M. (1994). Comparisons of children's cognitive representation of number: China, France, Japan, Korea, Sweden, and the United States. *International Journal of Behavioral Development, 17*, 401–411.

Miura, I. T., Okamoto, Y., Kim, C. C., Steere, M., & Fayol, M. (1993). First graders' cognitive representations of number and understanding of place value: Cross national comparisons. *Journal Of Educational Psychology, 85*, 24–30.

Moore, D. S. (1997). Infant mathematical skills? A conceptual replication and consideration of interpretation. Poster presented at the Biennial Conference of the Society for Research in Child Development, Washington D.C., April 1–3.

Morehead, D. M., & Ingram, D. (1976). The development of base syntax in normal and linguistically deviant children. In D.M. Morehead and A.E. Morehead (Eds). *Normal and deficient child language* (pp. 209–238). Baltimore, MD: University Park Press.

Moyer, R. S., & Landauer, T. (1967). Time required judgments of numerical inequality. *Nature, 215*, 1519–1520.

Munn, P. (1994). The Early Development of Literacy and Numeracy Skills. *European Early Childhood Education Research Journal, 2*, 5–18.

Munn, P. (1995). The role of organised preschool learning environments in literacy and numeracy development. *Research Papers in Education, 10*, 217–252.

National Council of Teachers of the Deaf Research Committee (1957). The teaching of arithmetic in schools for the deaf. *The Teacher of the Deaf, 152*, 165–172.

NFER-Nelson (1994). *Mathematics 7* through *Mathematics 10*. Windsor, UK: NFER-Nelson Publishing.

Noel, M.-P., & Seron, X. (1993). Arabic number reading deficit: A single case study of when 236 is read (2306) and judged superior to 1258. *Cognitive Neuropsychology, 10*, 317–339.

Nolan, D. R., Hammeke, T. A., & Barkley, R. A. (1983). A comparison of the patterns of the neuropsychological performance in two groups of learning disabled children. *Journal of Clinical Child Psychology, 12*, 22–27.

Nunes, T. (1992). Ethnomethodology and everyday cognition. In D. A. Grouws (Ed.), *Handbook of research on mathematics teaching and learning* (pp. 557–574). New York: Macmillan.

Nunes, T., & Bryant, P. (1996). *Children doing mathematics*. Oxford: Blackwell.

Nunes Carraher, T., & Schliemann, A. D. (1990). Knowledge of the numeration system among pre-schoolers. In L. P. Steffe and T. Wood (Eds.), *Transforming children's mathematics education.* (pp. 135–141). Hillsdale, NJ: Erlbaum.

Nunes, T., Miranda, E. M., & Silva, Z. H. (1991). *The development of the understanding additive composition: A predictive and an intervention study.* Paper presented at the Meeting of the Association of Portuguese Psychology, Braga, Portugal.

Nunes, T., & Moreno, C. (1990). The Signed Algorithm and its bugs. *Educational Studies in Mathematics, 35*, 85–92.

Nunes, T., Schliemann, A. D., & Carraher, D. W. (1993). *Street mathematics and school mathematics*. Cambridge: Cambridge University Press.

O'Hare, A. E., Brown, J. K., & Aitken, K. (1991). Dyscalculia in children. *Developmental Medicine and Child Neurology, 33*, 356–361.

Ozols, E. J., & Rourke, B. P. (1988). Characteristics of young learning-disabled children classified according to patterns of academic achievement: Auditory-perceptual and visual-perceptual abilities. *Journal of Clinical Child Psychology, 17*, 44–52.

Parkin, A. J. (1996). *Explorations in Cognitive Neuropsychology*. Oxford: Blackwell.

Pastore, N. (1961). Number sense and "counting" ability in the canary. *Zeitschrift für Tierpsychologie, 18*, 561–573.

Pau, C. S. (1995). The deaf child and solving problems of arithmetic: The importance of comprehensive reading. *American Annals of the Deaf, 140*, 279–286.

PeBenito, R., Fisch, C. B., & Fisch, M. L. (1988). Developmental Gerstmann's syndrome. *Archives of Neurology, 45*, 977–982.

Pepperberg, I. M. (1987). Evidence for conceptual quantitative abilities in the African Gray Parrot: Labeling of cardinal sets. *Ethology, 75*, 37–61.

Perry, M. (1991). Learning and transfer: Instructional conditions and conceptual change. *Cognitive Development, 6*, 449–468.

Perry, M., Van der Stoep, S. W., & Yu, S. L. (1993). Asking questions in first grade mathematics classes: Potential influences on mathematical thought. *Journal of Educational Psychology, 85*, 31–40.

Pettito, A, L., & Ginsburg, H. P. (1982). Mental arithmetic in Africa and America: Strategies, principles and explanations. *International Journal of Psychology, 17*, 81–102.

Piaget, J. (1926; 1929). *The child's conception of the world.* London: Routledge & Kegan Paul.

Piaget, J. (1973). Comments on mathematical education. In A. G. Howson (Ed.), *Developments in mathematical education: Proceedings of the second international congress on mathematical education* (pp. 79–87). New York: Cambridge University Press.

Piaget, J., & Szeminska, A. (1941; 1952). *The child's conception of number.* London: Routledge & Kegan Paul.

Pirolli, P., & Recker, M. (1994). Learning strategies and transfer in the domain of programming. *Cognition and Instruction, 12*, 235–275.

Platt, J. R., & Johnson, D. M. (1971). Localization of position within a homogeneous behavior chain: Effects of error contingencies. *Learning and Motivation, 2*, 386–414.

Posner, M. I., & Snyder, C. R. R. (1975). Facilitation and inhibition in the processing of signals. In P. M. A. Rabbitt & S. Dornic (Eds.), *Attention and performance: V* (pp. 669–682). New York: Academic Press.

Power, R. J. D., & Dal Martello, M.F. (1990). The dictation of Italian numerals. *Language & Cognitive Processes, 5*, 237–254.

Pritchard, R. A., Miles, T. R., Chinn, S. J., & Taggart, A. T. (1989). Dyslexia and knowledge of number facts. *Links, 14*, 17–20.

Pullan, J. (1969). *The History of the Abacus.* New York: Praeger Publishers

Quine, W. V. O. (1960). *Word and object.* Cambridge, MA: MIT Press.

Rapin, I. (1986). Helping deaf children acquire language: Lessons from the past. *International Journal of Paediatric Otorhinolaryngology, 11*, 213–223.

Raven, J. C. (1985). *Coloured progressive matrices.* London: H.K. Lewis.

Renkl, A. (1997). Learning from worked-out examples: A study on individual differences. *Cognitive Science, 21*, 1–29.

Renton, M. (1992). *Primary school children's strategies for addition.* Ph.D. thesis. University of London Institute of Education:

Resnick, L. B. (1982). Syntax and semantics in learning to subtract. In T. P. Carpenter, J. M. Moser, & T.A. Romberg (Eds.), *Addition and subtraction: A cognitive perspective* (pp. 136–155). Hillsdale, NJ: Erlbaum.

Resnick, L. B. (1994). Situated rationalism: Biological and social preparation for learning. In L. A. Hirschfeld & S. A. Gelman (Eds.), *Mapping the mind: Domain specificity in cognition and culture* (pp. 474–493). New York: Cambridge University Press.

Resnick, L. B., & Omanson, S. F. (1987). Learning to understand arithmetic. In R. Glaser (Ed.) *Advances in instructional psychology*, (Vol. 3, pp. 41–95). Hillsdale, NJ: Erlbaum.

Reynolds, A. J., & Walberg, H. J. (1992). A process model of mathematics achievement and attitude. *Journal for Research in Mathematics Education, 23*, 306–328.

Reynolds, D., & Farrell, S. (1996). *World's apart? A review of international surveys of educational achievement involving England.* London: HMSO.

Richardson, F. C., & Suinn, R. M. (1972). The Mathematics Anxiety Rating Scale. *Journal of Counseling Psychology, 19*, 551–554.

Rickard, T. C., & Bourne Jr, L. E.,. (1996). Some tests of an identical elements model of basic arithmetic skills. *Journal of Experimental Psychology: Learning, Memory, and Cognition, 22*, 1281–1295.

Riley, M., Greeno, J. G., & Heller, J. I. (1983). Development of children's problem solving ability in arithmetic. In H. Ginsburg (Ed.): *The development of mathematical thinking.* (pp. 153–196). New York: Academic Press.

Rilling, M. E. (1967). Number of responses as a stimulus in fixed interval and fixed ratio schedules. *Journal of Comparative and Physiological Psychology, 63*, 60–65.

Rilling, M. E., & McDiarmid, C. (1965). Signal detection in fixed ratio schedules. *Science, 148*, 526–527.

Rittle-Johnson, B., & Alibali, M. W. (1998). Conceptual and procedural knowledge of mathematics: Does one lead to another? Manuscript submitted for publication.

Rosenberger, P. B. (1989). Perceptual-motor and attentional correlates of developmental dyscalculia. *Annals of Neurology, 26*, 216–220.

Ross, S. H. (1986, April). *The development of children's place-value numeration concepts in grades two through five.* Paper presented at the annual meeting of the American Educational Research Association, San Francisco, CA.

Rourke, B. P. (1993). Arithmetic disabilities, specific and otherwise: A neuropsychological perspective. *Journal of Learning Disabilities, 26*, 214–226.

Rourke, B. P., & Finlayson, M. A. J. (1978). Neuropsychological significance of variations in patterns of academic performance: Verbal and visual-spatial abilities. *Journal of Abnormal Child Psychology, 6*, 121–133.

Russell, R. L., & Ginsburg, H. P. (1984). Cognitive analysis of children's mathematics difficulties. *Cognition and Instruction, 1*, 217–244.

Salthouse, T. A., & Babcock, R. L. (1990). *Computation span and listening span tasks.* Unpublished manuscript. Atlanta: Georgia Institute of Technology.

Saxe, G. (1979). Developmental relations between notational counting and number conservation. *Child Development, 50*, 180–187.

Saxe, G. B. (1982). Body parts as numerals: A developmental analysis of numeration among remote Oksapmin village populations in Papua New Guinea. *Child Development, 52*, 306–316.

Saxe, G. B. (1977). A developmental analysis of notational counting. *Child Development, 48*, 1512–1520.

Saxe, G. B. (1982). Developing forms of arithmetical thought among the Oksapmin of Papua New Guinea. *Developmental Psychology, 18*, 583–594.

Saxe, G. B., Guberman, S. R., & Gearhart, M. (1987). Social processes in early number development. *Monographs of the Society for Research in Child Development, 52*, Serial No. 216.

Saxton, M., & Towse, J. N. (1997). Linguistic relativity: The case of place value in multidigit numbers. *Journal of Experimental Child Psychology, 68.*

Schaeffer, B., Eggleston, V. H., & Scott, J. L. (1974). Number development in young children. *Cognitive Psychology, 6*, 357–379.

Schank, R. C., & Abelson, R. (1977). *Script, plans, goals, and understanding.* Hillsdale, NJ: Lawrence Erlbaum Associates Inc.

Secada, W. G. (1984). *Counting in Sign: the number string, accuracy and use.* Unpublished Ph.D. dissertation, Department of Education, Northwestern University, Evanston, (IL).

Sekuler, R., & Mierkiewicz, D. (1977). Children's judgements of numerical inequality. *Child Development, 48,* 630–633.

Seron, X., & Noel, M.-P. (1995). Transcoding numbers from the arabic code to the verbal one or vice versa: How many routes? *Mathematical Cognition, 1,* 215–243.

Seron, X., Deloche, G., & Noel, M.-P. (1992). Number transcribing by children: Writing arabic numbers under dictation. In J. Bideaud, C. Meljac, & J.P. Fischer (Eds.), *Pathways to number: Children's developing numerical abilities.* Hillsdale, NJ: Erlbaum.

Sewell, B. (1981). *Use of mathematics by adults in daily life.* London: Advisory Council for Adult and Continuing Education.

Shafrir, U., & Siegel, L. S. (1994). Subtypes of learning disabilities in adolescents and adults. *Journal of Learning Disabilities, 27,* 123–134.

Shalev, R. S, Manor, O., Amir, N., Wertman-Elad, R., & Gross-Tsur, V. (1995). Developmental dyscalculia and brain laterality. *Cortex, 31,* 357–365.

Shalev, R. S., Weirtman, R., & Amir, N. (1988). Developmental dyscalculia. *Cortex, 24,* 555–561.

Share, D. L., Moffitt, T. E., & Silva, P. A. (1988). Factors associated with arithmetic-and-reading disability and specific arithmetic disability. *Journal of Learning Disabilities, 21,* 313–320.

Shipley, E. F., & Shepperson, B. (1990). Countable entities: Developmental changes. *Cognition, 34,* 109–136.

Siegel, L. S. (1982). The development of quantity concepts: perceptual and linguistic factors. In: C. J. Brainerd (Ed.) *Children's logical and mathematical cognition. Progress in cognitive developmental research.*

Siegel, L. S., Lees, A., Allan, L., & Bolton, B. (1981). Non-verbal assessment of Piagetian concepts in preschool children with impaired language development. *Educational Psychology, 2,* 153–158.

Siegel, L. S., & Linder, A. (1984). Short-term memory processes in children with reading and arithmetic disabilities. *Developmental Psychology, 20,* 200–207.

Siegel, L. S., & Ryan, E. B (1989). The development of working memory in normally achieving and subtypes of learning disabled children. *Child Development, 60,* 973–980.

Siegler, R. S. (1987). The perils of averaging data over strategies: An example from children's addition. *Journal of Experimental Psychology: General, 116,* 250–264.

Siegler, R. (1988). Strategy choice procedures and the development of multiplication skill. *Journal of Experimental Psychology: General, 117,* 258–275.

Siegler, R. S., & Crowley, K. (1991). The microgenetic method: A direct means for studying cognitive development. *American Psychologist, 46,* 606–620.

Siegler, R. S., & Crowley, K. (1994). Constraints on learning in nonprivileged domains. *Cognitive Psychology, 27,* 194–226.

Siegler, R. S., & Engle, R. A. (1994). Studying change in developmental and neuropsychological contexts. *Cahiers de Psychologie Cognitive/Current Psychology of Cognition, 13,* 321–349.

Siegler, R. S., & Jenkins, E. (1989). *How children discover new strategies.* Hillsdale, NJ: Erlbaum.

Siegler, R. S., & Robinson, M. (1982). The development of numerical understandings. In H. Reese & L. Lipsitt (Eds.), *Advances in child development and behavior* (Vol. 16, pp. 241–312). New York: Academic Press.

Siegler, R. S., & Shrager, J. (1984). A model of strategy choice. In C. Sophian (Ed.), *Origins of cognitive skills* (pp. 229–293). Hillsdale, NJ: Erlbaum.

Simon, T. J., Hespos, S. J., & Rochat, P. (1995). Do infants understand simple arithmetic? A replication of Wynn (1992). *Cognitive Development, 10,* 253–269.

Sinclair, A., Siegrist, F., & Sinclair, H. (1983). Young children's ideas about the written number system. In D. Rogers and A. Sloboda (Eds.) *The acquisition of symbolic skills.* New York: Plenums.

Singer, H. D., & Low, A. A. (1933). Acalculia (Henschen): A clinical study. *Archives of Neurology and Psychiatry, 29,* 476–498.

Slade, P. D., & Russell, G. F. M. (1971). Developmental dyscalculia: A brief report of four cases. *Psychological Medicine, 1,* 292–298.

Snowling, M. (1991). Developmental reading disorders. *Journal of Child Psychology and Psychiatry, 32,* 49–77.

Sokol, S. M., & Macaruso, P. (1994). Developmental dyscalculia and cognitive neuropsychology. *Developmental Neuropsychology, 10,* 413–441.

Sokol, S. M., Macaruso, P., & Gollan, T. H. (1991). *Patterns of impairment in developmental dyscalculia.* Presentation at the Society for Neuroscience meeting, New Orleans, LA.

Sokol, S. M., Macaruso, P., & Gollan, T. H. (1994). Developmental dyscalculia and cognitive neuropsychology. *Developmental Neuropsychology, 10,* 413–441.

Sokol, S. M., & McCloskey, M. (1988). Levels of representation in verbal number production. *Applied Psycholinguistics, 9,* 267–281.

Sokol, S. M., & McCloskey, M. (1991). Cognitive mechanisms in calculation. In R. Sternberg & P.A. Frensch (Eds.), *Complex problem solving: principles and mechanisms.* Hillsdale, NJ: Erlbaum.

Sokol, S. M., McCloskey, M., & Cohen, N. J. (1989). Cognitive representations of arithmetic knowledge: Evidence from acquired dyscalculia. In A.F. Bennett & K. M. McConkey (Eds.), *Cognition in individual and social contexts* (Proceedings of the XXIV International Congress of Psychology, Vol. 3). Amsterdam: Elsevier.

Sokol, S. M., McCloskey, M., Cohen, N. J., & Aliminosa, D. (1991). Cognitive representations and processes in arithmetic: Inferences from the performance of brain-damaged subjects. *Journal of Experimental Psychology: Learning, Memory and Cognition, 17,* 355–376.

Sophian, C. (1987). Early developments in children's use of counting to solve quantitative problems. *Cognition and Instruction, 4,* 61–90.

Sophian, C. (1988). Limitations on children's knowledge about counting: Using counting to compare two sets. *Developmental Psychology, 24,* 634–640.

Sophian, C. (1995). Representation and reasoning in early numerical development: Counting, conservation, and comparisons between sets. *Child Development, 66,* 559–577.

Sophian, C. (1997). Beyond competence: The significance of performance for conceptual development. *Cognitive Development, 12,* 281–303.

Sophian, C., & Kalihawa, C. (in press). Units of counting: Developmental changes. *Cognitive Development.*

Sophian, C., Wood, A., & Vong, K. I. (1995). Making numbers count: The early development of numerical inferences. *Developmental Psychology, 31,* 263–273.

Sowder, J. T. (1992a). Estimation and related topics. In D. A. Grouws (Ed.), *Handbook of research on teaching and learning.* New York: Macmillan.

Sowder, J. T. (1992b). Making sense of numbers in school mathematics. In G. Leinhardt, R. Putman, & R. A. Hattrup (Eds.), *Analysis of arithmetic for mathematics teaching.* Hillsdale, NJ: Erlbaum.

Spelke, E. (1990). Principles of object perception. *Cognitive Science, 14,* 29–56.

Starkey, P. (1992). The early development of numerical reasoning. *Cognition, 43,* 93–126.

Starkey, P., & Cooper Jr., R. G. (1980). Perception of numbers by human infants. *Science, 210,* 1033–1035.

Starkey, P., Spelke, E. S., & Gelman, R. (1990). Numerical abstraction by human infants. *Cognition, 36,* 97–127.

Steffe, L. P., Thompson, P. W., & Richards, J. (1982). Children's counting in arithmetical problem solving. In T. P. Carpenter, J. M. Moser, & T. A. Romberg (Eds.) *Addition and subtraction: A cognitive perspective* (pp. 83–96). Hillsdale, NJ: Erlbaum.

Stevenson, H. W., Chen, C., Lee. S. (1993). Mathematics achievement of Taiwanese, Japanese, and American children: Ten years later. *Science, 259*, 53–58.

Stevenson, H. W., Lee, S., Chen, C., Stigler, J. W., Hsu, C., & Kitamura, S. (1990a). Contexts of achievement. *Monographs of the Society for Research in Child Development, 55*.

Stevenson, H. W., Lee, S., Chen, C., Lummis, M., Stigler, J., Fan, L., & Ge, F. (1990b). Mathematics achievement of children in China and the United States. *Child Development, 61*, 1053–1066.

Stevenson, H. W., Lee, S., & Stigler, J. W. (1986). Mathematics achievement of Taiwanese, Japanese, and American children. *Science, 231*, 593–699.

Stevenson, H. W., & Stigler, J. W. (1992). *The learning gap: Why our schools are failing and what we can learn from Japanese and Chinese education.* New York: Summit Books.

Stigler, J. W., Chalip, L., & Miller, K. F. (1986). Consequences of skill: The case of abacus training in Taiwan. *American Journal of Education, 94*, 447–479.

Stigler, J. W., & Fernandez, C. (1995). Learning mathematics from classroom instruction: Cross-cultural and experimental perspectives. In C. Nelson (Ed.), *Contemporary perspectives on learning and development; Twenty-Seventh Minnesota Symposium on Child Psychology* (pp. 103–130). Hillsdale, NJ: Erlbaum.

Stigler, J. W., Fuson, K. C., Ham, M., & Kim, M. S. (1986). An analysis of addition and subtraction word problems in American and Soviet elementary mathematics textbooks. *Cognition and Instruction, 3*,153–171.

Stigler, J. W., Lee, S., Lucker, W., & Stevenson, H. W. (1982). Curriculum and achievement in mathematics: a study of elementary school children in Japan, Taiwan, and the United States. *Journal of Educational Psychology, 74*, 315–322.

Stigler, J. W., Lee, S., & Stevenson, H. W. (1987). Mathematics classrooms in Japan, Taiwan, and the United States. *Child Development, 58*, 1272–1285.

Stodolsky, S. S. (1985). Telling math: Origins of math aversion and anxiety. *Educational Psychologist, 20*, 125–133.

Stone, C. A., & Connell, P. J. (1993). Induction of a visual symbolic rule in children with specific language impairment. *Journal of Speech and Hearing Research, 36*, 599–608.

Strang, J. D., & Rourke, B. P. (1983). Concept-formation/non-verbal reasoning abilities of children who exhibit specific academic problems with arithmetic. *Journal of Clinical Child Psychology, 12*, 33–39.

Strang, J. D., & Rourke, B. P. (1985). Arithmetic disability subtypes: The neuropsychological significance of specific arithmetical impairment in childhood. In B. P. Rourke (Ed.), *Neuropsychology of learning disabilities: Essentials of subtype analysis.* New York: Guilford Press.

Strauss, M. S., & Curtis, L. E. (1981). Infant perception of numerosity. *Children Development, 52*, 1146–1152.

Stuart, M., & Howard, D. (1995). KJ: A developmental deep dyslexic. *Cognitive Neuropsychology, 12*, 793–824.

Suchman, L. (1987). *Plan and situated actions. The problems of human machine communication.* Cambridge: Cambridge University Press.

Suinn, R. M., Edie, C. A., Nicoletti, J., & Spinelli, R. (1972). The MARS, a measure of mathematics anxiety: Psychometric data. *Journal of Clinical Psychology, 28*, 373–375.

Suinn, R. M., Taylor, S., & Edwards, R. W. (1988). Suinn Mathematics Anxiety Rating Scale for Elementary School Students (MARS-E): Psychometric and normative data. *Educational and Psychological Measurement, 48*, 979–986.

Sullivan, K. S., Macaruso, P., & Sokol, S. M. (1996). Remediation of Arabic numeral processing in a case of developmental dyscalculia. *Neuropyschological Rehabilitation, 6*, 27–53.

Svenson, O., & Sjoberg, K. (1978). Subitizing and counting processes in young children. *Scandinavian Journal of Psychology, 19*, 247–250.

Swanson, H. L. (1993). Working memory in learning disability subgroups. *Journal of Experimental Child Psychology, 56*, 87–114.

Swart, W. L. (1985). Some findings on conceptual development of computational skills. *Arithmetic Teacher, 32*, 36–38.

Takeuchi, M., & Scott, R. (1992). Cognitive profiles of Japanese and Canadian Kindergarten and first grade children. *The Journal of Social Psychology, 132*, 505–512.

Temple, C. M. (1986). Developmental dysgraphias. *Quarterly Journal of Experimental Psychology, 38A*, 77–110.

Temple, C. M. (1989). Digit dyslexia: A category-specific disorder in developmental dyscalculia. *Cognitive Neuropsychology, 6*, 93–116.

Temple, C. M. (1991). Procedural dyscalculia and number fact dyscalculia: Double dissociation in development dyscalculia. *Cognitive Neuropsychology, 8*, 155–176.

Temple, C. M., & Marshall, J. C. (1983). A case study of developmental phonological dyslexia. *British Journal of Psychology, 74*, 517–533.

Thomas, R. K., Fowlkes, D., & Vickery, J. D. (1980). Conceptual numerous judgments by squirrel monkeys. *American Journal of Psychology, 92*, 33–43.

Thurstone, L. L., & Thurstone, T. G. (1941). Factorial studies of intelligence. *Psychometric Monographs, No. 2.*

Tobias, S. (1979). Anxiety research in educational psychology. *Journal of Educational Psychology, 71*, 573–582.

Tocci, C. M., & Engelhard Jr., G., (1991). Achievement, parental support, and gender differences in attitudes toward mathematics. *Journal of Educational Research, 84*, 280–286.

Towse, J. N., & Hitch, G. J. (1995). Is there a relationship between task demand and storage space in tests of working memory capacity? *The Quarterly Journal of Experimental Psychology, 48A*, 108–124.

Towse, J. N., & Saxton, M. (1997). Linguistic influences on children's number concepts: Methodological and theoretical considerations. *Journal of Experimental Child Psychology, 66*, 362–375.

Trick, L. M., & Pylyshyn, Z. W. (1993). What enumeration studies can show us about spatial attention: Evidence for limited capacity preattentive processing. *Journal of Experimental Psychology: Human Perception and Performance, 19*, 331–351.

Trick, L. M., & Pylyshyn, Z. W. (1994). Why are small and large numbers enumerated differently? A limited-capacity preattentive stage in vision. *Psychological Review, 101*, 80–102.

Turner, M. L., & Engle, R. W. (1989). Is working-memory capacity task-dependent? *Journal of Memory and Language, 28*, 127–154.

Ueno, N. (1996). *Cutting metals as situated practice.* Paper prepared for the symposium for Vygotsky/Piaget Conference in Geneva.

Ueno, N. (1996). Resources for organizing collaborative activities. *Cognitive Studies: Bulletin of the Japanese Cognitive Science Society, 3(2)*, 5–24.

Uller, M. C., Carey, S., Huntley-Fenner, G. N., & Klatt, L. (1996). *The representations underlying infant addition.* Unpublished manuscript.

Van der Lely, H., & Howard, D. (1993). Children with specific language impairment: Linguisitic impairment of short-term memory deficit? *Journal of Speech and Hearing Research, 36*, 1193–1207.

Van Loosbroek, E., & Smitsman, A. (1990). Visual perception of numerosity in infancy. *Developmental Psychology, 26*, 916–922.

Vernon, P. E., & Miller, K. M. (1976). *Graded arithmetic–mathematics test.* Sevenoaks, UK: Hodder & Stoughton.

Vygotsky, L. S., & Luria, A. R. (1930/1993). *Studies on the history of behaviour: Ape, primitive and child.* (V. I. Golod & J. E. Knox Trans). Hillsdale, NJ: Erlbaum.

Vygotsky, L. S. (1962). *Thought and language.* Cambridge, Mass.: MIT Press.

Wagner, S. H., & Walters, J. (1982). A longitudinal analysis of early number concepts: From numbers to number. In G. E. Forman (Ed.), *Action and thought* (pp. 137–161). New York: Academic Press.

Wang, J. (1995). *Chinese children's understanding of the numeration system.* Unpublished Masters dissertation, Child Development and Learning, Institute of Education, University of London.

Warrington, E. K. (1982). The fractionation of arithmetical skills: A single case study. *Quarterly Journal of Experimental Psychology, 34A,* 31–51.

Watts, W. J. (1981). The performance of deaf, partially hearing and normally hearing children on conservation tasks of cardinal number, discontinuous quantity and length. *Journal of the British Association of Teachers of the Deaf, 5,* 11–19.

Watts, W. J. (1982). The performance of the deaf, partially hearing and normally hearing children on conservation tasks of weight and area. *Teacher of the Deaf, 6,* 5–9.

Weaver, J.F. (1954). Differentiated instruction in arithmetic: An overview and a promising trend. *Education, 74,* 300–305.

Webb, S. (1995). *Children's use of derived fact strategies in addition and subtraction.* Undergraduate project. University of Oxford.

Webster, R. E. (1979). Visual and aural short-term memory capacity deficits in mathematics disabled students. *Journal of Educational Research, 72,* 277–283.

Wechsler, D. (1991). *Wechsler Intelligence Scale for children, 3rd Edition.* San Antonio, Texas: Psychological Corporation.

Weddell, R. A., & Davidoff, J. B. (1991). A dyscalculic patient with selectively impaired processing of the numbers 7, 9 and 0. *Brain and Cognition, 17,* 240–271.

Widaman, K. F., Geary, D. C., Cormier, P., & Little, T. D. (1989). A componential model for mental addition. *Journal of Experimental Psychology: Learning, Memory, and Cognition, 15,* 898–919.

Wigfield, A., & Meece, J. L. (1988). Math anxiety in elementary and secondary school students. *Journal of Educational Psychology, 80,* 210–216.

Wilder, R. L. (1968). *The evolution of mathematical concepts.* Chichester, UK: Wiley.

Wilkinson, A. C. (1984). Children's partial knowledge of the cognitive skill of counting. *Cognitive Psychology, 16, 28–64.*

Wittgenstein, L. (1958). In G. E. M. Anscombe and R. Rees (Eds.), *Philosophical investigation, 3rd Edition.* Oxford: Blackwell.

Wollman, D. C. (1965). The attainments in English and arithmetic of secondary school pupils with impaired hearing. *The Teacher of the Deaf, 159,* 121–129.

Wood, D., Wood, H., & Howarth, P. (1983). Mathematical abilities of deaf school-leavers. *British Journal of Developmental Psychology, 1,* 67–73.

Wood, H. A., Wood, D. J., Kingsmill, M. C., French, J. R. W., & Howarth, P. (1984). The mathematical achievement of deaf children from different educational environments. *British Journal of Educational Psychology, 54,* 254–264.

Woods, S. S., Resnick, L. B., & Groen, G. J. (1975). An experimental test of five process models for subtraction. *Journal of Educational Psychology, 102,* 734–736.

Wynn, K. (1990a). The development of counting and the concept of number. Unpublished doctoral dissertation, MIT, Cambridge, MA.

Wynn, K. (1990b). Children's understanding of counting. *Cognition, 36,* 155–193.

Wynn, K. (1992a). Addition and subtraction by human infants. *Nature, 358,* 749–750.

Wynn, K. (1992b). Evidence against empiricist accounts of the origins of numerical knowledge. *Mind & Language, 7,* 315–332.

Wynn, K. (1992c). Children's acquisition of the number words and the counting system. *Cognitive Psychology, 20,* 220–251.

Wynn, K. (1992d). Issues concerning a nativist theory of numerical knowledge. *Mind and Language, 7,* 367–381.

Wynn, K. (1996). Infants' individuation and enumeration of sequential actions. *Psychological Science, 7,* 164–169.

Wynn, K. (1998). An evolved capacity for number. In D. Cummins & C. Allen (Eds.), *The evolution of mind.* Oxford: Oxford University Press.

Xu, F., & Spelke, E. (1997). Large number discrimination in 6-month-old infants. In M. G. Shafto & P. Langley (Eds.), *Proceedings of the Nineteenth Annual Conference of the Cognitive Science Society.* Hillsdale, NJ: Erlbaum.

Young-Loveridge, J. M. (1991). *The development of children's number concepts from ages five to nine: Early mathematics learning project. Phase II.* Education Department, University of Waikato: New Zealand.

Zacks, R. T., & Hasher, L. (1994). Directed ignoring: Inhibitory regulation of working memory. In D. Dagenbach & T. H. Carr (Eds.), *Inhibitory processes in attention, memory, and language* (pp. 241–264). San Diego, CA: Academic Press.

Zbrodoff, N. J., & Logan, G. D. (1986). On the autonomy of mental processes: A case study of arithmetic. *Journal of Experimental Psychology: General, 115,* 118–130.

Author Index

Subject Index